THE FOREIGN POLICIES
OF WEST GERMANY, FRANCE,
AND BRITAIN

THE FOREIGN POLICIES OF WEST GERMANY, FRANCE, AND BRITAIN

Wolfram F. Hanrieder

*University of California,
Santa Barbara*

Graeme P. Auton

Whitman College

PRENTICE-HALL, INC., Englewood Cliffs, New Jersey 07632

Library of Congress Cataloging in Publication Data

Hanrieder, Wolfram F.
    The foreign policies of West Germany, France,
and Britain.

    Bibliography: p.
    Includes index.
    1. Germany, West—Foreign relations.
2. France—Foreign relations—1945–
3. Great Britain—Foreign relations—1945–
4. North Atlantic Treaty Organization.
5. Germany, West—Politics and government.
6. France—Politics and government—1945–
7. Great Britain—Politics and government—
1945–   I. Auton, Graeme P., joint author.
II. Title.
DD259.4.H238   320.9'4'055   79–14688
ISBN 0–13–326397–5

© 1980 by Prentice-Hall, Inc.
Englewood Cliffs, New Jersey 07632

Printed in the United States of America

10 9 8 7 6 5 4 3 2

Editorial/production supervision
and interior design by Lynda Heideman
Cover design by Allyson Everngam
Manufacturing Buyer: Harry P. Baisley

PRENTICE-HALL INTERNATIONAL, INC., *London*
PRENTICE-HALL OF AUSTRALIA PTY. LIMITED, *Sydney*
PRENTICE-HALL OF CANADA, LTD., *Toronto*
PRENTICE-HALL OF INDIA PRIVATE LIMITED, *New Delhi*
PRENTICE-HALL OF JAPAN, INC., *Tokyo*
PRENTICE-HALL OF SOUTHEAST ASIA PTE. LTD., *Singapore*
WHITEHALL BOOKS LIMITED, *Wellington, New Zealand*

For
Kehaulani
and
Betty

Contents

3

Reunification and *Ostpolitik*

50

4

Foreign Policy and Domestic Politics

74

FRANCE

5

Security and the Western Alliance

97

10

Political and Economic Reconstruction
215

11

Decolonization and the Third World
244

12

Foreign Policy and Domestic Politics
264

CONCLUSION

13
Transatlantic Relations, Economic Interdependence, and the Confluence of Domestic and Foreign Policy
281

For Further Reading
297

Index
301

Introduction

Politics is the art of the necessary as well as the art of the possible. The connection between necessity and possibility is especially apparent in the foreign policies of secondary powers like West Germany, France, and Britain. They are not able to shape the power configurations of international politics as can the superpowers, even though they are essential elements of the international system. Middle-level powers have to adjust their foreign policies to circumstances that are not primarily of their own making and that they can manipulate only within certain limits.

But power is a many-faceted concept, the sum of a great variety of elements (some intangible and hence immeasurable). Thus, classifications such as "superpower" or "secondary power" are ambiguous, relative, and contingent. For example, one of the consequences of the growing global economic interdependence is that such measures of power as military capacity are becoming less relevant. A secondary power like Germany may well be a "primary" power with respect to economic and monetary capabilities, and in certain circumstances and time periods, economic power may be a more effective instrument of diplomacy than military power. Moreover, the superpowers do not operate without restraints of their own. Freedom of action is checked by power relationships between the superpowers—for instance, the military-strategic balance between the United States and the Soviet Union— as well as by demands placed upon them by secondary powers and to which they feel obliged to respond. Stanley Hoffmann puts it this way, "The superpowers are like two giants who try to walk through a crowded room, in which they are not only slowed down by a packet of midgets but pushed aside by men of normal size, and cannot hit back."*

Even so, the three nations whose foreign policies we will examine in this book have faced a compelling and inescapable context of necessity. After World War II the ends as well as the means of German, French, and British foreign policy were imposed by international circumstances over which these countries had little control. The case of West Germany is perhaps the most clear-cut example. The defeat of Nazi Germany, the years of political impotence and economic deprivation during the occupation, and the Cold War not only gave rise to the major foreign policy issues that were to preoccupy West Germany for decades but also mapped or foreclosed the roads that could be taken toward their resolution. Indeed, the Federal Republic (as well as the German Democratic Republic) owed its very existence to the disagreements between the Soviet Union and the Western powers that prevented joint administration of Germany in the years following World War II. The creation of the two German states in 1949 seems, in retrospect, to have been a logical outcome of Cold War differences over the nature of the postwar European order. But the division of Germany did not put an end to the East-West conflict; instead, control of Germany remained the pivot and most coveted prize of the Cold War.

The postwar foreign policies of France and Britain also evolved under a variety of constricting influences. First, although the two countries emerged from World War II as victorious powers, their military, economic, financial, and diplomatic resources were diminished to the point of exhaustion; and France, in addition, had suffered the humiliating and deeply divisive experience of German occupation, a national trauma that affected French political life in subtle but profound ways for years to come. Second, while both countries still retained far-flung and extensive colonial holdings, the foundations of their empires were shaken in part as a consequence of the events of World War II and its aftermath, and in part because of inherent processes of fragmentation that could not be contained. Finally, the center of global power had shifted away from Europe. International leadership now rested with the United States and the Soviet Union, both relative newcomers to the game of world diplomacy—one in possession of the atomic bomb and an overwhelming economic capacity, the other in control of an immense land mass and superior conventional armed forces.

The context of necessity imposed upon Germany, France, and Britain in the post–World War II era was also reflected in the striking continuity with which they pursued their foreign policy goals. While these goals have been modified in light of failures and successes and in response to changes in international and domestic politics throughout the postwar period, they have

---

*Stanley Hoffmann, *Gulliver's Troubles, Or the Setting of American Foreign Policy* (New York: McGraw-Hill, 1968), p. 70.

remained closely tied to three major interconnected issues: security, political and economic recovery, and national self-definition.

The concern over national security arose from the Cold War struggle between the Communist and non-Communist alliances, and continued to be an important theme even after the climate of confrontation cooled, leading to the uneasy truce of coexistence and thence to the era of detente. But the way the West perceived the security issue began to change during those decades. With time Europe came to see the Soviet threat less in terms of physical aggression than the political uses to which Soviet military capabilities could be put. Also, as the Soviet Union achieved nuclear parity with the United States and the credibility of the American nuclear guarantee for Europe weakened, serious differences developed between Washington and its allies. American and West European security interests began to be less compatible than in the first postwar decade. At the same time, American nuclear protection of Western Europe took on more of a political than military meaning, and all parties—Washington, Moscow, Bonn, Paris, and London—resorted to military-strategic concepts to express what were at bottom political purposes.

Aside from grappling with the problem of security, West Germany, France, and Britain all faced the awesome task of reconstructing shattered and dislocated domestic economies after World War II. They encountered three critical problems in the process. First, their economic relationship with the United States, which was critical to European recovery in the early postwar period, later became a major source of tension when Washington attempted to extend its privileged position in the international monetary and economic system. Second, pressure for European integration originated from needs that sometimes came into conflict: the structural need to rationalize domestic economies, the political need (perceived by France and Britain) to contain a West German resurgence, and the security need to retain an American commitment to Europe by presenting to Washington a picture of a united West European effort. Third, all three countries had to meet mounting social welfare demands, demands that could only be satisfied by diverting resources from both domestic and international investment (especially in Britain and France) and by finding a way to balance domestic social and economic requirements and broad opportunities for economic growth. As with the goal of security, the meaning of the goal of economic recovery (and its political dimension) altered as time went on. For example, analysis of German monetary and economic policy vis-à-vis the United States and the European community in the sixties and seventies demonstrates the leverage of the Federal Republic in these areas and renders "economic recovery" a somewhat inappropriate label for Germany's recent foreign policy objectives in the area of economics.

The third key issue that shaped the foreign policies of West Germany, France, and Britain was how to define themselves politically, psychologically, and territorially within a radically transformed international system. In the Federal Republic's case this entailed seeking to end the division of Germany, which imposed upon Bonn its most intractable foreign policy task—a task that was not accomplished. France and Britain, in turn, had to adjust to the disintegration of their colonial empires. With loss of great-power status, they became simply European powers with limited European interests. There is no need to press too insistently the similarity between the goal of reunification in the German case and the goal of "imperial devolution" for France and Britain; it is sufficient to say that in terms of their emotional, psychological, and political impact, the two objectives were highly comparable. Furthermore, for all three countries the process of national self-definition was closely tied to policies regarding West European integration. As time passed, the specific meaning of the goal of national self-definition for each nation changed, as had the other two foreign policy goals. In the case of Germany, for instance, the earlier aim of reunification was eventually drastically reformulated.

It is the purpose of this book to trace the pursuit of three major sets of foreign policy goals—security, political and economic recovery, and national self-definition—by West Germany, France, and Britain during the period from the end of World War II to the late seventies. We shall deal with these goals both in their international context and in their domestic context, covering why and how the goals were sought, what obstacles and opportunities were met in the external environment, and who supported or opposed them in the internal environment of domestic politics.

As reflected in the chapter organization of the book, our analytical orientation strongly emphasizes the goals of foreign policy. It is a truism to say that foreign policies are intended to bring about results that the makers of foreign policy deem desirable. But goals are of central importance in analyzing foreign policies because one of the most important questions one can ask about any human activity is, Why is this being done, and what purposes are to be accomplished? Only after attaining an answer to that question—ambiguous, uncertain, and preliminary as that answer may be—can one proceed to raise additional questions about how these purposes were advanced, why they succeeded or failed, and in what ways they were reshaped or abandoned.

There are also more specific factors that make a goal-oriented analysis useful. First, German, French, and British foreign policy objectives have been rather succinct, and there is wide agreement among scholars as to their nature, content, origin, and development. Second, among the goals of each of the three countries were some that were contradictory and some that were compatible. As a result, success in seeking certain objectives precluded or complicated the attainment of others; while still other sets of goals proved to be compatible and could be effectively advanced together. Compatibility and contradiction among goals constitute a fundamental feature of German,

French, and British foreign policy and can be elucidated most clearly if we concentrate our attention on the goals themselves. Third, by emphasizing goals we can demonstrate the conflicts *among* the three countries as they advocated differing programs to bring about a new European order. Finally, emphasis on goals permits the reader as well as the analyst to make better-informed normative judgments about foreign policy. By concentrating on the question of what was to be accomplished, one also raises the question of whether the goals were worthy of accomplishment.

Our point of view is not only directed toward the external aspects of foreign policy but also toward the domestic factors affecting the pursuit of foreign policy. It is too one-sided to stress only the international forces at work in determining foreign policy, for such an analysis implies a kind of fatalism, an acceptance of inevitable historical necessity that denies the possibility of choice. Although international circumstances may indeed have limited foreign policy paths, the responses of the German, French, and British people and their decision makers were shaped by impulses that came from within as well as from without their political systems. Domestic and foreign politics were inextricably tied together.

In a fundamental sense, the domestic debates within West Germany, France, and Britain over foreign policy questions revolved around what the governments' opposing parties regarded as possible to accomplish or, given the incompatibility of some foreign policy goals, what they viewed as appropriate choices among mutually exclusive alternatives. National concern over foreign policy took on a special meaning and intensity because from the beginning of the postwar period most political groups in these three nations assumed, quite correctly, that foreign policy had a direct impact on political and socioeconomic developments at home. Especially in the case of Germany and France, international military, political, and economic commitments set the stage for the future direction and content of their internal order.

Without letting them intrude too insistently, we have applied two concepts—compatibility and consensus—in organizing and analyzing our historical materials.* With the first concept, compatibility, we assess the degree of feasibility of foreign policy goals given the obstacles and opportunities of the *international* system; with the second concept, consensus, we assess the measure of agreement (or disagreement) over the ends and means of foreign policy on the *domestic* political scene.

By considering the conditions of the international system and a particular foreign policy goal to be compatible, we mean that the goal has a reasonable chance of realization if implemented in a way that an outside observer would

---

*For a more extensive discussion of these concepts and their theoretical implications, see Wolfram F. Hanrieder, "Compatibility and Consensus: A Proposal for the Conceptual Linkage of External and Internal Dimensions of Foreign Policy," *American Political Science Review* (December 1967), pp. 971–82; and Wolfram F. Hanrieder, *Foreign Policies and the International System: A Theoretical Introduction* (New York: General Learning Press, 1971).

deem appropriate. The degree of complementarity *among* goals is also very important, especially if circumstances do not permit success in all of them. Thus if one goal seems compatible with prevailing international conditions, but the pursuit of this goal is perceived as having a negative effect on another goal's chances of attainment, we conclude that these two goals are incompatible.

Clearly, the concept of consensus is of a different order because it pertains to the domestic-internal dimension of foreign policy. In domestic politics there is no standard of feasibility that corresponds precisely to the one the international system provides for assessing the chances of success of foreign policy goals. Still, the concepts of compatibility and consensus have some similarity. If consensus is defined as the existing measure of agreement on foreign policy projects among the elements involved in a nation's decision-making process, then the degree of such agreement also limits what a political system can do without risking fragmentation. In that sense consensus is also a standard of feasibility, especially in a democratic political system. It determines, in the long run, what foreign policy goals a government can pursue without losing popular support and office.

We shall therefore be concerned with two sets of relationships. The first is the one between foreign policy goals and the conditions of the international environment in which they are pursued. Here the key concept is compatibility. The second set of relationships is the one between foreign policy goals and the domestic political environment. Here the key concept is consensus (or lack of it). In the concluding chapters for each country, we shall trace the shifting configurations of consensus that have emerged from the attitudes and conduct of political parties, pressure groups, and public opinion. In the final chapter of the book we shall connect the patterns of compatibility and consensus for all three countries, address specifically the question of interdependence, and talk about problems of the Atlantic Community.

The "division of labor" we have employed in writing this book is relatively simple. Wolfram Hanrieder has written the first and second parts, "West Germany" and "France"; Graeme Auton has written the third part, "Britain." The concluding chapter is a joint effort. Both of us, of course, have been involved in all chapters of the book, and we share responsibility for errors of fact and judgment.

THE FOREIGN POLICIES
OF WEST GERMANY, FRANCE,
AND BRITAIN

WEST GERMANY

1
Security and the Western Alliance

Perhaps the most fundamental question one could raise about West Germany's goal of security—understood as the preservation of territorial integrity from outside intrusion—is whether it was a plausible concern to begin with. Was German security threatened by the Soviet Union at any time during the postwar era? A full answer to this question would take us far afield, and it seems sufficient for our purposes to demonstrate that the West German people and their decision makers perceived a threat to exist.

But the question is put too narrowly in any case. Security policy always has two dimensions, defense and diplomacy; and West Germany (as well as France and Britain) has been acutely sensitive to this dual perspective and how it could be used to serve the national interest. The connection between defense policy and diplomacy is central for an understanding of postwar German foreign policy. Even today, when fear of Soviet physical aggression has waned in Western Europe, the political dimensions of security policy continue to be crucially important.

Since no West German armed forces were established until the late fifties, the security of the Federal Republic was in the beginning entirely determined by the capabilities and intentions of the Soviet bloc and the countervailing power and purpose of the Western alliance. The Bonn government's decision to rearm as a member of the Western alliance had several immediate and important consequences. First, rearmament initiated the country's increasingly important contribution to the Western defense system. Second, rearmament became the linchpin that held together the entire foreign policy program of the German government. West Germany's chances of achieving its foreign policy goals—security, political and economic recovery, and reunification—were directly affected (positively in the case of security and recovery, and negatively in the case of reunification) by the decision to join the Western

3

defense system. Rearmament thus connected the international environment with the whole range of West German foreign policy goals. Without the Cold War there would have been little reason for the Western powers to press for Germany's rearmament a few years after the end of World War II. Without the need to rearm Germany, there would have been little incentive for the Allies to accommodate the West German government in its pursuit of political and economic recovery and its attempt to unify Germany. Rearmament was the link between the Cold War and the successes and failures of Bonn's foreign policy.

THE ROAD TO GERMAN REARMAMENT, 1949–55

After several years of Cold War tensions, and following the creation of the North Atlantic Treaty Organization (NATO) in 1949 and the outbreak of the Korean War in 1950, the Western allies (and in particular the United States) began to regard the rearmament of West Germany as indispensable to Washington's containment policy in Europe.

It appeared to many in the West that, in light of the superior Soviet ground forces, the only way to deter Soviet aggression was with the threat of rapid nuclear escalation—a punishment that would be catastrophic as well as likely, given America's nuclear monopoly. Since the Western powers felt they could not match Soviet ground forces, the threat of nuclear strikes against the Soviet Union seemed to be the only deterrent that would be plausible as well as cost-efficient.

Although the United States had a nuclear monopoly, Washington viewed the rearmament of West Germany as essential for creating an effective forward line of defense with conventional ground forces. The newly established government in Bonn, under Chancellor Konrad Adenauer, was cooperative. The main problem was how to control a West German military contingent, since Bonn's future allies wanted security *from* Germany as well as security *for* Germany.

The question of control raised some serious problems within NATO. The United States recommended that German units be no larger than a division, and that ten such divisions be included in a NATO defense force. But a deeply apprehensive France objected, proposing instead the so-called Pleven Plan for a European Defense Community (EDC). The plan was designed both to satisfy American pressures to rearm Germany and to allay fears over the control of German military units by extending the concept of European integration into the military sphere. The Pleven Plan called for German units much smaller than divisions and for the "complete fusion of all human and material elements" of the proposed European forces under a unified Atlantic command. The United States and France also disagreed over French attempts to limit German military functions to an essentially auxiliary role and to curtail German political influence in the EDC. After protracted negotiations, the Allies agreed that Germany would provide twelve divisions within a European army, and that while technically the country would not receive NATO status, it would become a de facto member of the alliance since the EDC would itself be part of NATO. The only major concession to French demands was the provision that German contingents be merged with other Allied forces at the corps level, thus preventing German generals from commanding German national corps.

By the time the EDC treaty was signed by the Federal Republic, France, Italy, and the Benelux countries* in May 1952, the connection between West German rearmament and West German sovereignty had become formally acknowledged. The day before the signing of the EDC pact, the occupying powers and the West German government had concluded the so-called Bonn Conventions that provided for an end to the occupation regime through abolition of the Occupation Statute and the Allied High Commission. The conventions also anticipated the restoration of German sovereignty in external and internal affairs, though with certain reservations. The Western Allies retained the right to station troops in Germany and to decide questions involving the whole of Germany—including reunification, a final peace treaty, and Berlin. The conventions were to go into effect at the same time as the EDC treaty.

Meanwhile, the question of German rearmament had become even more pressing for the members of NATO. There was a feeling of increased urgency since the Soviet Union had already exploded nuclear devices, and it was expected that as a result American strategic nuclear superiority would gradually diminish and—as the United States became more vulnerable to nuclear attack—NATO conventional forces would take on added importance. Thus, at the Lisbon Conference of February 1952, NATO members were urged to establish ninety-six army divisions, of which thirty-five to forty would be battle-ready on the line and the remainder capable of mobilization within a month after D-Day. Given these military requirements, it was not surprising that the Allies saw a German military contribution as essential.

The implications of the Lisbon strategy aroused misgivings in Bonn, however—misgivings that foreshadowed much more serious concerns voiced in later years. To be sure, Adenauer fully appreciated that rearmament could provide valuable political leverage toward gaining West German sovereignty and achieving his fundamental goal of equal partnership for West Germany in a West European union. Rearmament presented Bonn with a chance to trade German support of the West for Allied political and economic concessions. Nonetheless, the Lisbon Plan caused some concern in Bonn because there apparently was an acceptance of the possibility of a "limited war" in Europe in which the Federal Republic, due to its forward geographical posi-

*The Benelux countries are Belgium, the Netherlands, and Luxembourg.

tion, would necessarily suffer the most. It was this concern—that West Germany could become a battlefield in a nonnuclear but (for Germany) total war —that became the central theme of the Federal Republic's preoccupation with security.

As it was, the conventional force goals envisaged at Lisbon were unrealistic. Implementation would have been both costly and politically controversial. Morever, many Europeans regarded conventional forces primarily as a tripwire that would trigger an immediate American nuclear response if they were attacked. For this purpose a much smaller contingent seemed sufficient —and, in fact, a larger one would have been detrimental—especially since the most effective tripwire forces, American units, were already deployed at the Iron Curtain. The Atlantic alliance, therefore, continued to rely largely on the American nuclear deterrent, and when the Eisenhower administration announced its doctrine of "massive and instant retaliation" by means and at places of Washington's choosing, this merely added a catchy slogan to the existing and accepted deterrence posture.

The "automaticity" of an American nuclear response to conventional provocation, which was reemphasized in the doctrine of massive retaliation, was highly attractive to Bonn. It seemed to reinforce the credibility of deterrence and reduce the likelihood that West Germany would become a battlefield in a conventional war. But Washington's strategy was called into question by the shifting power relationship between the United States and the Soviet Union. Massive retaliation depended heavily on B-47 bomber bases overseas, which were beginning to become vulnerable to Soviet attack —in August 1953 the Soviet Union set off its first H-bomb, and during 1954 Moscow began to display a considerable number of long-range bombers. Meanwhile, NATO's Lisbon military plans remained far from implementation.

Both the increase in Soviet strength and the Atlantic powers' failure to meet the Lisbon force goals led NATO to announce in December 1954 a revision of the Lisbon plan: thirty standing divisions would be deployed in the central defense sector, and they would be supplied with tactical nuclear weapons. These battlefield nuclear devices had been developed by the United States during the previous year and were scheduled to be ready for deployment soon. Tactical nuclear weapons seemed attractive since they were expected to make up for America's gradual loss of its nuclear monopoly by providing an additional "firebreak" between conventional provocation and all-out nuclear war. NATO planning was now officially based on the principle that tactical nuclear weapons would be used to counter almost any type of aggression.

The Adenauer government could hardly neglect to exploit the political leverage provided by the decision to fortify NATO with battlefield nuclear weapons. Under the new strategy, West German conventional forces were needed even more than before. The twelve divisions that West Germany had agreed to provide were now assigned two important functions: (1) to carry the major burden in defending the European central front (especially since the other NATO members had not met their share of the Lisbon force goals), and (2) to provide the strong forward contingent of ground troops required by the new strategy to force the enemy to attack in concentration, so as to make tactical nuclear counterstrikes effective. In addition to being part of the Western ground forces, the planned German contingents had become an integral element in Washington's attempt to reinforce the American strategic nuclear position. Without having proceeded beyond the planning stage, German rearmament, which initially had been regarded only as complementing American nuclear superiority, had become an essential part of a new nuclear strategy for Europe.

But in August 1954, when the French National Assembly failed to ratify the 1952 EDC treaty, the structure that was to rearm the Federal Republic, and also restore German sovereignty by enabling the Bonn Conventions to go into effect, collapsed. The entire Western defense system seemed threatened, and the United States hinted it might disengage from Europe because of French obstructionism. The situation appeared especially serious because of the plans to deploy tactical nuclear weapons on NATO's forward line in Germany, plans that assigned new and crucial functions to the proposed German contingents.

In the wake of these disquieting developments the Allies agreed that Germany should join NATO and also become part of an expanded and revived Brussels Treaty Organization. The Brussels Treaty of March 1948 between Britain, France, and the Benelux countries had been little more than a mutual defense agreement, and the organization had become practically obsolete with the establishment of NATO in 1949. The enlarged Brussels Treaty Organization was renamed the Western European Union (WEU), and it obligated Britain to maintain an army on the Rhine, established institutions to check on Germany's rearmament, and placed German contingents under NATO control, thus meeting some of the French objections to German rearmament.

This outcome was a full success for the Federal Republic. Germany was granted full equality as a member of NATO, agreeing to establish a national contingent of twelve divisions wholly under NATO command. In return, the members of NATO pledged to use all diplomatic means to support the reunification of Germany and to regard the West German government as the only legitimate spokesman for all of Germany. A condition of joining NATO was that Bonn renounce the manufacture of atomic, biological, and chemical weapons, certain other types of arms such as guided missiles and rockets, and submarines and other types of vessels. Because these provisions did not preclude Germany's possession or use of nuclear weapons, Bonn was renouncing not a nuclear strategy but rather the independent production of nuclear weapons on German territory. Some of the other restrictions (the ban on producing submarines, for example) were subsequently abandoned.

MASSIVE RETALIATION
AND CONVENTIONAL FORCE LEVELS

As we have seen, the Eisenhower administration, while stressing massive nuclear retaliation against conventional provocation, also considered conventional troops to be highly important. The question was not so much what forces were required as who would provide them. Admiral Arthur Radford, chairman of the Joint Chiefs of Staff, argued in 1956 for a global "balance of forces" toward which the United States would contribute its nuclear striking power while America's allies would contribute the bulk of ground forces and local naval and air power. This theme of a strategic division of labor among the Western alliance partners had already been voiced by British government spokesmen, who held that the American argument also applied to Britain's situation.

In Bonn, the Radford Plan was viewed with mixed feelings. In Western capitals there were already doubts about whether a full-blown American response could be relied upon in light of Soviet nuclear military capability. A strategic division of labor, which would reduce the American conventional force level on the Continent and diminish the credibility of the American commitment, could only deepen these anxieties. At the same time, full-fledged preparations for a conventional response (which were enhanced by the presence of a strong American conventional force) suggested that an American nuclear response might not be automatic, that it might be delayed. It has been convincingly argued that the West at that time should have attempted to match the Soviet Union at all levels, conventional as well as nuclear, and that establishing sufficient conventional forces was in fact essential for a credible strategic nuclear deterrence posture. But because of its forward position, West Germany could not view the prospect of deterring Soviet ground forces with Western ground forces as very appealing.

As a result, the American plan to deploy tactical nuclear weapons in Europe—weapons that were publicized as deterrents rather than as potential instruments of defense—was attractive to Bonn. The Eisenhower administration reasoned that the implicit threat of an immediate nuclear response, which was created by denying the likelihood of a conventional response, would deter a Soviet conventional attack. As long as it was reasonably credible, this deterrence posture appealed to Western European powers, especially the Federal Republic. It was widely believed in Germany and elsewhere in Europe that preparation for a conventional response would increase the likelihood of war by undermining the credibility of massive retaliation and would in fact encourage American "nuclear disengagement" from Europe. Since even a limited engagement with conventional forces would make Germany a battlefield, from Bonn's perspective it seemed better not to extend the range of retaliatory options because this seemed to weaken the automaticity of a nuclear response.

By 1956, the Federal Republic had begun to reappraise its security policy. The government now shifted from arguing that German rearmament would help deter Soviet aggression to stressing that German force levels would aid in deterring nuclear war. This shift could in part be explained by the fact that by 1956 the fear of Soviet conventional aggression had diminished and been replaced by the fear of nuclear arms. This change in the East-West power relationship was forcefully demonstrated when the West failed to come to the aid of the Hungarian revolutionaries and when the Kremlin threatened to employ missiles during the Suez crisis. At the end of the year, the Bonn government for the first time expressed an interest in obtaining tactical nuclear weapons for West Germany's armed forces.

To explain this shift in policy, Adenauer argued that a nonnuclear NATO response to a Soviet attack was no longer likely in light of the ramifications of the Radford Plan, France's transfer of troops to Algeria, Britain's reliance on nuclear defense, and Belgium's reduction of its period of conscription. In effect, Bonn implied that the West could continue to rely on nuclear deterrence and that Western Europe's conventional capabilities were now so depleted that NATO had no choice but to use tactical nuclear weapons to respond to a Soviet attack.

Bonn's position reflected a lack of confidence in NATO's ground forces. The concurrently waning credibility of the American nuclear commitment, and the failure of the West to intervene in Hungary, provided Bonn with a strong incentive for seeking a voice in the nuclear decision making of the Western alliance. The Bonn government began to doubt the value of a large German conventional contingent because this would provide NATO with a wider range of responses that seemed to undermine nuclear deterrence and increase the risk that Germany would become a battlefield in a conventional war. Bonn's misgivings were reinforced by reductions of conventional forces in other NATO countries. These reductions further emphasized the existing division of labor between Germany's conventional force responsibilities and America's nuclear obligations to NATO—the less West Germany's allies were involved in the early stages of a Soviet attack, the less likely, or the more delayed, would be American nuclear retaliation. Because Germany could not accept a substitute for a "forward strategy," Bonn consistently aimed to fully engage the Allies at its borders. German co-management of nuclear weapons was expected to reinforce the Western nuclear presence at the East German border and extend Washington's nuclear commitments more unequivocally to cover the Federal Republic.

NATO's new defense strategy, which began to rely heavily on tactical nuclear weapons, meant that West Germany and other European allies were becoming more and more dependent on weapons over which they had no control. The tactical nuclear warheads that were deployed in increasing numbers with American ground forces in Germany were kept under tight American control, and the Adenauer government found itself largely excluded from planning for their use and deployment. Bonn's misgivings over this arrangement were shared in other European NATO capitals. France, in particular, was interested in developing its own strategic nuclear capability, which would permit the French to join the special Anglo-American nuclear relationship as an equal partner—as General Charles de Gaulle proposed in 1958 when he called for a NATO nuclear triumvirate. After de Gaulle returned to power in 1958, France and Germany also reportedly discussed the establishment of some type of nuclear partnership between the two countries. Nothing came of the talks, however; it is not certain whether France was unwilling to share nuclear control and technical secrets, or whether Bonn felt the time had not come to engage in such a politically controversial venture. The conclusion that de Gaulle drew from the changing East-West nuclear balance—namely that France needed an independent national nuclear deterrent—could not be implemented by West Germany in any case, even if the Bonn government had so desired. Strategic considerations made it seem imperative for West Germany's defense posture to remain closely tied to American strategic nuclear capabilities, and there were political and legal obstacles as well. Also, Bonn feared expansion of the nuclear club, since the trend was fracturing the NATO alliance and thus undermining the basis of West German security.

The logical middle course between an independent nuclear capability and no sharing of control at all was a tightly integrated nuclear alliance with equal sharing of control. West Germany now aimed to increase its military and political influence not so much on the basis of a "special understanding" with the United States or through the quest for a national nuclear arsenal, but rather by stressing the need for political and military integration of the alliance and for a larger German role in the control of nuclear weapons. In the fall of 1960, the Bonn government began to express cautious interest in an integrated NATO nuclear force as an alternative to the national nuclear force favored by de Gaulle. At this point Germany primarily sought to achieve participation in nuclear planning, rather than joint sharing of nuclear control.

An interest in joint nuclear management was expressed by other European capitals as well. During the late fifties and early sixties they offered numerous proposals for a jointly controlled NATO force (or at least for consultation and common planning). This posed a delicate problem for American policy. The Eisenhower administration had consistently sought to prevent nuclear proliferation and would only permit nuclear control arrangements that would allow NATO members to decide jointly about use, reserving a veto for the United States. In December 1960 the United States offered

NATO five submarines with eighty Polaris missiles, to be delivered by 1963 on the condition that the NATO powers agree on a multilateral control scheme. But in view of the impending change of administration in Washington and the need for Congressional approval of the offer—which most likely would mean that warheads would remain in American custody—the NATO Council issued a noncommittal communiqué in response to the American proposal.

THE DOCTRINE OF FLEXIBLE RESPONSE

The NATO debate about the role of nuclear and conventional forces became even more heated when the Kennedy administration began a thorough revamping of American strategy. Soon after taking office, President John F. Kennedy repeated rather half-heartedly Eisenhower's offer to provide NATO with five submarines. But he added the important proviso that NATO's conventional force level (twenty-two divisions at the time) would have to be raised to thirty divisions prior to any joint nuclear arrangement.

More importantly, whereas the Eisenhower proposal had been put forth in the context of the doctrine of massive nuclear retaliation, the Kennedy proposal was related to a more flexible American strategic doctrine, which was designed to multiply Washington's strategic and tactical options and which required a conventional force buildup. The new administration wanted to reverse the trend toward reliance on strategic and tactical nuclear weapons and began to stress a more flexible and "graduated" scale of responses. Kennedy felt the West ought to be fully prepared on all levels, including the conventional level, in order to avoid the dilemma of having to choose either a nuclear strike (with the risk of a Soviet counterstrike) or the politically disastrous consequences of doing nothing at all. In short, the Kennedy administration wanted to provide a credible retaliatory response to every possible level of provocation.

By 1962 President Kennedy and Defense Secretary Robert S. McNamara had presented a "doctrine of flexibility," which involved contingency planning that tacitly admitted the possibility of a limited conventional war in Europe. McNamara suggested that because of the shifting nuclear balance of power, nuclear arms had become NATO's shield and conventional arms its sword (thus completely reversing the strategic principles of the Radford plan). He thus implied that a nuclear strike countering a conventional attack might be delayed. In broad terms, the new strategy signaled that the United States would not use nuclear weapons at the outset of hostilities except in reply to a nuclear attack; that small-scale attacks would not elicit a nuclear response at all; and that even in case of a massive attack, NATO would first use conventional troops to allow time for negotiations with the opponent and for consultations among the Allies about the initial use of nuclear weapons. Central to the new strategy was the concept of "graduated deterrence," which postulated an initial Soviet attack without nuclear weapons that might lead to a series of controlled steps of escalation, ranging from the conventional force level to the "selected and limited use" of tactical nuclear weapons, the more general use of these weapons, and ultimately the threat of a strategic nuclear attack on the Soviet Union. In short, the new doctrine was intended to provide a more considered and effective meshing of military and diplomatic action.

The doctrine of flexible response required, above all, a substantial increase in NATO's conventional forces. But even though Washington argued that a conventional force buildup would enhance the credibility of the American nuclear deterrent, European NATO capitals were not reassured. The increase in ground forces demanded by Washington would not be large enough to provide for a viable local defense strategy, they felt; yet it seemed to render the threat of a United States nuclear counterstrike less plausible. In addition, while Western Europe agreed with Washington that NATO's deterrence posture should be strengthened, a response to a conventional attack with conventional forces held little attraction. It meant total, if nonnuclear, war. Because of its forward position, West Germany in particular feared a conventional war; and the possibility of a "conventional pause," during which Washington would determine whether nuclear retaliation was appropriate, necessarily made Bonn nervous.

Changes in the deployment and tactical disposition of NATO's defenses added to Bonn's security concerns since they seemed to weaken the principle of forward defense. NATO's defense planning during the Kennedy administration gradually shifted to a tactical doctrine of "fluid defense" and mobility, with designated but not otherwise prepared defense positions. This "defense in depth" required not only time to assess the opponent's major thrusts and to direct counterforces to critical sectors of the front, but also space—and both commodities would be crucial for Germany in case of attack, because time and space would determine the extent of destruction on German territory.

West Germany and other NATO allies had additional sources of disagreement with the Kennedy administration. Washington sought to strengthen the credibility of its nuclear deterrent by stressing the feasibility of controlling nuclear war and preventing "spasmic," irrational nuclear exchanges. This created a conflict of interest in the alliance because the European powers believed they could gain most by emphasizing the uncontrollable nature of nuclear war. Furthermore, the Cuban missile crisis and the Nuclear Test Ban Treaty strongly pointed to a Soviet-American common interest on nuclear questions. To many Europeans the treaty, which followed the allies' exclusion from Washington's deliberations on the Cuban confrontation, indicated that in case of a major European crisis the two nuclear superpowers might settle the issue bilaterally and that the White House would add diplomatic flexibility to the Pentagon's doctrine of strategic flexibility.

MULTILATERAL FORCE PROPOSALS

During the last years of the Adenauer government, and throughout the Erhard administration (1963–66), Bonn expressed considerable interest in participating in a multilateral nuclear force (MLF). As already noted, proposals for a jointly controlled NATO nuclear force were put forth in Europe in the late fifties, and elicited only perfunctory responses from Washington. But the Skybolt controversy of December 1962 triggered a series of events that made it appear the United States might respond to such proposals somewhat more earnestly.

London had anticipated that the Skybolt, a two-stage ballistic missile being developed jointly by the United States and Britain, would be carried by British raiding bombers and thus prolong the bombers' usefulness (they were becoming vulnerable to Soviet antiaircraft missiles). In other words, the Skybolt was to be a modernized delivery system for Britain's independent nuclear deterrent. But in November 1962, after extensive cost-effectiveness evaluations, the United States decided to scrap the Skybolt development program. This meant, in effect, that Britain would either have to abandon plans for an independent nuclear capability because of lack of an adequate delivery system or develop the Skybolt on its own at exorbitant costs. To make up for the loss of Skybolt, at a meeting in Nassau in December 1962 President Kennedy reached an agreement with British Prime Minister Harold Macmillan to sell American-made Polaris submarine missiles to the British on the condition that they would assign such Polaris-equipped submarines to a NATO command, whenever established, as the nucleus of a NATO nuclear force. A similar offer was made to the French, who had neither the warheads for the missile nor the submarines to launch it.

The Germans felt they had been excluded from these deliberations and the resulting agreement, and were not reassured by the ambivalent strategic-military implications of the Nassau arrangement. At the same time, there was some hope that Bonn would gain a voice in nuclear decision making—a hope that was raised by the language of the agreement, which toned down its bilateral features and stressed the potential for multilateral nuclear control (the agreement called for the creation of a multilateral force of nuclear-armed ships and submarines with integrated crews drawn from the NATO members).

The MLF idea not only made little military sense (President Kennedy himself viewed it as a fake), but also its anticipated political value turned out to be even more doubtful. European control-sharing in a nuclear force would not have been increased substantially had the MLF proposal been implemented since the United States still controlled the buttons, and the Nassau agreement was seen by the French president as additional evidence that Britain would be an American "Trojan horse" in Europe. Furthermore, even though Bonn had shown an early interest in the collective nuclear force concept and later became its only enthusiastic European supporter, the MLF project was designed not to satisfy but to forestall West Germany's alleged desire to become a nuclear power. Following French rejection of both the Nassau agreement and Britain's application to join the Common Market, and after the signing of the Franco-German cooperation treaty of 1963, Washington began to view the MLF primarily as a way to prevent a possible nuclear pact between Paris and Bonn. In short, much of the initial support for the MLF came from Washington rather than Europe, and was based on the expectation that the MLF would vitalize NATO and prevent nuclear proliferation by preserving the Western alliance's "nuclear centralization." At best, it was hoped, the MLF would genuinely further integration; failing that, it would at least temporarily paper over the fissures in the Western alliance.

Far from being a harmless palliative, however, the MLF proposal turned out to be a troublesome liability for American policy. It jeopardized an arms control agreement between the United States and the Soviet Union, since Moscow opposed the entire MLF notion as a scheme to place nuclear weapons in the hands of West Germany. Neither did the MLF succeed in symbolizing American-European interdependence or in furthering the integration of Europe. The military-strategic shortcomings of an American-dominated joint force could hardly foster a feeling of interdependence in Europe. In addition, Franco-German relations, which had been strained throughout the years of the Erhard administration, were further burdened by the divisive issue of the MLF. De Gaulle wanted a French-dominated European defense arrangement and adamantly opposed German participation in nuclear decision making because it would tie Bonn more closely to the United States.

In 1965 President Lyndon Johnson scrapped the MLF scheme, causing Chancellor Ludwig Erhard considerable embarrassment. Sacrificing the MLF was relatively easy for the Johnson administration, since neither Britain nor France wanted to see Germany admitted to nuclear policymaking and in any case most NATO members had shown no real interest in an MLF arrangement. Also, the Soviet Union had repeatedly made it clear that Washington would have to choose between a nuclear nonproliferation treaty and the MLF.* The Germans, of course, felt that their deep-seated suspicions about a possible Soviet-American deal were confirmed by Washington's about-face

---

*The nonproliferation treaty, concluded in the early summer of 1968, was the result of six years of negotiations at the Geneva disarmament conference. The treaty was sponsored by the United States, the Soviet Union, and Britain (France and China had indicated they would not accede to such a treaty). The pact's intent was to restrain lesser powers from acquiring nuclear weapons and to prevent their use in regional conflicts that might escalate into a global nuclear holocaust, thus forestalling the destabilizing effects expected from further nuclear proliferation. To insure the security of nonnuclear ratifying states during the twenty-five-year span of the treaty, the sponsoring powers pledged to act through the UN Security Council and agreed in Article VI to pursue in good faith negotiations on arms control and nuclear disarmament.

on the MLF. Moreover, Bonn's security concerns became even more pressing after de Gaulle announced French withdrawal from the integrated NATO command in February 1966. NATO's forward strategy, which had always appeared rather impracticable, was now further undermined by the loss of French troops, soil, and airspace. This made it seem imperative for West Germany to gain a voice in nuclear councils, especially since Washington spokesmen suggested that the French withdrawal might compel NATO to use nuclear arms earlier than previously planned because the possibility for defense in depth had been reduced—thus implying that West Germany previously had been considered expendable before nuclear weapons would be used.

THE NONPROLIFERATION TREATY

Throughout 1966, the Soviets emphasized that any German "association" with nuclear weapons (except consultative arrangements) would stand in the way of a nonproliferation treaty. The Germans were just as adamant in insisting on participation in a nuclear force. Meanwhile, many Western leaders began to view German demands with a good deal of impatience. The nonproliferation treaty seemed to be in jeopardy, and there was little enthusiasm to begin with about a German finger on the nuclear trigger. The Germans, in turn, were highly suspicious of the idea of a nonproliferation pact. Considering the far-reaching repercussions of such an arrangement for German foreign policy, the Bonn government was probably justified in complaining about insufficient consultation. More important, even though German co-ownership of nuclear weapons seemed unlikely, the Germans saw a possibility of forcing some progress on the reunification issue by using opposition to a nonproliferation treaty as leverage. They had reservations about a nonproliferation agreement not so much because they wanted to own nuclear weapons but because they did not want to be deprived of the threat of acquiring them. The value of this threat was doubtful considering the widespread apprehensions about a German finger on the nuclear trigger, but the Germans were reluctant to forgo an opportunity to extract concessions on the reunification issue, since they had had so little leverage on that issue in the past and since it seemed as if the Russians' main purpose in negotiating the treaty was to deny nuclear arms to West Germany.

Chancellor Erhard must have viewed the likelihood of gaining German co-ownership of nuclear weapons as remote in any case, considering his troubled relationship with the Johnson administration. Among other issues, Erhard had difficulties with Washington over defense cost-sharing. American troops stationed in Germany had been a point of contention for a number of years because of their drain on the United States balance of payments. Washington wanted the Germans to continue easing the American balance-of-payments deficit through arms purchases from the United States, while the Germans insisted that they already had an adequate stock of military equipment. (During 1961–64 West Germany had purchased $2.5 billion worth of American arms and munitions.) The issue was finally resolved in the spring of 1967, during the early months of the Grand Coalition government that succeeded the Erhard administration. A compromise was reached (it had previously been proposed to Johnson by Erhard) that called for German-American monetary cooperation rather than for continuing German weapons purchases to offset the dollar cost of American troops. The new approach provided that Germany would not convert into gold the dollars earned from American troop spending in Germany (the central bank of West Germany in any case followed a general policy of not cashing in dollars for gold) and that Germany would purchase medium-term securities in the United States, thus relieving the American balance-of-payments position.

In December 1966 the Grand Coalition government replaced the Erhard administration, with Kurt Kiesinger of the Christian Democratic Union (CDU) as chancellor and Willy Brandt of the Social Democratic Party (SPD) as vice-chancellor and foreign minister. The Grand Coalition soon expressed misgivings about the nonproliferation treaty. The new government seemed less concerned about the linkage between nuclear self-denial and progress on the issues of reunification, or about obtaining nuclear co-ownership within the context of an allied nuclear force. Instead, the government's objections focused primarily on the implications of a nonproliferation treaty for the creation of a European nuclear force and for German participation in joint nuclear planning. Bonn succeeded in obtaining written assurances from Washington that the nonproliferation treaty, although it might preclude a NATO nuclear force, would not prevent the formation of a European nuclear force should a politically united Europe come into being. Bonn also stressed that West Germany's participation in NATO's Nuclear Planning Group should not be regarded as a substitute for a German role in a European nuclear force.*

Both points gained new significance when Washington's doctrine of flexible response, operative for the United States since the days of the Kennedy administration, became official and explicit NATO policy in May 1967. By the late sixties the Soviet Union had obtained an "assured destruction" capability against the United States, which meant that even after absorbing a surprise first strike, the Soviet Union could launch a massive retaliatory attack

---

*In December 1966, NATO established the Nuclear Planning Group to provide a forum where nonnuclear alliance members could share information and participate in nuclear planning and decision making. It consisted of four standing members (the United States, Great Britain, Italy, and West Germany), three to four rotating members (drawn from the other NATO members) serving terms of nine to eighteen months, and the Secretary-General of NATO acting as chairman.

upon the United States. Clearly, this development further undermined European confidence that the United States would resort to nuclear war in response to aggression by conventional means. Nonetheless, the doctrine of flexible response, while "logical" from a strictly strategic point of view, was especially perturbing since the use of conventional forces had become even more problematic with French withdrawal from NATO.

West Germany's security concerns, and the government's misgivings about the nonproliferation treaty, were further strengthened by the Soviet invasion of Czechoslovakia in August 1968. The Germans felt threatened by the increased strength and proximity of Soviet power across their borders, and they were hardly reassured by Russian attempts to justify the invasion with strongly worded statements claiming that a revanchist Germany had been a major driving force behind the "deviationism" of the Dubcek regime. Although the Grand Coalition had jettisoned the old demands for direct nuclear co-ownership and codetermination, Foreign Minister Brandt declared after the invasion that Germany would sign the treaty only if it would impose disarmament obligations on the nuclear powers, and would not endanger the security of Germany, delay the integration of Europe, or inhibit the peaceful application of nuclear energy.

Most other NATO members also expressed concern after the Soviet invasion. NATO's nonnuclear forces had been cut back for several years, particularly on the forward line in Germany, and the invasion called into question the prevailing Western assumption that post-Stalinist Soviet leadership had become too sophisticated to resort to large-scale force in the furtherance of political aims.

ARMS CONTROL, CONFLICT MANAGEMENT, AND THE INVASION OF CZECHOSLOVAKIA

The general question of European security was affected by the Soviet invasion in yet another way. During the previous few years various proposals for East-West security pacts and other military detente measures had been put forth in Western and Eastern Europe. They ranged from suggestions for the mutual reduction of force levels to demands for the dissolution of NATO and the Warsaw Pact. These proposals seemed to reflect an attitude shared by many within both blocs that NATO and the Warsaw Pact were not as important as before and that a formalized military detente would be mutually advantageous. Several proposals went beyond suggesting arrangements for the control and management of conflict situations and sought ways for the final resolution of East-West conflicts. In other words, military security arrangements were expected to facilitate a political reconciliation through increased East-West contacts and cooperative economic and diplomatic endeavors, in the hope that the political problems of Europe (such as the division of Germany and the unsettled frontier questions) would become more manageable.

Ever since the fifties, these two distinct aspects and purposes of European arms control—the military aspect, or conflict control, and the political aspect, or conflict resolution—had posed a dilemma for Bonn. Conflict control and crisis management were even more important to Germany than to its allies because of Germany's forward position. Nevertheless, Bonn had always felt obliged to reject arms control proposals because they did not seem to lead to a genuine resolution of conflicts but rather to the legitimization of the status quo in Central Europe, including the division of Germany. The East bloc's proposals of the mid-sixties could also be interpreted in this light. The Soviet Union and its allies renewed their proposals for a European security pact as an alternative to NATO and the Warsaw Pact, but their concept of "European security" also implied the dissolution of NATO and the withdrawal of the United States from Europe, as well as the legitimization of the East German regime.

Even so, Bonn's Grand Coalition was willing to reverse the Adenauer and Erhard governments' position that progress on reunification would have to precede an East-West detente. In fact, Bonn put forth its own ideas on a European settlement and suggested that such matters be discussed within NATO. From the beginning of the Grand Coalition, the possibility of mutual East-West troop reductions figured prominently in Bonn's detente program (although it was hard to see why the Soviet Union should have made any significant concessions since NATO was making unilateral reductions voluntarily).

The invasion of Czechoslovakia had repercussions on this issue. The show of force demonstrated unequivocally that the Soviet Union was determined to maintain control over Central Europe, thus diminishing Bonn's major long-range incentive for acceding to European arms control measures. On the other hand, the incentive of the other Western powers for conflict control remained unimpaired after Czechoslovakia, since the allies were primarily interested in military stabilization and detente in Central Europe. They had no major political demands to make on the Soviet Union and Eastern Europe; therefore they saw conflict control as much more urgent than conflict resolution. This difference between the interests of West Germany and the interests of its allies was of long standing, but the difference was reemphasized by the Soviet invasion, which had a much more damaging effect on the prospects of conflict resolution than on the prospects of conflict control.

This was clearly reflected in the rather innocuous Western response to the invasion. There were three major reasons for the mildness of the response: (1) budget-minded parliaments and voters in NATO countries were unwilling to finance a conventional force contingent that would match the capabilities of the Soviet bloc, and in any event NATO's nuclear deterrent strategy obviously could not be expected to apply in a situation involving the Soviet

Union and one of its client countries within the Soviet sphere of influence; (2) after the initial shock and consternation had worn off, the West began to view the Soviet action as a measure to maintain the status quo in Central Europe rather than as the first in a series of intemperate adventures to overthrow existing arrangements; and (3) most importantly, the United States and the Soviet Union were anxious to resume their bilateral negotiations on arms control, which had been interrupted by the invasion.

SECURITY, *OSTPOLITIK,* AND ARMS CONTROL

A coalition of Social Democrats and Free Democrats took over the Bonn government in October 1969, with the SPD's Willy Brandt as chancellor and the FDP's Walter Scheel as foreign minister. The new government did not intend to make significant changes in West German security policy but was determined, as had been every preceding German government, to make close German-American cooperation inside and outside of NATO the backbone of German foreign policy. Government spokesmen stressed their belief that an effective defense posture as well as a viable policy of detente could not be achieved without NATO. The SPD's Helmut Schmidt, who became the new minister of defense, had long been recognized as one of Germany's most sophisticated strategic analysts; and all indications suggested that the Brandt government would press for effective German-American or NATO consultative arrangements on allied strategy and contingency planning, and in general seek to enhance the cohesion and viability of the Western alliance.

The issue of West German security was deeply affected by Chancellor Willy Brandt's new Eastern policy, or *Ostpolitik* (more on this in chapter 3). Brandt sought an accommodation with the Soviet Union, East Europe, and East Germany on the basis of acceptance of the territorial status quo in Europe. Prior to this, in the fifties and sixties, the Federal Republic was the only European power to question the status quo by refusing to recognize East Germany and accept as permanent, under international law, the Oder-Neisse border between East Germany and Poland. Bonn's hard line, which was castigated as "revanchist" by the Soviet bloc, had the diplomatic support of the allies during the intense years of the Cold War. The West had nothing to lose by lending nominal support to West German aspirations for reunification since the prospects for German unity were dim in any case. During those years, Bonn's security policy, implemented through membership in the Western alliance, hindered reunification since every step undertaken to enhance West German security within the framework of NATO at the same time sharpened the division of Germany. (In contrast, the aspects of German security policy directed toward the West—i.e., integration into Western structures such as NATO and the Common Market—were compatible with another foreign policy goal, the rapid political and economic reconstruction of the Federal Republic. (This is a subject we will discuss more fully in chapter 2).

Unlike previous Eastern policies, Brandt's *Ostpolitik* was not incompatible with German security goals but rather became a complementary political part of German military security policy. When Chancellor Willy Brandt decided to fundamentally revise Germany's reunification policy by accepting the territorial status quo in Europe, including the division of Germany, German military security problems were tackled at their political roots. Germany's agreement to settle the fundamental political issues that had preoccupied the Warsaw Treaty Organization for decades removed Soviet incentives for military action outside the Warsaw Pact region—incentives that were perhaps small to begin with.

Ostpolitik aroused American suspicions that the new policy implied a weakening of Germany's ties to the North Atlantic Community and, in particular, to Washington. To reassure the West, Bonn reiterated that *Ostpolitik* was intended to further the goal of stability and reconciliation in Europe and that there was no desire on West Germany's part to follow a more independent security policy or to play off East against West.

The most convincing sign of the Brandt government's continuing commitment to the West—and at the same time, a step that furthered Bonn's dynamic new Eastern policy and desire for detente—was the willingness to sign a nuclear nonproliferation treaty without delay. At the same time, however, the Brandt government (as well as other West European governments) had some reservations about the treaty. Bonn was somewhat concerned that the treaty and the ongoing strategic arms limitations talks (SALT) between the United States and the Soviet Union might create a bilateral political-strategic understanding between the superpowers at the expense of European NATO members. A central aspect of this concern was the question of the continuing United States military presence in Europe. The substantial support given the Mansfield Resolution in the United States Senate seemed to reflect a widespread feeling in Washington that European NATO members were not carrying a fair share of their burden, and European NATO members feared that the United States would disengage from Europe as well as Asia.*

For Bonn, the political implications of a reduced American or NATO presence were much more serious than the purely military-strategic implications, because in the seventies direct military aggression from the East was not feared as much as political pressures, sustained by military means, that could hem in Bonn's room for political maneuvering. The West Germans were especially sensitive to the ramifications of either a unilateral Western force reduction or a mutual balanced force reduction (MBFR). Bonn was ambivalent about MBFR. On the one hand, the Brandt government did not oppose

---

*The Mansfield Resolution—which did not carry—called for the phased reduction of American force levels in Europe.

East-West force reductions—in fact, Bonn emphatically supported them, provided they were militarily equitable and politically acceptable. Moreover, the Germans viewed MBFR as a logical complement to *Ostpolitik:* the reduction of Soviet troop strength in Eastern Europe and in East Germany might lead to a more relaxed political climate, conducive to the psychological and political changes *Ostpolitik* sought to bring about. On the other hand, however, Bonn did not want to see NATO weakened further in light of the Soviet military buildup in Eastern Europe.

The close connection between Bonn's security policy and *Ostpolitik* became clear in 1971. The major results of Bonn's Eastern policy were the German-Soviet renunciation-of-force treaty, signed in August 1970; the German-Polish treaty, signed in December 1970; and the Big Four accord on Berlin of August–September 1971 that, in turn, prepared the way for the agreement on Berlin between East and West Germany of December 1971. Since none of these agreements would have been possible without the active support of the Soviet Union, there was a good deal of speculation about the Kremlin's motives. Most likely the Soviet Union intended to clear the way toward convening a European Security Conference, an objective Moscow had pursued for several years and that had aroused little enthusiasm in the West. Moscow hoped that the conference would provide a large and binding international framework within which there could be a permanent settlement of the major European issues that had developed in the aftermath of World War II. Above all, Moscow sought the freezing of postwar European boundaries and the full international legitimization of the East German state. Aside from the intrinsic importance of such a settlement for the Soviet Union—it would, for all practical purposes, serve as a belated World War II peace treaty and secure permanently the Western flank of the Soviet Union—resolution of these matters would allow Moscow to concentrate on domestic problems and unsettled issues with China, while simultaneously diminishing American influence in Europe.

Whatever the Kremlin's precise motives may have been, the Western powers, and especially the United States, viewed the Soviet conference proposal with a good deal of skepticism. In effect the West made participation conditional upon Russian cooperation on the Berlin question, successful completion of the SALT negotiations, and progress on MBFR. As in past years, however, the major problem of arriving at an equitable and truly balanced reduction of forces was to find a formula through which military asymmetries (such as differing troop strengths, especially between Soviet and United States forces in Europe) could be measured against political and geographical asymmetries (such as the internal security role played by the Soviet army in Eastern Europe and the fact that Soviet troops could withdraw from Central Europe by pulling back only 400 miles while American forces would have to cross the Atlantic).

This complex and interlocking set of issues, conditions, and expectations exemplified the degree to which German security policy had become saturated with purposes that were essentially political rather than military-strategic. The same held true for the security policies of all major powers and reflected the important new reality of the sixties and seventies that the likelihood of war in Europe had diminished substantially. Consequently, governments began to shift their priorities from strategic-military issues to political and economic goals. Europeans no longer feared a major conflagration on the Continent, and Washington had apparently changed its emphasis from the Cold War policy of region-by-region forward containment to the attempt to reach an essentially bilateral accommodation with the Soviet Union on matters of overriding mutual interest, such as stabilization of the global strategic balance of power. In other words, as the fear of military aggression receded over the years and as Soviet military might was seen more in terms of its diplomatic impact, containment at the periphery of the alliance blocs became supplemented by detente at its core and the Western powers were able to couch political purposes in military-strategic and arms control language—just as the Soviet Union had done in the mid- and late fifties. At the same time political and economic issues became the key instruments of diplomacy relative to military-strategic means (although the latter necessarily retained a good deal of importance because of the threat of global destruction). The meaning of security had thus changed significantly in the two decades between the fifties and the seventies, with significant consequences for relationships between the superpowers, between the superpowers and the secondary powers, and among the secondary powers themselves.

The general shift from military elements of power toward economic factors, as well as the political uses of strategic language and arms control proposals, had special implications for Bonn. The Germans were one of the main political beneficiaries of the shift from military to economic-monetary elements of power. Aside from the fact that Germany's political and diplomatic leverage increased along with its growing economic and monetary strength, economic and monetary language provided Bonn with an excellent opportunity to translate political demands—which might still have been suspect because of Germany's past—into respectable economic demands. Although the Germans grumbled a good deal about the fact that they were always called upon to pay "subsidies" of one sort or another to their allies, the relatively great economic strength of West Germany was highly advantageous to Bonn from a diplomatic point of view. (We shall return to this subject in chapter 2.)

In contrast, it was not as easy for West Germany to benefit from the shift toward political use of strategic language and arms control proposals. Owing to geography and history, the Federal Republic was from the beginning a NATO member with special inhibitions, obligations, anxieties, and opportunities. Whatever problems plagued NATO because of America's waning nuclear superiority were always felt more keenly in Bonn than in other West

European capitals. By the sixties it was apparent that there were conflicts of security interests not only between the United States and Western Europe but also between Western Europe and Germany. This was especially true regarding "lower" levels of provocation, since these would most likely involve West Germany because of its proximity to the Warsaw Pact countries. As a result, the big question of whether the defense of the Western alliance was indivisible was coupled with the equally big question for Germany of whether the defense of Western Europe was indivisible.

This alone would have made it difficult for the Germans to express political purposes in military-strategic language, but there were other inhibitions as well. Because of Germany's past, the West Germans could hardly couch political aspirations in terms of arms. Had they done so, they would have been accused of being unreconstructed militarists. Especially sensitive was the question of any kind of German association with nuclear weapons —the German finger on the nuclear trigger. Whenever German policy touched upon nuclear matters—talks about a Franco-German nuclear consortium in the early sixties, Germany's participation in the proposed multilateral nuclear NATO force, Bonn's footdragging on the nonproliferation treaty— anxiety levels rose in the West as well as in the East.

Arms control proposals played an important role in the East-West diplomacy on the German question, which explains in large part why the West Germans responded to such proposals with caution, suspicion, hesitation, and procrastination. In the mid-fifties, the Germans felt that the proposals for arms control and disengagement that were then put forth by the East bloc governments (as well as by influential public figures in the West) would reinforce the division of Europe and Germany. These proposals invariably provided that the status quo—the division of Germany and Europe—would serve as the basis for an agreement between the superpowers on arms control and that West and East Germany would participate in negotiations as equal partners. Thus, agreement on these terms would have led to a de facto recognition of the East German regime as well as to a weakening of the West's military presence at the periphery of the Soviet bloc. Disengagement would have ended plans for a West European Community and, by prying Germany from the Western alliance, would have undermined NATO's forward strategy, which the United States sought to strengthen for its symbolic effect and in order to make nuclear deterrence appear more credible. With these considerations in mind, the West rejected arms control proposals in the fifties.

As fear of the Soviet Union diminished, however, there was renewed interest, both in Western and Eastern Europe, for institutionalized European security arrangements. By the mid-sixties most of the major participants in the East-West dialogue on arms control had begun to use security policy to articulate and advance political objectives. But at first the trend toward translating political concerns into military-strategic rhetoric posed special problems for Bonn, because in this area the Germans had to speak softly indeed. Bonn's implied threats in the mid-sixties to carry a big stick by seeking joint nuclear control or by obstructing progress on detente through opposition to the nonproliferation treaty had met with considerable opposition from Germany's allies as well as opponents. The more cautious attitude adopted by the Grand Coalition and especially its successor, the Brandt government, stemmed from a realistic appraisal of the limits and opportunities of German policy. The Brandt government, in particular, was sensitive to the fact that German political interests would be ill-served by stalling European detente simply because it would bring with it a legitimization of the political status quo, that is, a legitimization of the East German state. Thus Bonn saw political advantages in backing detente and arms control measures, especially since the goals of *Ostpolitik* necessitated adopting a more conciliatory attitude toward the East.

GERMAN SECURITY AND NATO POLICY
IN THE SEVENTIES

Although Germany's security position was improved by *Ostpolitik* and other large trends in European politics that altered the nature of the Soviet threat, in some other respects Bonn's security concerns of the sixties persisted into the seventies. In particular, NATO's deterrence posture remained an issue. The NATO debates of the sixties over the use of tactical nuclear weapons were no longer publicly aired in the early and mid-seventies, most likely out of a desire to avoid aggravation of differences among the allies, but such differences had not really lessened. While the European NATO members, and above all the Federal Republic, saw their security interests best maintained by the early use of nuclear weapons, the United States wanted their use postponed as long as possible. While European strategists saw American tactical nuclear weapons as the essential link between United States strategic nuclear forces and American theater capabilities in Europe, symbolizing Washington's determination to risk escalation for the sake of its European allies, American strategists saw tactical nuclear weapons in a backup role should NATO conventional defenses fail. Such weapons were regarded primarily as a means of limiting conflict to the Continent and preventing escalation. These differing perspectives, which stemmed from the fact that the security interests of the United States and Western Europe were not fully coterminous, also led to differing views on the issue of the "conventional pause" (which went back to the McNamara doctrine of the early sixties) and the perennially troublesome question of forward defense.

Differences among the NATO allies received public attention in the summer of 1977. Rowland Evans and Robert Novak revealed in the *Washington Post* that the so-called Presidential Review Memorandum 10 to which they had gained access included a suggestion to President Jimmy Carter that, among other options, Western Europe might not be defended along the West-East German border but along the Weser and Lech rivers in West Germany. This would mean sacrificing about one-third of West Germany in the early phase of an attack from the East. In addition, the memorandum implied that even if the Weser-Lech perimeter were breached, the use of tactical nuclear weapons would by no means be assured. (Of course, the battlefield use of tactical nuclear weapons at that stage would in any case involve the West German population and for that reason would be problematical.)

President Carter, to be sure, reiterated the principle of forward defense and also did not exclude the use of tactical nuclear weapons on principle. The central question, however—the timing of a tactical nuclear response—remained as ambiguous as ever. Since many German military figures viewed tactical nuclear weapons as an essential link in the chain of escalation from a conventional response to a strategic nuclear exchange between the Soviet Union and the United States, American ambivalence as to when (or even if) tactical nuclear weapons would be used was seen as undermining the totality of NATO's deterrence structure. These anxieties were heightened by the conviction, shared on both sides of the Atlantic by political as well as military experts, that NATO's conventional capabilities were insufficient with respect to strength and preparedness either for purposes of deterrence or for purposes of defense if deterrence should fail.* A NATO strategy based on a time-buying conventional flexible response implied the sacrifice of West German territory for the overall benefit of the alliance. Since almost 25 percent of West Germany's population and 15 to 20 percent of its industrial strength are located within 100 kilometers west of its borders with the Warsaw Pact region, the Germans saw no alternative to the principle of forward defense.

The central dilemma of NATO became even more difficult to resolve during the seventies. The United States sought to limit the arms race and arrive at a stable nuclear balance and therefore was compelled to deal with the Soviet Union on the basis of *parity,* as reflected in the SALT agreements. But at the same time, Washington could not convincingly guarantee security for Western Europe except on the basis of an implied American nuclear *superiority.* This was a dilemma for which neither the United States nor West Germany could be blamed; nor was it likely that they could escape from it. When developments in weapons technology and Soviet determination to catch up with the United States brought about nuclear parity between the two superpowers, fundamental conflicts arose within NATO. Washington

---

*In order to compensate for these weaknesses, neutron weapons appeared attractive to European strategists since these "enhanced radiation" weapons could be deployed effectively against advancing tanks and armored vehicles. This explains the flap within NATO when President Carter vacillated over the decision to develop and deploy neutron weapons.

now had to take into account the potential nuclear devastation of the United States and therefore sought to delay the use of nuclear weapons, while America's NATO partners at the forward line of defense could not accept a strategy that implied sustained conventional warfare at the expense of their territory and population. The evident vulnerability of the United States to Soviet nuclear attack forced Washington to qualify the "automaticity" of its nuclear guarantee to Europe, impaired the credibility of even a qualified guarantee, and ultimately brought to the fore the strategically distinct positions of America and Europe. For Bonn, committed to the political as well as military-strategic purposes of the Western alliance and without an alternative to them, American military-strategic vulnerability threatened to become German political vulnerability.

2

Political
and Economic
Reconstruction

THE ROAD TO RECOVERY:
RESTORATION OF SOVEREIGNTY

The new German state established by the three Western occupation powers in 1949 was granted only a limited and revocable measure of sovereignty. The Allied High Commission, which succeeded the military governors of the occupation regime, for all practical purposes controlled the Federal Republic's political and economic relations with other countries and also had the power to regulate, or at least to supervise, domestic political and economic developments. The German government had only limited authority over domestic and foreign policy.

For Chancellor Adenauer and his supporters, the goal of political recovery meant the moral rehabilitation of Germany, the right to pursue its own foreign policy, and the return of a democratic Germany to the society of Western nations. Adenauer aimed to include Germany as an equal and respected partner in a Western European community, and he wanted Germany securely tied to the cultural, religious, and political traditions of Western Europe in order to forestall the recurrence of a dictatorial regime. Germany's society and politics were to be shaped by a close and permanent attachment to the cultural values of the Western democracies. These aims required a fundamental and lasting rapprochement with France and the United States and restoration of legal independence so that Germany could participate in European integration ventures as an equal, with freely given consent. The sovereignty that Adenauer sought for the West German state was thus of rather a special kind. Once sovereignty was attained, he was willing to give up certain rights and privileges and participate in international structures that would bind Germany to the West. As a consequence, Bonn could advance its demands for political and legal equality in the name of European integration and the Western alliance, rather than in the name of a discredited German nationalism. This theme characterized German foreign policy throughout the postwar period. Whenever possible, the Germans emphasized that meeting their demands would be good for Europe or the Atlantic alliance. Whether or not the argument was totally valid, the fact that it was plausible gave the Germans a certain political-psychological advantage. Their image of being "good Europeans" or "good Atlanticists" contrasted sharply with France's identification with obstructionism and nationalism, which stemmed from the fact that the French national interest seemed to call for a more independent course of action. Overall, however, the Germans' political-psychological advantage in the area of loyalty to the Atlantic alliance and to European integration was far outweighed by the burdens of Germany's historical past.

By the early fifties, German rearmament had become increasingly important to the Western alliance. Thus it is not surprising that Bonn's political leverage toward achieving the goal of sovereignty also increased. From the beginning the Western powers acknowledged the link between German rearmament and the restoration of sovereignty. In the fall of 1951, the West agreed that in return for remilitarization the Federal Republic would become fully sovereign and be admitted as an equal to the European Coal and Steel Community (ECSC), the first attempt at an integrated European economic structure. Since these so-called Bonn Conventions were to be implemented jointly with the treaty for the European Defense Community (EDC), Germany's progress toward political recovery seemed to come to an abrupt halt when the French National Assembly voted down the EDC treaty in August 1954. In fact, however, the Allies anticipated many of the provisions of the Bonn Conventions and from the outset acted in accordance with them as much as possible in their dealings with Germany.

In any case, NATO and the enlarged Brussels Treaty Organization quickly supplied an alternative contractual framework within which to restore German sovereignty. The Paris Agreements of October 1954 included essentially the same provisions as the Bonn Conventions of 1952. In addition to the restrictions placed on German armaments (mentioned in chapter 1), the three Western powers retained their rights regarding decisions on German reunification, a final German peace treaty, and Berlin. The political connections that throughout had linked a number of foreign policy issues were directly reflected in the legal interlocking of the components of the Paris Agreements. The following were signed together on October 23, 1954: the protocol for terminating the occupation regime, the declaration officially inviting Germany to join NATO and the Brussels Pact, the Saar Agreement, and the Status of Forces Convention (which retained certain rights for the Western allies). On the day the Paris Agreements took effect, May 5, 1955, the Federal Republic became a sovereign state.

The Western powers were not interested only in West Germany's military potential. They also wanted to achieve the permanent integration of West Germany into the Western alliance so as to bring about a German commitment to the Western system of values, interdependence of economies, political consultation with and perhaps supervision by the Allies, domestic consensus, and political stability. These larger considerations cannot be stressed too strongly because they gave Bonn much greater and more effective bargaining power in its quest for political recovery than the rearmament issue alone.

As the Federal Republic turned more and more toward the West the restoration of sovereignty became a less critical concession for the Allies, especially since many rights that came with the restoration of sovereignty were immediately "frozen" by the international organizations Germany joined (such as NATO, the Western European Union, and the European Coal and Steel Community). When Bonn made such deals the primary payoff came in equality, rather than independence. This met with no objection from the Bonn government. For Adenauer and other German "Europeanists," political recovery meant the integration of West Germany into a tightly knit West European community; hence it was not difficult to renounce some freedom of action in return for equal membership in international and supranational organizations. In turn, Bonn's continued agitation for political and economic concessions prompted the Allies to quickly set up integrative structures that could supervise the Federal Republic. Thus Adenauer's Europe-oriented policy was an essential precondition for political and economic recovery because the continued stress on European integration demonstrated Germany's willingness to tie itself to the West.

By providing mechanisms for controlling German sovereignty as soon as it was granted the integrative organizations joined by the Federal Republic made the restoration of sovereignty less risky and less painful for the Western powers, especially France. France not only saw such arrangements as imperative because they would help control German resurgence, but also because they might enlist for French purposes Germany's political and economic potential, thus buttressing the French position vis-à-vis the Anglo-American powers. At the same time, France consistently sought to curtail West German influence in these international bodies. The United States, in contrast, was constantly pushing for a solution that would be acceptable to Bonn and thereby bring West Germany into the Western military alliance as soon as possible.

Disagreements between the United States and France were not the only pressures on Bonn's goal of political recovery. Conflict arose from the dual nature of the goal itself. Prior to 1955, political recovery had two distinct aspects: the essentially *legal* aspect entailed in the restoration of sovereignty, and the more substantive *political* aspect, which for Adenauer meant the inclusion of Germany in a Western European union. The distinction took on special meaning after 1955 because although the legal goal had been attained, the political objective was still contested, both internationally and domestically. Even before 1955, however, tensions between the legal and political dimensions of recovery posed serious problems for Bonn. The Western powers had enough interest in German rearmament and European integration to allow the Federal Republic to pursue its recovery policy—in a European context—forcefully and effectively. In fact, the similarity of the French, Italian, Dutch, Belgian, and West German concepts of European integration immeasurably aided Bonn's pursuit of a viable Europe policy. But because of France's persistent attempts to curtail Germany's influence and deny the Federal Republic equality in the alliance, legal equality and the restoration of full sovereignty generally had the support of only the United States. At the same time, Adenauer's long-range political goals of a European union and reconciliation with France required France's sympathetic cooperation. Although this situation was at times awkward for Bonn, it was still manageable as long as the Western alliance was fairly cohesive and Germany could advance its interests in the name of an integrated Western alliance. But the pre-1955 tensions between the legal and political dimensions of recovery foreshadowed the much more serious dilemma that German leaders had to face in later years, when they saw that taking sides with either the United States or France tended to widen the developing fissures in the Atlantic alliance.

ECONOMIC RECOVERY
AND EUROPEAN INTEGRATION

The international developments that had such a profound effect on West Germany's political recovery were equally important for economic recovery. In the late forties and early fifties, there were four major hindrances to economic reconstruction: (1) a large quantity of industrial equipment had been destroyed or dismantled, and production in key industries was curtailed by Allied controls; (2) a severe balance-of-payments deficit hampered foreign trade; (3) insufficient investment slowed down economic growth; and (4) unemployment had risen to 10 percent of the labor force. Bonn's economic philosophy and program—the "social market economy"—assigned in theory and practice a considerable role to government but also relied heavily on individual incentive and the free play of market forces. Both elements would have been severely undercut by inflation, which by the early fifties had to be rigorously controlled. In the currency reform of 1948, through which the extremely inflated *Reichsmark* was replaced by the D-Mark, the monetary system had sustained a most drastic cure, and inflationary trends following on its heels would have had disastrous psychological and economic effects. Furthermore, inflation would have made it difficult for the government to fulfill its commitment to liberalize internal and external trade—a policy in which it believed on its own accord and that also was pushed strongly by the

United States. Without liberalization, exports would have suffered and the balance-of-payments problem could not have been remedied.

The situation called for a tight monetary and fiscal policy and whenever possible a balanced budget. In view of the high level of unemployment, such conservative measures were at times hard to adhere to and hard to defend. But they had very beneficial effects on German exports, which became highly competitive as a result of uninflated price levels and the domestic undercon-sumption caused by unemployment. Producers were forced to concentrate on export markets, and growing exports allowed a gradual liberalization of im-port restrictions. Liberalization of external trade complemented what Bonn was trying to achieve by relaxing controls on domestic markets. Moreover, the principle of liberalization was the central tenet of American global eco-nomic policy, and German policy dovetailed neatly with what the United States was trying to achieve. The groundwork for Germany's phenomenal economic and monetary success in the sixties and seventies was thus laid in the early fifties.

The Cold War had a profound, if somewhat indirect, impact on the course of Germany's economic revival. The economic reconstruction program ad-vanced by the American and British occupation authorities prior to 1949 guided the West German economy on a course that, although not irreversible, would have proven costly and disruptive if redirected fundamentally. In addition to initiating the currency reform, Allied economic policy made its most important and lasting impact on the economy by stressing the need for free markets and liberalized trade. These policies received an added and decisive impetus from the Marshall Plan, which was intended by Washington to bring about European recovery not only through the massive injection of American aid but also through the long-range liberalization of European trade-and-payments policies. To the extent that these developments were an outgrowth of tensions between the Soviet Union and the Western powers, the Cold War left an imprint on the West German economy even prior to the establishment of the Federal Republic. After 1949, East-West tensions con-tinued to provide an incentive for the Western powers, and especially the United States, to assist West Germany in the quest for economic recovery— if only to lay the economic and social foundations for political and military integration of Germany into the Western alliance.

Following the outbreak of the Korean War and the decision to rearm Germany, the Western powers gradually lifted their controls over production in key industries, and in 1955 the remaining controls were officially abolished. Between 1952 and 1954 exports and the gross national product continued to rise rapidly, and by the end of 1954 the gold and foreign-exchange reserves of the Federal Republic amounted to more than $2.5 billion.

The establishment of the European Coal and Steel Community (ECSC) is especially significant and illustrative in the context of Germany's rapid economic recovery. In May 1950, French Foreign Minister Robert Schuman presented a plan for a European common market for coal and steel that would include France, West Germany, the Benelux countries, and Italy. This proposal can be attributed to two aspects of the Cold War. In the first place, the rearmament of West Germany seemed inevitable, and France was determined to create at least a rudimentary international body for supervising German remilitarization before agreeing to it. International arrangements for regulating the production and marketing of coal and steel looked like an effective check on the war potential of Germany. Second, France was acutely conscious that German influence within the Western alliance was increasing. The Ruhr industrial complex was still under the control of the International Ruhr Authority, which had been created by the occupation powers, but French policymakers were afraid that the growing influence of Germany might lead to the scrapping of Allied restraints. To preclude exclusive German control over the industry of the Ruhr basin, France proposed the ECSC.

For West Germany establishment of the ECSC meant the abolition of the International Ruhr Authority and represented a significant advance toward the restoration of German sovereignty since Allied control would give way to an international organization in which the Federal Republic would participate as an equal. This promised gains for both the legal aspect of political recovery (restoration of sovereignty) and for Adenauer's larger aspiration—a fundamental reconciliation with France in the context of a West European community.

Throughout the early and mid-fifties, economic recovery was supported by the government's policy on political recovery—and of course by its policy on security and rearmament, on which the whole construct rested. In such ventures as the ECSC political and economic gains went hand in hand and were achieved through a calculated, coordinated strategy that encompassed both dimensions and advanced German demands in the name of European and Atlantic unity.

The compatibility of the political and economic aspects of Bonn's recovery goal was also exemplified by the European Economic Community (EEC), which was established in 1957 through the Treaty of Rome. After two years of negotiations, the six countries already joined in the ECSC—West Germany, France, Italy, and the Benelux countries—agreed to create in three successive four-year stages a common market for industrial and agricultural products by establishing a common external tariff. They also agreed to coordinate social policy and to create a European Atomic Community (Euratom). The understanding was that there would ultimately be a single administrative body for the ECSC, Euratom, and the EEC. French and Belgian overseas territories gained an associated status, and a joint development fund was established to help finance investments in these territories. Bonn gained the concession that trade between West Germany and East Germany would not be impeded by the Common Market's external trade barrier—an important issue since the government wanted to avoid creating a legal economic barrier between the two German states in addition to the already existing political and military-strategic barriers.

The political aspirations reflected in the Treaty of Rome, which specifically acknowledged that its signatories intended the Common Market to be the next phase in building a united Europe, gave rise to the hope among Europeanists that crucial and perhaps painful economic measures would be seen in light of the larger promise of political union. After attempts to unite Europe militarily through the EDC had failed, economic integration was regarded as a means of paving the way to political union; and Adenauer's goal of a united Western Europe seemed to have proceeded one step further. Although Adenauer himself assessed the value of the Common Market primarily in political terms, the long-range economic benefits for Germany were substantial. By 1957, the West German "economic miracle" was well under way (indeed, it would be inappropriate to continue talking about the goal of economic "recovery"). On the whole, the West German economy was well equipped to operate within economies of scale such as the EEC, especially in trading industrial products. The major trouble spot was agriculture, which traditionally had been shielded from foreign competition through direct and indirect subsidies. Nonetheless, German industrialists and economists believed that Germany could hold its own quite well in international markets, integrated or not. But they were concerned that the common external tariff, the characteristic feature of a common market, might impede Germany's extensive trade with countries outside the Common Market. For this reason German industrialists wanted a free-trade area arrangement with those European countries not wishing to join the EEC. The Germans saw greater advantages in a less protected Common Market arrangement than the French.

Economic misgivings over the Common Market, which were forcefully expressed within the Bonn government by Economics Minister Ludwig Erhard, were coupled with equally sensitive political considerations. Bonn had continually insisted on a broader EEC membership and especially the inclusion of Britain. But Britain showed no interest in joining, and de Gaulle, who had returned to power in 1958, was highly critical and suspicious of British (and American) influence in the realm of the Six. Although the Adenauer government paid lip service to the idea of a larger community, new developments soon demonstrated that the Germans could not change de Gaulle's policy of exclusion.

GERMANY, FRANCE, AND THE NEW EUROPEAN ORDER

Great Britain, having failed in its attempts to organize a seventeen-nation free-trade area—an issue that divided the Six for a long time—agreed with Norway, Sweden, Denmark, Austria, Switzerland, and Portugal to form the European Free Trade Association (EFTA), effective in May 1960. Intricate negotiations among EEC members took place over whether to allow an expansion of the Common Market to accommodate the proposed free trade area, and if so, under what conditions. Although Adenauer and de Gaulle had quickly established a remarkable rapport, Franco-German tensions were already developing—tensions that culminated in 1963, when de Gaulle vetoed British entry into the EEC.

The conflicts that developed between the Anglo-American powers and France during the late fifties and early sixties immensely complicated Adenauer's task of integrating Germany into a Western European community. Germany could hardly afford to weaken its military and political ties with the United States. But de Gaulle, the indispensable partner for Adenauer's Europe policy, was determined to shut out Anglo-American influence on the Continent, and he wanted the Germans to aid him in this effort. Moreover, it was becoming obvious that de Gaulle's concept of Europe was significantly different from Adenauer's. Both preferred a "little Europe" solution, but de Gaulle opposed genuine integration because that would curtail the national independence of France, and he apparently expected Germany to help the French regain their position in world politics by providing economic and political support. By that time, Bonn's Atlantic-oriented security policy was no longer compatible with its Paris-oriented recovery policy. The fundamental political objectives underlying Adenauer's recovery policy were concentrated on France because the French held the key to the West European community. In addition, Adenauer turned to Paris for support of his still conservative Eastern policy, since the United States and Britain appeared ready to reach an accommodation with the Soviet Union, perhaps on the basis of the status quo in Germany. In contrast, Bonn's security policy remained totally oriented toward the United States and NATO.

By early 1963, the choices confronting Adenauer allowed little equivocation in the developing tug-of-war between France and the Anglo-American powers. In the fall of 1962, de Gaulle and Adenauer had drafted a Franco-German friendship treaty providing for regular meetings between French and German officials, and although it contained no explicit provisions of great importance, to Adenauer this pact must have looked like the capstone of his policy of reconciliation with France. A few days before Adenauer was to arrive in Paris for the official signing of the treaty, in January 1963, de Gaulle announced the French decision to exclude Britain from the EEC.

For de Gaulle, proper timing was crucial. Adenauer was a lame-duck chancellor and his successor could not be expected to show equal understanding toward de Gaulle's ambitions in Western Europe. In fact, Adenauer had become increasingly isolated both at home and abroad. His relations with the Kennedy administration were strained, largely because of disagreements over United States policy toward the Soviet Union; his relations with London were at a low ebb because of his support of French interests; and at home, his increasingly authoritarian manipulations had split his own party and cabinet. By that time there were, in effect, two German foreign policies, not one. The first was Adenauer's, which resulted in the Franco-German friendship treaty and allowed de Gaulle to blackball Britain's membership in the

EEC with Germany's implicit acquiescence. The second policy direction was preferred by Economics Minister Ludwig Erhard and Foreign Minister Gerhard Schröder, who advocated a more flexible course and tended to support the Anglo-American position not only on the Common Market and the Atlantic alliance but also on a more imaginative Eastern policy.

When Ludwig Erhard succeeded Konrad Adenauer in the fall of 1963, the policy differences between France and Germany were leading to a major confrontation, if not a crisis. Almost every item on de Gaulle's agenda opposed German foreign policy at a time when the new chancellor in Bonn was much less sympathetic to French projects than Adenauer had been. The dilemma this created for Bonn became glaringly apparent during the "NATO crisis" of 1966. Bonn and Paris had for some years disagreed about the desirable future of the Western alliance, and a critical point was reached when de Gaulle announced early in 1966 that France would withdraw from NATO's command structure. De Gaulle declared that French troops (including those stationed in Germany) would no longer remain under NATO control and that NATO bases and the NATO command would have to be removed from French territory. This step posed a threat to German security and raised the touchy political and legal question of how French troops could remain in Germany (as the Bonn government hoped they would, for reasons of deterrence) once they were withdrawn from NATO control and returned to national French control. This question was finally resolved when the Germans consented to the continuing presence of French troops in their country on French terms.

Another source of tension between Bonn and Paris was the future of the Common Market. France and Germany disagreed about the optimal size of the EEC, because they had very different ideas of what the EEC ought to be. From the beginning of the European integration movement, economic structures such as the Coal and Steel Community, the Common Market, and Euratom were intended to pave the way for political integration. The executive authorities of these organizations were to be transformed into genuinely supranational governing bodies, responsive to policies made in a strengthened European Parliament rather than those promulgated by national representatives in the Council of Ministers. Although de Gaulle opposed any development that would undermine national sovereignty, there were no serious disagreements among the Six about the future of the Common Market's institutions so long as each member had a veto in the council. Beginning with the third stage of the Treaty of Rome in 1966, however, majority voting in the Council of Ministers was to be adopted, and there was great hope among proponents of political integration that this would begin the transformation of the Common Market into a supranational political union. The most that de Gaulle was willing to concede, however, was institutionalized, regular consultations among the governments of the Six, similar to the bilateral consultations arranged for in the Franco-German cooperation treaty.

Franco-German disagreements about political fundamentals were further aggravated by a clash over economic specifics. In the mid-sixties the Common Market went through crises over tariff policies, agricultural subsidies, and EEC funding, to mention just a few, and in 1965 the French staged a walkout over agricultural financing. De Gaulle's main objection, however, was not agricultural policy but supranationalism. By the time the issue of agricultural financing was resolved in May 1966, almost a year after the walkout, de Gaulle had critically reexamined the supranational potential of the Treaty of Rome. He set up three conditions for continued French participation in the EEC: that EEC members (1) agree on agricultural financing, (2) renounce the EEC Commission's supranational political-economic ambitions, and (3) delete the majority-voting provisions in the Treaty of Rome. In January 1966, the foreign ministers of the Six reached a compromise on de Gaulle's conditions. They agreed to retain the principle of majority voting, although the French also made it clear that they would reserve the power of veto when important French interests were threatened; and the EEC Commission's formal powers of initiative were left essentially intact, but the Commission's independence was significantly curtailed through the stipulation that member governments be consulted prior to making important policy proposals.

De Gaulle's timing was no coincidence. By 1965 the focus of the Common Market was shifting from removal of trade barriers within a customs union to the more ambitious project of adopting common commercial and monetary policies in an economic union—functions traditionally reserved for national governments. If this development had not been checked, the freedom of national governments to manipulate their economic, monetary, and social programs would have been curtailed, with far-reaching repercussions on foreign policy and defence policy—areas in which de Gaulle wanted maximum flexibility. This was the real issue underlying the Common Market crisis.

THE NEW LEADERSHIP IN BONN AND PARIS

The resignation of General de Gaulle in the spring of 1969 quite naturally led to speculation about the future of Franco-German relations. Both the German government (which faced an election in September) and the new French government under Georges Pompidou (which was preoccupied with the tasks of transition) preferred to postpone major initiatives until the fall. The new Brandt government achieved its first diplomatic success in Common Market policy when the EEC ministers for finance and agriculture agreed in November 1969 on a combined system of national and Common Market subsidies. This was of some importance to Germany because it allowed the compensation of German farmers for loss of income sustained by currency revaluations. The agreement, however, did not go very far toward settling the fundamental issue of the general financing of the Community's farm policy or the related question of British entry into the Common Market (which will be treated in later chapters). The French insisted on a common position of the Six toward Britain on as many outstanding issues as possible, because they felt that France's partners had in the past used French rejection of British entry as an excuse to play down their own reservations about the enlargement of the Community.

In early December 1969, the EEC chiefs of government, meeting at the Hague, fashioned an agreement whereby France consented to early negotiations for British entry into the Common Market as soon as a new EEC accord on farm financing—the overriding French interest—was concluded among the Six. This meeting provided the new German chancellor with an opportunity to demonstrate his European credentials (especially welcome because the Germans were embarked on a dynamic Eastern policy), but it also raised some troublesome political and economic issues for the new government. Willy Brandt and his Foreign Minister Walter Scheel, as well as their respective parties, the Social Democrats and Free Democrats, had long advocated British entry into the Common Market. The Brandt government expected economic benefits from British membership and, more important, felt that it would reinforce Western unity and provide added backing for *Ostpolitik.* But Bonn was much less enthusiastic about the possible implications of the common monetary policy for which Pompidou was pressing hard at the EEC summit. France wanted a common currency policy in order to guard against the powerful influence of the dollar in European economic and monetary affairs and to prevent the recurring currency crises that undermined the Community's common farm policy, of which France was the chief beneficiary. The Germans, on the other hand, although not opposed in principle to monetary coordination, feared that they would be called upon to bail out their weaker partners (whose sense of fiscal responsibility Bonn tended to doubt), in addition to continuing their costly subsidies of French agriculture. The Federal Republic wanted monetary-economic controls that could restrain fiscally profligate member states—a position strongly opposed by France.

In 1970, the Common Market moved from the so-called transitional period into its final and irrevocable stage. Two major problem areas had to be negotiated: the financing of a common farm policy, and the related issue of reinforcing the European Parliament's budgetary powers and thus giving the Common Market independent financial resources. With respect to farm financing, agreement was reached to continue the existing practice of drawing on direct national contributions (in addition to farm import levies to finance the farm fund) and to begin turning over to the EEC all tariffs on industrial imports (as well as a certain proportion of revenues collected through indirect taxation within member states).

During 1970 there were no major monetary disturbances in Europe, but there was a generally deteriorating climate in the economic relationship between the United States and Europe, with American spokesmen referring pointedly to the protectionist drive underway in the United States Congress and linking economic-monetary disputes to the continued presence of American troops in Europe. Partly in response to such external challenges and partly in response to internal dynamics, during 1970–71 the Community launched several new programs, all of which had important implications for German foreign policy and for the Common Market's relations with the United States. The organization established a common commercial policy; increased the number of preferential trade agreements; moved toward creating its own revenues; began negotiations to admit Britain, Denmark, Norway, and Ireland; and set up a timetable toward establishing a monetary union through the so-called Werner Plan.

The Werner Plan for a European Monetary Union (EMU) would have made the Common Market region into a single-currency area. But the steps toward this goal were hedged in important ways, and there was nothing irrevocable about the decision to carry them out. The plan provided that in the first and second stages of the EMU (1970–75) the exchange rates of EEC currencies would be moved close together and taxes would be harmonized. In the third stage (1976–78) EEC currencies would be so tightly locked as to be virtually one currency.

The political and economic calculations behind the response of EEC members to the Werner Plan were highly complex and far-reaching. All six members shared the major long-range goal of establishing a monetary-economic bloc that would guard the Common Market area against outside inflationary trends and disturbing capital transactions—especially by the United States—and provide an alternative to the dollar and sterling as reserve currencies. There was much less unanimity about the internal political and economic ramifications of the plan, since its implementation would have required the harmonization of a wide variety of monetary and fiscal policies that were still the prerogative of national governments. After long negotiations it was agreed that fluctuations among EEC currencies would be kept within a narrow range and that member currencies would move as a group with respect to outside currencies such as the dollar. This was the "snake in the tunnel"—the snake being the group of EEC currencies, the tunnel being the range or band of fluctuation with respect to outside currencies.*

The Germans pushed for the establishment of central institutions that would put teeth in the economic guidelines and monetary-fiscal targets called for by the Werner Plan. Bonn felt that unless the Common Market enforced economic and budgetary discipline on member states, West Germany would constantly be obliged to prop up economically weaker (and perhaps fiscally less responsible) EEC partners. Accordingly, Germany insisted on adding a provision to the Werner Plan making all agreements pertaining to the cur-

---

*This phase of the plan was put into effect in April 1972, but it ran into trouble very quickly. British sterling, the Italian lira, and the French franc began to float out because of their relative weakness, and the tunnel itself collapsed in March 1973 when the IMF–organized band disintegrated.

rency union invalid effective January 1976 unless EEC countries had by that time agreed on a binding stabilization program. As it was, the fate of the Werner Plan was tied to the larger international monetary picture, in which the policies of the United States were of crucial importance.

GERMANY, THE COMMON MARKET, AND THE UNITED STATES

In addition to internal difficulties the Common Market faced serious external problems, especially with the United States. These problems reached a crucial stage in 1970–71. The sources of Washington's displeasure with EEC practices were manifold but focused largely on three related areas: (1) the Community's preferential trade agreements with an increasing number of countries (notably in the Mediterranean), which tended to violate the most-favored-nation principle,* (2) the Community's general protectionist agricultural policy through which the prices of imported products were brought up to the inflated EEC level, and (3) the fact that the Community's large agricultural surpluses (encouraged by high, subsidized EEC price levels) were being dumped in traditional United States markets, especially the Far East and North Africa. Moreover, the United States feared these detriments to American trade would become even more formidable if Britain joined the Common Market and the other EFTA members gained associated status.

Common Market members, in turn, objected to American quotas on many important commodities and especially criticized the American policy of levying duties on chemicals based on their domestic prices in the United States rather than on their import prices. Above all, however, the Europeans felt that the central issue between the United States and the Common Market was money rather than trade. In the European view, the United States was acting irresponsibly in not taking drastic steps to remedy its chronic balance-of-payments problems and in shifting a major part of the resulting burden onto its European allies and trading partners. The United States had been running up deficits during most of the previous twenty years, with the dollar surplus countries for all practical purposes no longer even demanding American gold for American dollars. During 1970 the lowering of American interest rates as well as speculative dollar flights led to an even larger influx of dollars into Europe. The Europeans were sensitive to the rate fluctuations of the Eurodollar market, fed by surplus dollars, because these fluctuations directly influenced national monetary policies and they could be checked effectively only through intervention by a central EEC authority, as yet nonexisting. (In fact, this consideration had some bearing on the decision to establish a com-

---

*Most-favored-nation agreements concluded between the United States and European countries provided for mutual reduction of tariffs on a preferential basis.

mon EEC currency.) American investments in Europe were a touchy issue as well. The French in particular were concerned that the United States was buying up real value with inflated dollars. Other EEC countries also turned down attempts by American companies to acquire additional subsidiaries in Europe. Moreover, since United States exports to EEC countries consistently exceeded imports, the Europeans felt that American complaints about EEC trading practices were misplaced, that they were putting the cart before the horse.

The world monetary crisis of the summer of 1971, which brought to a head the economic-monetary controversies between the United States and the Common Market, was significant not only because of its intrinsic impor- tance but also because it affected all of the political-economic areas that we have discussed—the enlargement of the Common Market, the Community's plan to establish a common currency area, and the overall political-strategic and economic relationships between the United States and Europe. In effect, the world monetary crisis heralded a long overdue reorganization of the world monetary system, and revolved essentially around the economic, strategic, and political role of the United States in world affairs and what part of this role the allies were willing to continue financing.

President Richard M. Nixon's unveiling of a New Economic Policy in August 1971 amounted to a formal abolition of the Western monetary system established in 1944 at Bretton Woods. By breaking the dollar's tie to gold and by imposing a 10 percent surcharge on imports, the White House set in motion a series of events with far-reaching political and economic conse- quences. The immediate impetus for Nixon's decision was the United States deficit of $10.7 billion to foreign central banks in 1970, which had increased by $5 billion during the first quarter of 1971, a $20 billion annual rate. (In the *week* before the announcement, a speculative run to buy foreign currencies had amounted to an outflow of $4 billion!) Moreover, in 1971 the United States faced its first trading deficit since 1893; that is, United States imports had exceeded exports. The larger problem was that the chronic United States balance-of-payments deficit reflected a fundamental disequilibrium, causing a constant net outflow of funds, which Washington was apparently unable to redress. In other words, for a number of years the United States had been in a position that would have forced any other country to devalue its currency or impose other drastic remedies. But the United States government could avoid such steps as long as other countries continued to accept the role of the United States dollar as a reserve currency and were willing to adjust their own currencies to keep the central position of the dollar in the world monetary system intact. This led to a large accumulation of dollars by European central banks and increased the interdependence of national monetary systems.

When President Nixon ended the convertibility of dollars into gold and imposed a 10 percent surcharge on imports, he insisted that the United States would not devalue the dollar formally or change the price of gold—which amounted to the same thing since, under world monetary rules, a rise in the price of gold would have automatically devalued the dollar. Instead, Washington wanted other countries (especially Common Market members and Japan) to increase the value of their currencies and thus the cost of their exports. The 10 percent import surtax was intended to provide the leverage for Washington's negotiations with Japan and Europe. Basically, the American position was that the dollar's problems stemmed from the selfish trade and monetary policies of other countries and their unwillingness to share adequately in the defense burdens that the United States had shouldered for many years.

To the Europeans, it seemed preposterous to adjust their currency parities and make other concessions in order to absorb a huge amount of American goods and services for the express purpose of allowing the United States to continue investing abroad and propping up its military-strategic commitments around the world. United States allies felt they were already indirectly helping to finance the Vietnam War—during the sixties, the net United States balance-of-payments deficit on military expenditures amounted to $32 billion—while the United States was buying up European industrial plants with money that European countries were lending either directly or indirectly. In addition, the Community had a big trade deficit with the United States ($2.4 billion in 1970), which reflected the extensive and profitable nature of American trade with the Community, and the Common Market's tariffs averaged less than those of the United States (6 percent versus 7 percent).

The Europeans also argued that they had already helped considerably— the Germans had revalued the mark in May 1971, which caused a great many internal difficulties; EEC countries had helped establish the two-tier gold market system; Europeans (especially the Germans) had not demanded repayment of debts, accepting a huge amount of United States Treasury bills that yielded less than other holdings—while the United States had refused to change the value of the dollar or curb inflation. EEC members urged the United States to participate in a joint realignment of currency rates by devaluing the dollar, arguing that without this measure the value of their national gold reserves would be decreased, curbing world liquidity and hence trade expansion.

All parties agreed that in addition to the short-term problems caused by the monetary crisis, there was a need to reform the world monetary system itself. Fears were widespread that unless the differences between the United States and Europe and Japan could be ironed out speedily, amicably, and fundamentally, retaliatory protectionism between trading areas would result, impeding world trade and causing a disastrous reversal of the post-World War II trend toward relatively liberalized trade and investment policies. At the very least, the uncertainty over exchange rates and international trade arrangements could be expected to have a dampening effect on long-term economic planning and increase the dangers of world recession.

But the Europeans found it difficult to speak with a single voice. For although the Community's commitment to a monetary union and common currency was fundamentally at odds with the American desire for freely floating exchange rates, differences among EEC members (especially between France and Germany) made it difficult for the Community to articulate a common position. France opposed an appreciation of the franc relative to the dollar, and the Germans had already increased the value of the mark by having floated it. France controlled exchange rates with a dual standard—a "commercial" franc rate for foreign trade, and a "financial" franc rate for all other transactions—and after the August crisis, Paris held the commercial franc rate at the old dollar-franc parity (thus protecting French exports against an appreciation of the franc) but allowed the financial franc rate to rise in value by about 4 percent. This not only worked to the disadvantage of the United States by making it less attractive for American enterprises to invest in France but also met with objections from Germany. Bonn opposed dual markets (and other ways of controlling exchange rates), preferring a "free market" solution such as the floating of the mark. A concerted float against the dollar seemed a better solution, narrowing currency fluctuations among the EEC countries while letting European currencies genuinely float with respect to the dollar. This measure would have helped the United States by moving EEC currencies up toward the dollar, but the French were unwilling to help bail out the United States if that meant changing the franc's parity. Basically, the French and German economies required differing monetary policies. France was primarily interested in economic growth, and Germany in economic stabilization and control of inflation. Also, while France was Germany's most important trading partner, German exports to the United States were three times as high as French exports to the United States, and German exporters stood to lose much more by a continuing 10 percent surcharge than the French. At the same time, Bonn resisted a large increase in the value of the mark (which Washington desired) so long as France refused to revalue the franc upward, because that would have given France a considerable economic advantage in addition to what France had already gained because of the floating of the mark in May 1971.*

The economic-monetary disagreements between France and Germany—which were aggravated by personal disputes between their finance ministers, Valéry Giscard d'Estaing and Karl Schiller—were also tied to fundamentally conflicting political purposes. The German government did not want economic disagreements between the United States and Europe to escalate into political confrontation, fearing adverse consequences for Germany's *Ostpolitik* and the related issue of the continued American military presence in Europe. This made the Germans much more willing than the French to accommodate Washington—which tempted Washington into a clumsy effort to undermine the European bargaining position by holding out the possibility of bilateral

---

*Revaluation tends to increase the price of exports and lower the price of imports in the domestic economy. Devaluation has the opposite effect. Hence, a further revaluation (increase in the value) of the mark would have hurt the Federal Republic's trade position.

Washington-Bonn negotiations. At the same time, the concerted European float against the dollar advocated by Karl Schiller would have enhanced Germany's economic and political position among Community members. By narrowing the fluctuations among EEC currencies and shaping them into a more coherent monetary unit, the strongest currency (the mark) would inevitably push the others up to higher values against the dollar. This would have had deflationary consequences in all EEC countries, a welcome effect from the German point of view but something the other nations would be less willing to accept. In short, the partial harmonization of EEC exchange rates against the dollar would have tended to place the mark in a central position among EEC currencies—a likelihood that France found unacceptable for political as well as economic reasons. The French, therefore, advocated a large revaluation of the mark on top of the substantial upward revaluation that had already taken place since May and opposed adjusting the parity rate of the franc. (Although France did not favor a concerted float, wider trading margins among currencies were also unacceptable because then the mark and other currencies would have been allowed to drift down and put an end to the French franc's advantageous undervaluation.) These issues were ultimately resolved in a compromise, but they demonstrated once again that the economic and monetary interests of France and Germany were not fully congruent and that these differences strongly affected their political positions on European integration.

Concurrent with the Franco-German discussions, difficult and acrimonious negotiations were taking place between the United States and Western Europe. Washington was pressing for an upward revaluation of European currencies, specific and fundamental measures to lower barriers against American exports, and higher contributions to American military expenditures. The Europeans sought a devaluation of the dollar and a lifting of the import surcharge. While these negotiations were being held at various conferences of the International Monetary Fund (IMF), the Organization for Economic Cooperation and Development (OECD), the Group of Ten, and the General Agreement on Tariffs and Trade (GATT), the Europeans employed a variety of measures to keep their currencies from rising too high, including intervention in monetary markets, adjustment of interest rates, and exchange controls. But these measures were coordinated inadequately, if at all, because conflicting political and economic calculations of the various European countries did not allow a common position.

The protracted United States–European monetary talks were finally brought to an end in December 1971 in Washington. Nixon agreed to drop the import surcharge and devalue the dollar by 8.6 percent relative to the price of gold, which meant that the dollar was devalued 7.9 percent relative to foreign currencies. (Although this action was based on an increase in the price of gold from $35 an ounce to $38 an ounce, it did not mean that the United States Treasury would henceforth be willing to supply gold at the new price.) All in all, the formal devaluation of the dollar, together with the upward revaluation of foreign currencies, decreased the value of the dollar by about 10 to 12 percent. The German mark went up 13.5 percent against the dollar, and the French franc and British pound were revalued upward by 8.6 percent.

Nixon's characterization of the December 1971 accord as "the most significant monetary agreement in the history of the world" was something of an overstatement. The so-called Smithsonian Agreement was only a provisional settlement of the world's monetary problems. It left unresolved such important issues as the convertibility of the dollar balances held by central banks; the roles of gold, dollars, and Special Drawing Rights* in a new international monetary system; the problem of "hot" money speculative flows; and the touchy issue of negotiating trading arrangements between super-economies such as that of the United States and the European community.

Other troublesome issues remained in the wake of the Smithsonian conference. The realignment of currencies complicated the Community's agricultural financing system (as had the unilateral floating of the German mark in May 1971) because when EEC currencies fluctuated it became necessary to adjust prices with levies and subsidies so that prices could remain constant in terms of national currencies. These frontier "compensation taxes" were cumbersome and stood in the way of an integrated and complete agricultural market. Nor were the difficulties between the United States and the Community resolved in any thoroughgoing way. The dollar did not regain sufficient strength, which kept up pressure on the German mark and created new uncertainties about future monetary developments, and the dollar's nonconvertibility remained a problem, with Washington putting off any sweeping solution and the Europeans remaining anxious to obtain other reserve assets for the new dollar balances they had accumulated.

Most disturbing perhaps was the continuing American pressure to revise the EEC's farm support program. A basic change in the farm program would have shaken its very foundations because the central compact made between France and Germany in the mid-fifties would have been violated (the French had accepted industrial free trade in return for agricultural free trade, supplemented by a generous agricultural support system). Acquiescence in Washington's demands would have meant dismantling the agricultural basis of European integration, without which there could be no hope that a monetary, economic, and political union could be achieved.

TOWARD A NEW TRANSATLANTIC
AND EUROPEAN UNDERSTANDING

In the early and mid-seventies, the basic shift in American policy toward the Common Market (initiated during the Nixon administration and carried through by presidents Gerald Ford and Jimmy Carter) had far-reaching impli-

---

*A reserve asset created by the International Monetary Fund in 1969, made up of prescribed quotas of financial contributions remitted by IMF members.

cations for West German foreign policy because it signaled the abrogation of a tacit transatlantic agreement between the United States and Western Europe that had been forged in the postwar era. The essence of that bargain was that the United States, based on its hegemonic economic and monetary position in the postwar period, would be willing to make marginal economic sacrifices in return for political privileges and in order to advance the cause of European integration. During the sixties, as American hegemony declined relative to Europe and Japan, the United States allies felt increasingly restive about United States political and economic-monetary privileges. Europe pushed for an alteration of the framework within which these political and economic arrangements had been made.

This change in the basic understanding between the United States and Europe had two fundamental implications for West German foreign policy: (1) it affected the special ties between the United States and Germany, especially in the area of security policy—a policy for which Germany had no viable and responsible alternative; and (2) it affected Germany's position within the European Community and had a direct bearing on the Franco-German political-economic compact.

First, close relations between Washington and Bonn were as essential for West Germany in the early seventies as they had been at any time in the postwar period. The United States continued to be the indispensable guarantor of West German security—a consideration that remained important although a direct Soviet military threat had become unlikely—and Bonn's Eastern policy required American backing to obtain tangible results and avoid diplomatic isolation. To be sure, after initial hesitation the United States did not deny West Germany its support, but Washington's attitude implied that the American commitment to Europe was weakening on political-strategic as well as economic-monetary grounds. In the early years of the Federal Republic, the requirements of reconstructing Europe economically and containing the Soviet Union militarily were the same, from the perspective of the United States. When these requirements were no longer coterminous, the national interests of Bonn and Washington also diverged.

Second, the alteration of the transatlantic compact affected Bonn's European policy and Franco-German relations. The dilemma of choosing between Paris and Washington on major policy questions was not a new one for Bonn—it was the key problem of German policy toward the Western alliance in the sixties. But in the past, the choice seemed to be between two types of alliance options: the transatlantic option preferred by Washington, and the Gaullist European option preferred by France. By the early seventies, however, Washington became disenchanted with the Common Market. Washington thus implied that European integration in the larger context of the transatlantic alliance was no longer a primary American goal. As a result, Bonn's "traditional" dilemma was substantially changed. The integrative alliance option seemed to have vanished, and the Gaullist alliance option was also watered down (in any case the second option would not have provided a satisfactory alternative to Bonn for all the strategic, political, and economic reasons previously mentioned).

In other words, both the transatlantic and European alliances were fading —a process that seemed irreversible because the entry of Britain, Ireland, and Denmark into the Common Market dimmed even further the prospects for a politically integrated Europe and because the United States saw no way to revitalize the transatlantic compact of the fifties and sixties. The political dynamics of these two alliances had provided Bonn with many opportunities to implement German national interests. Bonn had always been highly effective in multilateral integrative settings—in contrast to France, whose foreign policy derived its vitality from a separatist line. As we have seen, this phenomenon dated back to the early fifties. By and large West Germany was very successful in turning international cooperation to national advantage. It was somewhat ironic that the integrative features of the transatlantic and European alliances, created in part to check the resurgence of Germany, were subsequently used by Bonn to increase its political leverage.

This also explains the central role that Bonn's international economic-monetary policy played in West German foreign policy. European and transatlantic institutions lent themselves well to transforming Germany's economic-monetary power into political leverage. Although the Germans frequently complained about always being called upon to pay subsidies of one sort or another to their allies, the integrative and coordinating features of the Western alliance provided the Germans with an excellent opportunity to translate political demands—which might still be suspect because of Germany's past—into respectable economic demands. The transformation of economic power into political power, and the translation of political demands into economic demands, compensated the Germans for their handicap of not being able to convert political demands into military-strategic language— which is what the French did so effectively under de Gaulle.

The Germans therefore faced a big paradox. On the one hand, as the importance of economic and monetary issues increased relative to military-strategic matters, German political leverage also increased. But on the other hand, this leverage could be best applied in integrative and coordinating structures, and those structures were either weakening (in the transatlantic context) or stagnating (in the European context).

The problems arising from this paradox became especially troublesome after Helmut Schmidt took over the chancellorship from Willy Brandt in 1974 —not because of the change in German leadership, but because Germany's dynamic Eastern policy had essentially run its course and because German domestic issues and the worldwide recession brought economic matters to the foreground. Compared to the economic malaise of many West European countries and the United States, West Germany stood out as a pillar of economic-monetary strength. Although real GNP growth was modest, the German economy was basically healthy, exports were booming, and the unemployment and inflation rates were among the lowest in the OECD area.

Even so, Bonn faced difficulties. In the fall of 1975, when the EEC Council of Ministers took up the Community's budget for 1976, Germany found itself outvoted on the issue of a substantially larger cut in the area of agricultural supports than the other eight countries viewed as desirable. Bonn did not resort to its right of veto, but spokesmen made it clear that Germany did not intend to be placed in such an isolated position repeatedly. As far as Bonn was concerned, the fundamental issue was the Community's unsound fiscal policy with regard to regional aid and social funds, assistance to nonassociated developing countries, and above all, the common agricultural policy. The Schmidt government took a much tougher stand than any previous German government on the issues of fiscal responsibility and reform of the Community's entrenched bureaucracies. Bonn made it clear that it would agree to monetary demands by EEC members only if they would seek to solve the larger structural problems of the Community. This was clearly a reflection of the personal convictions of the new chancellor. Although Schmidt was willing to be a "good European"—and in particular to support measures that could lead to a monetary union—he also demanded that fellow EEC members make reforms in return for Germany's heavy financial contributions to the Common Market. But France's decision to leave the European single-currency area (although Germany would have been willing to underwrite with substantial loans the costs to France), Italy's imposition of import controls (in spite of massive German financial assistance), the uncoordinated Community response to the energy crises, Britain's waffling over some aspects of its commitment to EEC, and several other smaller issues persuaded Bonn that criticism of the Community was justified. Correctly or not, the Germans felt that the economic and monetary plight of some EEC countries was in large part due to fiscal and political irresponsibility and that the sense of drift in the Community could be overcome only by political leadership that faced up to the challenges of the future and was more resistant to the day-by-day pressures of political expediency.

In the summer of 1978 Germany and France launched a major new initiative toward a European monetary union in a new attempt to coordinate more closely the currencies and economies of the EEC members. At the time the idea of the currency snake, in which the EEC currencies were held to a narrow range of fluctuation, had lost much of its meaning because of the overwhelming predominance of the mark. France, Britain, and Italy had been forced out of the snake because (1) their currencies had become too weak, falling below the bottom rate permitted by the snake, and (2) they could not afford to have their exchange rates locked to the strong mark, the value of which was increasing constantly as feeble dollars were converted into Swiss and German currency. The countries remaining in the snake were Germany, Belgium, the Netherlands, Luxembourg, and Denmark—countries that could afford to have their currencies rise with the mark or were helped by the Germans to do so. The Germans and the French proposed the creation of a European monetary fund in which EEC members would put one-fifth of their reserves and that would grant credit to members if they met certain conditions. This would lead to greater harmonization of national economic policies. The Germans also hoped that locking other EEC currencies to the mark in a proposed European Currency Unit (ECU) would ease excessive upward pressure on the mark by reducing speculative dollar investments in German currency and spreading such investments among other EEC currencies. This would, in addition, protect German exports, which were becoming very expensive, and make less glaring the political influence Germany had gained by having taken on a good portion of the dollar's reserve currency role.

The last point is particularly interesting since it reflected Chancellor Schmidt's sensitivity to the risks of having Germany appear to be pursuing national power and international leverage too assertively. Schmidt did not want to see the mark play too large a role as a clearly identifiable reserve currency because of the possible negative implications—politically, psychologially, and monetarily. Again, as in many other instances, the Germans preferred a European institutional context for implementing their policies, shying away from purely national policies and thus avoiding the implication that they were striving for national independence of action or heavy-handed political influence.

These considerations were especially delicate with respect to German relations with the United States, which were uneasy during the Schmidt chancellorship for several reasons. Schmidt opposed United States Secretary of State Henry Kissinger's tough attitude on "Eurocommunism," viewing it as nervous and shortsighted; the Middle East War in 1973 and the energy crisis caused irritations between Washington and Bonn; and the "off-set" agreements through which Germany had purchased American weaponry and United States bonds to finance American troop-stationing costs were for all practical purposes scrapped. During the early days of the Carter administration the issues of human rights, export of nuclear technology by Germany, Washington's failure to support the dollar in international markets, and the American demand that Germany help the world economy through a more dynamic spending program aggravated problems between Washington and Bonn.

It would be inaccurate to describe these policy differences as a "crisis" in United States–German relations. Nonetheless, Bonn's policies and attitudes were signals that the Germans believed that their economic and monetary power—Germany's monetary reserves were the largest in the world, twice those of the United States—carried with it a sense of responsibility. This was reflected in an intensive German diplomatic effort, sustained by development aid, in the Third World, and in general a more assertive foreign policy. By and large, this was not done in a heavy-handed way. From Bonn's point of view, the Germans were propping up the United States as well as the European Community: they were asked to support the French farmers as well as the American dollar; they were expected to underwrite Italy's attempt to overcome economic and political disarray; they were supposed to pay the lion's share of the cost of the EEC nuclear research program as well as American defense costs in Europe; and they were to continue to subsidize the Community's regional development programs and absorb a major portion of the cost of petrodollar recycling. At the same time, the Germans saw themselves being asked to undermine the very basis of their economic well-being through what they considered ill-advised economic and monetary policies. In short, they felt that the "equalizing" measures suggested to them were a leveling down to a lower common denominator, when they believed that the process should be the reverse—that Germany's partners should make stronger efforts to match the Federal Republic's economic and monetary performance.

3

Reunification and *Ostpolitik*

Reunification proved to be the most troublesome foreign policy goal for West Germany. The division of Germany had been a direct consequence (as well as an important cause) of the disagreements that developed between the victorious powers soon after World War II. Due to Cold War tensions the four states that occupied and controlled Germany in the postwar years—the United States, France, Britain, and the Soviet Union—found it impossible to exercise the joint control and administration of Germany they had agreed upon. Finding it impossible to rule Germany together, and determined to deny each other control over all of Germany, in 1949 the Cold War antagonists established client states in their respective zones of occupation—the Federal Republic of Germany (FRG) with its capital in Bonn, and the German Democratic Republic (GDR) with its capital in East Berlin. As the two Germanies became incorporated into the Western and Eastern spheres of influence, the Iron Curtain, which divided Central Europe as well as Germany, became the line of demarcation between the Cold War blocs and the forward line of defense for Washington's policy of containment.

THE PARTITION OF EUROPE
AND GERMANY, 1949–55

The Bonn government knew from the beginning that in contrast to other West German foreign policy goals—such as security, or political and economic recovery within the framework of the Western alliance—the unification of Germany required at least the acquiescence, if not the direct sponsorship, of both Cold War blocs. Consequently, Adenauer's long-range reunification strategy was based on two central assumptions: (1) that Washington and Moscow held the key to the German question, and (2) that with the passage of time the balance of power between the Cold War blocs would shift in favor of the West, thus allowing negotiations "on the basis of strength" that would induce the Soviet Union to settle the German question on Western terms.

The first of these assumptions was essentially correct. It followed that above all else, Bonn would need to gain political leverage within the Western alliance. Because of West Germany's postwar weakness and dependent status, the most immediate aim of Bonn's unification policy was to enlist the active support of the Western powers, especially the United States, and to ensure that the West would not treat the German question as a secondary issue that could conceivably be traded off in an overall American-Soviet settlement of the Cold War. The Germans realized that the Western powers would view the prospect of a unified Germany with apprehension. Thus, Bonn's unification policy required increasing German influence within the Western alliance in order to solidify on the political plane the legal and moral commitment of the Western powers to support reunification and acknowledge the Bonn government as the only legitimate spokesman for all of Germany. Bonn, in turn, pledged to implement Germany's treaty obligations, to forswear the use of force in seeking unification, and to develop a united Germany along peaceful and democratic lines.

The complementary aspect of this policy, the aspect oriented toward Moscow, was much more passive and vague because it was merely an appendage of Bonn's Washington-oriented policy. This was perhaps unavoidable. At the height of the Cold War, the Western powers most likely would have obstructed German overtures to the Soviet Union, and a more active Eastern policy would have jeopardized the entire treaty structure that was to restore sovereignty to the Federal Republic. This would have undermined the power base from which Adenauer expected to deal with the Soviet Union at some future date, not to speak of the risks Bonn would have incurred in dealing with Moscow independently. As a consequence, Bonn's Eastern policy inevitably appeared flaccid and unimaginative, especially in contrast to the political acumen and tenacity displayed by Adenauer in his dealings with the Western powers.

Bonn's Moscow policy was static because it consisted almost entirely of negative elements. West Germany refused to recognize East Germany or deal with it on an official basis, arguing that since the East Berlin government was not freely elected the Bonn government had the duty as well as the right of "sole representation" of all Germans, including those in East Germany. To buttress its claim of sole representation, and in order to isolate the East German regime diplomatically, in 1955 Bonn formulated the so-called Hallstein Doctrine on the basis of which the Federal Republic withheld or withdrew diplomatic recognition from governments that recognized the East German regime—except for the Soviet Union.

Bonn also refused to recognize the Oder-Neisse line as the permanent border between Poland and Germany. After the East German government and all the other East-bloc states accepted Poland's claim to the Oder-Neisse territories and East Prussia, the Bonn government adamantly refused to regard the territorial status quo in that area as anything but provisional and subject to revision. This refusal, which rested on the Potsdam Agreement's provision that no permanent revision of Germany's border could take place before a final all-German peace treaty, was supported consistently, if rather perfunctorily, by the Western powers until de Gaulle recognized the Oder-Neisse line as permanent in 1959.

Even though the Western powers backed Bonn's rigidly legalistic stand toward the Soviet bloc, they showed no great enthusiasm for the cause of German unity. Both Cold War camps considered it politic to give at least verbal support to German aspirations for unification, but neither the United States nor the Soviet Union wanted a unified Germany that would be genuinely free to conduct its own external affairs. The first choice of either side —to draw a united Germany into its respective orbit under effective supervision—could be prevented by the other side, given the power relations between East and West. On the other hand, securing the allegiance and power potential of the part of Germany that each Cold War camp already controlled promised a substantial increase of strength for each side. Power calculations allowed neither camp to go beyond repeating its interpretation of what constituted an equitable solution to the German problem.

As a result, the verbal exchanges between East and West on the German question became increasingly divorced from reality. Throughout the fifties, the Western powers, reasonably certain that a Germany united on the basis of free elections would side with the West and knowing that this prospect would be unacceptable to the Soviet Union, kept insisting on free elections in East Germany prior to the formation of an all-German government and on subsequent freedom of action for that government. In contrast, up to the mid-fifties the Soviet Union advocated the neutralization of a united Germany and the formation of a government in which East and West Germany would be represented equally. Agreeing to the Western proposals would have been risky for the Soviet Union, especially because loss of East Germany might jeopardize Soviet control over Eastern Europe, and by insisting on free elections and subsequent freedom to join alliances, the West asked the Soviet Union to face the likelihood that not only West Germany but a unified Germany would become a member of the Western alliance. The Soviet concept of reunification, on the other hand, threatened the West. Russian proposals such as the famous Soviet note of March 1952 allegedly aimed at Germany's unification, but most likely were primarily designed to prevent the rearmament of West Germany and to create political conditions advantageous to the Soviet Union. At a minimum the Soviet proposals would have deprived the West of the power potential of West Germany—a potential becoming more and more indispensable for NATO military strategy—and would have led to the de facto recognition of the East German regime.

At crucial junctures in the shaping of Bonn's rearmament policy, Moscow held out the prospect of unification if West Germany would abstain from military, economic, and political ties with the Western powers. But the Soviet Union demanded in effect that the West accept a probably unstable power vacuum in the heart of Europe (with many opportunities for Soviet manipulation and interference) at a time when clearly drawn spheres of influence seemed most promising for Washington's policy of containment. The line dividing the two power blocs in Europe, which ran through Germany, was clear-cut and manned on both sides by the armed forces of the major Cold War antagonists. This "tripwire" setting, and its opportunities for effective containment with a forward NATO strategy (as described in chapter 1), was precisely what the United States sought to establish on all Cold War fronts. It is easy to see why the United States was unwilling to replace this relatively tolerable and stable status quo with the uncertainties that would have followed if Moscow's unification proposals were implemented. For Adenauer, acceptance of Soviet plans for a neutralized united Germany would have meant the end of his most fundamental political aim—to include Germany in a West European union and to tie the future course of German society to the cultural, religious, and political values of Western Europe. The West, and Adenauer, had to weigh the uncertain and risky prospect of a neutralized Germany against the certainty of increasing Western power at a crucial stage in the Cold War.

In such circumstances, the military, economic, and political alignment of either West or East Germany with one of the Cold War blocs could not possibly have made unification acceptable to *both* superpowers. The Cold War camps faced a double-or-nothing situation, where each side had good reason to expect that acceptance of the opponent's proposals would result in a negative outcome. The stakes were high and involved not only the two Germanies but the cohesion of the two alliance blocs and the viability of their military-strategic planning. The very importance of the issue precluded a "global deal" between East and West at another front of the Cold War struggle to bring about a solution of the German question.

In short, although the first assumption of Adenauer's reunification policy —that Washington and Moscow held the key to the German question and that reunification required the consent of both—was correct, the German government found it impossible to advance a solution acceptable to both superpowers. By 1955, when West Germany joined NATO and East Germany became a member of the Warsaw Pact, the Western-oriented dimension of Bonn's policy had proven fairly successful. Germany had achieved a remarkable economic revival, Bonn's political leverage within the Western alliance had increased enormously since 1949, and the Western powers were at least paying lip service to the cause of German reunification. But the very success of this policy, through which Germany became the bulwark of Washington's containment policy, had further accentuated the Cold War division of Europe and sealed the division of Germany. Joining West Germany to the Western alliance thus aggravated the conditions that made unification difficult in the first place. After the Geneva Summit Conference of July 1955 Moscow clearly began to favor the status quo in Central Europe, and thereafter consistently sought to solidify the political division of Europe by following a two-Germanies policy and by seeking to gain Western recognition for the East German regime. It may well be that Soviet interest in a reunited Germany, under Russian predominance if not control, was a Stalinist phenomenon to begin with. In any case, when the Federal Republic joined the military, political, and economic structures of the Western alliance, a solution of the German question on terms Moscow could live with became unobtainable.

This is not to say that unification on a basis acceptable to the Bonn government could necessarily have been achieved if West Germany had *not* aligned itself with the West and joined NATO. The Soviet Union could have sabotaged unification at any point in the sequence of steps the Kremlin proposed for bringing about unification. If circumstances had remained the same, however, Bonn could not have hoped to improve chances for reunification by pursuing a policy of integration with the West.

The policymakers of the Federal Republic, and especially Konrad Adenauer, were fully aware of this. Their long-range calculations anticipated a future in which circumstances would *not* be the same, and Bonn's policies were designed to bring about these changes as quickly as possible. This was the second central assumption of Bonn's unification policy: with the passage of time the balance of power between the Cold War blocs would shift in favor of the West, allowing negotiations "on the basis of strength" that would induce the Soviet Union to settle the German question on Western terms. The single most important development that dashed these expectations was the Soviet Union's acquisition of nuclear weapons. A Western policy of "roll-back" and liberation of Eastern Europe, or even of applying strong pressure on the Kremlin, became inconceivable in light of the retaliatory power the Soviet Union was acquiring—as demonstrated by events in Hungary in 1956. Adenauer's "policy of strength," encouraged by the rhetoric of the first Eisenhower administration, had become illusory because the developing nuclear standoff was reflected in an East-West standoff on the German question: more than ever before, either side could deny the other control of both Germanies.

The Geneva Summit Conference of July 1955, which produced no agreement on the German issue, marked the end of a five-year period of East-West maneuvering during which the division of Germany had become increasingly solidified and uncontested. Moscow had failed to prevent West German rearmament; West Germany had become fully committed to a pro-Western course and had begun to form an integral part of the economic, military, and political structures of the Western alliance. But the failure of Moscow's Germany policy could not be converted into a success for Bonn's Germany policy, primarily because the Western powers had not achieved the superiority of power vis-à-vis the Soviet bloc that was the second central assumption of Adenauer's policy. To the contrary, the absolute and relative strength of the Soviet Union had increased substantially, and the Cold War balance of power was moving toward a deadlock of which the existing state of affairs in Central Europe was one manifestation.

STAGNATION AND LEGALISM, 1955–63

By 1955, the Soviet Union had come to accept the status quo in Central Europe and was beginning to turn to other Cold War fronts, especially in the Middle East and Asia. Instead of becoming more conciliatory on the German question with the passing of time, the Russians' attitude stiffened in exactly the way they themselves had predicted. After failing to prevent German membership in NATO, the Soviet Union shifted to a two-Germanies policy, which was specifically expressed in the Kremlin's readiness to establish diplomatic relations with Bonn in 1955.

This posed a dilemma for the Federal Republic. Establishing relations with Moscow underlined the division of Germany and lent it a certain de jure recognition. But Bonn knew that it could not block diplomatic channels of such importance for the German question, even if this step supported the Kremlin's contention that in fact two equal and sovereign German states had come into being. By 1955 Khrushchev and other Soviet leaders began to argue that the unification of such differently developing societies as those of East and West Germany could not possibly take place at the expense of East Germany, and during Adenauer's visit to Moscow late in 1955 Khrushchev even indicated he was no longer interested in bringing up the question of West Germany's withdrawal from the Western alliance. The Soviet Union thus became a status quo power in the European political arena, more interested in solidifying control over Eastern Europe and East Germany than in extending control to Western Europe.

Clearly, Adenauer's hope of dealing with the Soviet Union from a position of strength had not materialized by the mid-fifties. But the Western-oriented dimension of Bonn's reunification policy was also eroding, because the Western powers were anxious to move away from Cold War confrontations toward a more relaxed period of coexistence. These developments, which made Bonn apprehensive, were underlined by Soviet pressures on Berlin and by Soviet proposals for military disengagement.

In 1958, a decade after the Berlin Blockade and the Allied airlift, West Berlin again became the focal point of the Cold War in Europe. After the creation of two German states in 1949, Berlin had become the last clearly visible symbol of the Four Powers' responsibility for all-German affairs, and the Allied military and West German political presence in the western part of the city had been a constant source of irritation to the East German regime and the Soviet Union. Since the Soviet Union wanted to freeze and legitimize the political status quo in Central Europe, the isolated city presented Moscow with tempting opportunities to extract from the West de facto recognition of East Germany. The Soviets hoped to use Berlin to force the Western powers and the West Germans to deal directly with the East German regime. Berlin was a logical point at which to pursue such purposes because the city's political and legal status was not beyond challenge and because the access routes from the Federal Republic to West Berlin were the most vulnerable section of the Western defense perimeter. The Soviets had local superiority of power, and they could apply pressure and engineer provocations in fine gradations.

Late in 1958, after some preliminary harassing of Western transit to Berlin, the Soviet Union called for an end to the Western occupation of West Berlin and for the creation of a demilitarized "free city." Moscow talked about concluding a separate peace treaty with East Germany unless the West accepted these demands. The plan to establish a free city, perhaps under some form of United Nations supervision and independent of both East and West Germany, threatened vital West German interests. The proposal would have undermined the Four Powers' responsibility for all-German affairs and severed the tenuous political-constitutional link between West Berlin and West Germany. As reflected in the special provisions made for West Berlin in West Germany's constitution, the Western powers had never been enthusiastic about too specific and visible an integration of West Berlin into the Federal Republic, primarily because they wanted to preserve the legal claim that West Berlin was under the authority of the occupying powers. Although there was a de jure separation between West Berlin and the Federal Republic, there was a de facto economic, political, and symbolic connection that was as strong as that between East Berlin and East Germany—a connection that Bonn was determined to maintain. The creation of an isolated miniature state of West Berlin would have shut out the Western powers by abolishing the Four Power Agreement, and it would have excluded the political influence of the Federal Republic. A major political ambiguity standing in the way of the Soviet two-Germanies policy would have been clarified and resolved in Moscow's favor.

During the next three years, the Berlin question was bandied back and forth at East-West conferences held in Geneva, Camp David, Paris, and Vienna. The United States and Britain were apparently willing to come to some sort of terms with the Soviets, perhaps on the basis of a "symbolic" reduction of Western forces, but Adenauer and de Gaulle followed a much more intransigent line. The issue came to a head in 1961. In the intervening three years, refugees had poured into West Berlin from East Germany in increasing numbers, drawing manpower from the shaky East German economy and embarrassing the East German regime. The decision was made to stop this flow by erecting the Berlin Wall. In August, the East German People's Police and the National People's Army occupied East Berlin (taking over from the Russians in a symbolic as well as practical move) and began to block transit between East and West Berlin. This closed the last door between East and West Germany and destroyed the last symbol of the unity of Germany and Berlin. The division of Germany was complete.

The arms control and military disengagement proposals that the Soviets put forth during the mid- and late fifties were also intended to reinforce the division of Germany. They invariably called for the territorial status quo— that is, the division of Germany—to serve as the basis for an agreement between the superpowers on arms control and envisaged the participation of West and East Germany as equal partners. Thus, acceptance of these proposals would have led to a de facto recognition of the East German regime as well as to a weakening of the West's military presence at the periphery of the Soviet bloc. The *political* line of division in Central Europe would have been reinforced (reflecting Soviet interest in legitimizing the territorial status quo), and at the same time the East-West *military* boundary running through Germany would have been blurred (reflecting the Soviet interest in denying to the West the military and industrial power of West Germany). These proposals also threatened Bonn's growing interest in gaining a voice in nuclear decision making—which was undoubtedly one reason why disengagement proposals multiplied rapidly on both sides of the Iron Curtain. Adenauer viewed the military and political neutralization of Germany as a pseudo-solution without lasting value, and he believed disengagement would create a political no-man's land that could not maintain itself between two hostile blocs. Disengagement would have ended Adenauer's plans for a West European community and by prying Germany from the Western alliance would have undermined NATO's forward strategy, which the Pentagon sought to strengthen in order to make nuclear deterrence more effective. In some major respects, Soviet disengagement proposals would have accomplished the same purposes that the Soviet Union had sought to advance through its advocacy of a neutralized united Germany.

Bonn's suspicions appeared the more justified since the Soviet proposals were never specifically linked with unification but seemed primarily designed to disrupt NATO and to deny the Federal Republic a share in controlling nuclear arms. The Soviets always started with the assumption that two German states existed and that they should participate in negotiations as sovereign equals. Acceptance of even the initial stages of the Soviet plans would have implied Western recognition of the East German regime, which then could have sabotaged all further progress toward unification. Adenauer also distrusted Western disengagement proposals—which linked reunification with arms control and a European security system—because he suspected that they stemmed not so much from a desire to see Germany reunified as from the need to diminish East-West tension and to explore all possibilities for arms control.

Bonn's attitude toward disengagement highlighted a fundamental paradox of the unification issue. Bipolarities of interest and power were not conducive to the goal of unification; that was the lesson of the pre-1955 period. But the developing nuclear standoff between the United States and the Soviet Union, and the simultaneous political erosion of the two Cold War blocs, seemed no more likely to bring unification. The threat of nuclear war created between the Soviet Union and the United States an important common interest, which was demonstrated by the Cuban missile crisis and specifically acknowledged in the Nuclear Test Ban Treaty. Yet any lessening of tensions, coupled with intimations of Western flexibility, could be expected to diminish the importance of the German question. This was the fundamental dilemma for Bonn's unification policy: without an easing of East-West tensions neither side could afford to allow unification on the opponent's terms; yet an easing of these tensions might mean that the German status quo would get not only a tacit but also a legal blessing.

The political strains emerging within the two Cold War blocs during the late fifties and early sixties were not helpful either. On the surface it seems that these centrifugal tendencies would have enhanced Bonn's chances for manipulation and diplomatic flexibility. Moscow's forced relaxation of control over East Europe and the emerging Sino-Soviet dispute appeared to provide openings for Western probing actions, and conflicts within the Western alliance helped to make West Germany a pivot whose support was solicited by both Washington and Paris. Advisers and critics in Bonn and elsewhere urged Adenauer to adopt a more flexible and imaginative Eastern policy in order to take advantage of the fragmentation of the Soviet monolith; they suggested a more dynamic relationship with the nations of Eastern Europe and a less rigid stand on dealing with East Germany and the issue of the Oder-Neisse line. It appeared obvious that the Germans themselves ought to take some initiative on unification and that Bonn ought to modify its adamant Eastern policy and establish political and diplomatic contacts with the East European countries whose national interests were directly affected by the German question.

In fact, during the last years of Adenauer's administration Foreign Minister Gerhard Schröder initiated steps designed to gradually normalize relations with Eastern Europe and isolate the East German regime. But even though trade missions were established in Eastern Europe, Bonn remained unwilling to compromise its position on the Oder-Neisse line or the legal claims of the

Hallstein Doctrine and refused to deal with the East German regime on an official basis. This gave the Soviet Union a convenient rationale for maintaining its hold on Eastern Europe as the guarantor of the territorial status quo. In any event, it is unlikely that the East European countries would have aided Bonn's efforts to isolate East Germany politically and diplomatically, even though they were willing to expand trade agreements and normalize diplomatic relations. The unresolved German question helped contain centrifugal pressures in the Soviet bloc, because it symbolized an important common interest. Adenauer, of course, was convinced that the Soviet Union and its East European allies were not genuinely interested in seeing Germany unified; hence he clung even harder to his legalistic position, which would have been seriously compromised by shelving the Hallstein Doctrine and extending legitimacy to the East German government. Moscow's strategy to perpetuate the status quo inevitably shaped Bonn's unification policy and contributed to its stagnation. After 1955 West Germany did not really pursue a policy of unification, but rather attempted to prevent the legitimization of the status quo in Central Europe. This also meant that the primary function of the Western powers with regard to the German question was to deny to the Soviet Union and East Germany a legitimization of the German state of affairs.

The effects on the German question of fissures in the Western alliance were also problematical. Frictions between Washington and Paris caused difficulties for West German foreign policy in general, but they were particularly unpleasant for Bonn's Germany policy. Although de Gaulle had recognized the Oder-Neisse line in 1959, he was ready to help deny legitimacy to the status quo and to the East German regime. De Gaulle supported Adenauer's tough stand on the recurring Berlin crises, during which the United States and Britain were much more conciliatory toward the Soviet Union. Many in Bonn were convinced that in the long run the unity of Europe would be the key to the German question, and for this reason alone the support of France was indispensable. On the other hand, it was doubtful if France would favor unification itself. The hard line de Gaulle was taking on Berlin and the Soviet Union was not so much addressed to the Soviet Union as to those Germans who called for a more dynamic policy toward the East. In contrast, the United States and Britain could perhaps be counted on to support unification itself. In any event, the United States was the only Western power that could arrange an East-West deal that might result in unification. Yet here again, Bonn had to fear that it was precisely such a global deal that would in other ways work to the disadvantage of Germany. The tension between the two aspects of the German question—unification itself, and preventing the legitimization of the status quo—was emphasized by the centrifugal tendencies in both the Eastern and Western alliance. Short-run efforts to prevent the legal and political solidification of the status quo appeared to be incompatible with long-range planning for unification.

THE POLICY OF MOVEMENT, 1963–69

By 1963, when Ludwig Erhard became chancellor, dissatisfaction with the stagnation of Adenauer's Eastern policy had become widespread in West Germany. Although the new chancellor had no intention of departing radically from his predecessor's reunification policy, he did make cautious new beginnings, and the rethinking initiated by Gerhard Schröder toward the end of the Adenauer years now received at least halfhearted official blessing.

Erhard realized that de Gaulle's overtures to the Soviet bloc, and American and British efforts to nurture coexistence, were not bound to lead to reunification. To keep the German question alive within the Western alliance and to take advantage of the polycentric developments in the Soviet bloc, Bonn obviously would have to be more determined and innovative.

This task was very much complicated by the fact that during the three years of the Erhard administration many European countries (in both alliances) reassessed their national purposes and the role of international alliances. Bonn had to keep in step or risk diplomatic isolation for standing in the way of East-West detente efforts. As the two alliance blocs became less cohesive, Bonn had to deal with Eastern Europe as well as the Soviet Union in seeking a solution to the German question. Toward this end Gerhard Schröder, who remained foreign minister in the Erhard cabinet, continued his "policy of movement," which was intended to achieve an "opening to the East" by establishing closer economic, political, and diplomatic relations with Eastern Europe. As a result Germany set up trade missions in Warsaw, Budapest, Sofia, and Bucharest. This more flexible approach, which was coupled with a more pragmatic attitude on the Hallstein Doctrine, complemented French and American efforts to develop better relations with Eastern Europe.

The obstacles to West Germany's "policy of movement" were formidable —no less so because some of them were self-imposed. In the first place, Bonn's new efforts did not move far and fast enough. Bonn expressed good intentions, but did not scrap the Hallstein Doctrine or recognize the Oder-Neisse frontier. The government seemed insensitive to the fact that declarations of good will and of regret for the past meant little to Eastern Europe when they were coupled with implicit demands for territorial revisions. Moreover, the East European governments—which after all were allies of East Germany and sensitive to the guidelines set forth by the Kremlin—could hardly endorse Bonn's attempt to isolate the East German regime, which remained an essential part of the Federal Republic's Eastern policy.

Although Bonn was willing to trade and talk with the countries of Eastern Europe, the Erhard government, constrained as it was by ingrained habits of thought and by its conservative supporters, could not develop a more positive policy toward East Germany. Through this failure, the West German government denied itself the opportunity to pursue its Eastern policy on all three levels: toward Moscow, Eastern Europe, and East Berlin. Perhaps there was no real opportunity to do so. The East Germans were, at best, only interested in "confederation"; and by 1965, the East German regime had apparently stopped trying to obtain tacit recognition through increased contacts with the Federal Republic and had imposed considerably more stringent conditions (such as prior recognition) on negotiations with Bonn.

For the West Germans, even a partial modification of their position appeared risky. Bonn's diplomacy toward the Soviet bloc was pursued with logical (although self-defeating) consistency. Compromising one part would have compromised the whole, and scrapping one of its essential features would have caused the collapse of Bonn's entire legal-political Eastern policy. A dynamic diplomatic offensive in Eastern Europe would have required recognition of the Oder-Neisse line and abandonment of the Hallstein Doctrine. This would have undermined Four-Power responsibility for all-German affairs (since Bonn argued that Germany's definitive borders could not be settled prior to a final peace conference), as well as weakened Bonn's claim to sole representation of all Germans. In turn, the rationale for ostracizing the East German regime would have been destroyed. In toto, these changes would have signaled a major reversal of Bonn's longstanding Cold War posture, with important repercussions for Bonn's overall foreign policy program. Neither Erhard's temperament nor his quickly diminishing political fortunes allowed such drastic revisions of German foreign policy.

The government's reunification policy was further complicated by the fact that Erhard and Schröder could not establish a working relationship with de Gaulle. Adenauer's central assumption that Moscow and Washington held the key to the German question continued to be valid in the sixties, but the assumption required some modification because the loosening of the Western alliance and the Soviet bloc had increased the importance of France in resolving the German question. There was an increasing realization in Bonn—though one that Erhard and Schröeder did not manage to act on—that reunification could be accomplished only within the context of a larger European settlement and that in this context France was at least as crucial a partner for Germany's opening to the East as the United States.

This line of argument appeared especially plausible to the Gaullists in Bonn, since the Johnson administration's growing involvement in Vietnam reflected a general shift of American concern away from Europe. During the Johnson years, the United States practically had no European policy. Yet de Gaulle's determination to exclude the United States from a "Europe from the Atlantic to the Urals" was unacceptable to the Germans because of security concerns, and they also suspected that de Gaulle sought a solution to the German question that would fall short of reunification and that he was really only interested in resolution of the issue to speed American and Soviet withdrawal from Europe.

In sum, Adenauer's problem of having to make choices between Washington and Paris became even more pronounced during the Erhard administration, when the centrifugal tendencies within the Eastern and Western alliance systems increased the leverage of France. In opting for the United States on most issues that divided Washington and Paris, Erhard also opted for a fundamentally static and conservative reunification program, because Washington (as well as Moscow) found the status quo in Europe entirely acceptable. France, on the other hand, pursued a dynamic foreign policy intended to exploit the changes taking place in Western and Eastern Europe. This might have led to a political arrangement conducive to German reunification, but de Gaulle could not be expected to support the cause of reunification itself except perhaps in the restraining context of a Franco-Soviet security system.

The Grand Coalition of Christian Democrats and Socialists that replaced the Erhard government late in 1966 was determined to overcome the impasse of Bonn's reunification policy and to avoid, as much as possible, the damaging consequences of making choices between Washington and Paris. Chancellor Kurt Georg Kiesinger declared the Munich Agreement of 1938 (which gave Germany territory in Czechoslovakia) no longer valid; he expressed Bonn's desire for reconciliation with Poland; and he intimated that even though the Bonn government could not drop its legal claim to sole representation of the German people, West Germany was prepared to accept the East German regime as the de facto government and would not object to a European renunciation-of-force agreement that both Germanies would sign. There followed an unprecedented exchange of letters and other communications between Chancellor Kiesinger and Willi Stoph, head of the East German cabinet, that was notable not so much for its content—both sides reiterated their familiar positions—but for the fact that for the first time intra-German contacts took place on a semiofficial basis.

West Germany's policy initiatives did not go far enough, however, to suit the Russians and East Germans. In late 1967 and early 1968 Bonn and Moscow held discussions on multilateral declarations abdicating the use of force, but the talks failed because the Soviet Union insisted on incorporating highly controversial political issues, such as recognition of East Germany and the existing European borders, and the permanent nuclear abstention of West Germany. In 1968 the East Germans put new pressures on access routes to West Berlin, imposing even more stringent passport and visa requirements.

East European governments responded more favorably to the Federal Republic's initiatives. Diplomatic relations were opened with Rumania in January 1967, a trade mission was established in Prague in August 1967, and diplomatic relations were resumed with Yugoslavia in early 1968 (they had been severed in 1957 when Tito formally recognized East Germany). Although Bonn reemphasized its claim to sole representation of the German people, it was clear that the claim and its diplomatic corollary, the Hallstein Doctrine, were in effect being shelved. It would have been difficult to maintain that the Hallstein Doctrine was in full effect when two German states, each speaking for its own territory and population, were fully accredited in Bucharest as well as in Moscow. Even so, the Grand Coalition, under pressure from conservative elements, sought to maintain the legal shadow if not the political substance of the doctrine. In order to exempt the East European countries from the doctrine, Bonn now argued that the policy should not apply to countries that had no free choice in the matter of recognizing the East German regime because of their dependence on Moscow. This so-called "birthmark" theory could not cover Yugoslavia, of course, since of his own volition Tito had recognized the East German government in 1957. Before making an exception for Belgrade, Bonn was careful to ensure that this further watering down of a watered-down version of the Hallstein Doctrine would not trigger a mass recognition of East Germany by Third World countries. Bonn's legalism had reached its peak.

The Grand Coalition's difficulties in Eastern Europe resulted not only from the resistance of East Germany (which put pressure on its allies to support its demands) but also from the Bonn government's own political and conceptual inhibitions. Some of these inhibitions seemed unavoidable. Germany's Eastern policy could not possibly have been as flexible and consistent as France's because the Germans could not afford to match de Gaulle's disavowal of NATO or his disdainful attitude toward the United States. Other handicaps were largely self-imposed. Although the new government in Bonn moved beyond the entrenched Cold War positions of its predecessors and revised long-established principles of Germany's Eastern policy, the Grand Coalition was encumbered by its conservative members and supporters. Bonn continued to seek concessions from the Soviet bloc in return for a more accommodating West German stand on West Berlin, the nuclear nonproliferation treaty, the recognition of East Germany, or the Oder-Neisse line.

The issue of the German-Polish frontier is a case in point. Bonn's position had been ambivalent and inconsistent all along. In spite of its efforts to normalize relations with Eastern Europe, the Erhard administration had persisted in arguing that only an all-German government could bring about a final settlement of Germany's eastern borders. Thus Bonn held out to Warsaw the unacceptable prospect of having to deal with a united Germany on a question of vital importance to Poland. This made it easy for the Soviet Union to pose as the guarantor of Polish security vis-à-vis West Germany and to accuse Bonn of being revanchist. East European and Soviet attitudes on the Oder-Neisse issue symbolized the convergence of Communist and East European national interests—a frequent characteristic of other East bloc policies toward the Federal Republic as well. This convergence of Soviet and East European interests had been cemented by the intransigent Eastern policy of the Adenauer government. As long as Bonn expected a Four-Power agreement to lead to German unity there was at least some rationale for refusing to sanction the existing East German–Polish border. When this expectation was replaced with the premise that reunification required accommodation with Eastern Europe, obstinacy on the Oder-Neisse question became even more damaging to the prospects of reunification, and more at odds with the basic strategy for its realization, than during the Adenauer period.

Influential policymakers in Bonn realized, of course, that reunification and frontier revisions were incompatible goals. In his inaugural statement, Chancellor Kiesinger made no mention of Bonn's traditional demand for the "borders of 1937," and he implied that Bonn would accept the Oder-Neisse line as the eastern border of a united Germany. The Oder-Neisse issue strained the Grand Coalition from the beginning, and tensions were brought out in the open in 1968 when Foreign Minister Willy Brandt, speaking not in his official capacity but as the leader of the Socialists, defied the longtime policy of the Christian Democrats and called for "recognition and respect" of the Oder-Neisse border.

Bonn's own inhibitions, Moscow's unabated hostility, and a hard-line East German and Polish response had arrested Bonn's policy of movement even before the Soviet invasion of Czechoslovakia in August 1968. All the same, the invasion dealt Bonn's policy a blow that was not merely tactical.

In the first place, the central assumptions of Bonn's long-range unification strategy collapsed with the failure of the liberal experiment in Czechoslovakia, when it became clear that the Soviet Union and some of its client states were unwilling to allow a weakening of the bloc's forward position in Central Europe. It became apparent that Bonn's basic interest in changing, or at least loosening, the status quo in Central and Eastern Europe was in direct conflict with the interests of the Soviet Union—interests that seemed to dictate the status quo be maintained even if this required the use of brute force. The invasion was less significant for its effect on the actual prospects of reunification—even before August 1968 the outlook for achieving German unity had been dim—than for the feeling of frustration and resignation it engendered in West Germany. What had appeared to be a rational, temperate, and at least superficially plausible reunification policy had been invalidated by international developments, and the shaky measure of support the policy had received at home over the years met renewed attacks. The Grand Coalition government indicated that its policy of reconciliation with the Soviet bloc would continue, but it was clear that the obstacles were even more formidable than before. There was little reason to expect that meeting Soviet demands would advance the cause of German unity, since it now seemed likely that East European developments favorable to reunification would be met by the Soviets with a military "veto"—while Bonn's acquiescence in Soviet demands would further undermine the established foundation of its Eastern policy and arouse domestic criticism.

There was another subtle but important connection between Bonn's more flexible Eastern policy and the events of August 1968. Even though the Russians were interested in detente with Washington, they were dead set against allowing their allies to pursue their own coexistence policies toward the Western powers. Among other objections was the fear that this might upset the foundations for a Soviet-American understanding by erasing the dividing line between the two spheres of influence in Central Europe. For strategic as well as political reasons, the Soviet Union was especially sensitive to foreign policy "deviationism" in the northern countries of the Warsaw Pact since they were the anchor of Moscow's forward policy in Europe. When Bonn made the establishment of closer German–East European diplomatic relations a divisive issue in the Soviet bloc, this contributed to Russian fears. Thus, the smaller successes of Bonn's Eastern policy—in Bucharest, Belgrade, and potentially Budapest and Prague—helped start a chain of events that led to a larger failure. Even so, Moscow might have tolerated the increasing economic contacts between Bonn and Prague if by mid-1968 Czechoslovakia's liberalization efforts had not threatened the continued control of the Communist party in Czechoslovakia. Given the new relationships between East European countries and the West, a drastic transformation of the Czechoslovakian domestic order most likely would have led to a reorientation of Prague's foreign policy. This was a risk that the Soviet Union was not prepared to take. Since Bonn's softer line toward Eastern Europe gave Prague more room for extending its liberalization of domestic policy to foreign policy, the Kremlin's clampdown on Czechoslovakia simultaneously dealt Bonn's Eastern policy a decisive blow.

The invasion also had the effect of freezing the East European political arena for Bonn's probing actions, at a time when Bonn's "three-level" approach to the East—toward the Soviet Union, Eastern Europe, and East Germany—had just been put into tentative operation. This development tended to reinforce the importance of the other two arenas—Moscow and East Berlin. The freezing of the East European arena affected France as well as Germany. Whereas the polycentric developments of the early and mid-sixties in the Soviet bloc and in the Western alliance had increased the importance for German reunification not only of the East European countries but also of Germany's western neighbors, notably France, this trend was reversed after August 1968. The invasion of Czechoslovakia diminished the prospects for creating de Gaulle's "European Europe" within which a solution to the German question might be achieved, and thus renewed the importance of the Washington-Moscow level. But this came at a time when it was obvious that both the United States and the Soviet Union had tacitly agreed to respect one another's spheres of influence and were not about to redraw them. The "condominium" world system to which both superpowers apparently aspired was fundamentally conservative and hence aided Moscow in its attempts to solidify the political status quo in Eastern and Central Europe. The Johnson administration, bogged down in Vietnam and anxious to obtain an arms control agreement with the Soviet Union, was not about to make a big fuss over the invasion of Czechoslovakia or its meaning for the European political order.

It was the recognition of these developments, as much as the desire for a more flexible reunification policy, that led the Grand Coalition to reexamine West Germany's policy toward East Germany. It had become obvious that Bonn could no longer bypass East Berlin. But dealing with the East Germans was difficult and frustrating. The regime was rigid, defensive, and anxious to exact a price for having been ostracized by Bonn for so long. Over the years, Bonn had conducted its reunification policy in a style that could not help but grate the sensitivities of East German decision makers. There is a special psychological edge to the enmity between "brothers," and even the Grand Coalition's principle of "acceptance without recognition" was not sufficiently positive to cut through the long-accumulated layers of ill will. Bonn's softened attitudes did not seem to stem from a fundamental rethinking of the German question but appeared to be a grudging response to changing circumstances.

THE *OSTPOLITIK* OF WILLY BRANDT, 1969–74

Chancellor Willy Brandt's coalition government, which took office in October 1969, was determined to pursue a highly dynamic and innovative policy toward the East. This new policy—generally called *Ostpolitik*—led to a package of treaties with the Soviet Union, Poland, Czechoslovakia, and East Germany and was accompanied by a Four Power Agreement on Berlin and capped by some of the provisions of the European Security Conference.

The Brandt government was prepared to deal in a forthright and realistic manner not only with Moscow and the East European capitals, but also with East Berlin. The new policy initially aroused some suspicions and anxieties among the Allies, and Bonn took great pains to stress the continuity of German foreign policy toward the Western alliance (as well as toward the East). Throughout its negotiations with the East, the Bonn government was careful to keep the West informed, not only to avoid the impression that Germany might be toying with a seesaw policy between East and West but also because Bonn was genuinely convinced that its Eastern policy could succeed only with the backing of its Western partners. Moreover, on such issues as the status of West Berlin, the United States, Britain, and France were directly and formally involved; and since the Brandt government made a satisfactory resolution of the Berlin question the precondition of any West German accommodation with the East, the practical as well as symbolic involvement of the Western powers in Bonn's *Ostpolitik* was assured.

The foundation of *Ostpolitik,* the basis from which the Brandt government expected to deal with East Berlin and Eastern Europe, was an improved relationship between the Federal Republic and the Soviet Union. Twenty-five years after the end of World War II and fifteen years after the Adenauer government had gained formal reconciliation with the West in the Paris

Treaties of 1954, Chancellor Brandt was convinced the time had come to reach an accommodation with the East. He sought to move beyond the stale confrontations of the past and to make Bonn's foreign policy more realistic and dynamic. Brandt believed that for moral as well as political reasons West Germany should face up to the consequences of World War II and the Cold War and adjust the style as well as the content of German foreign policy to the realities of the seventies. This meant, above all, that Brandt was willing to abandon one of Adenauer's fundamental principles (which had already become eroded through the years), that progress on the German question would have to precede a fundamental East-West accommodation. Brandt was ready to replace this principle with its reverse, that the split between East and West Germany could only be narrowed on the basis of such an accommodation. The German question was no longer even defined as "reunification," a word that was quietly dropped from the government's terminology in speaking of intra-German issues and relations. In short, the Brandt government was prepared to do its part toward legitimizing the territorial status quo in Central Europe and bringing West German foreign policy in line with the explicit desires of the Eastern countries as well as with the tacit assumptions and policies of the Western allies.

Bonn's policy shift was not basically a reaction to an immediate danger of diplomatic isolation. It was more a question of timing and of keeping in step with the dynamics of large-scale developments between and within the two alliances. Both the Atlantic alliance and the Warsaw Pact were preoccupied with detente, as reflected by American, British, and French policies and NATO's adjustments to Soviet nuclear-strategic equality, as well as by the Soviet Union's overriding aim to secure its European flank with a European Security Conference. It was clearly in Bonn's interest to approach the Soviet Union, Eastern Europe, and East Germany with its own initiatives, maximizing whatever leverage might be available, rather than to have the most urgent issues between West Germany and the East negotiated in the wider context of a multilateral forum such as the European Security Conference. For this reason Bonn felt some urgency to have *Ostpolitik* launched and completed as quickly as possible—an interest shared by the Kremlin since one of Leonid Brezhnev's greatest ambitions was to see the European territorial status quo legalized by an overarching multilateral forum such as the European Security Conference.

The specific results of Bonn's willingness to formalize the status quo, and of Moscow's readiness to improve relations with West Germany, were the treaties signed between the Federal Republic and the Soviet Union in August 1970 and between the Federal Republic and Poland in December 1970. The provisions of the German-Soviet treaty, which was signed after intense and highly intricate negotiations, included mutual renunciation of the use of force and in its most important section a declaration by West Germany that it had no territorial claims against any country and that Bonn would "regard today and in the future the frontiers of all States in Europe as inviolable . . . including the Oder-Neisse line . . . and the frontier between the Federal Republic of Germany and the German Democratic Republic." Since the treaty provisions were in effect a legitimization of the territorial and political consequences of World War II, Chancellor Brandt was no doubt correct in saying "Nothing is lost with this treaty that was not gambled away long ago."*

Moscow's and Bonn's interest in the treaty went far beyond its specific provisions; they viewed the pact as an essential element in their overall foreign policy programs. West Germany's *Ostpolitik* became an important ingredient in an intricate set of dealings between and within the two alliances. These negotiations cut across several kinds of issues and were strung together by a series of preconditions, "prepayments," and quid pro quo's in which all parties sought to maximize their gains while hedging against possible losses. For Bonn, the treaty had an important symbolic and political impact. It was the first step toward a new relationship with the East, the basis from which West Germany could seek to normalize relations with Eastern Europe and East Germany and actively participate in the detente politics of the seventies. The Brandt government realized that a general rapprochement with the East, as well as a solution of the concrete issue of West Berlin, could be accomplished only by making it clear that Bonn accepted the European status quo and was willing to recognize it formally. The Soviet Union, in turn, considered the treaty a preliminary step toward a European Security Conference, for which the Kremlin was pushing hard in order to legitimize the European territorial and political status quo, reduce American influence in Europe in an atmosphere of detente, intensify economic and technological contacts with Western Europe, and concentrate on domestic issues and the China problem. The United States, however, was unenthusiastic about a European Security Conference out of fear that it could be turned into a big propaganda advantage for the Soviet Union and would accomplish little in terms of settling outstanding disputes. The Nixon administration demanded prepayments such as progress on the ongoing Strategic Arms Limitation Talks (SALT), mutual and genuinely balanced force reductions by NATO and the Warsaw Pact (MBFR), and a more solidly defined status for West Berlin. West Germany, on its part, agreed to support the idea of a European Security Conference in a declaration of intent that was attached to the German-Soviet treaty.

*When Chancellor Brandt signed the treaty in August 1970, he tied its ratification by the *Bundestag* to a successful resolution of the Berlin problem. This meant reaching a satisfactory general agreement among the Four Powers, to be followed by a subsidiary East-West German settlement of the issue of access to Berlin through East Germany and visiting privileges for West Berliners to East Germany and East Berlin, which had not been allowed since 1961. The Brandt government felt that in return for West Germany's acceptance of the general status quo in Europe, the Soviet Union should accept the status quo in Berlin —that is to say, reaffirm the continuing rights and responsibilities of the Four Powers and the political presence of West Germany that had developed over the past two decades.

The treaty between Bonn and Moscow also affected intra-alliance rela-tions. First, it set the stage for the treaty between the Federal Republic and Poland, which was signed four months after the Moscow agreement, in December 1970. The Warsaw treaty contained provisions similar to those of the Moscow treaty, and again its legal terms were less significant than the political, psychological, and moral ramifications of the pact. The document was negotiated during more than nine months of hard bargaining and essen-tially provided for West Germany's acceptance of the Oder-Neisse boundary as Poland's western border with East Germany. The treaty also provided for full diplomatic relations between the two countries and included renuncia-tion-of-force declarations. In a separate accord, Warsaw agreed to issue exit permits to a limited number of ethnic Germans living in Poland so they could be reunited with their families in West Germany.

Right from the beginning, the Bonn government faced great difficulties in coordinating a dynamic *Deutschlandpolitik* toward East Germany with an effective *Ostpolitik* toward Moscow and Eastern Europe. Although the Federal Republic was prepared to make major concessions to East Germany, negotia-tions between the two proved to be the most troublesome element of Bonn's Eastern policy. The set of agreements ultimately reached between the two Germanies, the so-called Basic Treaty, was not signed until late in 1972 and ratified in June 1973. The major stumbling block to the negotiations—quite aside from the fact that they took place in the acrimonious climate that had characterized East-West German relations for two decades—was that al-though Bonn had adopted a more innovative and flexible policy, it still stopped short of meeting major East German demands. During the first year of the Brandt government it gradually became clear that Bonn was willing to accommodate East Berlin to the extent of (1) accepting the reality of the German Democratic Republic as a state and dealing with it on the basis of full equality, (2) implicitly renouncing previous West German claims that only the Federal Republic could legitimately speak for all Germans, (3) treat-ing the frontier between East and West Germany as an inviolable political-legal border rather than a "demarcation line," (4) negotiating a treaty with East Berlin regulating the relations between the East and West German states, and (5) refraining from further interference with East Germany's trade and cultural exchanges with Third World countries.

Despite these concessions, however, Bonn was not willing to treat the German Democratic Republic like any other foreign country and to recognize it as a second German state in international law—which is in essence what the East German government insisted upon. In the face of this demand, the Brandt government reiterated its position that there was really only one German nation, that relations between East and West Germany could not be the same as those between foreign states, and that a treaty between the two would have to reflect a "coexistence" type of special relationship *(ein Nebenei-nander)*—one that could perhaps arrest the growing divergence between the social and political structures of the two states, and normalize relations between them. By reemphasizing the continuing Four-Power responsibility, Bonn suggested that in any case it could not legitimize on its own accord the permanent division of Germany. (Of course, Bonn's stress on residual Four-Power rights and responsibilities was also necessary for a more direct political purpose, that of obtaining a satisfactory Berlin agreement in the face of East German intransigence.) Moreover, in the Declaration of October 28, 1969, the Federal Republic made clear that it continued to prefer that allied and Third World countries not extend formal recognition to East Germany, although Bonn understood that an increasing number of countries, especially in the Third World, would in fact do so. Subsequently, however, the West German government indicated that it would not oppose the admission of both Germanies to the United Nations, an idea that was followed up later during the Bonn-Moscow treaty negotiations when West Germany and the Soviet Union explicitly agreed to promote actively UN membership of both German states.

East and West Germany played a wait-and-see game during their bilateral negotiations, realizing that the final outcome would be strongly affected by the larger context of East-West relations, as well as those among the members of the Warsaw Pact. The most specific example of these interconnections was the successful conclusion of a Berlin settlement. After almost seventeen months of negotiations, the Four Powers signed an agreement on the status of Berlin in September 1971, which went a long way toward meeting West German demands since essentially it provided for recognition of the status quo by the four signatories. In this so-called Quadripartite Agreement on Berlin, the Four Powers agreed that "irrespective of the difference in legal views, the situation . . . shall not be changed unilaterally." While the three Western powers thereby acknowledged that West Berlin was not a constituent part of West Germany, the Soviet Union in turn acknowledged that the ties between West Germany and West Berlin could be maintained, and that the Bonn goverment could perform consular services for the inhabitants of West Berlin and represent them in international organizations and at international conferences. The Western powers consented to the establishment of a Soviet consulate general in West Berlin (thus underscoring the city's separate status) and to expanded Soviet commercial activities, but the accord stipulated that the activities of this consulate would "not include political functions nor extend to matters connected with the rights and responsibilities of the Four Powers." The Western powers also agreed to discourage such "constitutional acts" on the part of West Germany as holding the election of the Federal chancellor or sessions of the *Bundestag* and *Bundesrat* in Berlin. On a matter of great importance to Bonn, access to West Berlin, the Soviet Union pledged that "transit traffic by road, rail and waterways through the territory of the German Democratic Republic of civilian persons and goods between the Western Sectors of Berlin and the Federal Republic of Germany will be facilitated and unimpeded," and that detailed arrangements would be negotiated subsequently. In short, the Soviet Union no longer maintained that West Berlin was part of East Germany or a separate entity, and played down the corollary claim that the East Germans had the right to control access to the city by the citizens of West Germany and the three Western powers.

No doubt the Four-Power accord on Berlin represented a diplomatic setback for East Germany, since East Berlin had to acknowledge the legitimacy of the West German and Western presence in West Berlin as well as the Soviet Union's continuing responsibilities in East Germany. The negotiations between East and West Germany over the supplementary agreement accordingly were tense and difficult, even though in early May 1971 East Germany's hard-line leader Walter Ulbricht was replaced by the somewhat more flexible Erich Honecker. After protracted and intricate negotiations, the two states finally reached a settlement in December 1971 on the subsidiary technical arrangements for transit traffic of civilians and goods. This intra-German agreement provided for (1) normalized access to West Berlin from West Germany, (2) an exchange of small enclaves between West Berlin and surrounding East Germany, and (3) improved visiting privileges for West Berliners to East Germany (from which most of them had been barred since 1952) and to East Berlin (from which most had been barred since 1966).

The settlement of the Berlin question was symptomatic of the shift in priorities that characterized the detente policies of both East and West in the seventies. The first formal accord between the two German states, which dealt with a major unresolved issue of the Cold War, reflected the fact that neither of the two Germanies could block detente efforts in the Western and Eastern alliance. In this detente setting, West Germany had some leverage against East Germany because Bonn could make a Berlin settlement the precondition for ratifying the Moscow and Warsaw pacts, which the Soviet Union viewed as an essential first step toward the multilateral legitimization of the European status quo that the Soviets expected to gain from a European Security Conference.

Although the East German government would clearly have preferred to hold out for more favorable terms on the Berlin issue and by all accounts felt heavily pressured by the Soviet Union to accede to the accord, this did not reflect a decline of East German influence in Moscow. East Germany was still the Soviet Union's most important partner in matters of European policy; the Soviet Union continued to support a clear-cut separation of the two Germanies; and the Kremlin shared East Berlin's overriding interest in stabilizing the territorial, political, and legal status quo in Central Europe.

Bonn's advantage vis-à-vis East Berlin stemmed from the inherent qualities of Willy Brandt's *Ostpolitik*. By attuning West German foreign policy to the dynamics of detente—the outstanding foreign policy aim of most members of the Warsaw Pact as well as of the Atlantic alliance—Bonn kept pace with developments and maximized German leverage in an East-West setting in which various kinds of political, strategic, and economic issues were coupled in multilayered connections. Bonn's *Ostpolitik,* which spanned all these issues and reached across the two alliances, was important to both East and West not because West Germany was able to act as a "balancer" between the two sides—that was neither intended nor possible—but because *Ostpolitik* was essential for the accommodation that both sides sought in Central Europe.

After concluding these treaties with the Soviet Union, Poland, and East Germany, the Federal Republic also achieved an understanding with Czechoslovakia, pertaining primarily to the legal and political implications of renouncing the Munich Agreement of 1938. Beginning in October 1970, Bonn and Prague held several rounds of talks and reached a compromise formula satisfying Czechoslovakia's demand for an *ex tunc* renunciation by West Germany of the Munich Agreement (declaring it invalid from time of its original signing in 1938) and Bonn's preference for an *ex nunc* renunciation (dating from the present).

With the completion of the Eastern treaties with the Soviet Union, Poland, and Czechoslovakia, the intra-German Basic Treaty, and the Four Power Agreement on Berlin—all of which were capped by the European Security Conference—the momentum of West Germany's *Ostpolitik* by and large was arrested. When Helmut Schmidt took over from Chancellor Brandt in May 1974, the intensive phase of Germany's *Ostpolitik* had ended and a period of uneasy consolidation began to set in. Almost from the beginning of Schmidt's administration, urgent domestic economic and fiscal problems required attention—problems closely connected to the general malaise of the Western economies, the energy crisis, and a variety of other issues that directed Bonn's focus more toward the West than the East. This shift in West Germany's concerns, although dictated by domestic and international developments, was enhanced by differences in temperament and political outlook between the new chancellor and the old. While Willy Brandt was more of a visionary and had other traits that made him probably the ideal chancellor for initiating and orchestrating Germany's *Ostpolitik,* Helmut Schmidt was a much more pragmatic politician, more inclined by temperament, training, and political experience to deal with practical issues such as economic, monetary, and military-strategic matters—in short, precisely those issues that were moving toward the center of Bonn's attention.

This is not to say that Bonn's relations with the East were neglected. During the mid-seventies a number of political, economic, and human rights issues were the subject of continuing discussions between Bonn and East Berlin, Moscow, and the East European capitals. But it was obvious that a period of consolidation had begun and that the most dramatic and fundamental aspects of *Ostpolitik* had been concluded. This period of consolidation was not an easy one, and one important reason was the continuing strain between

West Germany and East Germany. Both sides were constantly jockeying for positions that would underline and reinforce their respective understanding of the agreements between them. As they tried to test the legal parameters of the Basic Treaty in terms of elasticity and possibilities for interpretation, intra-German political, economic, and psychological arrangements were thrown into a state of flux. The relationship between the two sides became tense and ambiguous, cooperative in some respects but also charged with suspicion and conflict.

The larger context of Germany's *Ostpolitik* was also undergoing change. The basic aim of Willy Brandt's Eastern policy was to establish a European order within which East and West Germans might be able to reshape their relationship—remote as that possibility seemed. What type of relationship would evolve was of course uncertain and unpredictable, but it appears unlikely that Brandt himself perceived it in terms of "reunification." Dynamic as Brandt's *Ostpolitik* was in many ways, it was also fundamentally a policy of resignation, designed not so much to bring about changes for a foreseeable future as not to foreclose possibilities for an unforeseeable future. Brandt envisioned reconciliation of the two Germanies as taking place within a pan-European order of peace sustained by the United States and the Soviet Union—a structure sufficiently pluralistic to accommodate diverse national and ideological interests, and that would be held together by a sense of common destiny. During and after Brandt's chancellorship, the relationship between the two Germanies remained inextricably tied to global and European developments, developments in which the Federal Republic could participate but probably could not influence or direct in fundamental ways.

4

Foreign Policy
and
Domestic Politics

CONFRONTATION AND POLARIZATION, 1949–55

In a striking way, the East-West polarization of power during the fifties also polarized conflict on the West German domestic political scene. This was not because the government and opposition were divided along pro-Western or pro-Soviet lines, but because some of West Germany's foreign policy goals were incompatible. As we have seen, this was especially true during the formative years of West German foreign policy—from 1949 to approximately the mid-fifties. As it became increasingly clear that the government's wholehearted alignment with the Western powers aided the goals of security and political and economic recovery but failed to advance reunification, the question of priorities became crucial. Formulated as abstract goals, security, political and economic recovery, and unification were not contested; almost everyone supported them. But the apparent incompatibility between pursuing a pro-Western security and recovery policy and simultaneously advancing the cause of German unity led to sharp domestic conflicts over the implementation, proper order of priority, and content of foreign policy goals. So long as the opposition perceived acceptable alternatives to government policy, consensus was impossible.

It may well be that no acceptable alternatives to the government's course of action existed. The West was determined to enlist the Federal Republic in the Cold War struggle, and although the Adenauer government managed to extract from the former occupying powers important political and economic concessions, Bonn was not really free to pursue a flexible and dynamic foreign policy because the diplomatic-political, economic, and military instruments of that policy were embedded within the Western alliance structure. Washington's containment policy established a framework for the foreign policy projects not only of West Germany but of France, Britain, and other NATO countries as well.

The limited choices open to the German government were not unattractive to Adenauer, however, because they allowed him to pursue a foreign policy line that corresponded with his own preferences. The chancellor and his supporters in the CDU/CSU sought a European political order that would irrevocably tie German society to the cultural and political forces of Western Europe. This was to be achieved by making Germany an equal and respected partner of the Western powers and by forging a fundamental reconciliation between France and Germany. In the larger context of world politics, and especially for the purpose of meeting the communist challenge, a united Western Europe was to be anchored to the power of the United States within the framework of an Atlantic alliance.

Chancellor Adenauer, who also served as foreign minister during the early years of the Federal Republic and maintained effective control of his party, soon emerged as the towering influence in shaping Bonn's foreign policy. Even so, not everyone in his party, the heterogeneous CDU/CSU, shared in equal measure his overriding commitment to a Catholic-oriented, essentially conservative Western European condominium. Nor did the Free Democratic Party (FDP), the major partner joining the CDU/CSU in the coalition governments established after the 1949 and 1953 elections, fully endorse Adenauer's vision. The Free Democrats were largely backed by business interests who favored laissez-faire economic liberalism and by anticlerical middle-class voters who resented the Catholic tinge of the Christian Democrats. These groups would have liked Germany to play a more independent role than Adenauer's integrative, pro-Western program would allow, and they were not nearly as committed to his "little Europe" policy as were many of the Christian Democrats. The FDP favored a wider framework of European cooperation, which would include at least Britain; the party toyed with the idea of a "third force" in both international and domestic politics; and party spokesmen generally pressed more vigorously for unification than the CDU/CSU. But the FDP's emphasis on national interest and mobility in international affairs, coupled with the nationalistic sentiments of some groups in the party, posed no obstacles to pursuing a "policy of strength" and supporting Adenauer's rearmament-sovereignty barter with the Western powers.

Throughout the fifties, the Social Democratic Party constituted the most important and consistent opposition to Adenauer's foreign policy program. The Socialists' priorities were almost exactly the reverse of Adenauer's. They saw unification as most important, and although they had no intrinsic objections to Adenauer's policy of reconciliation with the West, they also believed that the commitments resulting from that policy—rearmament and membership in the Western alliance—were detrimental to the cause of German unity.

The SPD's deep commitment to reunification had two major sources. First, although the Socialists echoed the CDU's call for European integration and a rapprochement with France, they were apprehensive about the prospect of a West European community with strongly Catholic and conservative tendencies. Initially at least, the Socialists' blueprint for a new socioeconomic and political order was Marxist-reformist and had pronounced antibourgeois and anticlerical overtones. They had little hope that economic and political socialism would prosper in the West European union advocated by Catholic and essentially conservative Europeanists such as Adenauer, French Foreign Minister Robert Schuman, and Italian Prime Minister Alcide de Gasperi. The SPD felt much more comfortable with the sociopolitical and cultural values of Britain and the Scandinavian countries, which had been significantly influenced by their Socialist parties. A second source of the SPD's opposition to Adenauer's policies and the party's emphasis on reunification stemmed from the fact that the division of Germany had weakened the SPD by cutting the party off from the areas where it had enjoyed strong support during the Weimar Republic. Thus, reunification seemed essential not only for establishing the political order the Socialists wished to foster in postwar Germany but also for solidifying and extending the party's power base. The Socialists as well as the Christian Democrats regarded foreign policy as an instrument to guide West German society in the direction they favored, and they consistently evaluated foreign policy projects in terms of domestic party aims.

This explains in large part the intensity, and at times the acrimony, that characterized foreign policy debates in Bonn during the fifties. The Socialists agreed with the Christian Democrats that unification should be pursued only by peaceful means and that democracy would be the only acceptable political order in a united Germany. But the SPD was much more willing than the government to test Soviet proposals and to assume that the Russians were at least partially acting in good faith; and they frequently accused the Adenauer administration of dragging its feet on unification, of letting opportunities for profitable negotiations pass by, and of lacking initiative, flexibility, and foresight. SPD spokesmen argued constantly that the German question could only be resolved by lifting the two parts of Germany from the grasp of the Cold War blocs, and that this would require a more accommodating posture toward the East bloc and abstention from political, economic, and military association with the Western powers. Since all of the government's foreign policy aims and means were inextricably interlocked, the Socialists were led to a sweeping and often indiscriminate condemnation of the entire range of Bonn's pro-Western policies: they fought rearmament and membership in the European Defense Community, the Coal and Steel Community, and NATO, and they acquiesced only reluctantly and with grave reservations in plans for a Common Market. The Socialists also opposed rearmament because they felt that since the Western powers were occupying Germany the Allies should be responsible for Germany's defense and that West Germany should not rearm unless sovereignty were restored.

This latter point was one reason why the SPD found it difficult to gain widespread support for its adamant opposition to rearmament. For although most West Germans were not eager to rearm and join EDC and NATO, they were aware that Adenauer's foreign policy program was making progress—especially in the areas of economic reconstruction and restoration of sovereignty—and that continued success depended upon German participation in the Western military alliance. The practical and immediate requirements of economic reconstruction, the desire for an adequate standard of living after years of deprivation, the gains promised in return for collaborating with the Western powers—in short, the recognition that Adenauer's policy showed a way toward stability, recovery, and international "respectability"—made opposition to rearmament an essentially emotional issue that had to stand up against the test of expediency and the hope for normalcy.

Perhaps the major problem the Socialists faced in converting the general desire for unification into votes was the goal's lack of immediacy. This is not to say that the German people did not want unification. But in contrast to the prompt economic and political benefits that resulted from the government's pro-Western policies, the question of unification became increasingly abstract and hypothetical. The distant nature of the goal stemmed not only from the obvious risks and obstacles of implementing a unification policy diplomatically but also from the problem of relating the goal to more immediately relevant and concrete issues of the day. West Germans were constantly being asked to choose between unification and the possible loss of democratic freedoms and failure to attain political and economic normalcy. Even if a large part of the population had been willing to pursue unification with determination, the daily realities of political and economic life would have stood in the way.

The problems of advancing reunification on the international scene were thus strikingly reflected on the domestic political scene. The Western-oriented dimension of Adenauer's unification policy—which sought to strengthen the Western alliance and obtain political leverage for Bonn through rearmament—gained the support of powerful German interest groups and a large proportion of the electorate because these policies also yielded extensive economic and political benefits. In contrast, the Socialist strategy for achieving reunification—an accommodation with the Soviet Union on the basis of a neutralized united Germany—was rejected by the Western powers and thus could not have produced payoffs for the Federal Republic in terms of sovereignty and economic reconstruction. The FDP deliberately attempted to bridge these two conflicting strategies for reunification by pursuing a basically "pro-West" line but always making clear that the party was ready to explore any openings to the East that appeared to advance reunification. But the FDP's attempts to occupy the center were undercut on the domestic political scene both from the Right and from the Left, and most importantly, from the Christian Democrats who appealed to a wide group of supporters with the prospect of political and economic normalcy.

For all parties, the crux of the matter was the question of how to exercise the rights of sovereignty being restored to the Federal Republic. Because sovereignty was always legally and politically tied to rearmament and participation in Western integrative structures, the rights won by the Bonn government were not able to be used for purposes other than the ones earmarked in international treaties. Whereas the interests of the Western powers obviously complemented Adenauer's plans for joining Germany to a West European union, they were necessarily adverse to the SPD's call for mobility of action that might lead to reunification and detrimental to the SPD's long-range plans for Germany's domestic order as well. For Adenauer, necessity was combined with virtue; for the Socialists, the international barter that restored sovereignty in exchange for rearmament was objectionable on most grounds.

The Socialists' dilemma extended into the area of economic reconstruction. The Schuman Plan for the European Coal and Steel Community was an important milestone on the way to economic and political recovery because it provided for German participation on an equal basis and removed raw-material bottlenecks that had hampered the revival of German industry. Although the Socialists did not oppose European integration as such, their objections to the Schuman Plan were sweeping and led to some of the most abrasive political fights in the *Bundestag.* The Socialists argued that the ECSC would become a conservative regional alliance for the perpetuation of capitalism, they objected to French attempts to admit the Saar to the ECSC as an autonomous entity, and in general they attacked the Schuman Plan as an international conspiracy to impede unification and handicap Germany's ability to compete with France on world markets.

In 1954 the Socialists drastically reversed their position. They no longer objected to the transfer of economic authority to international agencies but stressed instead the democratic-parliamentary methods by which that transfer ought to be accomplished. The SPD now called for extended economic planning, supranationally coordinated economic analyses, and countercyclical measures and investments. By 1955, the Socialists advocated internationally coordinated investment policies and business-cycle controls, and began criticizing the ECSC for not having gone far enough in this direction.

In part, the SPD's about-face can be explained by the change in the complexion of the Saar issue, a matter that had figured prominently in previous objections to the Schuman Plan and that was now basically settled by the pro-German plebiscite (more on this in chapter 6). Also, the SPD feared that a totally negative attitude would freeze out Socialist influence and allow industrial interests to gain control of the ECSC. Thus political isolation at home and changes abroad had led the SPD to reverse itself on a major foreign policy issue.

The Socialists' turnabout on the Schuman Plan was the first of a series that gradually narrowed the gap between government and opposition. Even so, by 1955 the domestic contest over foreign policy was still very much polarized, reflecting tensions between the goals of rearmament and reunification on the international scene. Important changes in the global configuration of power after 1955 provided a different backdrop for the domestic dialogue over foreign policy and produced corresponding realignments in the domestic patterns of conflict and consensus.

TOWARD A PARTIAL CONSENSUS, 1955–63

Domestic conflict over foreign policy gradually diminished in the late fifties and early sixties. By the end of the Adenauer era in 1963, the bitter contest over foreign policy had given way to a significant (if limited) measure of consensus.

As in the period before 1955, it was the international environment that set the boundaries for the domestic debate on foreign affairs. Most important, the choice of security, recovery, and democratic freedoms on the one hand, or unification on the other, had become a moot issue after Germany joined NATO and West European integration efforts. Also it was now becoming obvious that unification on terms other than those proposed by the Soviet Union was not likely. This freed the Socialists from their preoccupation with unification and allowed them to assess other foreign policy issues on their own merits and with more detachment. The points of agreement that had existed before 1955 among the major political parties and interest groups increased, a process aided by the fact that the more flexible elements in both the CDU/CSU and the SPD had become stronger. Narrowing the gap between the parties was not as hard for the Christian Democrats as for the Socialists, who were more ideological and somewhat removed from the mainstream of German politics. But adjustment was made slightly less painful by the fact that other political elements—notably the FDP—were going through a similar process.

The Socialists did not drop their opposition to the government's rearmament and military-strategic policy until the early sixties, when it became obvious that even the most conciliatory overtures to the Soviet Union would not aid unification. Prior to this, in the late fifties, the Socialists had intensified the contest over rearmament that had begun before West Germany's accession to NATO in 1955. The party felt vindicated in having argued that rearmament and membership in NATO would diminish the prospects for German unity while increasing the chances that Germany would become a battlefield in a "hot war." And although on the one hand they objected to the buildup of German conventional forces because they did not want a new German army to become NATO's foot soldiers, on the other hand they rejected the only possible alternative—American strategic nuclear deterrence via the doctrine of massive retaliation. During 1956 and 1957, when the recruitment method and makeup of the West German armed forces became an issue, the Socialists argued against conscription and rejected deployment of nuclear arms on German soil. Following the fall 1957 election (which was widely regarded as a popular endorsement of Adenauer's foreign policies), the SPD renewed its efforts to stir up popular opposition to nuclear weapons.

The SPD's antinuclear stand was linked to hopes for unification. Although the prospects for unification were becoming increasingly dim, the Socialists were encouraged by military disengagement proposals put forth on both sides of the Iron Curtain. The SPD's own plans called for withdrawing or thinning out conventional forces, keeping nuclear weapons off German territory, and neutralizing a united Germany in the context of a European security system. It was largely for this reason that the Socialists opposed having American nuclear weapons on German territory—they felt this would complicate disengagement schemes.

Despite the fact that nothing came of early military disengagement proposals, the Socialists intensified their commitment to this goal. In 1959 they presented another detailed Germany Plan, which advocated step-by-step military disengagement and gradual political and economic integration of the two Germanies. This plan offered a concession that not even the Socialists had proposed before—withdrawal of foreign troops from West and East Germany without prior agreement on unification—and it embraced the Soviet idea of a "confederated" Germany by proposing the establishment of all-German institutions, in which Bonn and East Berlin would be represented equally. The issue of free elections in both parts of Germany was left to the final phase of the three-stage integration plan.

But even this accommodating proposal was rejected by the Soviet bloc, and a year after its inception the Socialists themselves considered it a thing of the past. The party did not immediately lose interest in disengagement, but the building of the Berlin Wall in 1961 finally pushed them toward resignation on the question of unification. During the 1961 election campaign, the SPD began to endorse most aspects of the CDU's Western alliance policy; and Willy Brandt, mayor of West Berlin and the SPD's candidate for chancellor, admitted that the security of West Germany, rather than reunification, had become the primary issue. With this announcement the great reversal of the SPD's policy priorities was now specifically acknowledged.

The FDP's commitment to unification was subject to the same pressures. During the 1961 campaign, the Free Democrats still called for a more "independent" foreign policy for West Germany and asserted that the Germans themselves, rather than the Four Powers, were ultimately responsible for reunification. As late as the beginning of 1962, the FDP proposed that Bonn should hold bilateral exploratory talks with the Soviet Union, and some elements of the party were apparently flirting with the prospect of a bilateral German-Soviet understanding. But shortly thereafter party chief Erich Mende declared that the FDP had reconsidered its foreign policy stand and that it was now opposed to Germany's neutrality and disengagement projects for Central Europe. The party renounced its suggestions for bilateral discussions with the Soviet Union and instead emphasized the need to encourage liberalization of the East German regime so as to better the lot of the East German people.

Meanwhile, the Socialists' utter disappointment with the Soviet reaction to their Germany Plan for disengagement led them to readjust their entire foreign policy program. The SPD began to support a full-fledged German defense effort within the Western alliance and to offer suggestions for enhancing the alliance's deterrence posture. By 1963 the SPD regarded itself as the true champion of NATO, urging Adenauer to resist de Gaulle's disruptive NATO policies. The party even supported Washington's doctrine of flexibility, agreeing with its premise that the Western alliance needed more conventional forces. While the Adenauer government was critical of the strategy advocated by United States Secretary of Defense Robert S. McNamara and was beginning to question some of NATO's military planning, the Socialists and the Free Democrats were moving much closer to the American position. It was not so much that the Socialists were fully persuaded by the United States' military-strategic rationale but that the party viewed NATO as a restraint on a closer Bonn-Paris military tie. They feared that de Gaulle would succeed in persuading Adenauer to place Germany's security under the protection of the French rather than the American nuclear umbrella. Thus at a time when Adenauer began to criticize the revamping of American strategic doctrine, his most vociferous critics began to endorse his earlier unqualified support of NATO.

The Socialists and Free Democrats also opposed the government's European policy, which was based on the close relationship between Adenauer and de Gaulle. De Gaulle had agreed to support Adenauer's hard line vis-à-vis the Soviet bloc if Adenauer would support de Gaulle's little Europe policy restricting membership in the Common Market. The SPD opposed both positions. Still hoping that the loosening of the Soviet bloc might aid reunification, the Socialists favored a much more flexible policy toward the Soviet Union and Eastern Europe and wanted the government to resist de Gaulle's attempts to limit Common Market membership.

The SPD's position on the Common Market had been cautious from the beginning. The Socialists had no use for de Gaulle's little Europe concept, which would favor the conservative elements in Western Europe and highlight the bipolarization of the Continent and the division of Germany. But it was politically risky to attack the government's proven economic policy, and in the end the Socialists guardedly endorsed the Common Market, hoping that it could be turned into a supranational organization for economic planning.

For some time the party continued to voice misgivings about the EEC. Some of these objections were shared by important German political and commercial circles. The German business community was far from united in assessing the implications of the Common Market. One element saw great opportunities for exploiting a large "internal" European market, while another group, for whom the CDU's Ludwig Erhard and the Free Democrats became the spokesmen, feared the possible loss of markets outside the EEC. This group was not impressed with the argument that the Common Market could lead to the political integration of the Six, but rather was afraid that Britain and the Scandinavian countries would be excluded indefinitely. Prominent businessmen were also suspicious of the threat of economic planning, and some opposed the EEC because it included the loss of tariff protection. Farmers were particularly alarmed by the prospect of losing the tariff protection that had traditionally shielded them from foreign competition.

The cross-pressures felt by industrial interests, and the fears of agricultural interests, raised some intricate political questions. Erhard's supporters in the CDU/CSU (who did not share the ardent Europeanism of some Adenauer supporters and who preferred a larger Common Market) came very close to the FDP on this issue, and the dividing line between the FDP and the CDU's Erhard group became fuzzier. Agricultural interests had powerful spokesmen not only in the Bavarian CSU but also among some elements of the fragmented FDP. They were courted as well by the Socialists, who were seeking to overcome their traditional handicap in rural areas.

The situation became even more complicated after the establishment of the British-led European Free Trade Association. Again, the SPD, the FDP, and the Erhard supporters in the CDU/CSU—a somewhat awkward coalition —pressed for Britain's admission to the Common Market and warned that the reduction of tariffs within EFTA and EEC, coupled with the common external EEC tariff, would create tension between the two economic organizations and push up prices in Germany. All the political elements taking this position were careful, however, not to give the impression that they did not identify with EEC objectives—as long as these objectives did not preclude a Common Market with larger membership.

The SPD's international economic policy was by now close not only to the position of the FDP and some factions of the CDU but also to that of the United States. Although Washington supported the EEC rather than EFTA for political-strategic reasons, the Kennedy administration nonetheless favored a less exclusive Common Market because an economic split within non-Communist Europe would aggravate American balance-of-payments problems and undermine the economic foundations of the Western alliance. Furthermore, the preference for a larger Common Market shared by the Socialists, Free Democrats, and liberal Christian Democrats dovetailed neatly with their agreement with other goals the United States sought—support of NATO, and opposition to de Gaulle's design for a West European alliance under French hegemony and the protection of a French-led European nuclear umbrella. These divergent groups were much less willing than Adenauer to make allowances for de Gaulle's foreign policy, which was disrupting the Western alliance and which they perceived to be contrary to Germany's political, economic, and military-strategic interests. On political as well as economic and military-strategic grounds, they had the common objectives of (1) thwarting de Gaulle's design for a European order under French leadership, (2) admitting Britain to the Common Market, (3) embarking on a more flexible and imaginative policy toward the Soviet Union and Eastern Europe so as to further the cause of German unity, (4) pursuing an enlightened and undoctrinaire security policy based on close cooperation with NATO and the United States, and (5) seeking a change of regime in Bonn. It was on this basis that the Socialists, the Free Democrats, and the liberal wing of the CDU established a tenuous, implicit, partial—but nonetheless important—consensus.

The fundamental impulses for such political realignments continued to come from changes in the international system. The apparent hopelessness of unification and the gradual fragmentation of the Western alliance, whose harmony of purpose had been the prerequisite for the domestic as well as the international success of Adenauer's foreign policy program, forced a reconfiguration of domestic political forces. As it became necessary to choose between Washington and Paris, longstanding tensions within the governing coalitions and within the CDU could no longer be contained. The disagreements between the United States and France not only created serious problems for Bonn's foreign policy but, because of the sensitivity of the West German political process to external influences, undermined Adenauer's domestic support on foreign policy issues even within his own party.

The attrition of support for Adenauer's foreign policy program was accelerated by an erosion of the chancellor's personal authority. In 1959, Adenauer displayed a good deal of cynicism and lack of respect for the democratic institutions of the West German state when he vacillated about whether he wished to succeed Theodor Heuss to the largely ceremonial office of president of the republic. Adenauer's power plays during that episode—which were obviously designed to perpetuate his influence on foreign policy in the event of his retirement as chancellor—cost him a good deal of support and prestige not only in political circles but also among the people. After the 1961 elections, these developments came to a head. The Free Democrats made considerable gains (at the expense of the CDU/CSU, since the Socialists had also been successful) and now insisted that they would rejoin the governing coalition only if Adenauer agreed to step down as chancellor by 1963. Precarious to begin with, the 1961 coalition collapsed after one year.

The FDP was finally persuaded to join a reshuffled cabinet after Adenauer threatened to create a Grand Coalition between the CDU/CSU and the SPD. Although the Free Democrats were restrained for the time being, the internal cohesion of the CDU/CSU had been shaken at the core. Adenauer was a lame-duck chancellor, and in 1963 could not even prevent the chancellorship from going to Ludwig Erhard, whom Adenauer had opposed and openly humiliated all along with allegations that he was insufficiently astute in international affairs and lacking in political acumen, vision, and experience.

THE ERHARD CHANCELLORSHIP, 1963–66

The partial and tentative consensus on foreign policy that had emerged in Bonn by 1963 was symbolized in the person of the new chancellor. Ludwig Erhard was the very embodiment of Germany's successful quest for normalcy. He was the patron saint of the "economic miracle," and his appeal to voters had been an important factor in his selection as the CDU's choice for chancellor. Erhard was obviously less authoritarian than Adenauer, and he had himself suffered from the high-handedness with which his predecessor gradually alienated even his supporters. The new chancellor represented the pro-Atlantic consensus (manifested in staunch support of NATO and an increase in the membership of the Common Market) that reached across Bonn's political spectrum, and he seemed to favor a less doctrinaire and more flexible policy toward the Soviet Union and the countries of Eastern Europe.

On the surface it would seem as if Bonn could now face foreign policy issues with resolution and on a secure foundation of domestic support. Several factors, however, worked in the opposite direction. Although the partial consensus on foreign policy issues appeared to offer a chance for turning West Germany's political energies inward, it soon became apparent that the international environment was as intrusive and compelling as it had been before and that external events continued to raise controversy in Bonn. The biggest obstacle to effective policymaking was the widening conflict between the United States and France during the mid-sixties. As it became clear that Erhard was inclined (as well as induced by circumstances) to support Washington rather than Paris, the consensus that had been in the making proved insufficiently broad. A polarization of political viewpoints soon developed, but in contrast to the interparty differences of the fifties, the debate between the Gaullists and the Atlanticists reached within as well as across party lines —with the majority party, the CDU/CSU, containing strong advocates of both sides.

At the core of the Gaullists' disagreement with the Atlanticists was a considerable disenchantment with the United States. The Gaullists feared that the Kennedy administration might make deals with the Soviet Union over the heads of Germany and other European states. In contrast, de Gaulle's policy clearly sought to maximize the leverage of Europe, and in that context the leverage of Germany might increase as well. For these reasons the Gaullists stressed close Franco-German cooperation, sustained by the economic and military potential of the Common Market, and they were unenthusiastic about the prospect of British membership in the EEC.

The rapid deterioration of Franco-German relations and Erhard's lack of success in Washington, especially with respect to proposals for the MLF (multilateral nuclear force, discussed in chapter 1), aggravated tensions within the CDU/CSU. The Gaullists opposed Erhard not only because of what they viewed as his misguided and naive pro-Atlantic policy but also because of the government's more flexible Eastern policy (largely initiated by Schröder), which they regarded as similarly lacking in realism and determination. The Gaullists were much more closely identified, by conviction as well as past association, with the orthodox Cold War position of the Adenauer years. The concept of a loose community of Eastern and Western European states, which seemed to serve as the basis of the Gaullists' reunification policy, clearly implied a weakening of the Soviet position in Eastern Europe. In particular, they opposed any modification of the Hallstein Doctrine and the official government position on the Oder-Neisse border issue, and they generally followed a hard-line policy toward the East German regime.

While Erhard and Schröder were attacked by the Gaullists within their own party for making a dangerous opening to the East, they were chided by their coalition partners, the Free Democrats, for not making the opening wide enough. Although the Free Democrats were conservative on economic and social issues and in favor of the government's Common Market policy, the FDP's abiding commitment to a dynamic reunification policy led them to attack the Christian Democrats' hesitant gestures toward Eastern Europe much more stridently than did the Socialist opposition.

Even so, the SPD remained in the foreground of the debate on the German question. Almost all political groups agreed that the changing international circumstances, especially in the Soviet bloc, required new initiatives in Bonn; but they disagreed on how far and in what direction a revised reunification policy should go and on how to deal with East Germany. On the Left, critics of the government's Eastern policy argued that it would prove ineffective unless Bonn also revised its orthodox position on the Oder-Neisse line, the Munich Pact, and the attempted isolation of East Germany. They favored increased contacts between the two Germanies, even on an official level, in order to avoid widening the gap and to encourage liberalization of the East German regime.

The opposition on the Right was doubly effective because of its leverage in both the cabinet and the CDU/CSU. The Gaullists were determined to restrain the moderately progressive Eastern policy of Erhard and Schröder. They obstructed the establishment of diplomatic relations with Rumania and resisted opportunities for exploratory talks with Czechoslovakia on this issue, and they prevailed upon the government to modify the conciliatory language of Erhard's "Peace Note."

The lines between the government and the opposition became blurred. The CDU/CSU (and to some extent also the FDP, its coalition partner) not only played the role of the party in power but also acted as the unofficial opposition on some major foreign policy issues, while the official opposition, the SPD, shared several of the government's policy preferences and tried to straddle the fence on the issues that divided the majority party. The resulting ambiguity of party images may have helped the CDU/CSU in the lackluster 1965 election campaign, since Erhard proved to be a very formidable vote getter and almost regained for his party the absolute majority that was lost in 1961. In 1965, in contrast to previous years, a vote for the CDU/CSU expressed ambivalence about foreign policy and could be interpreted as a refusal to choose either a pro-Atlantic or pro-Gaullist position.

Although the traditional CDU/CSU-FDP coalition was reestablished, this was widely viewed as an interm solution. Erhard's ineffectiveness as chancellor and loss of prestige was already so great that at the very moment of the CDU/CSU's electoral triumph, to which he contributed substantially, rivals within his own party were making plans to topple him.

The jockeying for position in Bonn led to a curious and paradoxical interplay between domestic and foreign policy considerations. In their determination to ultimately wrest power from Erhard and preclude Schröder from succeeding him, the Gaullists rather than the Atlanticists flirted with the prospect of a Grand Coalition with the Socialists—even though the foreign policy conceptions of the SPD were much closer to the Erhard-Schröder line on Atlantic policy and to the FDP line on Eastern policy, and hence in conflict with the preferences of the Gaullists. By contrast, Erhard, Schröder, and others feared that a Grand Coalition with the Socialists, although acceptable to them from the viewpoint of foreign policy matters, would lead to the absorption of their power in a conglomerate "national front." The Free Democrats also opposed a Grand Coalition. Constantly afraid of winning less than the 5 percent of the vote required for representation in the *Bundestag* and threatened with exclusion by proposed changes in the electoral law, the FDP needed to maintain its third-party image and leverage in order to survive— even though the major foreign policy lines of a CDU/CSU–SPD Grand Coalition probably would have proven acceptable.

Clearly, all this contrasted with the situation in the fifties, when the line dividing the government from the opposition was sharp, when foreign policy preferences generally complemented domestic policy preferences and power calculations, and when viewpoints were articulated by specific parties in fairly clear-cut confrontations. The intricate patterns of alignment and opposition in the sixties, and their connections with domestic and foreign policy considerations, were in a sense doubly involuted. The need to choose between Washington and Paris led to domestic political differences similar to the polarization of the fifties. But the polarization of the sixties developed over different issues, which meant that the constituency of one viewpoint, Atlanticism, was dispersed over a wide political spectrum and not concentrated in a single political party. To be sure, advocates of the opposing viewpoint, the Gaullists, were located primarily within one party, but groups within the CDU/CSU were also the major spokesmen for Atlanticism.

The blurring of the line between government and opposition made for a greater readiness to adjust foreign policy preferences to gain domestic political advantage, as compared to the fifties—especially since politics had become more pragmatic and less ideological. All elements of the political spectrum sought, in an almost promiscuous way, to entice more or less likely bedfellows to join them in small or grand coalitions. At the same time, the disagreements between Atlanticists and Gaullists in the CDU/CSU were sharpened by the Gaullists' efforts to dislodge the chancellor. This forced both sides to endorse foreign policy alternatives that were basically unrealistic. For even though the United States and France were genuinely at odds, the positions of the Atlanticists and Gaullists in Bonn were not truly aligned with the positions of Washington and Paris. As a result the apparent foreign policy interests of the Federal Republic—whether interpreted by the Atlanticists or the Gaullists—were no longer fully compatible with those of either the United States or France. As Fritz René Allemann has noted,

The "Gaullists," while eager to move closer to Paris, did not at all see eye to eye with President de Gaulle's Eastern European policies and were rather frightened by his visions of a Greater Europe embracing the Communist East. The "Atlanticists" were lured by the dream of German participation in nuclear defense and of a kind of "special relationship" between the United States and the Federal Republic, even long after it had become clear that Washington had dropped the MLF concept and was as interested as de Gaulle himself in furthering an understanding with the Soviet Union and with Moscow's Eastern European allies. To a large extent, the controversy between these schools of opinion was something like a tragi-comedy of errors: the German clients of France and America still fought out battles which their foreign friends had already abandoned. In reality, however, these battles only masked a fight for power which had little to do with ideological labels.*

These political complexities would have been a challenge for any chancellor. Erhard, handicapped by a divided party and coalition as well as by his personal shortcomings, was doubly ill-equipped to deal with the situation. Throughout 1966, a series of political misfortunes befell the chancellor and led to his forced resignation late in the year. In foreign affairs, Erhard's diplomacy seemed to consist almost entirely of pro-Atlantic gestures and occasional pro–de Gaulle rhetoric, sustained primarily by good will and personal bonhomie. He had failed to persuade the Johnson administration to

*Fritz René Allemann, "The Changing Scene in Germany," *The World Today,* February 1967, p. 54.

come around to the German viewpoint on the MLF, Franco-German relations were at their lowest point since the establishment of the Federal Republic, and the government's halfhearted overtures to Eastern Europe only annoyed the right wing of the CDU/CSU without particularly impressing the Free Democrats or the Socialists.

On domestic issues, things were not going much better. For the first time since the launching of the "economic miracle," a serious recession hit West Germany, causing unemployment and aggravating budgetary and fiscal problems. When Erhard returned in the fall of 1966 from a trip to Washington without having gained a reduction or even delay of Bonn's payments commitment toward United States military costs in Germany, the last remnants of the chancellor's prestige evaporated. The immediate occasion for Erhard's demise—the resignation of the FDP ministers over budgetary matters in October 1966—was thus only the trigger and not the cause of the Erhard administration's collapse.

THE GRAND COALITION, 1966–69

In December 1966, for the first time since the establishment of the Federal Republic, the Christian Democrats and the Social Democrats joined forces in a national coalition government, which gave them an overwhelming majority —447 out of 496 seats in the *Bundestag*.

The extensive deliberations and negotiations that preceded the formation of the new government—during which all parties considered joining in every possible coalition arrangement—demonstrated the growing pragmatism and de-ideologization of the political process, exemplified by a willingness to adjust party policy to gain political advantage. But the Grand Coalition that resulted was an uneasy one from the beginning. The final composition of the new government reflected the precarious balance struck among various party wings, policy orientations, and personalities. Kurt Georg Kiesinger, the CDU/CSU's choice for the chancellorship, was a compromise candidate. He was acceptable to both Gaullists and Atlanticists, and he also obtained the support of Franz-Josef Strauss, head of the powerful Bavarian CSU, who thus secured his own return to the cabinet. Many Socialist parliamentarians and party officials would have preferred a mini-coalition with the FDP, but Willy Brandt's position as SPD leader was at no time seriously challenged and he become vice-chancellor and foreign minister.

The achievements of the Grand Coalition were not spectacular. The government managed to revive the economy but international and domestic factors combined to make it almost impossible to revitalize foreign policy. The international environment continued to be troublesome, and institutional responsibility for the conduct of foreign affairs was blurred. Kiesinger, as chancellor, had the constitutional right to determine the general direction of policy, but Brandt, in the foreign office, was clearly the innovator in foreign policymaking.

Even before the Soviet invasion of Czechoslovakia the Grand Coalition was working at cross-purposes, with the more conservative CDU/CSU elements acting as a constant brake on more innovative SPD elements. The invasion of Czechoslovakia, from which neither the reformists nor the conservatives could derive any comfort, tended to strengthen the position of the conservatives. It seemed to confirm their argument that the reformists, with no guarantees from the Soviets, were undermining the consistency and legitimacy of the orthodox German viewpoint in the face of an unreconstructed Soviet imperialism.

There was also a clash over the nonproliferation treaty. Each side in the debate claimed, with some justification, that it was being "realistic." The groups that favored (or were resigned to) German participation in the treaty —most of the Social Democrats, and CDU moderates—knew that it would be costly to reject an important arms control measure that was widely supported by Bonn's allies as well as its opponents. Arguing most vocally against the treaty was Franz-Josef Strauss, who characterized it as a "Versailles of cosmic proportions." Ex-chancellor Adenauer (prior to his death in April 1967) and several other CSU and CDU leaders also opposed the treaty, seeing it as another example of Soviet-American complicity, damaging to vital German national interests, and impairing Bonn's present and future mobility.

In the election year of 1969, programmatic differences within the Grand Coalition intensified and led to greater stagnation of German foreign policy. This was especially problematic because foreign policy was supposed to have been the cement holding the government together—on domestic issues the coalition members could hardly be expected to see eye-to-eye. However, the peculiar calculations that had brought the coalition partners together in the first place made them mute public controversy while simultaneously trying to gain electoral advantage. None of the parties wanted a full and open break before the September vote because they anticipated that the election results might force them to continue the coalition. A second Grand Coalition would have been hard to justify if the first had ended with an open admission of failure.

The SPD adopted an election strategy based on a division of labor. Economics Minister Schiller, who could take credit for having led the German economy from the recession to the heights of a new boom, served as an ideal symbol of the party's trustworthiness in domestic, and especially economic, affairs. Willy Brandt represented the SPD's flexibility and "modernity" in foreign affairs. In short, the SPD hoped to outmaneuver the Christian Democrats by moving to the Right on economic issues to gain ground among moderates, while shifting somewhat to the Left on foreign policy issues. All told, however, foreign policy did not play a very significant role in the campaign.

THE BRANDT CHANCELLORSHIP, 1969–74

The coalition government of Social Democrats and Free Democrats, established on the basis of the September 1969 election results, rested on a slim majority in the *Bundestag.* An even more important source of difficulty for the new government—under the SPD's Willy Brandt as chancellor and the FDP's Walter Scheel as vice-chancellor and foreign minister—was the structural weakness of the coalition. The two coalition partners did not fully agree on all the issues they had to face in the fall of 1969. Although the Socialists and Free Democrats shared common ground on foreign policy matters—above all, the determination to try new approaches to the East and to enlarge the Common Market—they were much further apart on domestic affairs. Particularly in the areas of economic and social policy, the Free Democrats were closer to the Christian Democrats than to the Socialists. In addition the Free Democrats had a reputation for lacking party discipline, a result of internal tensions within the FDP, and some Socialists feared the Free Democrats could not always be relied upon to back a Socialist chancellor.

The latter point was especially pertinent since some elements of the FDP were not enthusiastic about entering into a coalition with the Socialists. A handful of "national conservatives," led by former party chairman Erich Mende, opposed the dynamic Eastern policy mapped out by Willy Brandt and FDP party chairman Walter Scheel, and there was a real possibility that FDP backbenchers might defect on important votes. In fact, Brandt was elected chancellor by a margin of only three votes even though the SPD and the FDP had a twelve-vote margin in the *Bundestag.*

In spite of these difficulties, both coalition partners were eager to join forces. The Free Democrats hoped to create a more distinct image for their party, thus staving off its threatened demise. The SPD wanted to prove itself capable of governing responsibly and was anxious to form the first Socialist-led government in Germany since 1930.

The tensions between the SPD and the FDP on economic issues and the tenuous coalition majority in the *Bundestag* pushed the new government to emphasize foreign policy, where its base of support was apparently most secure. But the government faced a determined and powerful opposition, which put additional strain on the coalition. The Christian Democrats, out of office for the first time in the history of the Federal Republic and bitter because they were denied a voice in government although they had drawn the most votes in the election, were eager to act as vigilant, exacting, and vociferous critics of the SPD–FDP coalition in the hope of toppling it as soon as possible. In November 1969, the CDU/CSU sparked a major debate in the *Bundestag* on the question of Germany's acceptance of the nonproliferation treaty. Although the party emphasized its reservations about the treaty, ratification could not be prevented and the party generally found it difficult to get much political mileage out of the issue. Most of the background deliberations on the treaty had already taken place during the years of the Grand Coalition, and Washington had made reassurances on the questions of greatest concern, including the nuclear powers' commitment to engage in serious arms control and disarmament talks.

From the beginning, it was the coalition's *Ostpolitik* that drew the opposition's most intense fire. Throughout 1970 and 1971, when the Bonn government negotiated the Moscow and Warsaw treaties and the inter-German accord on the Berlin question, the CDU/CSU attacked what was viewed as a dangerous departure from Bonn's postwar foreign policy line. The Christian Democrats contended that *Ostpolitik* would allow the Soviet Union to extend its influence in Central and Western Europe and lead to a weakening of the Western defense effort and a reduced American commitment to Europe. Former Foreign Minister Gerhard Schröder, probably the most sophisticated opposition spokesman on foreign policy matters, was a very effective critic because of the intellectual thrust of his arguments and because he was not unsympathetic to the general direction of *Ostpolitik*. Other opposition spokesmen, including CDU/CSU floor leader Rainer Barzel (who became chairman of the CDU in October 1971), called for a number of preconditions for accepting the treaties—among others, a satisfactory Berlin settlement, progress in East-West German relations, specific Soviet "recognition" of the Common Market, explicit repudiation of Moscow's claim to have the "right of intervention of victorious powers" under the UN Charter, reiteration in the treaties of the German right to self-determination, and clarification of treaty provisions that were subject to differing interpretations by Bonn and Moscow. The right wing of the opposition, and especially CSU chief Franz-Josef Strauss, accused the government—and by implication the Western powers— of selling out German interests. Strauss called the Four Power accord on the status of Berlin a "rubber treaty" that would help to extend Soviet influence in Berlin and left the status of the city insufficiently clarified. Critics also insisted that final border arrangements would have to wait until a peace treaty for all of Germany was concluded. Nonetheless, the Christian Democrats indicated that they favored a policy of rapprochement with Moscow and would regard the treaties, if ratified, as binding on a future CDU/CSU government. On the other hand, the opposition pledged that if the treaties were defeated they would reopen negotiations with Moscow for more favorable conditions.

In the spring of 1972, the controversy over *Ostpolitik* reached a critical point—in part because the Moscow and Warsaw treaties were going through preliminary debates in the *Bundestag*, and in part because the SPD–FDP coalition had become so shaky that the survival of the government itself appeared to be at stake. Although these two factors were related, the difficulties of the government stemmed from causes that went beyond *Ostpolitik*, important as that issue was. Mostly as the result of FDP defections over *Ostpolitik*, in February 1972 the coalition was left with a majority of one, creating a serious crisis of confidence. The crisis, although occasioned by the issue of the government's Eastern policy, had other sources as well. In an effort to maintain the coalition's narrow base of support in the *Bundestag*, and in order to shield the foreign policy consensus of the cabinet from disruptive domestic issues, the government had been obliged to shelve the ambitious domestic reform program announced in the fall of 1969. This was politically risky, however. The 1969 election had been fought primarily on domestic rather than foreign policy issues, raising expectations that were not being fulfilled. Inflation and economic stagnation made economic and social reform seem all the more urgent. At the height of the coalition's crisis over *Ostpolitik* in the spring of 1972, quarrels continued within the government over tax reform and related issues.

The political consequences of the government's inability to solve economic problems, especially inflation, were particularly serious since the controversy over *Ostpolitik* prevented the coalition from falling back to a safe position on foreign policy matters. In short, the inner contradictions of the coalition prevented it from acting decisively on domestic issues, while the coalition's fundamental raison d'être, foreign policy, rested on the narrowest of margins in the *Bundestag* and was forcefully attacked by the opposition.

The opposition was not without problems of its own. The Christian Democrats were (at least initially) uncertain in their unaccustomed role of being the party out of power, and their diverse constituency made it difficult to formulate a coherent program. In addition, serious leadership problems arose when party chiefs sought to replace Kiesinger as chairman of the CDU. In the scramble to succeed Kiesinger, the major contenders—Rainer Barzel, the party's floor leader; Helmut Kohl, minister president of Rhineland-Palatinate; former foreign minister Gerhard Schröder; and Franz-Josef Strauss, chief of the CSU, as kingmaker—sought to establish their reputations as foreign policy spokesmen. Barzel's success in becoming party chairman (with the help of Strauss) signified a definite move to the Right on foreign policy questions.

The intense debate over *Ostpolitik* could not hide the fact that Bonn's Eastern policy was irreversible. The connections between *Ostpolitik* and other issues of great importance to both East and West—such as a European Security Conference, the SALT talks, MBFR, and a general East-West detente—meant that a collapse of *Ostpolitik*, through failure of the *Bundestag* to ratify the Moscow and Warsaw treaties, would dismay not only Bonn's opponents in the East but also its allies in the West. The Christian Democrats realized that by bringing down the treaty structure of Bonn's *Ostpolitik*, they would shoulder the responsibility of having obstructed the central foreign policy goal sought by both East and West during the seventies. Moreover, the opposition found it difficult to offer a realistic alternative to the government's foreign policy program—a situation reminiscent of the fifties when the Socialists were in opposition.

In the *Bundestag* election of 1972, the SPD–FDP coalition won a 46-seat majority and the SPD for the first time gained more votes than the CDU/CSU. The election could be interpreted as an endorsement of the government's *Ostpolitik* (especially since the economy was not an important issue), and not even the opposition could overlook the implication that the German electorate wished to clarify the issues by giving the architects of *Ostpolitik* a more clearly expressed endorsement. Even so, the intra-German Basic Treaty also had rough going during the *Bundestag* ratification process in 1973, which was complicated by legal-constitutional maneuvers initiated by the opposition. By 1974, when Willy Brandt felt compelled to resign over the discovery that his personal assistant, Günther Guillaume, was an East German spy, the dynamics of his *Ostpolitik* had largely run their course.

THE SCHMIDT CHANCELLORSHIP

The new coalition team, headed by the SPD's Helmut Schmidt as chancellor and the FDP's Hans Dietrich Genscher as foreign minister (with Walter Scheel becoming president of the republic), soon became preoccupied with domestic and international economic problems. This is not to say that *Ostpolitik*, and especially relations between West and East Germany, was neglected by either government or opposition. But a significant shift of priorities was taking place. In the two years between the formation of the Schmidt-Genscher coalition and the *Bundestag* election of 1976, economic and social questions—particularly on the domestic front—began to come to the fore. The three major parties, gearing up quite early for the 1976 campaign, began to take stands on the major socioeconomic issues in the minds of the voters.

The CDU/CSU was handicapped by internal dissension. Although the two parties within the Union traditionally campaigned on the basis of a common platform, they were in a sense independent entities outside of the *Bundestag*, with the CDU competing in all German *Länder* and the CSU (tightly controlled by Franz-Josef Strauss) being the sole representative of the Union in Bavaria. Helmut Kohl, minister president of Rhineland Palatinate and the Union's candidate for chancellor, had considerable difficulty establishing a convincing profile for himself (especially in foreign affairs), a problem aggravated by the constant and highly visible efforts on the part of Franz-Josef Strauss to maximize his influence over the election platform and the political direction of the CDU/CSU in general.

The CDU/CSU followed a strategy of attacking the governing coalition on economic policy, arguing that the SPD in particular was undermining and endangering the "social market economy" principle that had proved so beneficial for Germany since the days of Adenauer and Erhard. The Christian Democrats also charged that *Ostpolitik* had been more advantageous for East Germany than for West Germany and had resulted in greater Soviet influence over Europe. They also raised a law-and-order theme with respect to developments within Germany, accusing the government of having been insufficiently firm in dealing with radicals and terrorists and singling out the SPD for being too tolerant and responsive to its young, left-wing activist members.

Some of these charges were not very plausible. Placed in an international, comparative context, the economic record of the government was by no means bad. Neither the chancellor (a trained economist) nor his economics and finance ministers could be accused of lacking judicious and responsible attitudes and policies. The government could point out that it had shielded the West German economy quite successfully from the impact of the international recession; that West Germany enjoyed an enviably low inflation rate; that the growth rate of production, although not spectacular, was at a level that prevented the economy from overheating; and that exports and the international position of the German mark were cause for a sense of satisfaction. With respect to *Ostpolitik,* the government argued that the opposition had failed to come up with a reasonable alternative that would not aggravate international tensions; that everything possible was being done to increase human contacts between the two Germanies; and that the more hard-line attitude advocated by the opposition would be unrealistic and self-defeating. The charge of having coddled left-wing dissidents within the SPD seemed especially ironic since Schmidt and the party apparatus in general, including most of the SPD contingent in the *Bundestag,* were themselves extremely annoyed and embarrassed by the more radical left wing and had been subject to attack from that direction.

In the 1976 election the governing SPD–FDP coalition won, but it was a narrow victory. The coalition lost 3.8 percent to the Christian Democrats, which reduced the government's majority from 46 to 10.

By the late seventies, thirty years after its establishment, the Federal Republic had become much more concerned with economic well-being and related social questions than with military-strategic issues and large-scale political designs. In a sense, Willy Brandt's *Ostpolitik* was the last remnant of West Germany's preoccupation with the big, "classical" foreign policy issues of the previous two decades. More and more, in Germany as well as in other European countries, economic and monetary issues began to come to the foreground, and it became harder to draw distinctions between foreign and domestic policies. This development was accelerated by economic interdependence in the context of regional and global politics, a process enhanced by European economic integration. Foreign policy and domestic economic and social issues thus increasingly became fused in a highly intricate way, leading to a change in the way foreign policy issues were debated and evaluated on the domestic political scene.

FRANCE

5

Security and the Western Alliance

Similar to the case of Germany, France's postwar foreign policy goals were characterized by a remarkable continuity. Although this in large part was a consequence of international circumstances, the French historical experience also played an important role. The meaning of France's national interests, during the Fourth as well as the Fifth Republic, grew out of French perceptions of the past as well as the present.

Above all, the traditional hostility between France and Germany—dating at least from the Franco-Prussian War of 1870–71 and enflamed again during World War I and II—had left a deep residue of bitterness. The conviction that French national interests required a weak Germany was only strengthened by the rapid defeat of the French armed forces in May and June of 1940, by the four-year German occupation, and by the fact that France could not have been liberated without massive Allied support.

In this light, France considered it imperative to take steps to permanently alter the Franco-German balance of power after Nazi Germany's defeat in 1945. Two choices presented themselves. One involved permanently weakening Germany either through partition or effective international control; the other, as a corollary to the first, involved creating a European order in which France would play a flexible, independent, and hence predominant role as the continental "balancer" of power relations—a role that would maximize French power relative to Germany and also relative to Britain, the United States, and the Soviet Union. Keeping Germany in a subordinate position would also advance a much larger purpose: restoration of France as a global power, capable of reasserting control over her far-flung empire and gaining an effective voice, as one of the Big Four, in the rearrangement of the postwar international order.

Considering the physical and psychological exhaustion of the country, the confused political process during the years immediately following the liberation of 1944, and the disarray of relations within the empire, it was apparent that French foreign policy goals—if they were realizable at all—would have to be pursued with the utmost skill and circumspection. Moreover, these goals were not precisely defined, nor did a blueprint exist in anyone's mind for their implementation. Even General Charles de Gaulle, in charge of France for eighteen months between the liberation in 1944 and the establishment of the Fourth Republic at the end of 1945, lacked a strategy for translating French aims into diplomatic action. The flux and pressure of events allowed only tactical responses.

Even so, the "goals of 1944," as Alfred Grosser has called them,* had already begun to take shape in their general outlines:

1 *Permanent security, primarily with respect to Germany.* This meant working toward a favorable international climate as well as seeking to create a French sphere of influence over the Saar territory, establish an autonomous Rhineland, and install a special regime, perhaps under Four-Power responsibility, for the Ruhr. In short, France wanted to regain what was perceived as the country's "natural" frontiers and to keep Germany weak under a Four-Power control arrangement in which France would be an equal partner.

2 *Political and economic reconstruction.* Political reconstruction meant, above all, restoring independence, flexibility, and dynamism to France's dealings with the Allies so as to place French aims vis-à-vis Germany on a solid footing and underline the country's position as one of the victorious Big Four. The need for this reassertion of French power was brought home not only by the wartime experiences of General de Gaulle but also by the country's exclusion from the Yalta Conference of February 1945. It was only because of the insistence of Prime Minister Winston Churchill and President Franklin Roosevelt that the Allies created a French zone of occupation in Germany (carved out of the British and American zones) and established a French seat on the Allied Control Council. The economic aspect of the recovery goal involved rebuilding a prosperous national economy. Like most other European nations emerging from the devastating effects of the war, France suffered from shortages of goods and hard currency reserves, unsatisfactory trade relations with other countries, unemployment in certain sectors of industry, and other forms of economic and social dislocation. Recovery was as much a foreign as a domestic policy project. France's resources alone could not accomplish the task of economic reconstruction, and the coun-

*Alfred Grosser, *French Foreign Policy Under de Gaulle* (Boston, Mass.: Little, Brown and Co., 1965), pp. 2–5.

try's monetary and trade problems could be solved only through foreign aid and international cooperation.

3 *Adjusting to decolonization.* A third set of foreign policy goals revolved around France's colonial territories or, as the empire was officially called after the Brazzaville Conference of January 1944, the French Union. Although the conference was touted as the beginning of a process of decolonization, the French had no intention of loosening their grip on possessions in Africa and Indochina. They sought, instead, to develop a "modernizing" framework that would perpetuate French control. There existed a widespread national feeling that the country's cultural, political, and moral prestige was at stake in the empire and that France would in a sense no longer be France if the nation were to divest itself of a civilizing vocation by giving up the colonies entirely. Similar to the German goal of reunification, the issue of decolonization became for France a question of national self-definition.

We will discuss each of these sets of French foreign policy goals in the three chapters that follow. A fourth chapter will relate the domestic political process to the three sets of goals.

THE DILEMMA OF FRENCH SECURITY

At the end of World War II, the military power of France was as depleted as that of defeated Germany. The French armed forces were small, scattered, and overcommitted; the nation's human and physical resources were exhausted. As a result, the goal of security had to be implemented by means of diplomacy —by convincing France's wartime allies to build a European and global order in which French security interests would be adequately satisfied. This was not an easy task, even before the beginning of the Cold War. De Gaulle achieved some success in this direction in 1945 by obtaining Big-Power status for France through recognition as the fourth occupying power in Germany and by gaining for France a permanent seat on the United Nations Security Council. In addition, the proposal to detach the Saar from Germany met a favorable initial response from the Allies.

But the aim of dismembering Germany—the central French security objective until the beginning of the Cold War—and the goal of occupying the Rhineland had to be abandoned. The Anglo-American powers and the Soviet Union refused to give a "western settlement" of the German issue their full support. This created an asymmetry in European power relationships, as de Gaulle noted in September 1945. At the end of the war, he pointed out, "Germany was amputated in the East but not in the West. The current of German vitality is thus turned westwards. One day German aggressiveness might well face westwards too. There must therefore be in the West a settlement counterbalancing that in the East."

But the Franco-Soviet alliance of 1944 did not prevent the Kremlin from opposing French aims regarding Germany; the alliance with Britain (formally instituted at the beginning of 1947) could not divert Britain from its "special understanding" with the United States; and Washington, suspicious of French colonial policy in Indochina and Africa, became increasingly annoyed with French obstructionism in the Allied Control Council and with the way the French exploited their zone of occupation in Germany.

With the outbreak of the Cold War, French security goals toward Germany became even more complicated. France's new "goals of 1947"—security from the Soviet Union, and economic reconstruction through foreign aid— were difficult to pursue simultaneously with the major "goals of 1944," primarily Big-Power status and security from Germany. Success in one area was bound to be achieved at the expense of success in the other, for seeking to accomplish both would overtax France's limited resources. France's internal weakness was underscored in 1947–48, when most of the French became concerned over not only the possibility of Soviet military aggression but also a communist takeover in France itself.

To counter these threats from both internal and external sources, France required American aid. But American military protection through NATO and economic assistance via the Marshall Plan could only be secured at a costly price. The United States, determined to implement its containment policy on a multilateral European basis, insisted on French support of German reunification (France signed the London Agreement of June 1945), German rearmament, and German participation as an equal in an integrated Europe. In other words, France had to abandon expectations of territorial satisfaction and political predominance over Germany. Furthermore, the bipolarization of international politics resulting from the Cold War immensely weakened France's diplomatic leverage in her dealings with the West as well as with the East and placed French security goals on an even more precarious footing than during the immediate postwar years.

NATO AND EDC

Considerations of both defense and diplomacy determined France's attitudes toward the two military-strategic frameworks within which the government sought security and influence: the North Atlantic Treaty Organization and the abortive attempt to establish a European Defense Community. For France both of these arrangements were second best, acceptable only out of necessity. The French would have preferred to rest their security on an independent national military posture, which would allow greater diplomatic flexibility.

In 1949, when both NATO and the Federal Republic of Germany were established, the contradictions between France's security policy toward the Soviet Union and toward Germany became fully visible. French policymakers were compelled to deal with the issue of security toward the Soviet Union and the issue of restraining West Germany within the same political context —the Western alliance. This was extremely disadvantageous for French policy because the highest priority of the Western alliance (as an instrument of Washington's Cold War policy) was the containment of Soviet power, whereas the highest priority of France was the containment of German power. This dilemma was demonstrated in the heated debates in the French National Assembly in July 1949 over ratification of the Atlantic Pact. There was less controversy over entering an alliance directed against the Soviet Union (only the Communists were opposed on those grounds) than dismay over the prospect that the Atlantic Pact would sooner or later open the door to German rearmament. Although the supporters of the pact in the Assembly denied this possibility (Robert Schuman: "Germany still has no peace treaty. It has no army, and it must not have one. It has no weapons, and it will have none."), the Pentagon was already making plans for German remilitarization. A year later, President Harry S Truman and the United States State Department formally proposed establishing ten German divisions under NATO command.

The French position was a difficult one. The invasion of South Korea by North Korea in 1950 followed a series of hostile Communist acts—the Berlin blockade, pressures on Iran and Turkey, the Kremlin's adamant opposition to the Marshall Plan, establishment of the Cominform, Soviet support of French and Italian strikes, the takeover of Czechoslovakia—and many West Europeans feared that the Soviet Union might pursue its ambitions in Europe even with military means. France had joined Britain and the Benelux countries in the mutual assistance arrangements of the Brussels Treaty of March 1948, but was fully aware that these assurances had only nominal value and that its security depended on the North Atlantic Treaty Organization. Paris had pledged twenty-four divisions to NATO, but could muster only three divisions in West Germany and six in France, with ten divisions pinned down in Indochina. German rearmament thus seemed to promise substantial savings for France and, above all, to strengthen a forward NATO strategy in which not France but Germany would stand on the first line of defense.*

These were compelling arguments for German rearmament. But France (as well as other West European countries) considered rearming Germany to

---

*French politicians were interested in a forward strategy not so much because they expected an immediate Soviet attack but because they feared that if an attack occurred the United States would conduct its liberation efforts from behind the Pyrenees or from an even more remote staging area. Thus although experts had always questioned the military value of a forward strategy, a verbal commitment to it seemed absolutely necessary on political and psychological grounds.

be premature and insisted on strong safeguards against a revival of German militarism. Also, French decision makers knew that the German government intended to use rearmament to advance its goals of political and economic recovery, goals the French government viewed with apprehension because the power relationship between France and the newly established Federal Republic would shift in Bonn's favor. It seemed only natural, therefore, to come up with a proposal for controlling German rearmament analogous to the Schuman Plan (announced in May 1950), which had as one of its central purposes the continued surveillance of German coal and steel production under supranational auspices.

France's proposal for a European Defense Community sought to restrain German rearmament through the tight integration of small German units within international divisions of a European army. Such an arrangement would have denied the Germans national control and given them little influence over recruitment, disposition of forces, command functions, contingency planning, and so forth. The French government also hoped to use EDC to obtain greater British and American commitment to Continental defense and to pressure West Germany to renounce control over the Saar.

In many respects, though, the EDC proposal was a fake. Its military value was doubtful, its political ramifications were ambivalent (the United States at first opposed it as unrealistic, the British were lukewarm, and the Germans demanded major revisions), and it would have raised practical and legal problems of implementation. The fate of the EDC plan illustrated the French government's general problem in the early fifties of trying to implement its policies in the face of conflicting pressures—from the East; from the United States, Britain, and West Germany; and (last but not least) from the government's constituency in the National Assembly and in the country at large.

The final demise of the EDC in August 1954, when it was voted down by the French National Assembly, and the Western powers' reaction demonstrated the differing priorities of the members of the Western alliance, especially the United States and France. The United States was preoccupied with the Soviet Union; France was preoccupied with Germany. The United States was in a hurry to implement its containment policy through the rearmament of Germany; France wanted to postpone unpleasant decisions as long as possible and chose the response of the weak—delay. But French procrastination hurt the country's prestige and influence, annoyed the United States, and put France out of touch with military-strategic and political developments. While France delayed, German leverage increased—in part because the decision to deploy tactical nuclear weapons in Europe made German rearmament even more important.

Generally, the United States applied to France a carrot-and-stick approach. On the one hand, Washington sought to reassure France by stressing the continuing American commitment to NATO and the EDC (as a protection against West Germany as well as the Soviet Union) and by holding out the promise of continued military and economic aid. At the same time, the Eisenhower administration threatened to cease its aid program in an "agonizing reappraisal of basic United States policy" if France blocked an integrated Western defense system in which West Germany would be an equal partner. (An amendment to the Mutual Security Program appropriation for 1953–54 made half of the military aid measures envisaged for Europe contingent upon passage of the European Defense Community treaty.) The French felt especially unfairly treated because they viewed their war in Indochina as helping to contain world Communism. Although in 1952 the United States paid for about one-third of the annual cost of the Indochina war, France had spent more on it over a five-year period than the entire amount the nation received under the Marshall Plan.

NATO AND THE FRENCH NATIONAL
NUCLEAR FORCE

When the Eisenhower administration announced its massive nuclear retaliation doctrine in January 1954, France reappraised her own security policy and announced that the country would build an independent national nuclear force and reduce the conventional force contribution to NATO.

The French decision did not lack a certain persuasive military rationale. Washington's new strategy discouraged the Europeans even more than before from building up their conventional forces, since they believed that if nuclear weapons compensated for conventional firepower in the American armed forces the same should hold true for NATO as a whole. Moreover, the conventional troop strength of NATO was so weak, relative to that of the Soviet bloc, that matching it seemed like a hopelessly unrealistic goal. Economic and political considerations also played a part in France's decision. Like other European governments, she was preoccupied with economic reconstruction and felt domestic political pressures to reduce spending for armaments. Although France's neighbors continued to rely on the American nuclear deterrent (the only one available, in any case) and hoped that technology could be substituted for manpower and money, French decision makers felt that joining the privileged Anglo-American nuclear club as soon as possible would solve many of the nation's political-military and fiscal problems —especially now that official NATO strategy stressed nuclear weapons rather than conventional forces.

The French decision to develop a national *force de frappe* was not just a response to the revamping of NATO's strategic doctrine or a nationalistic remedy for the political frustrations of the Fourth Republic. There were larger reasons as well. In the mid-fifties, as tensions between East and West relaxed and the Cold War began to enter a less volatile stage, there was less fear in Western Europe that the Soviet Union would resort to direct military aggression. After the two German states joined their respective alliances a certain measure of stability was restored on the divided continent, particularly since the Soviet Union now seemed prepared to live with the status quo in Central Europe. In addition, the economic integration of Western Europe was in its planning stages, economic reconstruction was proceeding well, and Europeans were becoming more self-assertive and expected once again to play a significant role in shaping the destiny of their continent.

Against this background, the technical arguments for a French nuclear capability—that it might trigger an American nuclear response, or that a French nuclear force would compensate in the credibility of its use for what it lacked in size and sophistication—seemed much less important than France's larger political aims. French policymakers hoped that a national nuclear arsenal could help France escape from the grip of the superpowers, whose superiority had paralyzed the nation's foreign policy in the postwar years, and enable France to regain flexibility in dealing with her allies as well as her opponents. The linkage between military strategy and diplomacy was not discovered by de Gaulle; his predecessors in the Fourth Republic were fully aware of it.

The connection between security and diplomatic flexibility was clearly demonstrated during the Suez crisis of 1956. When American pressure forced France and Britain to withdraw from their ill-considered invasion (undertaken by the British to regain control of the Suez Canal and by the French to consolidate their position in North Africa and Algeria), both countries began to feel that they could not always depend on the United States for protection and that Washington might even side with the Soviet Union in certain circumstances.

During the following years France pursued, with varying emphasis and success, three avenues toward increasing her leverage in nuclear strategic matters. First, development of an independent arsenal of nuclear weapons and delivery instruments continued. The first French nuclear explosion took place in 1960, and further nuclear development was restrained only by considerations of cost. Second, France sought to gain a voice in NATO's nuclear decision making process. The Eisenhower administration strongly opposed such efforts, causing, as we shall see, a serious rift between Washington and Paris after Charles de Gaulle returned to power in 1958. Third, France explored the possibility of exploiting a European or Franco-German nuclear consortium for French interests. Although the six members of the European Community signed an agreement in 1957 to develop jointly a program for the peaceful application of nuclear energy, France did not succeed in becoming the nuclear spokesman for the group nor could the joint nuclear pool be converted into an instrument of national strategic-diplomatic leverage.

NUCLEAR STRATEGY AND CHARLES DE GAULLE

The return to power of General de Gaulle in June 1958 added a new sense of urgency and determination to the French quest for a national nuclear capability. The steady evolution during the Fourth Republic toward making France a nuclear power was now capped with a well-articulated foreign policy program that stressed movement and put a premium on independence and flexibility. De Gaulle was convinced that being a nuclear power would contribute substantially toward these ends, regardless of whether the cost of a small national *force de frappe* was justified on purely strategic grounds. For de Gaulle, the technical inadequacies and high cost of a French national arsenal were outweighed by the perfect logic with which the plan fit into his global political program.

That program envisioned the transformation of the European and world political order in a direction that would enable France to regain the independent and dynamic role to which the nation was, in de Gaulle's view, naturally entitled and predestined. De Gaulle saw NATO and the Warsaw Pact perpetuating the division of Europe into two camps for the benefit of an American-Soviet world dominion, and thus obstructing the legitimate aspirations of the European nations. Therefore he strove to end the division of Europe and the Continent's subordination to the powers responsible for its partition, the United States and the Soviet Union. This required elimination of the two military-political blocs so as to end the superpower duopoly over Europe and strengthen the trend toward an East-West detente. By improving France's rapport with the Soviet Union and Eastern Europe and by seeking to weaken the American position on the Continent, de Gaulle attempted to speed up the fragmentation of both alliances, hoping this would culminate in a new European political order in which France would play a prominent role. Toward this end it was essential to reach a settlement of the German question—short of the actual reunification or close confederation of the two German states —since one of the major reasons for the superpowers' continuing presence in Europe was the unresolved issue of a divided Germany. De Gaulle also thought it important to check the Common Market trend toward political integration, not only because he wished to reserve independence of action for France but also because the door had to be kept open for the states of Eastern Europe to join in an arrangement larger than that of the Six. In short, de Gaulle desired to overcome the consequences of World War II and the Cold War—especially the bipolar balance of power that had imposed such severe restraints on French maneuverability—and take the lead in creating an all-European security system, consisting of sovereign states acting in concert.

In September 1958, after a few months in office, de Gaulle made a proposal to the United States and Britain for the creation of a NATO tripartite directorate that would include France. He suggested that NATO's strategy and diplomacy be extended worldwide and that the directorate make joint decisions on global problems. As a result, the Western Big Three (each having a veto) would shape NATO policy in Asia, Africa, and other areas outside the North Atlantic region.

Had it been accepted, this proposal would have significantly advanced de Gaulle's ambitions in at least five respects:

1 Broadening NATO's geographical and political scope would have shifted the alliance's traditional emphasis on Western Europe. As a result, NATO's explicit anti-Soviet orientation would have diminished, at least symbolically. This would have given France a freer hand in exploiting the movement toward detente in Western and Eastern Europe.

2 Membership in a tripartite NATO directorate would have made France the supreme strategic spokesman for continental Europe. De Gaulle hoped to gain access to the nuclear decision making process that was dominated by Britain and the United States, and thereby obtain for France a superior status vis-à-vis the nonnuclear NATO members, especially Germany.

3 France sought more influence in Washington to forestall the possibility that the United States would either fail to defend Europe or involve the Continent in wars peripheral to French interests. By involving France in the global politics of the Western alliance, de Gaulle hoped to guard against American adventurism as well as American lack of resolve.

4 De Gaulle wanted to enlist the support of the alliance for French ambitions in the Third World. The unhappy Suez episode of 1956 (see chapter 9) had demonstrated Washington's unwillingness to automatically support French interests in Africa, and most NATO powers strongly criticized France's policy in Algeria as crass colonialism and an obstacle to French fulfillment of her NATO commitments because large numbers of French troops were kept tied down.

5 De Gaulle wished to gain formal recognition of France as an equal partner of the Anglo-American powers.

The Eisenhower administration was not willing to grant de Gaulle's demands. Washington pointed out that as a member of both SEATO and NATO France was already offered an opportunity to collaborate with her allies on a global scale, that the forum of the NATO Council was particularly well suited for discussion of worldwide matters, and above all, that the French proposal would be unacceptable to other NATO partners and thus cause friction within the alliance. Throughout the next few years this issue stood between the United States and France, with de Gaulle pressing for a formalized Big-Three status for France and Eisenhower holding out the possibility of close consultations but refusing to set up an exclusive tripartite directorate that would dictate major policy choices to other NATO allies. To make matters worse, in October 1958 the United States entered into test ban negotiations with the Soviet Union at Geneva, which implied an American commitment to prevent the spread of nuclear weapons and information—especially to nations like France that had already proclaimed they would not be bound by such a treaty. The United States was in effect siding with the Soviet Union in opposing France's aim of gaining nuclear equality with Britain, a position Washington took for the sake of upholding the principle of nuclear nonproliferation (a principle France was certain to violate in any case).

Between 1958 and 1960, when France exploded its first nuclear device in the Sahara, the United States considered various arrangements for nuclear sharing—including a proposal by NATO's Supreme Commander, General Lauris Norstad, that NATO itself become the fourth nuclear power—in order to stave off pressures for independent nuclear arsenals. But aside from the difficulty of gaining Congressional approval, such schemes were strongly opposed by the Soviet Union, and it was highly doubtful that they would be supported by France, their primary target. This rendered such exercises largely academic.

Nor was de Gaulle interested in the multilateral control arrangements for a NATO missile force that were tentatively advanced by Washington toward the end of the Eisenhower administration. It therefore came as no surprise when France reacted coolly to Kennedy's revival of Eisenhower's control-sharing proposal, which gradually began to focus on the concept of a multilateral nuclear force (MLF). French objections to the idea focused primarily on four aspects: the MLF would be militarily ineffective; it would provide for German access to nuclear weapons, divide Europe, and undermine the Franco-German friendship treaty of 1963; it perpetuated American control since there was little chance that a European authority would come into being; and it stood in the way of a detente with Eastern Europe and the Soviet Union.

Washington's MLF proposals were not the only source of France's dissatisfaction with the policies of its allies. The revamping of NATO's strategic doctrine under the Kennedy administration and especially the new emphasis on "flexible response"—which assigned to the Europeans an even larger conventional force role—was directly opposed to the French goal of nuclear self-sufficiency. The Skybolt controversy (discussed in chapters 1 and 9) also helped to convince de Gaulle that his suspicions of Washington and London were well-founded and bolstered his view that France was embarked upon the proper course in seeking independence and maneuverability.

As a result, the French decided to formally disengage from NATO. De Gaulle announced in February 1966 that France would claim control of all foreign bases on French soil. Subsequently France withdrew its forces from NATO, demanded the removal of all NATO command organizations from the country, and cancelled a number of bilateral agreements with the United

States, Canada, and West Germany pertaining to their military installations in France. Although France remained nominally a member of the alliance, operational connections with NATO were severed and NATO headquarters subsequently moved from Paris to Brussels.

De Gaulle's independent security policy culminated, on the doctrinal level, in the formulation of a deterrence strategy publicized by General Charles Ailleret in December 1967. This so-called "all azimuths," or "all-horizons" defense doctrine was intended to complement de Gaulle's political-diplomatic program. By threatening nuclear retaliation against any global target (on the face of it a rather unlikely contingency), France was expressing in strategic terms what were essentially political purposes. The Ailleret Doctrine symbolized that France wished to stand apart from the United States as well as from the Soviet Union and that French interests were worldwide and could not be satisfactorily pursued within the confines of the Western alliance.

The military justification for the all-points deterrence doctrine rested basically on three interconnected points:

1 France, as a nuclear power, was no longer adequately served by NATO because its primary raison d'être, the threat of Soviet aggression, had diminished and because NATO had fallen under excessive American control.

2 In spite of reduced East-West tensions, threats to France's security existed because American, Soviet, and (within a few years) Chinese missiles would have the capability of intersecting over France and because trouble spots existed in the Third World that might lead to an all-out conflagration involving the superpowers and their allies. The first-generation French nuclear forces (essentially Mirage airplanes) did not provide adequate protection, and even the second-generation forces being developed were technologically insufficient.

3 Therefore, France required sufficient intercontinental ballistic missiles and an omnidirectional thermonuclear strategic force to safeguard French security interests in the years to come, weapons capable of linkup with a future military outer-space force.

The Ailleret Doctrine evoked a good deal of controversy in France and elsewhere. French critics pointed out that the new strategy, which relied fully on the French national nuclear arsenal, underestimated the quantitative and qualitative shortcomings of a national *force de frappe* and overestimated the security it could provide. Moreover, it was argued, the high cost of the new strategy would absorb a disproportionate share of military expenditures and increase the dangerous imbalance between France's nuclear and conventional capabilities. For de Gaulle, however, technological and purely military-strategic considerations were of secondary importance. He viewed the *force de frappe* as a supremely political instrument, and it is unlikely that he anticipated circumstances in which France would actually have to stand alone in confronting one or several of the superpowers.

The timing of the announcement of the Ailleret Doctrine most likely was designed to accelerate the European and global political developments that de Gaulle considered essential for his entire foreign policy program. This program rested on three major assumptions about the future:

1 The security of Europe would continue to be assured by the nuclear balance between the superpowers.

2 The fragmentation of the two alliance blocs would proceed symmetrically, leading to a decreasing role in Europe for both the United States and the Soviet Union.

3 United States–Soviet tensions would ease, a development that, along with the resurgence of Europe, China, and Japan, would transform the bipolar Cold War system into a more traditional multipolar balance of power.

The first assumption was central for de Gaulle's foreign policy in general and for the articulation of the Ailleret Doctrine in particular. Had de Gaulle not felt that he was running no real security risks, he could not have pursued an independent diplomatic and military-political strategy. The second and third assumptions about the future depended on proper timing. De Gaulle's aim of creating an all-European security system required the fragmentation of the two alliance blocs. In his view, the reconciliation between Western and Eastern Europe, based on a solution of the German problem short of reunification, would lead to a breakup of the alliance blocs and eliminate the main reason for an American and Russian presence in Europe. This would also pave the way toward an all-European security system based on political rather than technical-military grounds. Therefore de Gaulle felt that arms control arrangements, which would most likely be part of an all-European security system, should be discussed after a political understanding between Eastern and Western Europe was reached. Otherwise NATO and the Warsaw Pact would be the negotiators of arms control measures, and any resulting agreement could reinforce Washington's and Moscow's position in Europe. In other words, de Gaulle was much less interested in the technical side of arms control than in its relationship to fundamental political issues. The timing of arms control talks was thus crucial.

During 1966 and 1967, de Gaulle's timetable became skewed because both arms control talks and political developments proceeded simultaneously. Between de Gaulle's decision to remove French troops from NATO control in 1966 and the invasion of Czechoslovakia in 1968, many changes took place in the European political-strategic picture. The United States was preoccupied in Vietnam and exercised no leadership in Europe; the future of West European integration seemed less and less clear; the Soviet Union and East European states expressed an interest in a European security system; the new Grand Coalition government in Bonn appeared to be aiming at a more independent diplomatic policy; the United States and the Soviet Union initiated bilateral discussions on strategic arms control; the Sino-Soviet conflict loomed larger than ever; and the doctrine of flexible response, operative for the United States since the Kennedy administration, became official and explicit NATO policy in May 1967. All these events and trends, to mention only the most important, made for a very complicated international situation, characterized by flux and uncertainty.

In 1968, two major events severely jarred de Gaulle's grand calculations and led to a revision of his security policy: the Soviet invasion of Czechoslovakia in August, and the financial crisis of November, which was a consequence of domestic disturbances in France during May and June.

The Soviet occupation of Czechoslovakia called into question some of de Gaulle's central assumptions about trends in world politics and how to achieve the favored reorganization of Europe he sought. In the first place, the invasion invalidated de Gaulle's expectation that Russia would back off from Eastern Europe. The events of August 1968 demonstrated that there was a fundamental imbalance in the softening up of the two alliance blocs: while the Western alliance was becoming less cohesive, the Soviet Union was determined to maintain its position in Central and Eastern Europe, by brute force if necessary. Even mutual troop reductions now seemed unlikely since the Soviet military presence in Central and Eastern Europe had become a matter of internal security. Czechoslovakia had pointed up the limits of the Soviet capacity for disengagement from Europe.

Meanwhile, as the Soviet Union reinforced its hand in Europe, the Johnson administration was almost totally preoccupied with the war in Vietnam. Yet at the same time American interest in a fundamental accommodation with the Soviet Union seemed to be increasing. Washington was so determined to conclude a nuclear nonproliferation treaty with Russia that the invasion of Czechoslovakia hardly even interrupted United States–Soviet deliberations. Most West European governments applauded the superpowers' arms control efforts, but complained about not being sufficiently consulted and realized that a nonproliferation treaty would deny them nuclear sharing within NATO. Although at this stage de Gaulle was not interested all that much in participating in NATO nuclear decision making, he saw the treaty as foreclosing France's own opportunity to obtain American assistance on nuclear matters in the future. De Gaulle also objected to the treaty talks as an example of Soviet-American collusion.

Moreover, the exploratory discussions between the United States and the Soviet Union about strategic arms limitation (SALT) meant that United

States–Soviet nuclear parity was becoming institutionalized. This, coupled with the possibility that the United States could unilaterally reduce its conventional troop strength in Europe, weakened the American presence in Europe while the Soviet presence had become stronger than at any time since World War II. Consequently de Gaulle's go-it-alone approach toward East-West relations, which heretofore had not lacked a certain plausibility and had gained a measure of grudging respect among the Western allies, now began to look like a dangerous miscalculation.

To make matters worse, in 1969 de Gaulle faced the most serious domestic political crisis of his ten years in office. Dissatisfied French workers paralyzed Paris in May and June of 1968 in a series of violent riots and crippling strikes. In order to satisfy the labor unions' demands for higher wages, the French government arranged for inflationary wage settlements, causing an increase in France's balance of payments deficit. In turn, this contributed to the crisis of the franc in November. Rather than devalue the franc, de Gaulle imposed severe austerity measures and curtailed military spending. The nuclear testing program planned for 1969 had to be postponed, and production of the French missile system delayed. The whole concept of the *force de frappe* began to seem shaky as the French national nuclear arsenal became too expensive and the invasion of Czechoslovakia created doubts about the political value of de Gaulle's independent strategic posture—which all along had been seen as much more important than its purely military value.

FROM NUCLEAR INDEPENDENCE
TO FLEXIBLE INTERDEPENDENCE

In combination, these external and internal developments led de Gaulle to revise his foreign policy in the fall of 1968. Most noticeably, there was a definite improvement in relations with the United States. This policy shift stemmed primarily from the realization that the French policy of detente in Europe was checked for the time being and that France should help in redressing the Soviet-American balance of power. There were also more specific factors encouraging de Gaulle to change his attitude toward the United States —a new administration in Washington; United States determination to wind down the Vietnam War, thus removing an issue that had troubled Franco-American relations for some time; the buildup of Soviet naval forces in the Mediterranean, which caused concern; and the possibility held out by President Nixon of American technical assistance to French nuclear submarine and missile projects. Aided by Nixon's visit to France in March 1969, relations between Paris and Washington became so cordial that some European NATO members grew a little nervous about what they perceived to be an impending Franco-American "special relationship."

De Gaulle's diplomatic rapprochement with Washington was accompanied by another important development—a cautious strategic rapproche-ment with the NATO alliance. This came as a result of a rethinking of French military-strategic doctrine initiated by de Gaulle in the fall of 1968. The specifics of the new policy became public in an article by France's Chief of Staff, General Michel Fourquet, in the *Revue de Défense Nationale* in May 1969, one month after de Gaulle had left office. The so-called Fourquet Plan differed from the Ailleret Doctrine in two major respects:

1 In contrast to the "all azimuths" orientation, the Fourquet concept identi-fied a potential enemy, the Soviet Union and its East European allies; envisaged French nuclear forces as taking part in the defense of the West; and rejected the notion that an independent nuclear arsenal would ensure French neutrality in an East-West war.

2 The Fourquet Plan stressed a carefully graduated, flexible response strat-egy—*la réplique graduée.* Very similar to McNamara's NATO strategy, the new French plan sought to enlarge the range of French responses to a variety of military-political challenges. The strategy relied heavily on the use of tactical nuclear weapons in the early stages of battle (partially in order to establish a triggering link with the American strategic deterrent), with strategic weapons serving as the ultimate deterrent against an all-out attack on French territory. In this way France could avoid the dilemma of having to choose between strategic surrender and national suicide.

In short, the Fourquet Plan was a pragmatic response to the political and strategic implications of the Soviet invasion of Czechoslovakia: it implicitly denied the validity of de Gaulle's previous assumption that political and strategic bipolarity was giving way to a multipolar international configuration (in which several nuclear powers were conceivable opponents) and that France needed a fully independent strategic capability to complement the independent diplomacy such a system would have allowed.

De Gaulle's revised strategic outlook, as reflected in the Fourquet Plan, continued to be the core of French strategic policy under President Georges Pompidou and Prime Minister Jacques Chaban-Delmas. The new strategy reflected a major change in thinking in that it was not totally based on political doctrine but was much more sensitive to technical requirements, technological capabilities, and cost factors. Given this more pragmatic doctri-nal underpinning, French security policy—while still designed to serve politi-cal purposes and to maximize diplomatic flexibility—became somewhat more accommodating, at least in its style and rhetoric. The inherent logic of the Fourquet Doctrine suggested that limited cooperation with NATO would be advantageous, if only to coordinate French tactical nuclear forces with NATO contingency planning. But the new policy did not mean a fundamental change of attitude toward NATO. Even though French strategy was not as glaringly independent as before, the Pompidou government still was not willing to assume a greater share of NATO's burdens. France also opposed the integrative features of NATO. The government initially was unwilling to participate in NATO's Nuclear Planning Group, notwithstanding the fact that this body's main function was precisely that of coordinating Allied contingency planning. France continued to find it unacceptable to integrate command structures and technical facilities, especially since the French (just as the Germans) distrusted the NATO principle of a "conventional pause," which they considered detrimental to French security interests and in any case impossible to implement because of NATO's inadequate conventional troop level. The French also saw a conflict between the defensive principles of NATO's contingency planning and the French principle of "active defense," which was designed to enhance the credibility of the French deterrent by assuring a step-by-step confrontation with the enemy during which France's determination would be demonstrated by a series of escalating measures, if that should be necessary.

In the early seventies, the principles and implications of the Fourquet strategy did not receive a great deal of public attention. When President Valéry Giscard d'Estaing entered office in 1974, however, French strategic planning began to move even further away from the Ailleret Doctrine. Initially the new president reaffirmed the traditional Gaullist principle of an independent French nuclear force and the corresponding idea that France would decide for itself to what extent and in what ways collaboration as a member of the Western alliance was desirable. Nonetheless, French military cooperation with NATO improved somewhat (for example, French forces participated in NATO exercises more frequently and in greater numbers), and in the early part of 1975, Prime Minister Jacques Chirac announced that French security could not be isolated from its European context and that the notion of France as a self-reliant "sanctuary" would have to be reexamined. Although strategic nuclear weapons would remain at the core of the French deterrence posture, he said, a "certain equilibrium" was needed among nuclear-strategic, nuclear-tactical, and conventional forces to provide for greater versatility. In other words, Chirac implied that the new government was connecting deterrence with defense (by then a well-established NATO principle), and he suggested that by creating a "triad" of arms components French national strategy could be linked with NATO's doctrine of flexible response.

Chirac's somewhat tentative and carefully phrased reappraisal became more explicit about a year later. In March 1976, General Guy Méry, Chief of Staff of the Armed Forces, strongly criticized the concept of massive retaliation (which was still official doctrine), advocating instead a "graduated response" concept that could cover a wider array of possible military threats. He also rejected the notion that France was an "absolute sanctuary" as being unrealistic and impractical. In arguing for an "enlarged sanctuarization"—which would extend beyond France to a wider European context—Méry also rejected the notion that the country was militarily strong enough to pursue a policy of global intervention. In other words, the principle of an "enlarged sanctuary" was presented as a middle course between a global strategic posture and a narrow national one, with the logical consequence that French armed forces had to become more mobile and versatile.

One of the most sensitive aspects of Méry's strategic concept was its implication for the extent and timing of French participation in the defense of NATO's central sector. For over a decade, the official French doctrine had distinguished between a "first" battle, fought by NATO in West Germany, and a "second" battle, fought on the French border and perhaps on French soil. At the core of that doctrine was the idea that French forces would be held back during a "first" battle, leaving that engagement to NATO, and would be used primarily in a "second" battle, buttressed at that point with the threat of nuclear weapons. Méry now suggested that although French forces would not participate in NATO's forward defense preparations in times of peace, France would be willing to take part in a forward "first" battle. The role of tactical nuclear weapons was also a crucial element of the Méry doctrine. Méry contended that if tactical nuclear weapons could not be avoided in order to turn the tide of battle, they should be employed not so much as a spectacular gesture but in order to affect the outcome of the engagement. In sum, the Méry Doctrine stated that French forces would participate (in certain circumstances) in the NATO defense of West Germany, that France would be willing to take part in a tactical nuclear engagement close to the French border area, and that strategic nuclear arms would serve as the ultimate backup for the defense of French territory.

Amid the polemic created by Méry's argument—strong attacks coming from both the French Right and Left, as well as from military experts—President Giscard made clear that his own views were the same as Méry's. He supported in particular Méry's ideas on the use of tactical nuclear weapons and conventional forces, and the related concept of an "enlarged sanctuary" that would place the defense of France within the context of a wider European framework. Giscard reiterated what Chirac and Méry had stated earlier: the impossibility of separating France from Europe, since its territory was an inextricable part of the European-Mediterranean environment. France acknowledged that the defense of Central and Western Europe was indivisible.

6

Political
and Economic
Reconstruction

France's Fourth Republic was established in 1946 after de Gaulle resigned as head of the provisional government that had ruled the country since the liberation in 1944. Because France was a fully sovereign state under international law there was no need to pursue a legal-political recovery goal, in terms of international juridical status, as had been the case for the Federal Republic of Germany when it was established in 1949. Nevertheless, in a very broad sense political recovery was a fundamental French foreign policy goal, pursued with intensity during both the Fourth Republic and Fifth Republic.

Most basically, political recovery meant a renewal of the French nation, a quest for self-definition and self-assurance after living through the humiliating conditions of the German occupation and the political uncertainties that followed in the wake of the liberation. The need to reassert France's greatness was especially pressing and psychologically complex, because no justifications for this greatness could be found in the immediate past (except for the Resistance and de Gaulle) and because a new national affirmation seemed so difficult to achieve in the present and future. The institutions of the Fourth Republic were not well-suited to this task. French politics, contentious to the point of immobility and self-destruction during the prewar Third Republic, were equally divisive in the Fourth Republic. The political energies released by the liberation were as fiercely competitive as they had been before the war (in fact, they were fed by new grievances stemming from the war years). Moreover, social and political structures in the Fourth Republic were ill-designed for dealing with these conflicts and were strained by them to the breaking point. There were no powerful symbols or institutions capable of unifying the country. The National Assembly, although itself often immobilized through lack of majorities, was nonetheless effective in checking the hand of the executive.

Political recovery soon became predominantly defined in terms of foreign policy. There were several reasons for this. For one, disappointment with the domestic political process provided an impulse to pursue national self-assertion through foreign policy. Second, the glory of France had been reduced by forces on the international scene, the more reason, therefore, to seek to reestablish the nation's glory in the same arena. A third factor was the international setting in which France found itself after World War II. Almost every aspect of French politics was linked to foreign policy, exemplified in French dependence on American economic aid but visible also in many other areas of public life.

As a foreign policy goal, political recovery meant—for the French people as well as for French politicians—reclaiming the nation's prewar status as one of the great powers. France would thereby regain freedom of action, flexibility of diplomacy, international prestige, and national pride. But the discrepancy between France's present position and future prospects seemed enormous. The quest for independent action, which was at the heart of France's recovery goal, made a collision course with the United States almost inevitable. France wanted independence, maneuverability, and the opportunity to assert itself against other European powers (especially Germany). The United States, whose primary foreign policy goal became containment of the Soviet Union, strove for coordination within a Western alliance in which America would predominate and the nations of Western Europe (including Germany) would be equal, with Britain being a little more equal than the others. As a result, right from the beginning of the postwar period tensions developed between the United States and France, with each side showing insufficient understanding of the priorities and the psychological needs of the other. The United States—self-confident and secure in its great power status, unambiguously recognized as a victorious power, rationalistic and "management-oriented" in the conduct of foreign policy—equated its national interests with those of the Western alliance and saw opposing viewpoints as remnants of a discredited nationalism. The French, on the other hand— deeply frustrated by the fact that they had all the attributes of a great power except power—were doubly sensitive to real or imagined slights. France's status as one of the victors of World War II was ambiguous because it was conferred by the Allies politically rather than having been earned militarily. The French were determined to compensate for their lack of real power with a style of politics and diplomacy that would maximize national individuality and independence.

The difference between the French and the German goals of political recovery made a big difference between United States–French relations and United States–German relations. American annoyance with France contrasted sharply with the cordial relationship between Washington and Bonn that developed during the Eisenhower administration in the early fifties. Whereas the integrative, alliance-oriented, and accommodating German goal of political recovery fit neatly into the context of America's containment policy, the self-assertive and independent French version of political recovery undermined the cohesion of the Western alliance. Washington (and especially the Pentagon) considered the value of the potential German military contribution to the Western alliance as higher than that of France in any case, not only because geography put West Germany on NATO's forward line but also because the United States distrusted the erratic politics of the Fourth Republic. For military-strategic, political, and psychological reasons, Germany's importance to the Western alliance increased enormously relative to that of France, with consequences that affected the entire range of French, as well as German, foreign policy aims. Thus a few years after the end of the war, at a time when important issues were still pending between France and Germany and when French foreign policy goals could not be achieved without the support of the United States, Germany began to gain a political edge over France. These developments could only sharpen French resentments against Germany, and also the United States. Yet the more Paris procrastinated and objected to American policies, the more the United States was irritated and France's position within the alliance was weakened. Paris was in a fundamental bind—Cold War tensions put a premium on alliance cohesion and reduced the opportunities for French diplomacy.

Another obstacle to French freedom of action was the country's dependence on the United States, nowhere more clearly visible than in the economic sphere. Economic reconstruction was from the beginning a French foreign policy goal par excellence—for like political recovery, economic recovery was linked to international politics and international aid.

In the mid- and late forties and early fifties, four major problems hindered French economic reconstruction. First, there was a good deal of physical destruction, especially of transportation facilities. Second, French industry and commerce were inefficient. The typical French industrial unit was small (it was frequently a family enterprise), which impeded the modernization of production, the risk-taking necessary for expansion, the reinvestment of capital, and the adaptability to change. Larger firms could no longer rely on assured national and international markets, dividing them up through cartel agreements and shielding them from competition. French agriculture was also inefficient and, for a variety of complex historical and socioeconomic reasons, highly resistant to change. The industrial revolution had practically bypassed the French peasant, and there was little modern agricultural machinery. Third, the French economy suffered from serious inflation, fed by international price increases, the cost of colonial wars, a large national debt, and a chronically unbalanced national budget. Finally, France suffered from a dollar shortage and had difficulty earning hard currencies through exports. French producers were not competitive in international markets, especially relative to German exporters, and in the late forties and early fifties France ran up large balance-of-trade deficits with the United States and the sterling area.

Overcoming these obstacles required help from the United States, and the aid that France received was substantial. Almost $3 billion in Marshall Plan funds, one-fifth of the amount advanced to all European countries under the program, poured into France. After the outbreak of the Korean War in 1950, when the United States aid program began to emphasize military purposes, the French received additional dollars through American weapons purchases from France, the construction of a NATO communications network, and offshore procurement arrangements.

But it seemed to Washington that American aid was not used for a genuine modernization of the French economy. France appeared to be financing a series of stopgap measures designed to plug up budgetary deficits, thus encouraging stagnation rather than long-range reform. This added yet another point of friction to the relationship between the United States and France.

FRANCE AND EUROPEAN INTEGRATION

Economic difficulties and political frustrations shaped French attitudes and policies toward European economic and political integration. These attitudes and policies were highly ambivalent because the issues were too complex for clear-cut answers and because of tensions between short-range and long-range interests.

There were several reasons why the French needed to support European integration. France's primary motive was to encourage the development of international and supranational organizations that could provide ways for controlling Germany. Since France feared that West Germany's political and economic recovery would proceed along national lines, international arrangements for supervision seemed imperative. At least they would help control German resurgence, and at best they might enlist for French purposes Germany's political and economic potential. But such considerations could not alter the fact that Bonn stood to gain more from integration than Paris. For example, by becoming a member of the European Coal and Steel Community the Federal Republic not only gained economically but also politically by obtaining equal legal status in the organization. France, on the other hand, gave up a measure of economic and political mobility that ran counter to the self-assertive, independent aspect of her goal of political recovery.

The French, of course, also expected more positive benefits from European integration. France stood to gain economically, at least in the long run, and integration would create a potential French power base on the Continent. In addition, some influential French public figures (such as Robert Schuman, Jean Monnet, and others) supported the cause of European integration on its own merits. Generally, however, it was necessity rather than choice that determined France's attitude toward European integration. The French were reluctant "Europeans" not so much because they were more nationalistic than the Germans but because they saw European integration from a different political, economic, and psychological perspective. Although emotions played an important part in French coolness toward European integration, political and economic realism suggested caution as well.

Thus the quest for independence and diplomatic self-reliance, which was the outstanding feature of the French goal of political recovery, conflicted sharply with the need to participate in European integration (required to check the resurgence of Germany) and the dependence on American aid (required for economic reconstruction, colonial policy, and the avoidance of national bankruptcy). The political and economic aspects of the French goal of recovery were contradictory, not complementary and reinforcing as in Germany. Nor was economic recovery aided by France's security policy, since that policy also sought to maximize independence and flexibility. As a result the French goals of political and economic recovery—in striking contrast to the German goals—were largely incompatible.

THE SAAR ISSUE

It was only natural that West Germany should occupy a prominent place in the formulation of the French goal of political recovery. The growing influence of the Federal Republic was seen as an obstacle to regaining French influence in Western Europe, and several issues arising from France's political recovery objectives severely strained relations between Paris and Bonn. One of the most important of these issues—and certainly the most instructive as a case study of the nature of Franco-German relations in the early and mid-fifties—was the question of who would control the Saar territories.

The Saar conflict provides four lessons:

1 It illustrates the impact of Germany on the French goals of political and economic recovery.

2 It demonstrates the decisive effect of the Cold War on intra-alliance relationships, which worked largely to the advantage of the Federal Republic.

3 It exemplifies the close political, economic, and psychological connections between European integration and the resolution of a highly charged political issue.

4 It shows how an intensely contested issue between France and Germany was finally resolved because both countries recognized how crucial it was to nurture a Franco-German reconciliation.

During World War II, the Allies had repeatedly discussed the future status of the industrial complex of the Saar basin and agreed that it ought to be split off from Germany. Absorption of the Saar into the French economy, as well as separation of the Ruhr and the Rhineland from Germany, became major goals of France.

At the end of the war, however, Paris received little support for these aims. France was not represented at the Potsdam Conference, and since the Anglo-American powers opposed a final settlement of Germany's borders before a peace conference (in order to avoid legitimizing the de facto annexation of the Oder-Neisse territory and East Prussia by Poland and the Soviet Union), they could hardly support a permanent revision of Germany's western borders. France was also disappointed because the Potsdam Agreement envisaged the ultimate establishment of a central German government and the treatment of Germany as an economic unit. France intended to exploit its zone of occupation as much as possible and feared that setting up some form of central German political structure would consolidate Germany's western borders and frustrate French plans to pry the important industrial and natural resources of the Saar from international control.

Failing to gain the support of the wartime Allies, the French decided to take action on their own. In December 1945 France sequestered the Saar mines, which were in the French zone of occupation, and a year later French customs officials manned the administrative boundaries between the Saar and Rheinland-Pfalz and began to control the passage of goods, money, and persons. In other words, the Saar was administratively carved out of the French zone of occupation and economically tied to metropolitan France. Britain reacted with ambivalence, the Soviet Union objected strongly, and the United States criticized the move as a unilateral decision that circumvented the authority of the Allied Control Council.

From here on, the French sought to obtain the Allies' legitimization of measures they took to consolidate the Franco-Saar economic union politically and contractually. Although the United States and Britain could not approve of the plan officially, they soon gave their implied acquiescence. There is little doubt that Allied support for France's economic annexation of the Saar was given in return for French agreement to the formation of a West German government. In April 1948, the Saar was formally united economically with France, and commercial dealings between the region and Germany were henceforth treated as foreign trade operations.

The unresolved political status of the Saar territory became a major obstacle to Franco-German reconciliation. The issue greatly complicated negotiations on the Schuman Plan for a European Coal and Steel Community and the European Defense Community, and threatened the entire treaty structure that was to rearm the Federal Republic and restore German sovereignty.

Soon after the establishment of the Federal Republic, the French government renewed efforts to obtain a treaty that would legalize the de facto union of the French and Saar economies. Early in 1950 the French and Saar governments negotiated the so-called Franco-Saar Conventions, which further solidified French control over the Saar economy, especially in the mining and steel industries. The reaction in Bonn was extremely sharp. The Adenauer government issued a lengthy memorandum asserting that the Saar was part of Germany as defined by the Allied declaration of June 1945 and that consequently there could be no legal change of the 1937 German frontiers prior to a peace treaty.

Both France and Germany were very much aware that the Saar dispute was strongly affected by larger developments. Timing became a crucial consideration. Bonn, confident of improving its bargaining power within the Western alliance because of Germany's commitment to Western defense, sought to keep the Saar situation in a state of flux. Paris, for the same reason, was in a hurry to obtain a treaty that would be difficult to renegotiate and would permanently settle the question in France's favor. When the Schuman Plan was being negotiated France tried to have the Saar admitted to the ECSC as an autonomous political entity, underlining its separation from Germany. The Bonn government suggested that the Saar be placed under the supervision of a European organization such as the ECSC Council of Ministers and insisted that Germany's economic relations with the Saar must be essentially the same as France's. The German demands were largely met in a Franco-German agreement signed in May 1954, but the head of the French delegation could not get his government to accept the pact. Three months later, with the defeat of the EDC in the French National assembly, Prime Minister Mendès-France thought he had the lever he needed to improve the French bargaining position. It seemed that France could now deny the Federal Republic access not only to the Atlantic alliance but also to sovereignty. But this proved to be a miscalculation when Germany became a member of NATO.

As part of the Paris Agreements of October 1954, France and Germany finally reached a compromise settlement. It provided (1) that the Saar would be placed under a European statute within the framework of the Western European Union and that this statute, after referendum approval by inhabitants of the region, would not be called into question until the conclusion of a peace treaty; (2) that a European Commissioner would represent the Saar in foreign affairs and matters of defense; and (3) that France would retain close economic ties with the Saar, with Germany moving toward the same arrangement over a period of time.

This outcome was a compromise for both Paris and Bonn. There was, of course, the strong implication that the Saar was the price for French acceptance of German membership in NATO. Nevertheless, the Germans denied that the agreement meant a permanent separation of the Saar from the Federal Republic, and events were soon to prove them right. When the European statute was submitted to the Saar voters in October 1955, it was rejected by a large majority. For the time being this merely meant continuation of the status quo, but both France and Germany interpreted the referendum as a vote for reunion with Germany. In December, the Saar's incumbent pro-

French government was decisively defeated at the polls. A pro-German majority gained control and forthwith declared its intention to end the separation of the Saar from Germany. Negotiations between Paris and Bonn produced an agreement in October 1956 providing for the restoration of German political sovereignty over the Saar on January 1, 1957. France was given twenty-five years to phase out its mining of the lucrative Warndt coal deposits; Germany agreed to deliver 1.2 million tons of coal annually beginning in 1962, plus a third of the total output of the Saar mines; and French demands for a Moselle canal were accepted with the understanding that Germany would make a large financial contribution toward its construction. Economic reunification with Germany was accomplished in July 1959, when the Saar was included in the German currency and customs system as an integral part of the Federal Republic.

The resolution of the Saar issue in Germany's favor was symptomatic of the difficulties that France experienced within the Western alliance in pursuing its goal of political recovery. Although Germany had to make concessions on the Saar question to obtain French acquiescence in the Paris Agreements —which paved the way for West German membership in NATO and the restoration of sovereignty—Bonn's political leverage was nonetheless increasing because of Cold War tensions and the growing importance of West German rearmament. On the other hand, French diplomatic mobility was severely restricted by the Cold War alliance blocs, which required her to lean on the Anglo-American powers so as to avoid political isolation.

FRANCE AND THE COMMON MARKET

The resolution of the Saar issue in 1955 coincided with a resurgence of the movement toward European economic integration and political union. This movement had suffered a severe setback with the demise of the EDC treaty in August 1954, and even the European Coal and Steel Community had come under attack because it had made little progress in increasing productivity and trade during its first two years. But the cause of European integration received an impetus in the next few years that was unequaled at any time during the postwar period.

Most important, the six member states of the ECSC agreed to expand the common market for coal and steel to other commodities. In part, this decision was made possible, economically as well as politically, because the Coal and Steel Community was finally succeeding owing to the general economic expansion in Europe during the mid-fifties. Another important reason for proceeding with European integration was that the political situation in Central Europe had stabilized considerably, with West Germany joining NATO and East Germany joining the Warsaw Pact. This signaled the end of a distinct phase of postwar political developments and set more predictable boundaries

—geographically as well as politically—for creating integrative structures for Western Europe. The coldest phase of the Cold War was over, fear of the Soviet Union had diminished, economic reconstruction was completed, and Europe was beginning to feel a new sense of vitality.

France also experienced new energies and a sense of purpose. The Indochina war finally had been brought to a conclusion with the 1954 Geneva agreements, lifting from France a tremendous military, fiscal, and political burden (although the Algerian war would soon reimpose it). Above all, the French economy was in the midst of an upswing every bit as remarkable as the German "economic miracle." These developments allowed the French to view the prospect of joining a Common Market of the Six with self-confidence, especially since France's trade with Germany was already expanding rapidly (by the mid-fifties, France had become Germany's largest customer and second-largest supplier, and Germany had become France's second-largest customer and supplier).

France hoped for substantial benefits from the abolition of trade barriers and the harmonization of social legislation among the Six. French farming interests expected large gains from the Common Market because they were producing a substantial surplus and the other EEC countries were large importers of agricultural goods. Although some sectors of French industry (for example, textile producers) were concerned about competition, others (for example, the steel, automobile, paper, and electrical engineering sectors) felt certain they would prosper in an economic community.

But economic integration was not an easy task to accomplish, and many troublesome differences among the Six remained to be negotiated. The question of harmonizing social programs among the Six was arranged by meeting the French demand that the other EEC partners enlarge their social programs so that France would not have to water down its extensive program or see its producers become less competitive because of their higher contributions to the French program.

On the whole, while the anticipated economic consequences of French membership in EEC were positive, the political aspects of European integration were complicated and ambivalent. Euratom was a case in point. The French wanted to keep Euratom as separate as possible from the EEC and the ECSC so that other European countries, especially Britain, could join the Atomic Community without simultaneously joining the other organizations. France also hoped for military benefits from the nuclear energy program and wanted to give Euratom a monopoly of fissionable materials. Germany and other prospective EEC partners opposed the French proposals, but finally a compromise was reached. France agreed to a combined assembly for Euratom, ECSC, and EEC; the issue of military use of nuclear energy was postponed; and Euratom was given exclusive control over the selling and buying of fissionable materials.

One of the most troublesome issues in the European integration movement turned out to be the status of French and Belgian overseas territories. Both France and Belgium wanted to perpetuate their influence in these territories by giving them preferential treatment so that their exports to EEC members would not be hurt by the market's common external tariff. France and Belgium also sought joint investment financing by the Six in these areas. The Germans had no desire to be associated with what they considered colonial policy. On the other hand, they themselves tried to obtain special arrangements for trade between West Germany and East Germany to avoid creating an economic barrier between the two on top of the already existing political, legal, and military-strategic barriers. Eventually both sides essentially gained their objectives, and special terms were agreed upon to satisfy French and Belgian as well as German interests.

When Charles de Gaulle returned to power in 1958, many "Europeanists" feared that the general, known for his disdain of supranationalism, would sabotage the Common Market at its inception. But de Gaulle cooperated so completely that by 1962, at the beginning of the EEC's second stage of implementation, the process of establishing a customs union was considerably ahead of schedule, France was ready to move toward a common agricultural policy, and negotiations over British entry into the Community had been launched. The integration of French industry and agriculture into the Common Market had proceeded so smoothly that safeguards included in the Treaty of Rome at French insistence had not been used.

It was not that de Gaulle had been converted to the cause of European supranationalism. De Gaulle viewed the three integrative organizations as bodies of experts whose primary task was to assist the member governments in making and implementing decisions. He welcomed certain joint economic decisions on political as well as economic grounds—and he was fully aware of the inseparability of the two—but he was also determined to retain political control over economic matters so as to maximize French national interests and use the Community as much as possible to serve his overall foreign policy program.

By the mid-sixties, however, de Gaulle must have realized that he could not advance his basic political purposes through the EEC. His attitude became much tougher as threats to his political program came from inside as well as outside the Common Market.

By 1965 the focus of the Common Market was shifting from the removal of trade barriers within a customs union to the more ambitious project of adopting common commercial and monetary policies in an economic union —functions traditionally reserved for national governments. If this development had not been checked, the control of member states over their economic, monetary, fiscal, and social policies would have been curtailed, also hemming in the conduct of foreign policy and defense policy—areas in which de Gaulle wanted maximum flexibility. In addition, it had become obvious that France's

Common Market partners would accept neither de Gaulle's disruptive military policy nor his attempt to dominate the EEC.

De Gaulle's realization that neither the EEC nor NATO could be bent to his will and put to work to achieve his grand design for Europe led to the declaration of a French boycott of the EEC Commission and Council of Ministers in 1965 (which ultimately led to a setback of the EEC's supranational principles), and French withdrawal from NATO's integrated command structure in 1966. Similar considerations had been at the bottom of de Gaulle's veto of British membership in the Common Market in 1963. De Gaulle feared that through Britain, the United States would gain excessive influence in the EEC and that this would be an obstacle to the realization of his vision of Europe. Although external threats to de Gaulle's vision for the Common Market could be dealt with by exclusion, by 1965 it had become clear that the internal dynamics of the EEC were a threat to his foreign policy program.

The Luxembourg accords of early 1966 ended the French boycott of the EEC. Although France retained the economic advantages of membership in the Common Market, political ground had been lost because the position of Germany in the Community was strengthened. The Five had hammered out a series of compromises, fighting hard to prevent the weakening of the fundamental principles of the Community. At the same time the Germans had become more assertive in their Common Market dealings.

The French veto of British membership in the EEC in 1963, the boycott of the Common Market in 1965, and withdrawal from NATO in 1966 were vivid expressions of de Gaulle's attempt to gain more independence, mobility, and flexibility for French foreign policy within the Western alliance. The second British application to the Common Market in May 1967 could hardly count on a more conciliatory French attitude. In rejecting British membership once again, the French essentially repeated the reasons put forth to justify the 1963 veto. First, France contended, because of historical, geographical, economic, political, and cultural factors, Britain was more closely aligned with the United States, the Commonwealth, and EFTA countries than with Western Europe. Second, British membership would open up the Community to American influence, transform it into a loosely knit free-trade area, disrupt EEC agricultural arrangements, and in any case weaken the predominant position that France wished to obtain in European affairs.

In the wake of the French veto, Belgian Foreign Minister Pierre Harmel offered a highly complicated proposal to strengthen the EEC "in the political, military, technological, and monetary fields," using the Western European Union (WEU) as the institutional device. He implicitly threatened that a fully implemented common agricultural policy might not come about if Britain were excluded from membership. Harmel also proposed compulsory consultations in foreign affairs once Britain became a member. Paris opposed all aspects of the Harmel Plan, and by 1968 France had maneuvered itself into an increasingly isolated position in the European as well as the Atlantic community.

FRENCH MONETARY PROBLEMS

De Gaulle's foreign policy goals ran into difficulties over European integration and monetary problems. In turn, these monetary problems were partly the result of his foreign policy program. In the fifties and sixties, the French government gave precedence to economic expansion and full employment over price stability—in part for domestic reasons, and in part to catch up with West Germany's industrial boom. France strongly supported fixed exchange rates that would allow the franc to remain undervalued and create higher foreign demand for French products, thus contributing to the goal of growth and full employment. But this also fed inflation. Toward the mid-sixties, the franc had gradually begun to weaken, and a major crisis erupted in 1968.

Like most monetary crises, the 1968 crisis of the franc had its origin in a balance-of-payments deficit. For a number of years the French economy had suffered from moderate inflationary pressures (and moderate stagnation), which intensified greatly during the summer of 1968 after the government arranged for generous settlements with the labor unions in order to end a series of crippling strikes. These wage hikes, averaging 13 percent, coupled with an expansionist monetary policy designed to facilitate recovery and stimulate economic growth, substantially increased the amount of money in circulation and led to a rise in industrial costs and the cost of living. Inflation, in turn, raised the price of exports and increased the volume of imports to meet consumer demand. The resulting outflow of gold and hard currencies created a crisis of confidence in the franc, a crisis that was further aggravated as speculators sold francs for marks. Between June and November France lost more than $4.5 billion in reserves, and during the month of November alone West Germany acquired $2 billion in such speculative funds, with a sizable portion coming from France.

The 1968 crisis and de Gaulle's refusal to ease the problem by devaluing the franc led to serious disagreements with Germany. Both sides viewed the immediate monetary and economic issue as closely tied to fundamental political questions. For years, Germany's monetary policy had been the opposite of France's. The Germans, enjoying tremendous exports and monetary reserves plus full employment and a satisfactory growth rate, worried primarily about inflation. They saw no reason to revalue the mark upward in order to bail out the ailing franc but expected de Gaulle to revalue the franc downward —after all, it was the franc that was in trouble, not the mark. Moreover, the Germans felt that French economic and monetary policy had been used by de Gaulle to further his foreign policy programs, most of which they opposed.

In particular, Bonn resented being asked to help finance indirectly de Gaulle's costly nuclear strategy, which he put to political uses that were detrimental to German interests. In refusing to devalue the franc, West Germany felt, de Gaulle clearly intended to impose his will on Bonn once again and to extract concessions that would leave French prestige and political-economic maneuverability unimpaired.

De Gaulle's position on devaluation had some support from the United States and Britain. Although France's manipulations during the gold crisis of November 1967 had endangered the fixed gold-dollar-pound parity, the United States and Britain were highly sympathetic to the French plight one year later since they, too, suffered from balance-of-payments difficulties. Moreover, Britain expected that France's refusal to devalue the franc would work to British advantage, at least in the short run, by keeping French products from gaining a competitive edge over British exports and averting immediate danger to the pound. From Washington's point of view, a moderate upward revaluation of the mark had long been favored, and in fact it was American pressure that had forced the Germans to revalue in 1961.

During the November 1968 Bonn conference of the finance ministers of the ten leading financial powers, de Gaulle, who had characterized the possibility of devaluing the franc as the "worst of absurdities," instructed his negotiators to push for an upward revaluation of the mark. The United States and Britain backed his position; Germany was strongly opposed. The German viewpoint ultimately prevailed, but the finance ministers placated Paris by agreeing to make available to France $2 billion in credits, of which Germany contributed more than half. (Bonn reportedly had offered Paris a unilateral loan of $1 billion even before the conference, which was apparently turned down because Germany refused to revalue and demanded that the French impose additional anti-inflationary measures.)

The agreements reached at the November meeting were not contingent on French devaluation, but it was widely assumed that Paris had little choice but to devalue the franc between 10 and 15 percent. It came as a surprise, therefore, when de Gaulle made a terse announcement that the franc would not be devalued, which was soon followed by a statement spelling out a tough domestic deflationary program to help correct France's economic difficulties and keep the franc afloat. Aside from incurring intangible political costs, the program required postponement of some of de Gaulle's most cherished foreign policy-related ambitions, such as the development of intercontinental ballistic missiles, the equipment of the French army with tactical nuclear weapons, and the completion of the H-bomb testing program in the Pacific. Moreover, the austerity measures he imposed—price and wage freezes, spending cuts, increased "value-added" taxes to reduce the volume of imports, currency exchange controls, and several others—were politically controversial and threatened the nation's precarious domestic tranquility, which had just recently been restored. (These factors most likely contributed to de Gaulle's decision to retire in April 1969.)

Most likely, de Gaulle's reaction to the controversy over the franc was influenced by the humiliating circumstances in which devaluation would have been carried out and by his resentment of the way in which German economic power was being translated into political power. The irritations that had been building up on both sides during years of controversy made the outcome of the currency confrontation not only a matter of economic import but also a question of national prestige, with great psychological and political significance.

DE GAULLE'S EASTERN POLICY

French aims conflicted with German aims on another important front—the pursuit of a dynamic policy toward the Soviet Union and Eastern Europe. As it was, France's isolated position within the European Economic Community and her separatist military-strategic posture (reflected in French withdrawal from NATO and the Ailleret Doctrine) were not an ideal platform from which to launch initiatives toward the Communist bloc.

Deteriorating Franco-German relations played an important role in hindering the success of de Gaulle's Eastern policy. Previously, when Adenauer headed the German government (until 1963) and the Western alliance was still cohesive enough to force Bonn into making choices between Paris and Washington, the conflicts between France and Germany were manageable. But by the fall of 1963, when Erhard succeeded Adenauer, differences between France and Germany intensified and seemed to be leading to a major confrontation. The new chancellor in Bonn was much less sympathetic to French projects than Adenauer had been, and practically every item on de Gaulle's foreign policy agenda was opposed to German policy. NATO, the MLF, and the size and nature of the EEC were important elements in both sides' foreign policy programs, and disagreements on such topics resisted compromise solutions. De Gaulle's opposition to British membership in the Common Market was in direct opposition to the preferences of the "Atlanticists" in the Bonn government, who wanted a larger membership for precisely the reasons that de Gaulle objected to it. For years, Erhard and Foreign Minister Schröder had favored a larger framework for European integration than that provided by the Six, for economic and military as well as political and cultural reasons. Furthermore, they had consistently argued that such an expanded organization could, and should, be part of an Atlantic partnership with the United States. Thus while de Gaulle was opposing practically every facet of American foreign policy—NATO, the MLF, the Nassau agreement, the test ban treaty, Vietnam—Erhard was aligning Bonn with Washington's positions. In essence, Paris and Bonn were pursuing policies based on fundamentally different conceptions of a desirable political order, and the more de Gaulle widened the gap between American and French foreign policy, the more he forced Erhard to declare himself in favor of Washington.

At the same time, the Germans felt threatened by de Gaulle's increasingly conciliatory relations with the Soviet Union. Two crucial policy areas were at stake for both Paris and Bonn, and in both French policy seemed designed to frustrate German aims. Germany viewed with suspicion de Gaulle's dynamic policy toward the Soviet Union and Eastern Europe, highlighted by his state visits to Russia in 1966 and Poland in 1967. Bonn felt such moves reflected an important change in the Franco-German understanding on how to deal with the Soviet Union and Eastern Europe. De Gaulle skillfully exploited and accelerated the trend toward polycentrism and the general relaxation of East-West tensions with a foreign policy style eminently suited to the circumstances, demonstrating how a secondary power could stake out room to maneuver between the superpowers. But for a variety of political, strategic, and psychological reasons, the Germans could hardly emulate the example set by de Gaulle. Thus the French and German approaches to the Soviet Union and Eastern Europe were neither coordinated nor were their underlying purposes complementary.

De Gaulle's dynamic policy toward the Soviet Union and Eastern Europe, coupled with his loosening of France's ties with the Western alliance, were based on his expectation that French foreign policy could become more independent as the two Cold War blocs grew less cohesive and American and Soviet leaders began to show interest in peaceful coexistence. France was dealing with the Soviet Union from a weak position, however. Although polycentric tendencies in the two alliance blocs seemed to increase de Gaulle's maneuverability, he had weakened his position within the Western alliance through his policies toward NATO and the EEC. De Gaulle's vision of a Europe from the Atlantic to the Urals required reaching an accommodation with Moscow as well as curtailing the influence of Washington and Brussels, and it was rooted in the assumption that Moscow would see sufficient advantage in a gradual process of dissolving the two military blocs in Europe, even if this required a relaxation of Soviet power in Eastern Europe. But it is difficult to see how the Soviet Union could have perceived the situation in the same way, since Moscow was interested in solidifying the status quo, not in changing it. In any case, de Gaulle's expectation of a gradual erosion of the Soviet and American spheres of influence in Europe came to an abrupt end with the Soviet invasion of Czechoslovakia in August 1968.

De Gaulle's dynamic Eastern policy had, for all intents and purposes, been dealt a crushing blow from which it did not recover. This failure signified the end of a dynamic French Eastern policy. The initiative soon passed to Bonn, whose *Ostpolitik* was much more effective because West Germany could offer what the Soviet bloc wanted most: recognition of East Germany, the Oder-Neisse line, and the general territorial status quo in Eastern and

Central Europe. German *Ostpolitik* solidified the status quo, whereas French *Ostpolitik* had threatened it. Moreover, even if East Germany, Poland, and Czechoslovakia had preferred a relaxation of the Soviet hold over Eastern Europe, this could only have been accomplished subsequent to Bonn's willingness to recognize East Germany and the Oder-Neisse line and to normalize relations with Prague.

The Soviet invasion of Czechoslovakia, and the internal turmoil created by the May 1968 strikes in France, demonstrated dramatically that French resources—economic, monetary, political, and diplomatic—were insufficient to sustain de Gaulle's grandiose foreign policy program. De Gaulle's resignation in April 1969 over domestic issues—regional policy and Senate reform—and the selection of Georges Pompidou as president signified that domestic necessities had taken precedence over foreign policy.

THE PRESIDENCY OF GEORGES POMPIDOU

President Pompidou and his Prime Minister Jacques Chaban-Delmas, although restrained by domestic political considerations, quickly began a reorientation of French policy toward Europe. This took the form of a much more conciliatory attitude toward British entry into the EEC and a call for a summit meeting of heads of government and state. At the Hague summit of December 1969, with Willy Brandt in office as German chancellor, a compromise was reached that made renegotiations on enlargement of the Common Market dependent on the inclusion of all major farm products in the EEC's common agricultural program and on shifting the major burden of contributions to the program from national resources to the Community's own resources. Throughout 1970 and the early part of 1971, intricate negotiations on these issues took place during which it became clear that Pompidou was ready to make important concessions to facilitate British entry.

There were several reasons for France's change of attitude. Basically, Pompidou recognized that the political and economic reasons that had prompted de Gaulle to exclude Britain had been invalidated by the events of 1968 and 1969. Pompidou was determined to move France from its isolated position in the EEC toward a more flexible position, and British entry seemed essential for this purpose. British membership also seemed to fit into a modified Gaullist vision of a European order (a dimension not unwelcome to Pompidou since it allowed him to meet criticism from diehard Gaullists at home), for an enlarged EEC implied a wider framework for French foreign policy and might also serve as a check on Germany. Moreover, French fears of excessive American influence through British membership had declined. American foreign policy in the late sixties, preoccupied as it was with Vietnam, was much less concentrated on West European affairs, and it seemed as though the British Trojan horse of which de Gaulle had been so suspicious might turn out to be empty after all. French rethinking on British membership was also made easier because Britain, too, had become more conciliatory, making fewer and less important demands for exceptions and signaling a more convincing European stance. There appeared a real possibility that British links with the United States could be weakened and transferred to a European confederal context. Finally, Pompidou was much more willing than de Gaulle to deal with France's partners as equals, although he shared de Gaulle's belief that political agreement among community members had to come before the formation of community institutions.

The Pompidou government also took a more pragmatic attitude than de Gaulle had on monetary matters. A new crisis of the franc occurred in early May 1969, a direct result of de Gaulle's resignation. The crisis followed roughly the same pattern as that of November 1968, and Bonn reiterated its determination not to revalue the mark—a decision a government spokesman called "final, unequivocal, and for eternity." In August, the French government made the surprise announcement that the franc would be devalued by 12.5 percent.

In contrast to November 1968, there was relatively little international agitation and acrimony over the 1969 crisis of the franc. But the French devaluation once again raised intricate issues between Paris and Bonn because it affected the Common Market's farm pricing system. The EEC had to decide how to adjust uniform support levels for farm prices to the devaluation of the franc. Since EEC farm prices were based on a unit of account equal to one American dollar (with payments converted into national currencies), French farmers would have gained by the amount of the franc's devaluation, with the result that overall price increases would have diminished the anti-inflationary effects of the devaluation. Three major options were available to the Common Market negotiators. First, they could stand pat and allow rising French farm prices to push EEC farm surpluses, already high because of price supports, to even higher levels—a solution detrimental to the purposes the French government sought to further with devaluation and unacceptable to France's EEC partners because of the increasing financial burden of surplus subsidies. Second, they could devalue the unit of account—which is what French negotiators pushed for initially, but which was unacceptable to the Five because it would have hurt their farmers by automatically reducing their subsidized earnings. Third, they could suspend uniform support levels for farm products and "isolate" the French agricultural market for twenty-eight months, which together with fiscal manipulations would raise French farm prices only gradually—the solution they finally accepted.

The quarantine of the French farm market had several important implications. It required Pompidou to reverse de Gaulle's policy of insisting on a common agricultural policy among the Six, with the result that painfully forged agreements were being watered down and the cohesion of the Market was suffering. It also set a precedent that could work to Britain's advantage in seeking Common Market membership: once exceptions were being made on the sensitive issue of farm products for France, a country that had all along insisted on the speedy establishment of a common market for agricultural products, exceptions might also be made for Britain, a country whose major economic reservation about joining the EEC was the likelihood of higher food prices at home. Furthermore, now that the common farm program was suspended, President Pompidou's previous demand that agreement be reached on farm financing before negotiations on British membership would be reopened could no longer be met. Finally, the negotiations in Brussels again demonstrated that some of the issues dividing Germany and France could not be attributed solely to the personal idiosyncracies of the policymakers in Bonn and Paris but stemmed primarily from conflicting economic and political interests.

Although the question of agricultural finances was ultimately resolved in a compromise, the whole issue symbolized how Pompidou was forced by circumstances to deal with problems much more pragmatically than de Gaulle, a development that became even more pronounced under his successor.

THE PRESIDENCY
OF VALÉRY GISCARD D'ESTAING

In the presidential election of 1974, Valéry Giscard d'Estaing won a narrow victory over his Socialist opponent, François Mitterand. From the outset, Giscard faced serious economic and monetary difficulties. France suffered from a recession, high unemployment, and double-digit inflation, and after considerable pressure the franc had to be withdrawn from the "snake," the joint EEC currency float (see chapter 2). French monetary problems in the seventies were the outgrowth of some fundamental choices that had been made in the fifties and sixties—choices that, as we have seen, had contributed to previous French monetary problems with which Giscard was well acquainted, having served as finance minister in periods when these problems were most severe.

The immediate background to the monetary difficulties of the mid-seventies could be found in the events of the early seventies, while Pompidou was still president. Although at this time France's monetary problems were not as dramatic as they had been toward the end of the sixties, the major differences between French and German monetary policies remained because they stemmed from different underlying economic policies and from the much weaker position of the franc compared to the mark. In 1971, after EEC members had agreed on gradual monetary and economic integration on the basis of fixed exchange rates, a new dollar crisis deepened Franco-German monetary differences. The inflationary push of the dollar influx threatened

German interests while in the short run it served French interests because of increased liquidity. The Germans proposed a concerted float of European currencies toward outside currencies, which would have taken care of the dollar problem and at the same implied German willingness to absorb some of the imported inflation from fellow EEC countries. Finance Minister Giscard demurred, however, because he felt that the deflationary effects on the franc would be detrimental to France's full employment policy. In March 1973, after a variety of hedging measures had been agreed upon, Giscard did engage France in the joint float of five EEC members. But less than a year later the franc, along with the lira and pound, was lifted from the common EEC float. This reversal was caused by the deteriorating position of French monetary reserves (largely with respect to OPEC countries) and also by the fact that the European "snake in the tunnel," propelled by the upward trend of the German mark, deprived the franc of its competitive advantage against the floating dollar (and other currencies) that had developed after the 1969 devaluation of the franc. Also, even with exchange rates remaining the same, German exports were more competitive than ever because of the lower German inflation rate. By mid-1975, the franc had gained sufficiently against the mark (and inflation had become more manageable) to allow President Giscard, with some hesitation, to reenter the franc in the joint European monetary float. The franc was withdrawn from the float again, however, in March 1976.

In many respects, the Pompidou presidency had been a transition from de Gaulle's grandiose perspectives on Europe, East-West relations, and the Third World to the more pragmatic style of Giscard. A new orientation seemed to be taking shape. Jean Monnet observed in *Le Monde* (11 January 1974): "General de Gaulle had a policy which in his view was European; it certainly was not in mine. Pompidou took a series of measures towards building Europe, but Giscard has the conviction that Europe must be achieved and, consequently, it is not only a point of view, it is the heart that speaks."

A number of problems, however, plagued Giscard. As the domestic political scene moved toward an increasing cleavage between Left and Gaullist Right, it become difficult for Giscard to steer a middle road that would lead to a more pragmatic as well as a more committed European program. Giscard's European credentials were impressive (if not entirely unambiguous), and his more pragmatic style seemed to dovetail neatly with that of Helmut Schmidt, his counterpart in Bonn. Both were preoccupied with domestic policy, and both had little time (and inclination) to deal with large-scale global perspectives. The oil crisis, problems regarding raw materials, monetary issues, and related economic matters required immediate attention. But while the personal and political styles of the key decision makers in Paris and Bonn were complementary, the uneven economic and monetary performances of France and Germany did not permit a closer coordination of monetary and fiscal policies. Also, Schmidt's persistent criticisms of the EEC's common agricultural policy as outdated and wasteful, and his suggestion that Gaullist conservatives were in fact aiding the cause of communism in France, raised some uncomfortable issues for Giscard in his own domestic political context.

Giscard's ideas for a more streamlined Common Market "directorate"—consisting of Paris-Bonn-London-Rome—met with considerable resistance from the smaller EEC members. But at the economic summit meetings at Rambouillet in November 1975 and Puerto Rico in June 1976, only the Big Four were participants. In a sense, this directorate summitry, which Giscard also exploited for domestic political reasons, could be viewed as a further example of Giscard's commitment to the European cause since it seemed to elevate Common Market issues to the level "high politics." Giscard's appointment of Raymond Barre, a former vice president of the EEC Commission, as his second prime minister seemed to underline his intentions to strengthen the EEC. Giscard also suggested that the Community replace the requirement for unanimity with simple majority voting on questions not affecting vital national interests and set a date for the direct election of a European parliament.

Giscard's ideas about a confederated Europe came at a time when the prospects for European unity were not good, and the response of Community members was not enthusiastic. Moreover, Giscard's attempt to revive some aspects of de Gaulle's dynamic Eastern policy, without sufficient consultation with France's EEC partners, raised some question about whether his commitment to European unity and cooperation was as serious as he conveyed it to be and whether it extended into the area of coordinated foreign policies.

Giscard's hand was strengthened in the election of March 1978, in which the Center-Right coalition that supported him gained an impressive victory over the Left and the Gaullists. French policy became more confident, as reflected in a very tough stance against the United States at the Bonn economic summit in July 1978. But in contrast to de Gaulle's disagreements with the United States, which were at bottom political, Giscard's were economic and monetary and, moreover, were shared by his counterpart in Bonn, Helmut Schmidt. The French were defining their demands in terms of economic interdependence and the language of European collaboration.

7

Decolonization and the Third World

The postwar controversy over the status and disposition of the French empire was charged with an especially intense quality, because—like the German goal of reunification—French colonial policy was a matter of national self-definition. The question of what political and institutional role the colonies should play, and what principles should govern their relationship with France, had been discussed since the early days of the French empire. Although the eighteenth century *philosophes* had assumed that France would eventually divest itself of the colonies, the French Revolution had given rise to another point of view: the novel, and peculiarly French, idea that decolonization should result not in separation and independence from the mother country but in assimilation and association of these territories with France through parliamentary representation and extension of French citizenship to colonial subjects. The notion that the colonies were not foreign entities but in a sense an integral part of metropolitan France itself meant that colonial matters were not debated as foreign policy issues but as domestic issues. (As we shall see this was especially true during the days of the Fourth Republic, and in particular in regard to Algeria.)

The two diametrically opposed visions of the future of the French empire were never reconciled. The controversy became even more urgent in the wake of World War I when France's hold on its empire gradually became less secure and the myth of assimilation became more and more untenable. World War II, and the fundamental transformations in the world balance of power that followed, further undermined French power over its colonies. The nation's physical and psychological exhaustion at the end of the war, which had a decisive effect on shaping the goals of security and political and economic recovery, also had a deep impact on its colonial policy. France was overextended militarily, economically, and politically; and colonial involvements in the postwar period rapidly became a serious liability.

The most important factor leading to the eventual decolonization of France's empire was the inherent strength of indigenous emancipation movements. The Cold War provided a global framework for the decolonization process. France found it difficult to maintain a hold over its possessions without the support of at least one of the superpowers, for Paris was placed in a position similar to that of London—forced to contend with revolutionary forces of nationalism in an international context conducive to colonial emancipation, lacking sufficient leverage within the Western alliance to enlist its aid in keeping colonial control, but too weak to pursue a viable policy unilaterally.

The United States was ambivalent about the French dilemma. On the one hand, the United States viewed itself as an anticolonial nation—a position reflected in American sponsorship of the UN Trusteeship Council and the refusal in 1945 to give military aid to the French war effort in Indochina. On the other hand, Washington was aware that American assistance given to Paris for the purposes of domestic economic reconstruction could be diverted to colonial projects quite easily.

Another crucial factor influencing Washington's position was the connection between the Cold War policy of worldwide containment of communism and French colonial involvements. After the establishment of a communist regime in China in 1949 and the outbreak of the Korean War in 1950, Paris began to justify the war in Indochina as France's contribution to the containment of communist expansionism. It is unlikely that Washington was misled by the official rhetoric with which Paris justified the war in Southeast Asia. But French and American interests seemed sufficiently parallel for the United States to condone French colonial policy. In other colonial areas as well, Washington was placed in an ambivalent position. The United States managed to irritate the Dutch as well as the Asians over the Indonesian question, and in the fifties Washington was generally in an uncomfortable position in the UN with respect to the Moroccan, Tunisian, and Algerian issues, as American strategic and economic interests conflicted with Washington's avowed support of self-determinism and colonial emancipation.

The Soviet Union, too, turned the issue of Western colonialism into an instrument of Cold War policy. After the death of Stalin, the Geneva Conference of 1954, the Bandung Conference of 1955, and the stabilization of the Cold War front in Central Europe, it became apparent that Moscow intended to use colonial unrest as a door through which to extend Soviet influence in Africa and Asia. In Africa especially, where decolonization had reached a critical phase by the mid- and late fifties, Khrushchev's Third World strategy was pursued intensely—although it came too late to play a major role in the process of colonial emancipation. The UN served as the primary diplomatic forum through which both Moscow and Washington contended for the support of the newly emerging states and sought to enlist them for what were essentially Cold War projects.

Within this complex international context, France attempted to retain control over its colonial possessions. The goal jeopardized the nation's chances of achieving political and economic recovery and security, two other important postwar objectives. The diversion of scarce French resources to colonial projects caused tension between France and the United States, since Washington was more interested in the Cold War front in Europe; it weakened the French position relative to Germany within the Western alliance; it made it even more difficult for France to play the role of mediator and balancer; it stood in the way of political and economic recovery, straining economic and fiscal resources to the limit and causing domestic turmoil; and it damaged France's international image because of the organized brutality that accompanied French attempts to retain control over the colonial territories. The process of decolonizing the French empire became a painful, frustrating and demoralizing experience, which greatly weakened France on the international scene and contributed significantly to the collapse of the Fourth Republic.

FROM EMPIRE TO *UNION FRANÇAISE*, 1946–58

Toward the end of World War II, at the Brazzaville Conference of February 1944, the Free French under General de Gaulle began to make plans for the institutions that would govern the relationship between France and its colonies in the postwar world. Aside from a small number of African observers, no native leaders were present at the conference—the participants were high colonial officials and members of the Provisional Consultative Assembly.

The French realized at the time that the ideas and institutions of the prewar days were outmoded and that colonial policy would have to be adjusted to changing circumstances. Although this required taking a more equitable and far-sighted attitude toward Asian and African emancipation movements, there was a strong temptation to reassert French claims to being a major power by attempting to retain colonial control. This temptation was especially strong because metropolitan France had been defeated in the early days of World War II and because during the war the essence of Free France was located, physically as well as psychologically, in parts of the colonial empire, especially in Africa. (In May 1945, Gaston Monnerville, then a native deputy from Guiana and later President of the Council of the Republic, said in the Consultative Assembly: "Without the empire France would be no more than a liberated country today. Thanks to its empire, France is a victorious country.")

At Brazzaville, the old controversy over whether the relationship between the colonies and France should be one of assimilation or association lost much of its cogency (although the controversy was in no way resolved). The concepts of assimilation or association were replaced by the concepts of Community, French Union, and Federation. Paris decided to extend French citizenship to colonial subjects and establish colonial political bodies through the new French constitution. This would bring about some measure of integration among the various parts of the empire while leaving intact the empire's centralized governmental and administrative structures. The principles of internal autonomy and independence were firmly rejected at the Brazzaville Conference, and there was no question that France sought to retain as much control as possible.

The French Constitution of 1946 served as the institutional framework for governing the various parts of the French empire. It reflected a compromise between the principles of assimilation and federalism and sought to paper over their contradictions. Although the Constitution envisaged some measure of integration, it also reaffirmed the predominant position of metropolitan France over the territories. The Constitution also retained the distinction that had already been made during the days of the old empire between possessions considered an integral part of France and possessions such as protectorates and mandates that were more loosely attached to the mother country. Article 60 of the Constitution stated that "The French Union is formed on one side by the French Republic which comprises metropolitan France, the departments and overseas territories, and on the other by associated territories and states." This meant a classification along the following lines: overseas departments were Algeria and the four "old colonies," Martinique, Guadeloupe, Guiana, and Réunion; overseas territories were the colonies in Africa, Madagascar, and the Pacific; associated states and protectorates were Vietnam, Cambodia, Laos, Tunisia, and Morocco; and associated territories under mandate of the United Nations were Togo and the Cameroon.

The institutional and legal provisions of the 1946 Constitution were totally inadequate for governing French overseas possessions and for allowing genuine reforms. The centralized administrative apparatus anchored in the Constitution could not work because of political realities. The administrative process discriminated heavily against the native elites in the colonies who felt that this was just a new way to deny them a voice in governance, and French settlers in the colonies looked toward Paris as the protector of their privileges but at the same time wanted to strengthen their local political and administrative power. These political pressures on the administrative apparatus made its inherent contradictions even more visible. With respect to reform movements, the idea of granting French citizenship to all former subjects and giving them representation in the Republic left no alternatives to the opponents of this arrangement except secession. Reform of the French Union could be accomplished only by changing the structure of the French Republic itself. But the political process of the Fourth Republic was uncertain and fragile to begin with, and such a redefinition would have destroyed the state. In fact, the Algerian issue later on did just that—the conflict dealt the death blow to the Fourth Republic.

Moreover, the distinction made in the 1946 Constitution between overseas departments and other entities considered a part of metropolitan France (primarily Algeria) created profound political and psychological barriers to decolonization on the part of the French people. As a result decolonization, which had begun in every part of the empire after the Brazzaville Conference, was barely tolerated by some groups in French politics.

THE INDOCHINESE WAR, 1946–54

The war in Indochina, which turned into total defeat for France, exemplified the futility of French efforts to retain control over the empire.

The French position in Vietnam was extremely shaky at the end of World War II. In December 1946, after negotiations with nationalist leader Ho Chi Minh had broken down and the communist Vietminh established the Democratic Republic of Vietnam, France decided to wage war. To enlist as much indigenous help as possible, in June 1948 the French established a provisional central government in Vietnam, with former emperor Bao Dai as chief of state. (This state was recognized by the United States, Britain, and other Western powers, and the Democratic Republic of Vietnam was in turn recognized by the Soviet Union and the People's Republic of China in 1950.) But the Bao Dai regime had little grassroots support. It was supported by large landowners and commercial interests who had as much of a stake in the status quo as the French. The combined appeal of nationalism and social reform, which was at the heart of the Vietminh communist program, was much more powerful than what the French and the Bao Dai regime could offer and in the seven years from 1946 to 1953 the French were unable to achieve a decisive military victory over the Vietminh.

France viewed the Indochinese War as largely a domestic issue, and in the beginning was determined to shield the conflict from outside interference such as United Nations intervention and direct American involvement. France preferred obtaining American aid through the European Recovery Program and rechanneling these resources to the Indochinese conflict, thus avoiding direct American participation.

By 1953, the Vietminh controlled over half of Vietnam and considerable portions of Laos and Cambodia, and a negotiated settlement began to look attractive to some French political groups. Pierre Mendès-France, a deputy in the assembly and a former cabinet minister, proposed a full reversal of French policy toward Vietnam by granting the country genuine independence. But there were obstacles to such a move. First, there was the problem of which of the two Vietnamese governments to deal with, since Ho Chi Minh sought to bypass the Bao Dai regime. Second, many influential French deputies of the Right and Center were strongly opposed to granting independence.

Washington's position was ambivalent. On the one hand, the Eisenhower administration was dissatisfied with French conduct of the war, and Washington had urged the French to grant the Bao Dai regime some genuine concessions, if only to allow the government to compete more effectively with the nationalist appeal of the Vietminh. On the other hand, Washington did not apply effective pressures on France to strengthen the Bao Dai regime. The ambivalence of Washington's position reflected a deep-seated difference in the purposes that the United States and France sought to advance in Indochina. The overriding French purpose was to hold together the French empire, and genuine concessions to the Bao Dai regime, although they might have strengthened Bao Dai's hand vis-à-vis the Vietminh, would have undermined the very reason for the French effort in Indochina. The communist dimension of the Vietminh challenge did not perturb the French nearly as much as it did the Americans. The United States viewed Indochina as one of several strategic areas where communist expansion had to be checked. The global interests of the United States as a superpower, the belief that the communist threat was centrally directed from Moscow, and the fact that by 1953 the Vietminh were getting considerable support from the Chinese, led Washington to view the Indochinese War within the overall context of America's containment policy.

There were in fact direct connections between American containment efforts in Europe and Southeast Asia, which were fully appreciated in Paris and Washington because they touched upon vital national interests. The negotiations over the establishment of the European Defense Community occurred at a time when the French military effort in Indochina depleted the French military presence in Europe as well as in North Africa. The rearmament of West Germany envisaged in the EDC treaty thus appeared particularly threatening to French policymakers since it would make Germany the predominant military power on the Continent, especially if the United States and Britain should decide at some future date to withdraw their forces.

Given the energies of the Vietminh movement, which successfully combined a nationalist with a communist appeal, French attempts to retain Indochina would have faced great difficulties even if the larger political context had been favorable. But the internationalization of the Indochina war, in a Cold War setting, made it doubly difficult. The Vietminh were supported militarily, politically, and economically by the Soviet Union and China, which made it impossible for the French to achieve a decisive victory on the battlefield. At the same time, the French opposed genuine political and economic reform because in the short run their interests seemed better served by a conservative puppet regime. The United States constantly sought to divert France from its colonial purpose in Indochina and enlist the French effort on behalf of Washington's global containment policy. This strained Franco-

American relations considerably, especially since French policymakers felt that their major national interest in Europe—the control of Germany—was already being compromised for the purpose of strengthening Washington's Cold War posture in Central Europe. It is no wonder that French policymakers viewed the Cold War polarization of power and interest as fundamentally detrimental to vital French national interests. Major French foreign policy goals, in Europe as well as in Southeast Asia and elsewhere, were stymied because of the polarized global balance of power.

The final settlement of the war at the 1954 Geneva Conference resulted in partition of Vietnam. It signified the total defeat of French colonial aims in Indochina and had a strong effect on French colonial policy in other parts of the world.

BLACK AFRICA AND MADAGASCAR

Compared to the bloody and costly attempt to hang on to Indochina, the process of decolonization in Africa was relatively smooth (with the glaringly painful exception of Algeria, as we shall see). Aside from the Madagascar upheavals of 1947 and some minor incidents elsewhere, there was not much violence.

The black African colonies included the Central African Republic, Chad, Congo-Brazzaville, Dahomey, Gabon, Guinea, the Ivory Coast, Mali, Mauritania, Niger, Senegal, and Upper Volta, plus Madagascar. Under the *Union française* (1946–58), the African representatives in the French parliament did not command much real power. The device of a "double college" (where French citizens, including Africans who had acquired citizenship, were part of the first college and others were part of the second college) and the institution of the Territorial Councils (which gave advice to the governors) did not alter the fact that the governors held supreme power in the territories and that legislation continued to be enacted in metropolitan France. The reforms of 1946 increased the power of colonial subjects in a limited way. They triggered the establishment of the French African parties (and especially the influential *Rassemblement Démocratique Africain*, RDA), and it was important symbolically that black Africans now received equal treatment in the French Assembly. The experience gained by the African deputies in playing the parliamentary game, and the need to rally support in elections for the Territorial Assemblies and Councils, had a moderating influence on politics in the Territories and on the articulation of demands for independence and emancipation.

In its first ten years the *Union française* arrangement was stagnant, with only sporadic attempts at genuine reform or evolution. It was not until the adoption of the Framework Statute of June 1956, the *loi-cadre*, that the emancipation of sub-Saharan Africa began to make some progress. The *loi-cadre* was an enabling act, drafted with the participation of African deputies and passed by large majorities in the Chamber and Senate, which granted some measure of self-government to all French territories and which was to be followed by specific reform decrees tailored to the circumstances of the various territories. The bill granted the franchise to all French subjects; it allowed self-government in domestic affairs, with France retaining exclusive jurisdiction over foreign affairs, the armed forces, internal security, and the judiciary system for European Frenchmen; and it left other political matters to locally elected assemblies and their executives, retaining a veto power for the French governors.

It was understood by most concerned that the *loi-cadre,* important as it was in itself as a reform program, was only a transitional device toward more complete emancipation and self-government in the colonies. Under the *loi-cadre* the African possessions were still a part of the Republic, but there was some decentralization and delegation of power. Although the French Parliament retained most of its official jurisdiction and authority, this authority was beginning to crumble. Between 1956, when the *loi-cadre* was enacted, and May 1958, when Charles de Gaulle returned to power, the Fourth Republic was going through its final series of crises and Paris was simply incapable of mustering the political and psychological energy to handle pressures for emancipation in Africa. In September 1957, at Bamako (Soudan), the *Rassemblement Démocratique Africain*—the union of African parties—spelled out a common policy to which all affiliate parties were expected to adhere in order to confront France with a unified African position on matters of colonial emancipation. In effect, at Bamako the Africans put forth the concept of a Franco-African community (quite similar to the policy later implemented during the Fifth Republic by de Gaulle). But the Fourth Republic could not act on this proposal, preoccupied as it was with the Algerian issue and other political problems in metropolitan France. At the same time the Africans, while demanding independence, did not wish to lose French economic support for their modernization and development programs. Both sides were gaining a more realistic appreciation of what was possible and necessary, but the political process of the Fourth Republic was already so overloaded with problems and crises that it could not respond effectively to the requirements of the situation.

ALGERIA

Undoubtedly the war in Algeria was the most traumatic issue that confronted the Fourth Republic, and the failure to resolve the conflict contributed directly to the Republic's collapse.

During World War II a strong nationalist movement developed in Algeria, and in the early postwar years it quickly gained momentum. By that time the Algerian nationalists had totally rejected the idea of assimilation or integration and instead called for full self-determination and self-government. In 1947 an Algerian Statute was adopted under which France ruled Algeria until October 1958, but it did not give the Algerians more political influence—in part because it was not designed by Paris for that purpose, and in part because its major provisions were not implemented by the local administrators who were highly sympathetic to the cause of the French settlers in Algeria. Throughout the postwar years, the Algerians continued to be treated as subjects; they were deprived of effective political representation; and they remained underprivileged economically, socially, and educationally with no genuine improvements in sight. In late 1954, a short time after France had finally extricated itself from the war in Indochina, a major rebellion broke out in Algeria.

Most Frenchmen were emotionally involved with the Algerian issue—in sharp contrast to the public's indifference to black Africa—because they felt that Algeria was not a colony but an essential part of France. This was reflected constitutionally and administratively by the fact that Algeria was governed by the French Ministry of the Interior. As a result, in response to the rebellion in Algeria the Fourth Republic launched a formidable military effort. Eventually French forces in Algeria numbered half a million men, armed with modern weapons. Over the years neither the French nor the Algerians could achieve a decisive military victory, although this in itself represented a triumph for the rebels. The French forces were faced with the problem of chasing down guerilla units that sought to avoid large-scale engagements and preferred to strike at isolated outposts and terrorize settlements. The Arab guerillas denied the French secure pockets of control by shifting their attacks from place to place, undermining the French position politically and psychologically as well as militarily. The French position became even more precarious after Tunisia and Morocco gained independence because both countries offered sanctuaries for the Algerian forces who could cross the borders to and from Algeria as tactical circumstances required.*

When it became clear that the French armed forces could not gain victory, Paris initiated (or condoned) highly repressive measures and introduced emergency statutes that for all practical purposes left the administration of Algeria to the French army command. These statutes, passed in 1955–57, suspended civil rights, extended the jurisdiction of courts martial, allowed persons to be assigned to "forcible residence" (thus providing legal justifica-

---

*French withdrawal from Tunisia and Morocco proceeded relatively smoothly. By the early fifties, independence movements in both countries were growing substantially, and Prime Minister Mendès-France negotiated treaty arrangements that led to independence as part of his general decolonization policy. In March 1956, both countries gained independence with the abrogation of the Protectorate Treaty of 1881.

tion for confinement to concentration camps), and in general provided the legal basis for the cruelties that became part of the method with which the French sought to perpetuate their hold on Algeria.

As the war dragged on, the physical and psychological costs mushroomed. The war lasted seven years—from 1954 to 1962; it killed between half a million and a million Muslim Algerians, and about 80,000 French soldiers and civilians; and it cost France about $15 billion. Governments in Paris were formed and fell over the issue of Algeria, and the parliamentary politics of the Fourth Republic, inherently vulnerable, were brought to the point of disintegration. The French government was losing control, or in any case its authority, over the armed forces, and every element in the political spectrum, in Algeria as well as France, was advocating different solutions to the problem—ranging from integration (with complete equality of rights and a full merger of the French and Algerian economies) to partition and total and immediate independence. While the extreme Left and extreme Right managed to take clear-cut if opposing positions, the majority of Frenchmen held contradictory views—hoping to keep Algeria French but at the same time favoring an equitable and liberal solution. The dilemma was private as well as public, and French frustration grew along with emotional and moral uncertainty.

Aside from keeping domestic politics in a constant state of crisis, the Algerian war increasingly damaged French foreign policy. Following directly in the wake of the French defeat in Indochina, the Algerian War further weakened the French position in international politics—politically, militarily, economically, and morally—at a time when Paris sought to reassert its role as a world power and faced crucially important alternatives in Western Europe with respect to a renascent Germany and an emerging European community.

In retrospect, the failure of the French effort in Algeria seems to have been unavoidable. It might be of interest to quote extensively a French voice that deals with that issue. In drawing up a balance sheet of the Fourth Republic's record of involvement in Algeria, Guy de Carmoy poses the question "Why did the Algerian policy of the Fourth Republic fail?" and suggests the following answer:

> The coexistence of two communities, divided by religion, personal and economic status, and demographic pattern, created intrinsic difficulties that were aggravated by the Muslim population explosion and the resurgence of the Arab world. These difficulties, especially peculiar to colonies containing a minority group of settlers, were ignored as long as French domination went unchallenged. Subsequently, they were underestimated.
>
> The Fourth Republic's initial mistake was its persistent refusal to grant Algeria internal autonomy. The status of an associated state, which the Moslem members of parliament had suggested in 1947, was denied. The Statute of 1947 that called for some

measure of assimilation between Algeria and metropolitan France, and for the recognition of "the Algerian personality" was not applied. The fiction of Algeria as "an
integral part of the French Republic," based on the letter of the constitution, was
maintained. . . .

The Fourth Republic tacitly rejected integration. This solution appealed neither
to the nationalists, who wanted a homogeneous Muslim state, nor to the Algerian
Europeans, who were hostile to further assimilation. Nor did it appeal to metropolitan
France, which was beginning to assess the cost. But the idea of integration . . . was
not refuted by the various French governments. This ambivalence betrayed weakness
and was therefore a mistake.

Finally, the major error made by the regime was its refusal to realize the consequences of its relationship with three North African countries that belonged to the
Islamic world. There was a fundamental contradiction between willingness to grant
Tunisia and Morocco independence in 1955 and the determination to maintain an
authoritarian and centralized regime in Algeria in 1958.

The attitude of the authorities in Algeria was that of a series of refusals amounting to a total denial of reality. The truth was unbearable because it was tragic. A choice
had to be made between prolonging the war and granting independence (the latter
involving the departure of a large section of the European population). Faced with an
option that it could not bring itself even to state clearly, the government called up
additional troops in an effort to continue the war. But it was unable to define its war
aims. Consequently, it could not allay the weariness of the public or the anxieties of
the army.*

When Charles de Gaulle was brought back to power in May 1958 over
the issue of Algeria he most likely did not have very precise ideas about how
to deal with the situation, except perhaps to steer between the two extremes
of unconditional independence and of *Algérie Française.* It could not have
been easy for de Gaulle finally to arrive at the decision that the only workable
solution would be Algeria's independence, and it was even more difficult for
him to implement that decision. As de Gaulle's policy gradually moved from
vague and contradictory pronouncements to concrete negotiations with the
Algerian FLN, there were times when it seemed that the Fifth Republic, just
like its predecessor, would collapse over the Algerian question. The army was
thoroughly demoralized and rebellious, the Algerian Frenchmen were deeply
distrustful of de Gaulle's intentions although they had helped him return to
power, and the reshuffled executive and parliamentary structures of the Fifth
Republic could not completely shield the president from domestic political
pressures that stood in the way of a settlement.

In January 1960, the European settlers staged a rebellion in the streets of
Algiers. The local authorities and the French army were sympathetic to their
cause, but the army did not join the Europeans and after some uncertain days

*Guy de Carmoy, *The Foreign Policies of France, 1944–1968* (Chicago, Ill.: The University
of Chicago Press, 1970), pp. 165–66. Reprinted by permission of The University of Chicago
Press.

decided not to revolt against de Gaulle's authority. During the summer of
1960, de Gaulle began to negotiate in earnest with the Algerian rebels. The
two positions were still too far apart to result in concrete arrangements—with
de Gaulle hoping to be able to deal with a broader-based Algerian organization than the FLN—but the major outlines of a settlement began to emerge.

In January 1961 de Gaulle strengthened his hand by obtaining a vote of
confidence on his Algerian policy. A popular referendum in France resulted
in a 3 to 1 vote in favor of granting Algeria self-determination. Although
some of the French settlers and some elements of the army responded to the
referendum by forming a terrorist organization, de Gaulle announced in April
1961 that France would not stand in the way of complete self-determination
and self-government. After an unsuccessful coup by army officers in Algeria,
de Gaulle resumed negotiations with the Provisional Algerian Government.
These finally led to the Evian Accords of March 1962, which were a full
success for the Algerians. Among other items the accords provided for (1) a
cease-fire, and complete independence for Algeria pending approval by referenda in France and Algeria, (2) an arrangement whereby certain French economic interests would be safeguarded in return for French pledges to assist
Algeria with financial and technical aid, (3) reduction of French troops in
Algeria to 80,000 men within a year after the referenda, and their complete
withdrawal in another year, and (4) establishment of a Provisional Executive
to maintain security and to administer the Algerian referendum.

There remained the issue of the status of the French settlers, but in a
tragic way they resolved the problem themselves. In response to the Evian
agreements many went on a rampage of killing and destruction, and it became
obvious that the majority would have to leave along with the French armed
forces to escape retribution. Obliged to choose between "the suitcase and the
coffin," only a relatively small number of French settlers remained in Algeria.

The referendum on Algeria was held in France in April 1962 and led to
an overwhelming endorsement of the Evian Accords. In Algeria the referendum took place in July, also with a huge majority expressing approval of the
agreement, and in October Algeria took its seat in the United Nations as a
sovereign and independent state.

DE GAULLE AND DECOLONIZATION

Compared to the agonizing experience of settling the Algerian question, de
Gaulle met relatively few obstacles in seeking satisfactory institutional arrangements for the African territories.

The French Community, based on the 1957 reform proposal of the Africans, was intended by de Gaulle to replace the French Union and create a new
framework of relations between France and the African territories. The arrangement called for political autonomy for the African members and permitted France, through the Community organs, to influence policy in matters

that were specifically assigned to the Community's jurisdiction, such as foreign policy, defense, currency, common economic and financial policy, and policy on strategic raw materials. The Executive Council of the Community consisted of the chiefs of the territorial governments and the ministers charged with dealing in matters common to all members. The Senate was composed of representatives from the various member parliaments and on the request of the Community's president (who was elected by the territories and the metropole) was empowered to discuss economic and financial matters common to the Community. Effective legislative power, however, was retained by the French parliament, and the Community Senate was intended primarily as a deliberative rather than a decision-making body.

In proposing the Community framework, de Gaulle counted on the fact that self-interest—primarily the need for French economic, financial, military, and administrative assistance—would lead African leaders in the territories to join. This expectation was correct: twelve out of thirteen African territories opted for the Community, the exception being Guinea where Sékou Touré obtained an overwhelming vote for complete and immediate separation of the country from France in September 1958. As a result, when ordinances for the establishment of the Community were set up in December 1958 the Community included Senegal, Mali, the Ivory Coast, Dahomey, Upper Volta, Niger, the Central African Republic, Congo-Brazzaville, Gabon, Chad, Madagascar, Mauritania, and the UN trusteeships of Cameroon and Togo.

Imaginative as de Gaulle's initiative was, the Community was from the beginning a fragile and ineffectual structure that could not be held together because its benefits were relatively marginal. The Executive Council and the Senate met infrequently, the Court of Arbitration had not one case put before it, and the Community suffered from so many political and administrative disabilities that no sense of a common purpose could develop. The Africans were unwilling in the long run to accept limitations on their independence and to acknowledge France's privileged position in the Community, and the Community's institutions suffered from so many contradictions and inconveniences that no important decisions could be made or implemented. In September 1959 the Mali Federation (a newly established federation of Senegal and the old French Soudan) requested independence, with the states of West and Equatorial Africa soon following suit.

THE FIFTH REPUBLIC AND THE THIRD WORLD

As soon as General de Gaulle had completed the process of decolonization he turned to a policy of regaining and strengthening French prestige and influence in the Third World. Toward the end of the decolonization phase the image of France among Third World countries had suffered tremendously. After France gave up her empire de Gaulle could have chosen a policy of noninvolvement in the Third World, which might have led to a concentration of French political efforts in Europe. In choosing instead a policy of regaining French global influence through involvement with the underdeveloped countries, de Gaulle served notice to the superpowers that he intended to compete with them in a worldwide arena. France, liberated from the stigma of being a colonial power, was ready to reclaim a global role and provide an alternative to Washington's and Moscow's political presence not only in Europe but in the Third World.

The instruments of de Gaulle's policy were political and symbolic as well as economic and technical. De Gaulle repeatedly called on the superpowers to provide international assistance without interfering in the domestic politics of the recipient countries, he supported the industrialization of underdeveloped countries and the establishment of regional economic unions, and he was highly critical of the interventionist policies of the United States and the Soviet Union. French assistance in the sixties took various forms. Aside from a series of financial, economic, technical, and military aid measures, France entered into reciprocal preferential trade agreements, supported the international stabilization of prices for primary agricultural commodities (an issue of great interest to most underdeveloped countries as well as to France), helped balance budgets, and used the French monetary zone to facilitate commercial dealings. Although France gained certain commercial benefits from these arrangements, on balance they were a burden rather than an asset.

This burden was offset in other ways. Arrangements with the European Common Market obliging the other EEC members to share the cost of giving former French colonies aid were a great help to France. The Treaty of Rome provided for an assistance program for the colonial dependencies of member states, which was financed by the EEC members in a way that gave France a substantial net gain. A renewal agreement, the Treaty of Yaounde, was signed in 1963 between the Common Market and a large number of former colonies (mostly French), which extended this arrangement for another five years. The Yaounde Treaty also extended existing preferential tariff agreements for certain exports of the colonial dependencies to the Common Market countries. These arrangements, covering mostly tropical agricultural products, were also highly advantageous to France and her former colonies. The measures were strongly resisted by Germany and the Netherlands out of a desire to avoid offending their trading partners in Latin America and British Africa, whose tropical exports were being discriminated against through the Market's preferential arrangements with the former French colonies. The issue was finally resolved in a compromise: the tropical exports from French-speaking Africa were exempted from EEC customs duties, but the common external EEC tariff on tropical imports from other countries was lowered at the same time. The African countries in turn agreed, with certain qualifications, not to levy customs duties on imports from the EEC and to extend equal treatment to the commercial enterprises of all EEC members, avoiding discrimination in favor of the former colonial powers. Upon expiration of the original agreement, Yaounde II was negotiated in 1968–1969, taking effect in 1971. The basic provisions remained the same, but a coordinated investment plan was added.

De Gaulle's policy of regaining French influence in the Third World was not limited to former French Africa but extended globally. This reflected de Gaulle's desire to increase France's role as a great power, and it was also influenced by his failure to gain for France a more independent role within the Western alliance. In the mid-sixties Paris sought better relations with Peking and Havana; intensified French diplomacy with both India and Pakistan; called for the neutralization of Vietnam and castigated Washington's involvement; increased official contacts with Hanoi after breaking off relations with Saigon in 1965; and disassociated France from SEATO and the policy of Britain, Australia, and New Zealand in Malaysia. De Gaulle made two extensive visits to Latin America where he emphasized the cultural affinities between the continent and France, criticized Washington's excessive influence in the Southern Hemisphere, and called for economic diversification in developing countries and market stability for raw materials. De Gaulle was especially anxious to regain French influence in the Arab Near East, an area where French political, economic, and cultural involvement had been extensive until disrupted by the Algerian War and French participation in the invasion of Egypt during the Suez Crisis of 1956. In 1963 Paris restored diplomatic relations with Cairo (which had been broken in 1956), and in the late sixties, especially after the 1967 Six-Day War in the Middle East, France took an increasingly critical attitude toward Israel—clearly hoping to redress the power balance in the Middle East and regain for France a voice in an area of the world where the United States and the Soviet Union had become predominant.

On balance, the symbolic and psychological impact of de Gaulle's Third World policy was as important as its political and economic consequences. France lacked the resources to play the role of a superpower, and de Gaulle's aversion to the United Nations denied France a central role in the parliamentary politics of the General Assembly. French diplomatic successes in the Third World were mostly the result of de Gaulle's personal prestige rather than a reflection of the influence of France as such. It was de Gaulle's genius to convert the handicap of France's relative weakness into an asset of French diplomacy by stressing the empathy he felt with Third World countries in their desire to resist the pervasive global encroachments of the United States and the Soviet Union.

The highly personal diplomatic style of de Gaulle could not be continued by his successor. Although Georges Pompidou followed the major outlines of de Gaulle's policy toward the Third World, this policy became much more flaccid, less dramatic, less personal, and hence—given the psychology of this policy area where appearance was as important as reality—much less effective. Most important perhaps, Pompidou concentrated on the regional interests of France (especially in the Mediterranean area) rather than the grandiose global aims that de Gaulle had entertained.

This shift was especially noticeable in North Africa and the Middle East, where Pompidou pushed French interests intensely in a belated response to the Six-Day War in the Middle East in 1967. In its wake, France needed to choose between Israel and the Arab states. This was not easy. Relations between France and Israel during the Fourth Republic had been close, sustained by their common cause against the Arab countries that reached its peak during the strike against Egypt in 1956. Under de Gaulle French relations with Israel had remained cordial, and France sold a great many arms to Israel— including the Mirage bombers that had given Israel such an edge in the 1967 war. But siding with Israel after the war would have meant the end of French efforts to regain influence in the Middle East. It would have worsened relations with Algeria and other Arab countries at a time when France was trying hard to forge a Mediterranean policy that was internally consistent but would also take into account differences among the states in the area. As Edward Kolodziej has put it:

The problem was to define a policy that would strike yet another precarious balance and satisfy a number of conflicting demands. It would have to be a policy that would (1) maximize France's standing with as many Mediterranean states as possible; (2) slow the rate and minimize the magnitude of superpower penetration of the region; (3) draw advantage from the superpower conflict, including a privileged place for France at the Middle East negotiating table; (4) preserve the form and some substance of the growing alignment between France and the Soviet Union in the Mediterranean and in Europe; and (5) retain the security protection of the United States while combating American attempts to promote its competing political and economic interests to those of France's in both areas. . . . To achieve the Herculean tasks that the de Gaulle and Pompidou governments set for France, three intertwined courses of action were followed: (1) dealignment with Israel and alignment with the Arab position in the Middle East conflict; (2) continued French assertion of a big-power role in settling the conflict and the insulation of the region from superpower contention; and (3) efforts to regroup the western Mediterranean states around French leadership.*

These policies were only marginally effective. With respect to the superpowers' presence in the area, France did not have much leverage. The United States and the Soviet Union were engaged in important bilateral dealings, such as Strategic Arms Limitations Talks and President Nixon's call for superpower sponsorship of the Middle East peace talks in December 1973; they saw no reason to allow France to play a larger role. Nor were the Arab states inclined to enlist French diplomacy for the implementation of their interests.

---

*Edward A. Kolodziej, *French International Policy Under de Gaulle and Pompidou* (Ithaca, N.Y.: Cornell University Press), pp. 490–91.

In the mid-seventies, after the Yom Kippur War and the oil embargo, Soviet influence in the area declined and the United States became the major effective intermediary among Middle Eastern powers. But French influence did not grow. Even the expanding Soviet naval buildup in the Mediterranean hemmed in French maneuverability because it forced France to cooperate more extensively (although unofficially) with NATO naval forces.

France did expand commercial dealings in the Mediterranean area, but even there the French had to take second place to the Germans. Arms sales figured prominently in French exports to the region, both to Israel and the Arab countries, but the political hazards involved greatly complicated French diplomacy in an area that required a delicate juggling of highly diverse interests. Paris needed the support of the United States and the EEC partners for some projects, while other projects involved competition with them. In late 1973, Pompidou called for an emergency meeting of the heads of state and government to deal with the energy crisis and the Arab-Israeli conflict, and the nine EEC members subsequently announced a common position on the Middle East peace negotiations and issued a Dutch-German sponsored declaration on the oil embargo. But these attempts at a coordinated foreign policy with France's European neighbors did not have much impact, and Pompidou found it difficult to enlist the EEC partners for his regional policies, especially since the Europeans wanted to revise the privileges granted to France in the Treaty of Rome regarding its former possessions.

On the whole, the shift in emphasis from de Gaulle's globalism to Pompidou's regionalism did not ease French foreign problems but instead transferred them to a different context. This regional context—the Mediterranean area, and especially the Middle East—reflected many of the political features of the global context. The superpowers were engaged in intense diplomatic rivalry, France's Community partners had interests conflicting with those of France, and the differences among the countries of the area (including the Arab states) were so substantial that a policy designed to appeal to some was bound to offend others. If anything, regional problems were more difficult because they were more specific and could not be dealt with on the plane of lofty generalities. French diplomacy also was oriented toward a more multilateral framework than had been the case under de Gaulle. Pompidou used NATO and the WEU as well as the United Nations, the International Monetary Fund, and EEC structures to further French aims. This had become necessary to lift France from the increased isolation in which the nation found itself at the end of the de Gaulle era.

When President Giscard d'Estaing entered office in 1974, Europe was in the midst of a world economic crisis. This had an effect on French dealings with the Third World as well as with the European Community. Such issues as oil sources, raw material supplies, international monetary arrangements between the developing countries and the industrialized world, and related technical questions required immediate attention and could not be dealt with on the level of purely political considerations. Economic necessities took precedence over political choice. New circumstances required President Giscard to be much more pragmatic than de Gaulle or even Pompidou.

French Third World policy was also complicated by the fact that the enlarged European Community began to speak with a somewhat more coherent voice on Third World problems, especially in the United Nations, which forced France to coordinate policy with other Community members, especially Germany and Britain. (When West Germany was admitted to the United Nations in September 1973, all nine members of the Community were represented there.) The solidarity of the Nine at the United Nations was partial, but the EEC's political status was enhanced and there were more joint statements delivered by the representative of the EEC presidency on behalf of the nine member governments. Group cohesion of the Nine improved, especially on economic topics, when the EEC obtained observer status in the General Assembly and its seven committees in October 1974. Informal consultations among the Nine increased at the United Nations, and although it would be inaccurate to describe the resulting process as a totally coordinated UN policy, it was moving in that direction.

On such specific regional interests as the Middle East, the position of France (along with that of Italy and Ireland) was generally more pro-Arab than the positions of the other Six, reflecting the French attitude that Europe should play a larger role in the area because of important political and economic interests. As a permanent member of the Security Council (along with Britain), France had an opportunity to demonstrate its special status and the other EEC members were not regularly consulted about agenda items of the Security Council. Under Giscard, Paris continued to prize the symbolic representation of France at the UN as a power with "special global responsibilities."

Since much of the dealings between the industrialized world and the developing countries focused on financial and technical aid, equitable pricing arrangements for imports and exports, and other economic matters, the French position had to be coordinated with the German and British position. At the Lomé convention of February 1975, in which the Nine participated along with forty-six developing countries (including twenty-three from the Commonwealth), the Community undertook to provide the African, Caribbean, and Pacific countries with considerable aid. Such assistance was linked to more long-range and fundamental arrangements on trade promotion and trade access. Stabilization of export earnings for Third World countries, which would make them less vulnerable to price fluctuations, was an important measure in this respect. It was difficult for France, however, to play an especially dynamic role in these endeavors because the French monetary position was relatively weak.

Nonetheless, Paris continued to exert considerable influence in Africa, in part because of the significant (if small) French military presence. French troops were fighting rebel troops, supported by Libya, in Chad; French planes were used against the Polisario guerillas (supported by Algeria) in Mauritania; French forces were stationed in Djibouti to help protect it against the designs of Somalia and Ethiopia; and French troops were instrumental in repulsing invading forces in Zaire (formerly part of the Belgian Congo) in the summer of 1978.

8

Foreign Policy and Domestic Politics

"Can one really come to any other conclusion," Alfred Grosser has written, "than that the political life of the Fourth Republic was primarily and basically dominated by foreign policy? . . . The great distinction that one might make is that the Fourth Republic was preoccupied by foreign policy out of necessity, while General de Gaulle's preoccupation was one of taste. But in truth, the fundamental preoccupation with foreign policy was permanent."*

THE FOURTH REPUBLIC, 1946–58

The winners of the 1945 elections and the founders of the Fourth Republic —the Communists, the Socialists, and the Catholic *Mouvement Républicaine Populaire* (MRP)—emerged with a combined following of about 75 percent of the electorate. In subsequent years six major political groupings formed, of approximately equal strength: the Communists, the Socialists, the Radical Socialists, the Christian Democrats (MRP), the traditional conservatives, and the antiparliamentary Right. These groupings interacted in a highly complicated manner—not only because some of them were allies on certain issues while they opposed one another on others, but also because they were divided within themselves.

Throughout the years of the Fourth Republic foreign policy issues were contested intensely, making it extremely difficult for the various French governments to put together a coherent and effective foreign policy program.

---

*Alfred Grosser, *French Foreign Policy Under de Gaulle* (Boston, Mass.: Little, Brown and Co., 1965), p. 2.

Domestic politics were highly sensitive to foreign policy issues because of the nature of the goals themselves and because of the political and institutional disabilities of the Fourth Republic.

These disabilities were severe. Often the governments of the Fourth Republic operated on a narrow base of support, and the National Assembly, although fragmented because of unstable coalitions, was able to act as a powerful check on the executive. As a result it was difficult for governments to make long-range plans and hope to see them implemented. In turn, this gave the bureaucracy, conservative by temperament, an excessive measure of discretion over policies that were contested in the political arena. The bureaucracy, and the nature of the problems to be solved, provided the continuity that politics lacked. Other problems stemmed from the French proportional system of representation, which encouraged divisions among parties supporting generally similar programs. Even a small constituency in a few parts of the country assured representation in the National Assembly, and thus each party could act as a spokesman for highly specific socioeconomic and political preferences. Moreover, special interest groups found it quite easy to exploit a decision-making process that lacked a clear line of accountability. This, in addition to historical factors, inhibited modernization of the economy and equitable distribution of income. Economic conflicts were carried out in a static, deficit-ridden economy that was not sufficiently expansive, with the result that the economic success of one group was generally achieved at the expense of another group. The resulting feelings of frustration and discontent would have been difficult to handle in any society, but socioeconomic conflict in the Fourth Republic became especially politicized because the French state played such a large role in directing and administering the French economy.

Only a relatively small segment of the political spectrum supported the parliamentary regime of the Fourth Republic with any degree of loyalty and conviction. The Left was alienated from the Republic's institutions; the Communists as well as the left-wing Socialists considered them outmoded and incapable of solving socioeconomic and political problems. The extreme Right was equally disaffected, traditionally having been hostile toward democratic institutions and seeing no reason to revise this view in light of the Fourth Republic's ineffectual parliamentary performance. Even the moderate Right questioned at least some of the institutional and ideological bases of the Republic.

Consequently, throughout the life of the Fourth Republic domestic as well as foreign policy programs were pursued that were supported by only a minority, the majority being opposed. This was possible because both majority and minority were internally divided, which made it relatively easy for the "ins" and the "outs" to shift positions and to support some governmental measures but not others. The center, shifting in its own composition, was a highly unstable coalition of interests preoccupied with holding off the Gaullists and other groups on the Right and Communists and Socialists on the Left. It was easier to mobilize the electorate against a particular government or policy than for an alternative. In the electorate as well as among political parties and Assembly deputies, a "negative" majority was always ready to be activated, leading to what Roy Macridis has called "a government founded upon multiple *internal* oppositions and surviving only as long as the oppositional forces that surround it appear to be numerically either potentially or actually stronger."* Moreover, the inability of the government to solve concrete economic and social problems, the widespread disenchantment with the regime as such, and the fact that the multiparty system did not encourage programmatic compromises turned pragmatic political disagreements into ideological contests that further accentuated the cleavages among the French people.

Clearly, the institutions of the Fourth Republic and its political process were not sufficiently secure and resilient to accommodate foreign policy issues on top of domestic ones. Yet internal weaknesses pushed the Fourth Republic even more toward foreign policy matters. Unable to fashion an internal sense of community, the Fourth Republic sought to define itself through foreign policy. Yet far from providing a cohesive force, foreign policy goals, and the problems encountered in their pursuit, further fragmented French society. This was so not only because of the inherent institutional, economic, and political-psychological weaknesses of the Fourth Republic, but also because of the nature of the foreign policy goals themselves.

French foreign policy goals could not be compressed into polarized alternatives because of their complexity. Lack of polarized alternatives is not in itself a negative situation—as the German case indicates, polarization develops when foreign policy goals are strongly incompatible. But in the French case, the absence of polarized foreign policy alternatives meant that a fragmented set of foreign policy choices was placed before an equally fragmented domestic political system. Neither external nor internal politics permitted the simplification of foreign policy issues into clear-cut alternatives. Fragmentation rather than polarization characterized the external as well as internal dimensions of French foreign policy goals.

Security and the European Connection

The contradictions among French foreign policy goals, and the fragmented domestic political response to them, led to a highly complicated pattern of support and opposition on specific issues. The goal of security, and its various ramifications, is a case in point. In 1947–48, the security goal took on an anti-Soviet as well as anti-German dimension. Because there was a real possibility that the French Communist party would seize power in France, and as

*Roy C. Macridis, "Oppositions in France: An Interpretation," *Government and Opposition*, (Spring 1972), p. 170.

it became clear that security policy affected other foreign and domestic issues, the meaning of security itself became problematic and security issues became highly controversial.

The centrality of the security question was reflected in the domestic political arguments over French accession to the Atlantic Pact, German rearmament, and European integration. These issues were of course closely related, and the long debate on the ratification of the Atlantic Pact in the National Assembly (in July 1949) was at the same time a review of French policy toward Germany and Europe. But the proponents of the Atlantic Pact took great pains to deny any connection between these issues so as not to alienate potential supporters. By that time, the Assembly was already suffering from the fragmentation and paralysis that became the characteristic of the Fourth Republic's parliamentary life, and the coalition government that sought ratification of the Atlantic Pact in the Assembly consisted of a rather heterogenous grouping of Socialists, Radicals, and members of the *Mouvement Républicaine Populaire* (MRP) and the *Union Démocratique de la Résistance* (UDSR). The Communists vehemently opposed ratification, but so did the conservatives of the Right, with remarkably similar arguments. Both groups regarded Germany as more dangerous than the Soviet Union, arguing that the United States was rebuilding Germany economically and militarily to the detriment of vital French interests. Proponents of the pact insisted that ratification would in no way mean that Germany would be rearmed in the future, and Foreign Minister Robert Schuman of the MRP specifically denied the possibility that Germany would ever become a member of the pact. Although the Atlantic Pact was ratified with a healthy majority, there was much uneasiness in the Assembly because of the obvious contradictions between the anti-Soviet dimensions of the Atlantic Pact and the primary French concern to control the newly established Federal Republic.

Almost from the beginning of the debate over the future role of Germany and the issue of German rearmament, the possibility of some form of European unification played a considerable role. When the Federal Republic and the Western powers signed the so-called Petersberg Protocol in November 1949—which, among other features, expressed Bonn's desire to participate in a European community, paved the way for Germany to receive Marshall Plan aid, and generally enhanced the international position of the Federal Republic —the reaction in Paris was highly negative. Again, both the Communists and the Right were vehemently opposed, with the Communists castigating the Federal Republic as a reactionary, revanchist regime controlled by German and American finance capital, and the Rightists objecting to what they viewed as a return to a centralized state dominated by an international combine of big industry. Even some French Europeanists had misgivings; they were concerned that by restoring some measure of sovereignty to the Federal Republic, the Petersberg Protocol would become an obstacle to the integration of Germany into a future European structure. Although it was one of the most prominent French Europeanists, the MRP's Robert Schuman, who urged the Assembly to pass the Petersberg Protocol, there was little doubt that most deputies, including backers of the protocol, viewed this development in Franco-German relations with considerable apprehension.

The Schuman Plan for a European Coal and Steel Community

A few months after ratification of the Petersberg Protocol, in May 1950, Foreign Minister Robert Schuman announced his proposal to place French and German coal and steel production under a High Authority in an organization that would be open to other European countries. This proposal, which ultimately led to the creation of the European Coal and Steel Community, had its origin in a highly complex, but generally complementary and reinforcing, set of calculations. The primary motivation was political—above all, the desire to establish a binding framework within which to oversee the revitalization of Germany and Franco-German reconciliation. There were also some persuasive economic arguments for a common market for coal and steel. In the late forties, the French steel industry was in a state of crisis, suffering from lack of markets and sagging prices. Markets were restricted by national borders, and there were some signs that steel manufacturers were looking toward cartel arrangements to safeguard against costly market fluctuations. The French coal industry was in a similar situation.

The Schuman Plan departed radically from the traditional French foreign policy maxim that the only good Germany was a weak Germany, and replaced it with the principle that Franco-German collaboration would benefit the two countries and also serve as the foundation for a federated European order. Considering the Schuman Plan's far-reaching economic and political implications, it is not surprising that the proposal was hotly debated in France. Opponents argued that the German coal and steel industry would be the primary beneficiary, exporting much and importing little, while proponents viewed Franco-German economic relations as complementary and saw great benefits for both countries in an integrated base for economic development.

On the whole, French industry opposed the Schuman Plan. The trade associations of the steel industry and related metallurgical industries, as well as spokesmen for the chemical and engineering industries, small iron and steel producers, and the employers' association, argued that (1) the French coal and steel industry could not compete effectively with Germany unless existing protectionist features remained intact, including the deconcentration program for German industry and Allied control measures; (2) unless social security costs were equalized among the six projected members of the ECSC, French producers would be greatly disadvantaged because of their higher contributions; and (3) the plan would lead to an even more extensive role of the state in the economy.

The Communists attacked the plan as a device to build an economic base for American-German capitalism, from which a revanchist Germany would launch an imperialist war with the connivance of the United States. The right-wing, Gaullist *Rassemblement du Peuple Français* (RPF), thoroughly disaffected because of the weaknesses of the Republic's parliamentary regime, thought that France was no match against an economically powerful, politically aggressive Germany and should therefore negotiate integrative arrangements at a future date from a position of strength.

The major support for the European Coal and Steel Community came from the middle of the political spectrum—the Socialists, the MRP, the Radicals, and the Gaullists. Especially important was the support of Robert Schuman's own MRP. One of the party's major doctrinal commitments was the construction of a Western European federation. Between 1950 and 1954, the MRP sponsored four major plans for European integration: the Schuman Plan, the Pleven Plan for a European Defense Community, the plan for a European Political Community, and the Pflimlin Plan for pooling European agricultural markets. The party was determined to find a European solution to the problems that had divided France and Germany for such a long time and at such great costs.

The proponents of the Schuman Plan marshaled a good deal of public support, including that of influential news media and the federalist organizations, and they managed to carry the day in the Assembly. The government made ratification of the plan an issue of confidence, and in December 1951, the treaty was passed by a vote of 376 to 240, with 11 abstentions. The Communists and RPF voted against the treaty, but the Independent Republicans and the Peasant party split in their response to the treaty, assuring a comfortable margin for its passage in the Assembly. The Socialists, although no longer participating in the government at the time, also voted for the plan.

The Pleven Plan for a European Defense Community

In October 1950, a few months after Robert Schuman had proposed the European Coal and Steel Community and categorically denied the possibility of German rearmament, French Premier René Pleven proposed the establishment of an integrated European army incorporating a number of small German units. This reversal of policy, which the government justified by the outbreak of the Korean War, was made largely in response to American demands for Germany's speedy rearmament and demands by French Europeanists for extension of European integration from the economic sphere into defense and military areas of common concern.

In view of the Pleven Plan's military and political implications, it is not surprising that the idea of a European Defense Community evoked an intense controversy in France. The issues involved were similar to those raised in the debate over the Schuman Plan. The French government argued that the Schuman Plan and the Pleven Plan were complementary elements of the same European policy. But the tie-up between the ECSC and the EDC did not advance the government's case, especially when it became apparent that German membership in the EDC would lead not only to German rearmament but also to the restoration of German sovereignty. There were other obstacles to French acceptance of the EDC proposal: the Saar problem was not yet resolved; the size of the German contribution to the EDC was an issue between France and Germany; Cold War tensions seemed to have abated somewhat, making the need for German rearmament appear less pressing; Britain, although prevailed upon to maintain troops on the Continent, would not participate in the EDC because of its supranational features; and the French war in Indochina became an important consideration since it appeared that Moscow would be prepared to help arrange an acceptable armistice if France rejected the EDC.

From the beginning of the EDC debate in the National Assembly it was apparent that the idea of a European army was even more controversial than the idea of a European coal and steel community. More damaging than the attacks from the Right and Left was the gradual erosion of support in the middle. In the four years following the announcement of the Pleven Plan, each change in the makeup of the Assembly and the governments emerging from it was accompanied by a drop in support for the EDC. Prime Minister Mendès-France further weakened the EDC idea by proposing a compromise version of the treaty calling for suspension of the supranational features of the document for eight years. The modifications demanded by Mendès-France were unacceptable to the United States, Britain, and Germany as well as to the staunchest French supporters of the EDC. As a result, the treaty lacked the unequivocal support of even the French government.

The EDC proposal suffered above all from the fact that practically no major French political group supported the idea of a European army on positive grounds. The treaty's opponents objected to the EDC either because it spelled the end of a French national army (the main thrust of the Gaullists' argument), or because it meant rearming Germany (a prospect abhorrent to Communists and Progressives as well as to some Conservatives, Radicals, and Gaullists). Even some Europeanists were unenthusiastic about the EDC once its integrative features had been watered down. Most basically perhaps, it was the weakness of France—expressed in the fear of Germany and resentment of the American role in European affairs—that stood in the way of a more positive response to European integration in general and the EDC in particular. Thus when the EDC treaty was finally defeated in the Assembly in August 1954, it came as no surprise.

It was somewhat ironic that the construction of an alternative context for rearming West Germany—that of the Western European Union and the North Atlantic Treaty Organization—met with relatively few difficulties in the National Assembly. The NATO alternative for Germany's rearmament fragmented both the coalition that had favored the EDC and the one that had fought it. The Communists and the extreme Rightists were as opposed as ever to any kind of German rearmament, but the Gaullists were somewhat reassured because the French army remained intact under the new arrangement. The Socialists and the majority of the Radicals and the Gaullists saw the NATO solution as a device that would at least benefit the cohesion of the Atlantic alliance, and the MRP gradually moved from a posture of abstention to one of lukewarm support. At the end of December, the Assembly somewhat unenthusiastically approved the accession of Germany to NATO and the extension and modification of the Brussels Treaty.

The European Economic Community

The lengthy international negotiations over the establishment of the Common Market (EEC)—from the Messina Conference of June 1955 until the ratification of the EEC treaty by the French National Assembly in July 1957—had a beneficial effect. The economic and political pros and cons had a chance to be aired thoroughly in each country, making for a much more rational discussion than the debates over the Coal and Steel Community or the European Defense Community. In France, especially, there was a marked contrast between the moderation of the EEC debate and the divisive and acrimonious controversy over ECSC and EDC.

There were several additional reasons for the more favorable reception of the EEC in France. In the first place, in the mid-fifties the French economy as a whole was enjoying a remarkable upswing. Although the economic revival was unevenly distributed, it still created confidence that the French could hold their own against future EEC partners, especially Germany. Productivity was rising, in part because of the reforms that had modernized central sectors of the economy; the ECSC experiment seemed to be working, after some initial disappointments; and the French managers and technocrats who were committed to modernizing the French economy did not mind seeing it opened up to international competition, especially since the Common Market would primarily hurt the more inefficient French producers who had for so long enjoyed protectionist arrangements. This development was, in its way, as remarkable as the much more publicized German "economic miracle."

French industry was not unanimous in supporting the Common Market, however. Although the steel industry favored the EEC because it would complement the already existing integrative coal and steel arrangement, the metal-processing industries were afraid of German competition, arguing for the need to equalize welfare costs and protect French industries at least temporarily. Some industries, such as paper and automobile manufacturing and electrical engineering, were confident of their competitive position. Others, such as the chemical industry, were less worried about competition from future Common Market partners than fearful of losing protection against competition from the United States and Britain. This uneven but on the whole positive attitude toward the Common Market on the part of French industry was reinforced by the position of French agriculture. Agricultural production was high and could be pushed even higher, the national market for foodstuffs was unlikely to expand, and the other Common Market members, especially Germany, were heavy importers of agricultural products. After gaining assurances that the Common Market would develop a common agricultural policy, French agricultural interests supported the EEC wholeheartedly.

Another important reason for the relative moderation of the EEC debate in France was the skill with which the government involved the major employers' and employees' organizations and groups committed to a united Europe in all stages of the EEC negotiations. Some of these organizations had an international membership of prominent politicians and industrial leaders, and they in a sense lobbied for the EEC idea in the various European capitals. The alliance among many economic interest groups, their spokesmen in the political parties, and devoted Europeanists made for powerful support of the EEC treaty.

Adding to the favorable atmosphere toward the EEC was the fact that the political climate in the National Assembly and the makeup of the government during critical stages of the deliberations were more conducive to French participation in European projects than had been the case earlier. The government of Guy Mollet that was established on the basis of the January 1956 elections (which had given the Socialists the balance of power in the Assembly) was generally pro-Europe; the Gaullists had suffered severe losses; and the MRP, although not represented in Mollet's cabinet, could be counted on to support the Common Market as a new step toward the united Europe the party sought.

During the early summer of 1956, another integrative structure came before the Assembly for approval: Euratom, the common market for nuclear materials and equipment and coordinating agency for nuclear research and development. This raised a debate in the Assembly, with the Communists and Gaullists arguing against Euratom because it would primarily benefit Germany. But when the government gave assurances that Euratom would not hamper the French nuclear weapons program the Gaullists supported the arrangement. During the final ratification debate over Euratom and the EEC in July 1957, all Assembly commissions except one submitted favorable recommendations to the plenum. The discussions, although extensive and searching, were rational and lacking in the emotionalism that had character-ized previous controversies over European matters and Franco-German rela-tions, and the treaties were ratified by a vote of 342 to 239.

Decolonization and the Domestic Political Process

In the decade following the onset of the Cold War, during which France was compelled to revise its goals of security and recovery, the Fourth Republic was further strained by the divisive issues of decolonization and the Algerian question. The resulting political controversies proved so incapacitating that they finally led to the collapse of the Republic itself, not only because French foreign policy problems seemed insoluble but also because they touched upon the essence of France as a nation.

The costly war in Indochina, which lasted from December 1946 until July 1954, evoked intense domestic controversy when it became apparent that the French forces were making little military progress and the purposes for French involvement became increasingly questionable. Initially, efforts to gain a military victory over the Vietminh were not opposed in France—except for the Communists—but by 1953, when it had become clear that a military victory was unobtainable, pressures began to mount for a negotiated settle-ment. The major spokesman for such a settlement was Radical leader Pierre Mendès-France, long a critic of French policy in Indochina, who advocated disengagement and genuine independence for Indochina. Mendès-France narrowly missed becoming premier in June 1953, and although the govern-ment formed by Joseph Laniel (Independent) also favored a more flexible colonial policy, Foreign Minister Georges Bidault opposed the granting of independence and instead proposed association within the French Union. This solution was attractive to many deputies of the Right and Center, but it was opposed on the moderate Left and even within Bidault's own party, the MRP.

When Pierre Mendès-France became prime minister in June 1954, it was understood that his support in the Assembly was based solely on the premise that he would bring the war in Indochina to a speedy conclusion. He had no other mandate. Mendès-France undertook this task—a thankless one, which ended his political career—and arranged for French withdrawal from Indo-china in the summer of 1954. He also disengaged France from Tunisia and Morocco, which gained independence in 1955 on the basis of negotiations begun in 1954. But these moves were opposed by deputies of the Right and Center, many of whom feared that Mendès-France's dealings with Morocco and Tunisia would undermine the French position in Algeria.

Pressures continued to build for reform of the *Union française* framework, and once the Indochina war was settled the National Assembly began to concentrate on taking appropriate steps in that direction. The *loi-cadre* passed by large majorities in both Chamber and Senate in June 1956, although there was a good deal of disagreement over how it should be implemented.

Algeria, Suez, and the Demise of the Fourth Republic

The Algerian problem did not become a major electoral issue until the 1956 elections, although it had occasioned much debate prior to that. Some political figures favored the full political, economic, and social integration of Algeria and France, while others argued that full integration was unworkable because of cultural differences, the economic costs for metropolitan France, and the political chaos of having Muslim deputies in the National Assembly. The other alternative—independence—was unacceptable to the Center and Right as well as to many voters, and even left-of-center politicians found it difficult to abandon a million compatriots to the uncertainties that would have followed from granting sovereignty to Algeria. As a result, the National Assembly passed a series of "framework laws" that satisfied no one. They were essentially designed to perpetuate French sovereignty and offered little of real substance to the Muslims who remained second-class citizens in all areas of public life.

The struggle in Algeria was a struggle between two rival nationalisms. This meant that the legislative solutions attempted by the National Assembly were bound to fail since they were the result of mutual concessions and compromises among the political parties in the Assembly, while the two rival nationalisms were not willing to compromise. At the same time, the moral and political ambiguities of the Algerian war divided French public opinion even further; many voters who shared viewpoints on other important issues could not agree on the Algerian issue. This fragmentation was reflected in party politics, with the result that the political process of the Fourth Republic became even more ineffectual and divisive. Between November 1954 and May 1958 five cabinets were voted out of office, and with each crisis it became more difficult to put together a new coalition or to develop specific policy proposals that might work as well as attract political support.

The Mendès-France government lost power in February 1955 because of economic issues, loss of support by the Independents and nationalists, who accused Mendès-France of undermining the French position in Algeria as a result of his "weakness" in Tunisia and Morocco, and continuing resentment over Mendès-France's role in presiding over the French collapse in Indochina. After much controversy and more cabinet reshufflings during 1955, Algeria became the most prominent issue in the 1956 elections. But the political alignments in the Assembly and the government had been so complicated and transitory that it was difficult to assign responsibility for specific policies. Matters were further complicated by the fact that two new groups had emerged on the political scene. The Radical-Socialist party had split before the election and a majority, led by Mendès-France, had expelled Edgar Faure, the premier. Faure reacted by transforming the *Rassemblement des gauches républicaines* (RGR) from a coordinating committee for Radical Groups into a national party that appealed primarily to the party's right wing. Pierre Poujade's *Union et Fraternité Française* (UFF) also became an important political party, emerging from a tax reform organization that had appealed largely to French shopkeepers and small entrepreneurs. All this made for a great deal of confusion.

In the 1956 election the "Republican Front" won a moderate victory, with the Socialists (SFIO) and the Mendès-France Radicals its key elements. Although the Front was formed largely on the basis of shared dissatisfaction with the Algerian question, it could not produce a coherent Algerian policy. No specific mandate on Algeria had emerged from the election, and the Republican Front crumbled. Throughout 1956 and 1957 the debate became increasingly intense. The alternatives—integration, independence, or partition—all had their committed proponents and equally committed opponents, but none of the proposals could rally a majority either in the Assembly or among the public—in part because these alternatives were too clear-cut and radical. Consequently none of them were seriously considered by successive governments. Instead, "assimilation" was advocated, unrealistic as it had become.

Even more unrealistic was the assumption that the Algerian problem could be resolved by toppling Egypt's Abdel Gamel Nasser. The abortive Suez Canal campaign of 1956 did not initially hurt the government, under the SFIO's Guy Mollet, as a wave of nationalist sentiment swept over the country. When Mollet was turned out of office in May 1957, the immediate cause was economic issues rather than the Algerian War—although to be sure the two were closely related. By that time the Independents and the Right had become more and more disturbed by Mollet's economic and social policy, although they still supported him on Algeria, and the Socialists' tightrope act of appeasing the Right on either socioeconomic policy or Algeria had become difficult to sustain.

As the Suez debacle came to be perceived as a deeply humiliating experience for France, and the situation in Algeria deteriorated (with both sides increasingly resorting to cruelty and the government obviously incapable of keeping the military and popular forces in Algeria under control), a deepening and permanent crisis of the political process took hold. Mollet was succeeded by Maurice Bourgès-Maunoury, a young Radical who sought to continue the balancing act by keeping the hard-lining Robert Lacoste as governor-general in Algeria and by endorsing a program of social and educational reform. But he could not rally sufficient support for his policies, and his government was overturned after three months when his proposal for a revised "framework law" for Algeria was rejected by the Assembly. It took five weeks until a new government was formed in November 1957 under another young Radical,

Félix Gaillard. But this government, although it included the MRP and the Independents, had not significantly extended its basis of support since the backing of the Independents and Christian Democrats had been required all along. At that point, the very foundation of the Fourth Republic had become so fundamentally undermined that it could not be salvaged.

THE FIFTH REPUBLIC

When Charles de Gaulle returned to power in May 1958—after twelve years in political exile—he was determined to restore France to the position of power and respect he saw as the country's natural right and destiny. Ending the Algerian War was indispensable for this goal because it would heal France internally and allow Paris to champion the principle of national self-determination—a principle that could be applied to the Third World as well as to the transatlantic and East and West European alliances.

The relative ease with which de Gaulle managed to extricate France from Algeria was in part made possible by his own enigmatic and ambiguous stand before returning to power. While the rebellious army officers in Algeria who had backed de Gaulle expected that he would continue the war and bring it to a successful conclusion, political leaders in Paris expected the general to terminate the war and then return to retirement.

From the very beginning de Gaulle viewed his presidency as resting on the support of the French people, articulated through national referenda and presidential and parliamentary elections. This allowed him to dominate the institutional arrangements of the Fifth Republic and guide French foreign policy with a sense of purpose and direction that had been lacking in the Fourth Republic. According to the new constitution the president, elected by popular vote, wielded extensive legal-institutional powers, acted as commander-in-chief of the armed forces, designated his ministers of government, convened and presided over the Council of Ministers, negotiated international treaties, and appointed all high-level civil servants, officers, and judges —to mention only the most important of his powers and functions. De Gaulle also severely limited the discretionary powers of his successive prime ministers—Michel Debré, Georges Pompidou, and Maurice Couve de Murville.

As a result, during de Gaulle's eleven years in office he almost single-handedly determined the course of French foreign policy, without any real opposition. In none of the five referenda and four parliamentary elections held during his tenure was an important foreign policy issue at stake, with the exception of Algeria. Generally, the Gaullist party (which changed names several times) dominated the Assembly throughout the de Gaulle years, with the help of Valéry Giscard d'Estaing's Independent Republicans (although the Gaullists only had an absolute majority following the 1962 and 1968 elections). The Communist Party was remarkably moderate in its opposition largely because relations between Moscow and Paris had improved considerably. The Socialists also found it difficult to come up with an alternative foreign policy program. As a result only once, when the nuclear strike force was discussed in the National Assembly in 1960, did a majority turn against the government's proposals, opposing them as too costly.

De Gaulle's grip on foreign policy decisions was tight. At times his own ministers were kept in the dark about important impending decisions; the Assembly carried on no real foreign policy debates in its plenary meetings; the Senate, which tended to be anti-Gaullist, had only limited advisory powers; and public opinion was either indifferent to foreign affairs or, when opposed to government policy, was ignored (for example, on the *force de frappe* and the refusal to accede to the nuclear test ban treaty).

Even though there was little institutionalized opposition to de Gaulle's foreign policy program, there were areas of public policy in which foreign policy was closely connected with domestic issues. Such matters were closely contested because of their domestic dimension. For instance, throughout the sixties one reason why French planners sought to restrain private consumption and increase investments was to encourage economic growth so that French defense policy could be financed. This contributed to the climate of dissatisfaction that de Gaulle had to deal with toward the end of his tenure. The economic discontent that helped cause the May 1968 turmoil, and hence de Gaulle's resignation, can in large part be attributed to this mixed foreign-domestic type of policy. In the context of economic interdependence it became more and more difficult to distinguish between domestic and foreign aspects of economic and monetary issues. The various Economic Plans put forth during the Fifth Republic affected foreign policy as much as domestic policy since they dealt with trade, national and international monetary matters, agricultural policy, investment policy, and so forth. In other words, the government pursued a variety of policies (with both foreign and domestic policy considerations in mind) that were not contested as foreign policy issues but had a great impact on domestic politics and economics and were contested in that context. Contests over the domestic aspects of such issues were at the same time contests over their foreign policy aspects, whether or not this connection was always made clear during political debates. This point cannot be stressed too strongly, because the situation held true in the post-de Gaulle era as well and played a large role in shaping the domestic debate over "foreign" policy issues.

The Presidency of Georges Pompidou

The April 1969 referendum that was the immediate cause of de Gaulle's resignation was not called over matters of foreign policy as such—nor was the subsequent election, which brought Georges Pompidou to the presidency, fought over foreign policy questions. Nevertheless, foreign policy played a significant role in de Gaulle's decision to resign. As we have mentioned, the May riots resulted from economic problems generated in part by foreign policy-related programs. In addition, overextension of French resources, as well as the blow dealt to de Gaulle's Eastern policy by the invasion of Czechoslovakia, contributed heavily to his decision to resign.

Georges Pompidou had been groomed as de Gaulle's successor for several years. His prestige, although not to be compared to de Gaulle's, was considerable. Aside from differences in personality and temperament, there were some significant political differences between de Gaulle and Pompidou. Pompidou wanted to create a dynamic modern conservative party that would deal with pressing practical issues related to the goal of economic prosperity, rather than grandiose foreign policy projects. Other Gaullists, such as Michel Debré, followed a "purer" Gaullist line and sought to keep intact de Gaulle's vision as much as possible. Thus on the whole the Gaullist party was less cohesive under Pompidou than before. Nevertheless, the party still appealed to Centrist elements and continued to be allied with the Independent Republicans.

However, as time went on a gradual polarization of political forces became visible. The division between the Gaullist-conservative Right and the Socialist-Communist Left had already existed during the regime of de Gaulle. But de Gaulle's style of governing and his personal prestige, along with his deft manipulations of the Republic's institutions, allowed him to transcend parliamentary politics and appeal directly to the French voter through the use of plebiscites. But Pompidou could not place himself above party politics in this way. As parliamentary politics returned to normal and Pompidou had to deal on that level, the divisions between Left and Right became more obvious.

This return to more traditional party politics was also dictated by practical reasons. The concrete issues that Pompidou had to face could not be resolved with lofty generalities. Pompidou was forced to make specific decisions on economic and other domestic matters, and found it much more difficult than de Gaulle not to get involved in the prosaic, day-to-day process of parliamentary and party politics to obtain support for his policies. Pompidou had to take account of the various factions with his own party, for in the early seventies the Gaullists who favored economic planning lost some ground to the more laissez-faire oriented, conservative Gaullists. Pompidou also found it necessary to become politically aligned with elements of other parties. He took three Centrists into the cabinet and reinstalled Giscard d'Estaing of the Republican Independents as finance minister. His two prime ministers, Jacques Chaban-Delmas and Pierre Messmer, and their cabinets represented Gaullists, Democratic Centrists (led by Jacques Duhamel), and Independent Republicans (led by Giscard d'Estaing). In 1973, after the Gaullists lost the parliamentary majority that had been won in the landslide victory of 1968, Pompidou was forced to accommodate opposition Centrist leader Jean Lecanuet on some domestic issues.

Political realignments in the Assembly reflected the fact that the Right was not nearly as cohesive as it had been. This contrasted with the relative harmony on the Left, which was based on the electoral collaboration between the Communists and the Socialists. The parties had thereby gained respectable election results in 1967 and 1973, and they continued their partnership in backing the controversial Common Program of 1972. Among other items, the Common Program called for nationalization of all private banks and nine large companies, including two subsidiaries of United States–headquartered multinationals—ITT and Honeywell. As it turned out this alliance was not as solid as it seemed to be, collapsing in the election campaign of 1978. But in the early seventies, the unity of purpose on the Left provided a distinct contrast with the growing lack of cohesiveness on the Right.

The impact of these political shifts on Pompidou's foreign policy program was indirect. Pompidou's change of emphasis from a global orientation to a more regional one, efforts to improve relations with the United States (which had begun in the last year of de Gaulle's presidency), and the decision not to block British entry into the Common Market did not meet much opposition. Pompidou had impressive Gaullist credentials, and he left intact de Gaulle's legacy of an independent French defense effort. This policy appealed to traditional elements in his own party as well as to the Communists, and was tolerated by the Independent Republicans and Centrists who were more concerned with practical socioeconomic and monetary issues. The Independent Republicans in particular were interested in social and economic reform, hoping to create a "third" political force in the center between the Gaullists and the Left. They favored European confederation and persistently sought to push Pompidou toward a more positive European policy. On the whole, though, Pompidou succeeded in gaining support for his modified Gaullist foreign policy program—especially since the Assembly did not really play an important role in either setting guidelines for foreign policy or directing its daily conduct.

The Presidency of Giscard d'Estaing

Pompidou's failing health, and subsequent death, resulted in a regrouping of domestic political forces contesting for national leadership. In the 1974 presidential elections, the shifting political alignments of the previous years became solidified behind various candidates. Jacques Chaban-Delmas became the compromise choice of the Gaullist party after he edged out four others representing various spectrums of the party. Chaban-Delmas also gained the endorsement of some smaller groupings outside the party. Giscard d'Estaing was backed by his own Republican Independents and also received the support of smaller groups, including Lecanuet's *Centre démocrate* and a faction of the *Mouvement réformateur*. The Left nominated the Socialists' François Mitterrand as its candidate, with the Communists agreeing that Mitterrand would not run his campaign on the controversial platform of the 1972 Common Program. The two candidates who led the first ballot were Giscard and Mitterrand; in the second vote Giscard won narrowly, helped by Gaullist support. The campaign focused primarily on social policy, the economy, inflation, the Left's economic sense of responsibility, and related questions. Foreign policy was not an important issue, although in some campaign speeches Giscard argued that the resolution of socioeconomic problems required a more positive attitude toward the European Community.

The narrow majority of votes that brought Giscard to power in May 1974 could not be translated into a parliamentary majority. There remained a heterogeneous coalition in which the three components—the Gaullists, the Independent Republicans, and the Centrists—held conflicting views on a number of issues. During Giscard's presidency, the Fifth Republic became much more politicized than under his predecessors. De Gaulle's claim to authority and legitimacy had rested in his person, he had sought to embody a vision of France rather than advocate a specific program, and he had tried to place the governing of France above partisan politics. The supreme reflection of these characteristics of Gaullist leadership was in the area of foreign policy. After de Gaulle's death, Pompidou became the caretaker of the Gaullist movement. Although still powerful because of its political influence and its hold on the imagination, Gaullism became subject to fragmentation and dissent. With Giscard's presidency the Gaullist party began to look more like a traditional political party—though it had not yet fully developed the habits of thought and conduct, as well as the self-image, that characterized a modern, interest-oriented political party. No doubt, the fact that the president himself was not of the Gaullist party, although he had held cabinet posts under both de Gaulle and Pompidou, contributed to the transformation of Gaullism from a movement to a traditional political party. The change was underlined in August 1976 when Giscard replaced the Gaullist Jacques Chirac, his first prime minister, with Raymond Barre. Although this move was not caused by differences of policy as much as personal rivalry and election strategy, it meant nonetheless that for the first time under the Fifth Republic neither the president nor the prime minister were Gaullists. Giscard's action also emphasized his commitment to a pro-European policy since Barre had served for six years on the EEC Commission and had also been its vice president. (This did not greatly upset the Gaullists; Barre, although a Europeanist, was not an Atlanticist, and he had enjoyed good relations with de Gaulle.)

The transformation of Gaullism was coupled with a very broad development that affected many of the industrialized societies of Western Europe: economic and monetary interdependence, and the consolidation of the European Community, made it increasingly difficult to distinguish between foreign and domestic issues because they interlocked so extensively. At the same time, defense policy (always a supremely political instrument for

France) receded into the background compared to economic and monetary policy because a military confrontation in Europe seemed more and more unlikely and because defense policy had little utility in the day-to-day conduct of international negotiations and bureaucratic decision making. Bread-and-butter economic and monetary issues became predominant and required specific governmental programs. These programs affected the various socioeconomic groupings in France differently and were therefore contested on the political scene as domestic socioeconomic issues intricately connected with international events rather than as foreign policy issues in the more traditional meaning of the term.

Both these developments—the transformation of Gaullism and the "domestication" of foreign policy issues—affected Giscard almost from the beginning of his presidency. Giscard inherited serious economic and monetary problems and had great difficulty solving them. The French economy was drawn into the worldwide recession, and although Giscard applied a variety of fiscal and monetary measures, the economy remained sluggish. The government primed the economy and halted the decline in growth rates, but this did not much alleviate unemployment, and led to high budgetary deficits, a deteriorating trade balance and payments balance, and an even higher rate of inflation. Inflation and balance-of-payments difficulties forced the government to withdraw the franc once again from the European currency snake, in March 1976 (it had been withdrawn before in January 1974). This resulted in the depreciation of the franc, which in turn had an additional inflationary impact. The control of inflation became essential, and the so-called Barre Plan of September 1976 (named after Raymond Barre, who had become prime minister and finance minister the month before, after having served as minister of trade) called for a three-month price freeze, higher taxes, governmental guidelines for wage and price increases, more stringent exchange controls, and several other related measures.

Although these steps arrested "stagflation" (the economic problem of stagnation coupled with inflation) and improved the balance of payments, Giscard's governing coalition suffered a severe setback in the municipal elections of 1977. This led to a reshuffling of the cabinet amid renewed fears that a Left coalition (although strained by squabbles over the issue of nationalization) would gain a majority in the 1978 elections. This weakened Giscard's position.

Since Giscard's political difficulties were largely caused by economic problems, they were at least in part foreign policy problems; and their solution depended on the economic policy of Germany (France's largest trading partner), the OPEC countries' oil pricing policies, and changes in the whole complex of relationships that characterize economic interdependence. But Giscard had to deal with more traditional foreign policy issues as well. The Gaullists in the Assembly scrutinized foreign policy more intensely than before (former foreign minister Maurice Couve de Murville was chairman of the most important foreign policy committee), and although the Gaullists generally shied away from attacking Giscard on specific issues they criticized his general orientation as overly conciliatory toward the European Community and the United States. Many Gaullists opposed Giscard's support of a European parliament based on direct elections (which eventually took place in the summer of 1979), arguing that France would lose its independence and unity and that a more integrated Europe would be dominated by Washington, via Brussels. The Communists also opposed direct elections to a European parliament (as did a small minority of Socialists), but the idea was favored by Independent Republicans, Centrists, Radicals, Reformists, and a majority of Socialists.

Giscard's defense policy was especially problematic to the Gaullists. The revisions of French defense policy announced in 1975 and 1976 (especially the concept of an "enlarged sanctuarization" and the increased role of conventional forces) implied too close a cooperation with NATO and a weakening of French independence, they felt. The Communists joined the Gaullists in criticizing the revamping of French strategic doctrine, but the Military Plan embodying the new policy had no difficulty passing the Assembly. The Socialists waffled on the defense issue—in large part because they wanted to downplay defense policy, which was one of the most ambiguous items in their Common Program with the Communists. As it was, the Socialists were seriously at odds with the Communists on European policy. When the rift between them became wider in the fall of 1977, the immediate occasion— disagreement over the extent of nationalization—was as much an issue of European policy, because of its transnational impact, as it was an issue of domestic policy.

Since party alignments and cleavages were different depending on whether the question at hand involved purely domestic issues, traditional foreign policy issues, or mixed domestic-foreign policy issues, a highly complex pattern of support and opposition developed. On traditional foreign policy issues—defense, Atlanticism, fear of German predominance in Europe —no clear polarization was visible between Left and Right. In fact, there was a remarkable similarity of viewpoints on some issues. On purely domestic issues, however, and the mixed domestic-foreign policy issues that affected socioeconomic and monetary-fiscal programs, the cleavage between Left and Right was sharp. At the same time, the Communists and Socialists were divided on some aspects of these programs. The center, which Giscard sought to occupy and enlarge with his own party and its coalition partners, was forced into a delicate balancing act in order to maintain its own internal equilibrium and to extend itself toward the Left as well as the Right for electoral purposes. Different configurations of consensus and opposition developed, depending on what kind of foreign policy issue was at stake and on what connections were visible between foreign and domestic policy programs.

This delicate balancing gained for Giscard an impressive election victory in the spring of 1978, giving the Center-Right coalition a healthy majority in the Assembly. (The presidency itself was not at stake in the election since Giscard's term of office extended to 1981.) The Left's Common Program, which called for extensive nationalization of French industry and inflationary social programs, was decisively defeated, splitting the Communist-Socialist electoral alliance amid mutual recriminations. The election also weakened the influence of the Gaullist party and could be interpreted as an endorsement of the middle course that Giscard had long advocated. The *Union pour la Démocratie Française* (UDF), a loose group of parties supporting Giscard, received only slightly fewer votes than the Gaullists, breaking the Gaullists' long-standing hold over the Assembly. Although foreign policy issues per se did not figure prominently in the election, the solidification of Giscard's domestic political base could be expected to strengthen his foreign policy program as well.

BRITAIN

9

Security
and the
Western Alliance

Compared to a shattered Germany and a humiliated France, Britain emerged from World War II relatively unscathed. Victorious, the British could still have faith in their institutions and look upon themselves as a major force in world politics, one of the Big Three powers responsible for piecing together a new international system. The elements of continuity in British power and policy were impressive. Clement Attlee's postwar Labour government inherited long-term global commitments and an ability to deploy military force anywhere in the world, work continued on the creation of a British nuclear force, and British diplomacy was instrumental in organizing the Atlantic states behind the NATO alliance.

By the late forties some observers, adhering to the notion of continuity, saw Britain pursuing three security roles as (1) the center of a colonial empire and Commonwealth spanning five continents, (2) a major European power shoring up a crude political and military balance on the European continent, and (3) an Atlantic power with special ties to the United States. In 1948 Winston Churchill articulated this triadic commitment—what he called the Three Circles Doctrine—in almost poetic terms:

I feel the existence of three great circles among the free nations and democracies. . . . The first circle for us is naturally the British Commonwealth and Empire, with all that that comprises. Then there is also the English-speaking world in which we, Canada and the other British Dominions, and the United States play so important a part. And finally, there is United Europe. These three majestic circles are co-existent and if they are linked together there is no force or combination which could overthrow them or even challenge them. Now if you think of the three inter-linked circles you will see that we are the only country which has a great part in every one of them. We stand

177

in fact at the very point of junction and here is this island at the very center of the seaways and perhaps the airways also; we have the opportunity of joining them all together.*

This was obviously a parochial view: Britain alone had a place in all three circles (including a voice in a "United Europe" of which it would not be a member), and London was therefore entitled to a central role in international politics. The continuity of British policy distilled a durable configuration of global power.

But just as there were elements of continuity in British policy, there were also sources of profound change in the postwar world itself—in the rise of the superpowers, the growing political consciousness of the colonial areas, and the lingering economic effects of a half century of international turmoil.

First, although Britain was one of the Big Three and although British policymakers experienced no cathartic shocks that would cause them to change their fundamental outlook, the war years in fact saw a radical transformation of Britain's position vis-à-vis the other powers. By 1943 the United States had become the preeminent Allied partner, and at the end of the war two great extra-European powers dominated the international system and redefined its basic rules. A divided Europe became simply part of the global balance between Washington and Moscow. Britain occupied the eccentric position of being no match for the United States or the Soviet Union (which posed the major threat to British security after 1945), yet at the same time wielding far more power than any country outside the Big Three. London's role guaranteed it a wide range of continuing responsibilities, but without the incentive to reevaluate its responsibilities and world role, as had been forced upon the defeated and humiliated lesser powers.

Second, it quickly became evident that Britain's future as an imperial power would be circumscribed by the growth of nationalism in Asia and Africa and by a wave of anticolonialism in world public opinion. India and Pakistan gained independence in 1947, an event that greatly weakened the British position east of Suez; Burma and Ceylon became independent shortly afterward, and in 1957 the grant of independence to Ghana (formerly the Gold Coast) began the dissolution of the Crown's tropical African possessions. These developments were largely anticipated in London (as we shall see in chapter 11), and Britain—unlike France—withdrew from its possessions gracefully. Still, London at first assumed a large residue of responsibility for peacekeeping within the Commonwealth, and this responsibility occasionally conflicted with—or drew resources from—NATO commitments. Fortunately, with the exception of the 1962 Sino-Indian confrontation no member of the Commonwealth faced a serious postwar threat from a major power, and British governments avoided the kind of prolonged entanglements that en-

*Speech at Conservative Party Conference, Llandudno, 9 October 1948.

snared the French and Americans in Indochina. By 1971 Britain had abandoned its global role. If the events that brought this about were relatively peaceful, the magnitude of the transformation was nonetheless immense.

The third set of factors affecting Britain's international status was principally economic. The experience of two world wars and the Great Depression in a span of only thirty-one years stretched British resources to the limit and hastened the country's economic decline (which, in terms of the industrial competition with Germany and America, had actually begun at the turn of the century). During World War II the British were forced to liquidate extensive foreign investments in order to pay for the war effort, investments that had been an important source of external income. In 1945 the nation faced the awesome task of converting to a peacetime economy, rebuilding an independent base of foreign exchange earnings, and rejuvenating an aging and lackluster industrial structure. In addition, British political leaders had promised the public expensive social welfare reforms once the war was over. These programs were funded out of potential investment capital and at a cost of reduced government expenditures elsewhere.

Thus, the tug-of-war between limited resources and broad responsibilities that characterized all of postwar British foreign policy was more than simply a matter of competing external demands. It was also a matter of the competing demands of foreign and domestic policy. The allocation of resources in postwar Britain was heavily influenced by the rise of a consumer economy and welfare state, by broadly based efforts to modernize the economy, and by the government's policy of maintaining the international reserve role of the pound sterling (we shall consider sterling policy in detail in chapter 10). Although foreign policy issues seldom figured decisively in British electoral politics or became the major criteria of domestic political cleavages (in contrast to West Germany), domestic economic demands reduced the availability of resources for defense and foreign endeavors, often at precisely those times when international tensions were increasing. In turn, British domestic life was inevitably influenced by defense expenditures (which disrupted economic planning in the early fifties) and by the stringencies of the international economic system, especially the international weakness of sterling and the continued rise of more efficient industrial competition in Germany, Japan, and the United States.

THE "COGNITIVE LAG" CONCEPT

An important controversy centers around the extent of the "cognitive lag" generated in the British foreign policy and defense establishments by the gap between Britain's weakened international position and the fact that in the forties and fifties the country could still obviously lay claim to great-power status. To what extent did the British foreign policy elite, clinging to a timeworn global outlook, misunderstand or deliberately ignore the changes that had reduced Britain's relative power position and responsibilities? How much of British foreign policy was based on a faulty conception of the world? Although World War II produced drastic changes in the structure of global power, the repercussions for Britain were at first easy to ignore. The experience of the war had buoyed national self-confidence and underscored Britain's global role. The central elements of the postwar situation—the strategic role of nuclear weapons, the relationship between the two superpowers, and the alignment of world economic forces—could not for some time be clearly understood, and the immediately pressing problems of security and economic recovery left little time for any fundamental reappraisal of foreign policy principles. British leaders could perhaps be excused if their view of the world around them occasionally parted with reality; the reality was a complex one, and no government—especially not the United States or the Soviet Union—perceived it with perfect clarity.

The degree of British misperception, at least misperception by government officials, is often exaggerated. It would be wrong to attribute Britain's early failure to assume a leadership role in West European integration, or the persistent efforts of British governments to retain global commitments until 1967, exclusively to London's reluctance to recognize changed international conditions. This reluctance was balanced by a large measure of realism in postwar British foreign policy, which manifested itself throughout the Cold War (possibly excepting the 1956 Suez debacle) in an acute awareness of the limits of British power and resources. There is no better evidence of this realism than the Attlee government's decision to turn over support of Greece to the United States in the winter of 1946–47, the British diplomatic campaign for the creation of NATO down to 1949, and the relatively smooth and uncomplaining withdrawal from empire throughout the postwar era.

Nevertheless, some responsibility for failing to adjust to the postwar world must be assigned to Britain's leaders. The Attlee government perceived Britain's overcommitment in the late forties but was disturbed at the potential impact of admission of this fact on public opinion (and hence on its own electoral fortunes). It therefore argued that many foreign commitments could not be readily liquidated, despite the competing resource demands of new domestic programs. Subsequent governments evinced a similar trepidation about upsetting public confidence and national pride, and deemphasized foreign policy in their public statements. Unfortunately this resulted in a steadily widening gap between public and elite perceptions, a gap that reached its extreme during the last Macmillan government in the early sixties. In the end the process of readjustment, with public opinion following sluggishly behind, lasted thirty years—probably not, in retrospect, an unconscionable length of time when one considers the immensity of the task.

THE THREE CIRCLES DOCTRINE

To the extent that deception and lack of realism were present in postwar British foreign policy, a large measure of responsibility rested—in the first two decades at least—with Winston Churchill's Three Circles Doctrine. The doctrine deserves careful scrutiny. It has been invoked not only by British politicians, but also by academic analysts of British foreign policy on both sides of the Atlantic who have used it as an organizing paradigm. One of the standard interpretations of British foreign policy begins by pointing out the triadic nature of British commitments in 1945 (Commonwealth-Empire, American-Atlantic, and European), and then catalogues those political and economic pressures that caused London to abandon first one then two "circles" in its effort to restore the balance between commitments and resources. The ability of British leaders to choose effectively among three distinct external orientations was encumbered—the argument continues—by, first, their own pretensions and perceptual errors (the cognitive lag concept), second, the uncooperativeness of certain foreign governments (especially the French under de Gaulle), and third, the uncertainties of a constantly changing international environment. After fitful attempts to rely principally on Commonwealth ties and the American "special relationship," Britain realized the declining value of both these options and was forced down the tortuous path to an essentially European orientation (signaled by London's accession to the European Community in 1973).

Although this explanation is certainly a tidy one, it presents a number of problems. First, despite its ostensible concern with the cognitive lag notion, it incorporates many of the pitfalls of what Graham Allison has called the "rational actor" model of policymaking, which postulates the eventual maximization of national aims on the basis of a clear understanding of national alternatives.* The Three Circles paradigm assumes that British policymakers perceived themselves confronted by three distinct arenas of foreign policy activity and were guided by overarching foreign policy principles or rationales. This was not the case. British leaders not only failed to impose an organizing framework on the structure of British interests, but also were suspicious of any attempts to do so. British foreign policy through most of the postwar period was in fact conducted incrementally, responding to problems in a pragmatic way as they arose, and consequently was disjointed not only over time but also in the sense of a serious dissonance between the perceptions of the diplomatic establishment on one hand and the defense establishment (which was more quickly affected by resource shortages) on the other. As Joseph Frankel has argued, "there is no indication in Britain's

---

*See Graham T. Allison, "Conceptual Models and the Cuban Missile Crisis," *American Political Science Review* (September 1969), pp. 689–718.

postwar record that perceptions in individual cases were strongly affected by any broad objectives or principles of foreign policy. . . . One is left with the impression of a pragmatic, case-by-case policy in which evaluations were based upon quite a realistic perception of each individual situation."* There were advantages to this style of policymaking. A pragmatic, disjointed, at times vacillating approach to such intractable problems as Palestine, Suez, and Rhodesia seemed to ensure flexibility and a recognition of the core facts of each situation—avoiding the rigidity of clear, doctrinally consistent policy. In significant respects British foreign policy goals were less clearly articulated than French and West German foreign policy goals.

Obviously, there was a price to be paid for the flexibility of "pragmatic" policies unsupported by a comprehensive framework of national purpose. Pragmatism obstructed long-range planning, tended to react to the actions of other governments instead of initiating action in accordance with a predetermined rationale, and caused policies in related and interdependent areas to be uncoordinated and even operate at cross-purposes. The disdain of "theorizing" and high principle in the foreign policy establishment led to an almost complete divorce of political action and theory, save in the sense of a truly vague and largely implicit understanding of broad national priorities. This militated against any systematic incorporation of the Three Circles Doctrine. British policymakers simply did not think in tidy academic terms of the progressive elimination of the Commonwealth and American "options" and the doctrinal reorientation of foreign policy to a fundamentally European outlook. There was a change in Britain's external outlook, to be sure. But it resulted less from a grand design than from the accretion of piecemeal and unintegrated policy decisions.

Second, the Three Circles paradigm is itself conceptually erroneous, obscuring more than it reveals about the structure of postwar British interests. Britain traditionally had not three but two external orientations: (1) a maritime strategy aimed at protecting overseas commercial and imperial interests, principally through naval supremacy, and (2) a Continental strategy aimed at protecting the British Isles through the maintenance of a European balance of power (that is, preventing any European state or combination of states from gaining hegemony over the Continent). Put perhaps too simplistically, the overseas orientation embodied economic security concerns, while the European orientation embodied military security and defense requirements. The two areas of interest were parallel and complementary, though from time to time first one would dominate, then the other. An alternating emphasis was necessary. At no point in modern British history was it assumed that the country could afford to pursue an aggressive policy in both areas at the same time. British resources were never secure enough, even at the height of impe-

---

*Joseph Frankel, *British Foreign Policy, 1945–1973* (London: Oxford University Press, 1975), p. 96.

rial power, to nurture a "myth of omnipotence" of the sort that characterized American foreign policy through much of the twentieth century.

Correspondingly, there were two major strands in British foreign policy after World War II: (1) the maintenance of overseas commitments and interests—a global disposition—combined with, as far as necessary and possible, a graceful dissolution of the British Empire, and (2) the defense of the United Kingdom itself and of the European approaches to the home island. Throughout the postwar period British foreign policy was dominated by the second of these concerns, European security and home defense. This meant that economic interests, many of them traditionally rooted in Britain's overseas connections, continued to suffer, a condition ameliorated only much later with the final reorientation toward Europe of British economic concerns and the realization in London that Europe provided a primary context of economic endeavor as well as a source of security worries—in other words, with the final confluence of Britain's economic and defense-related centers of attention.

The dominance of the European sphere over maritime concerns was not new. Since the beginning of the twentieth century, with the increasingly decisive impact of a unified Germany on the European balance of power, Britain had been unable to devote primary attention to overseas interests and had been preoccupied with home defense. The rise of Germany meant that Britain could not play its traditional role of "balancer" in Europe. This in turn necessitated the eventual intrusion of the Soviet Union and the United States. As F. S. Northedge has explained, "Whatever British government had been in office in the 1930s the result would almost certainly have been the same; that Germany could not be defeated without Soviet assistance, which implied Soviet paramountcy in Eastern Europe after the Second World War, and hence the necessity for a balancing United States presence in Western Europe. In turn, this meant a close alignment of British policy . . . with American policy after Germany's defeat in 1945."*

It is here that we see the roots of the "special relationship" between Britain and the United States. That relationship—based on cultural affinity, a common language and legal tradition, and mutual support in war—has been endowed by some writers with a certain timeless inevitability, as though a close tie between the two countries were a fixed and immutable feature of the modern international system. This is a misleading (and amazingly ahistorical) characterization, for British and American interests and responsibilities have not always coincided. In fact the Anglo-American special relationship really only dated from World War II and was "special" mainly for the British; it was not a separate sphere or circle of British foreign policy goals (as the Three Circles paradigm would suggest), but an important—indeed crucial—facet of

---

*F. S. Northedge, "The Adjustment of British Policy," *The Foreign Policies of the Powers,* ed. F. S. Northedge (New York: The Free Press, 1975), p. 162.

Britain's security interests in Europe. This point is underscored by the fact that *outside* Europe, London and Washington were at loggerheads throughout the Cold War: over Palestine and Suez, the pace of decolonization, China policy, the failure of British and American policies in Malaysia and Indochina to mesh, and—much later—approaches to the Third World oil cartel. It was only in Europe, where Anglo-American cooperation and the containment of the Soviet Union were opposite sides of the same coin, that relations between London and Washington had anything of a special quality—and then only into the sixties. Even the December 1962 Nassau Agreement, in which the British government asked the United States to supply the delivery vehicles for Britain's strategic nuclear deterrent, took place within the NATO framework and against the backdrop of a concern for European security.

The methods by which Britain sought to maintain an American commitment to Europe's future—and resist renascent American isolationism—emphasized the ultimate European focus of the special relationship. After World War II the British opposed institutionalizing a "two pillars" formula for European security, in which a coequal united Europe would share defense burdens with the United States. London preferred instead an "Atlantic" formula in which Washington would dominate in its relations with each European government. British policymakers suspected that successful West European integration—the creation of strong European defense and economic institutions—would encourage American isolationism, and they therefore favored the uneven dependency of a fragmented Europe on the United States. This became part of Britain's rationale for staying out of an integrated Europe. The British saw in American enthusiasm for European federation a barely disguised yearning for a return to isolationism, as well as a naive tendency to draw historical analogies from the United States' own federalist experience. In London's view NATO was a much more palatable solution to Europe's security worries than some sort of European community. NATO had no federal overtones, provided ample opportunity for great-power leadership, and—most important—institutionalized the American presence in Europe.

In short, the American and European dimensions of British foreign policy were inextricably woven together. London's prime postwar goal was to restore stability to Europe, and the Anglo-American special relationship was of major importance in achieving this goal. Thus there was no separate American "option"; the two sides of the Atlantic did not represent distinct alternatives for Britain. Under the circumstances the Three Circles paradigm was an erroneous and—what was worse—highly misleading concept, for scholars and politicians alike.

In the historical account that follows we need to consider not the tidy elimination of the Commonwealth and American "circles," but a more convoluted evolution of Britain's external policy. That policy shifted from two primary orientations, overseas and European, to one—a predominantly European outlook. But the change went beyond this. By 1970 the British no longer regarded Europe simply as a security concern, and therefore only temporarily salient, but also as a focus of British economic growth and political activity, and therefore permanently preeminent. Britain's decisive turn toward Europe between 1970 and 1974 happened to coincide with heightened economic and political tensions between most West European capitals and Washington. The Anglo-American special relationship—predicated upon Britain's role and interests in Europe—dissipated as part of a more general decline of Atlanticism, a growing realization that Europe and the United States had incompatible objectives on such questions as detente, monetary reform, and energy policy. By the mid-seventies Washington's relationship with London was not significantly more "special" than its relationship with Bonn or Paris.

All of this will become more clear as we trace the evolution of British security policy from 1945 to the present. It is useful to divide this era into four periods, each accounting for a distinctive phase in the evolution of London's security posture: 1945–49, the end of World War II to the establishment of NATO; 1949–56, the first months of NATO to the Suez crisis; 1956–67, the Suez crisis aftermath to the Wilson government's decision to withdraw from "east of Suez"; and 1967–80, the period of Britain's persistent —and finally successful—effort to abandon a global role and decisively join Europe.

BRITAIN AND THE ATLANTIC ALLIANCE:
PHASE ONE, 1945–49

Some writers have argued that Britain's immediate postwar security posture was uncertain, that the deep East-West antagonisms of the Cold War took time to surface, and that Whitehall to begin with had no particular foe in mind in fashioning British defense policy.* The Soviet Union, in this view, was not perceived as a major threat until late 1947 or early 1948, in part because the more provocative aspects of Soviet policy did not emerge for some time, but also because large segments of Clement Attlee's ruling Labour Party (which won the 1945 general election) were ideologically sympathetic with Soviet goals and even with Soviet visions of socialism.

This interpretation is really only partly accurate, however. Soviet and British views of the postwar situation in fact clashed quite early—over German reparations and the Polish frontier at the Postdam Conference; over Soviet behavior in Poland and the character of Soviet-imposed regimes in Rumania, Hungary, and Bulgaria at the September 1945 Council of Foreign Ministers meeting; and, at most of the Big Three parleys of 1945–47, over

---

*See R. N. Rosecrance, *Defense of the Realm: British Strategy in the Nuclear Epoch* (New York: Columbia University Press, 1968), pp. 52–54.

Moscow's desire to extend its control to the Mediterranean and Southern Europe. Nor did the leaders of the new British Labour government mince their words. Foreign Secretary Ernest Bevin as early as 1945 accused Moscow of substituting one kind of totalitarianism for another in Eastern Europe, compared the Soviet foreign minister to Hitler, and alienated still naive left-wing Labour members of Parliament by denouncing the Soviet Union as the principal threat to European security. As for the Conservative Party opposition, Winston Churchill in March 1946 delivered his famous Fulton, Missouri speech in which he asserted that an "iron curtain" had descended across the middle of Europe and argued that the Soviets desired "the fruits of war and the indefinite expansion of their power and doctrines." By comparison Washington was still much more conciliatory in its approach to Moscow.

Still, the international picture was not immediately clear. There were also large differences of opinion between Britain and the United States. Washington's abrupt cessation of Lend-Lease in August 1945, Congressional passage of the McMahon Act forbidding American nuclear sharing with Britain in August 1946, and President Harry S. Truman's decision to support the creation of a Jewish state in Palestine in October 1946, all served to exacerbate tensions between the two allies. Washington's abrogation of the wartime Hyde Park Agreement establishing full Anglo-American cooperation in nuclear matters was easily the most vexing issue. It not only encouraged the Attlee government to move ahead with construction of an independent British nuclear deterrent, but also—as Secretary of State Dean Acheson, who sympathized with the British position, noted—cast doubt on the value of solemn commitments made by the United States.

Security without NATO

Until 1949 there was no formal American commitment to European security, though there were American occupation forces in Germany, and a limited amount of ad hoc cooperation between American and British military staffs continued. The Attlee government, though it remonstrated against Soviet behavior in Eastern Europe and perceived the Soviet Union as a long-term threat, at first did not organize defense planning around the possibility of East-West military conflict. It sought instead (1) to shore up the stability of newly reinstalled continental European governments, especially the French, without committing Britain to a permanent military presence on the Continent unsupported by the United States, and (2) to impose order and an organizing rationale on British military and political commitments around the world, a task requiring substantial rethinking in view of the promised independence of India and other South Asian possessions. Both tasks were made more difficult by the prospect of dwindling foreign policy and defense resources as a larger portion of government expenditures was taken up by new domestic programs, and by the fact that British forces were spread thin during

1945–47—in Germany, Austria, Greece, Venezia Gulia, Palestine, Indochina, Japan, and at scattered points throughout the Near and Far East and Africa. Some of these deployments could soon be scaled down; others could not.

In working toward the first goal, European stability, it seemed obvious to the British that Europe would have to be roused from its postwar shock and depression. Primarily that implied the restoration of France. Britain in 1945–46 became the chief advocate of France's return to great-power status, obtaining for Paris an occupation zone in Germany, a seat on the Allied Control Council for Germany, and permanent membership on the United Nations Security Council. On March 4, 1947, London signed the Anglo-French Treaty of Dunkirk, which reassured the shaky Fourth Republic of British support in the event of future German aggression—an assurance that retained some of its significance in subsequent years as West Germany was integrated into Atlantic security arrangements. (The Dunkirk agreement did not, however, imply that London still saw Germany as the prime threat.) These measures seemed important at first, since President Franklin D. Roosevelt had told the British at Yalta that American forces would be withdrawn from Europe two years after the end of hostilities. Until 1948 this was the limit, however, of the Attlee government's commitment to Europe. Although it was obvious that Soviet power presented the major potential danger, Britain deferred a permanent European arrangement for dealing with this threat until the direction of long-term American policy could be known. Washington at first was distrusted, especially in the Parliamentary Labour Party, though this changed once Marshall Plan aid began flowing, much of it financing Labour's social welfare programs. It was not until 1948 that events forced Britain into an intense effort to secure a permanent American commitment to Western Europe's security.

London's second foreign policy task, that of imposing order on the structure of British global commitments, was heavily influenced by the overextension of the nation's military forces and the declining availability of resources. Withdrawal from immediate postwar responsibilities, such as the occupation of southern Indochina, was implemented as quickly as possible in combination with a general reduction of forces (though in 1946 Britain still had twice the percentage of its population under arms that the United States had). The real press of resources came in the winter of 1946–47 and throughout 1947. A fuel shortage, combined with unexpectedly high inflation and the steadily weakening position of sterling against the dollar, forced the government to cut heavily into defense expenditures, which fell from £1,667 million in 1946 to £899 million in 1947. Early in 1947 it was decided that Britain could no longer afford economic and military aid to Greece and Turkey (projected to cost $250 million in 1947 alone), despite the fact that both Mediterranean countries faced formidable communist pressure (Greek communists had been waging a civil war since December 1944). In February the Attlee government appealed to Washington to take over this responsibility, claiming economic exhaustion. The appeal was couched in Cold War language, which painted a picture of a still prostrate Western Europe being outflanked in the Eastern Mediterranean by Soviet power—a prospect made all the more worrisome by the size of the French and Italian Communist parties.

President Truman responded favorably to Britain's request. In March 1947, in a speech before a joint session of Congress, he called for $400 million in aid to Greece and Turkey. But Truman was really asking for much more: an open-ended American security commitment to governments outside the Western Hemisphere. By presenting the specter of a Soviet threat to Mediterranean, European, and ultimately American security, the president got what he wanted, and the Truman Doctrine of global containment of Communism became part of United States policy. Still, many in Congress opposed a formal alliance with European governments, arguing that London and Paris should accept Washington's assurances at their face value instead of pressing for binding agreements.

Throughout 1946–47 British military planners sought a strategic doctrine that would take account of the nation's diminishing resources and the uncertainty of American intentions, while at the same time provide a nexus between Britain's continental European and global security interests. Whitehall at first adopted what has been called a "functional" defense doctrine—functional in the sense that it was not directed at any specific enemy, but simply sought to maintain certain commitments against all possible contingencies. This doctrine had three components: (1) a traditional commitment to ensure the security of overseas possessions and keep open the sea lanes; (2) preservation of British interests in the Middle East and North Africa, areas crucial to both European security and imperial communications; and (3) long-term development of an independent nuclear deterrent. It was assumed that no major conflict involving Britain would occur for at least ten years and that during the late forties military equipment would be provided largely out of World War II stocks. The nuclear weapons program would progress at only a leisurely pace since it was expensive (the United States McMahon Act forced Britain to duplicate research already done under the joint wartime Manhattan Project), since more advanced jet bombers to deliver nuclear weapons were still a decade off, and since the strategic consequences of nuclear weapons were still uncertain (though the February 1948 Defence White Paper argued that such weapons would ultimately be decisive). Finally, Whitehall's policy provided that the British Dominions of Canada, Australia, New Zealand, and South Africa would henceforth be responsible for their own defense because Britain's meager resources would be tied down elsewhere. In significant respects, of course, the refusal to build strategy around an identified future threat was the exact antithesis of an "organizing rationale" for British military and political commitments; it was in the end simply an economizing expedient, one more incremental measure intended to reduce responsibilities and cope with immediate problems.

The lines of East-West confrontation solidified in late 1947 as Western governments perceived a growing military and ideological threat from the East, and as the Kremlin perceived a corresponding economic and political threat from the West. On July 2, 1947, the Soviets rejected United States Marshall Plan aid; Poland, Czechoslovakia, and Finland, under pressure from Moscow, followed suit. In November opposition parties in Poland and Hungary were dissolved. Three short months later, in February 1948, a coup in Prague led to the installation of a pro-Soviet Czechoslovak government, outraging Western opinion. It became evident that there would be no postwar peace settlement for all of Europe.

Establishment of NATO

By January 1948 Foreign Secretary Bevin had decided to seek a military relationship with Western Europe that might eventually include the United States. He proposed to the House of Commons a collective defense treaty comprising Britain, France, and the three Benelux countries (Belgium, the Netherlands, and Luxembourg). The immediate result was the Brussels Treaty, concluded March 17, 1948 between the five governments. At its signing Bevin dispatched a telegram to Washington expressing the hope that this first step would lead to a broader, transatlantic defense grouping. On April 23 Bevin renewed the overture to Washington in a secret telegram. He argued that the United States should convene a conference to discuss North Atlantic defense arrangements, that only within the framework of an Atlantic defense pact would West European nations stand up to new acts of aggression, and—furthermore—that only within the context of such a pact would France agree to rebuilding Germany. Under pressure from Bevin and the example of the Brussels Treaty, and impelled by recent Soviet hostility, a faction of the United States Senate on June 11, 1948 pushed through the Vandenberg Resolution calling for regional security arrangements based on self-help. By now a permanent American commitment to European security was a major objective of British foreign policy.

Events moved quickly. Moscow, responding to what it saw as Western antagonism (particularly political and monetary arrangements for West Berlin and the prospect of a sovereign West Germany), imposed the Berlin Blockade on June 20, 1948. The Berlin crisis catalyzed Western resistance to Soviet power. As part of the emergency the Pentagon in July dispatched nuclear-capable B-29 bombers to Europe, and in the same month United States and Canadian military representatives met with the Brussels Pact Military Committee in London. In August the United States Joint Chiefs gathered at Newport, Rhode Island, to draw up plans for the defense of Western Europe. It was a short step from this to the Truman administration's open approval of the Atlantic pact idea in January 1949, and to final American signature of the North Atlantic Treaty on April 4, 1949.

The establishment of NATO constituted the realization of London's prime foreign policy goal. Anglo-American tensions continued, of course, especially over the nuclear sharing problem, but at least there was now a permanent American commitment to the future of Europe. By 1949 even rank-and-file Labour opinion in Britain found little to object to in this. American cooperation rendered the Attlee government's Europeanist emphasis on continental and home defense feasible and promised to reduce the drain of military expenditures on domestic programs.

BRITAIN AND THE ATLANTIC ALLIANCE: PHASE TWO, 1949–56

The strategic situation became radically altered in 1949. First, both Britain and the United States were now formally committed to the defense of Western Europe. Second, the Soviet Union conducted its first atomic test in August, forcing Whitehall—along with the rest of NATO—to drastically rethink ideas about European security. Although Soviet deployment of nuclear weapons in significant numbers was some time off, Moscow's new capability in the long run meant that Britain could not be defended against strategic annihilation, since only a few Soviet aircraft (later missiles) would have to penetrate home defenses in order to destroy British cities. Indeed, the United Kingdom —like West Germany—was uniquely vulnerable to nuclear attack because of its high urbanization, compact size, and close proximity to the Soviet bloc. National security would depend upon Britain's ability to deter such an attack rather than defend against it, which in turn would require a viable British nuclear force—perhaps linked to the American strategic umbrella.

Impending Soviet possession of nuclear weapons also meant that in a future European war a seaborne invasion of the Continent such as Operation Overlord in 1944 would no longer be possible. The Soviet army would have to be prevented from overrunning the Continent in the first place. There would be no time for Britain and the United States to mobilize for this, so NATO would have to maintain a sizable standing army on the Continent in peacetime—large enough, at least, to stall an attack until American strategic air power could take its toll. The immediate implications were clear: West European countries would have to increase their conventional defensive capabilities, and the United States would have to speed expansion of its nuclear deterrent (Britain's role in the grand scheme of European defense was, however, less certain).

For the next three or four years the new Atlantic alliance thought principally in these terms. The Hague and London NATO meetings of April and May 1950 dealt with the division of labor among alliance members and with a Medium Term Plan for conventional defense of the European central front. The September 1950 New York meeting, held shortly after the beginning of the Korean emergency, devised a forward strategy for defending Western Europe as far east as possible. And the February 1952 Lisbon meeting proposed high conventional force goals (ninety-six divisions by 1954), which for economic and domestic political reasons were never met (see chapter 1).

British strategy at this time was more than ever circumscribed by the need to limit spending as the nation faced a continuing financial crisis. The defense estimates for 1949–50 and 1950–51 envisaged budgets of only £759 million and £780 million respectively. These resources had to be shared between Britain's conventional forces in Europe (the British Army of the Rhine [BAOR]), the counterinsurgency effort against communist guerrillas in Malaya (which began in 1948), and continued development of the nuclear deterrent, as well as base commitments around the world. In an effort to save money London in December 1949 offered to terminate its atomic research if Washington would provide Britain with atomic weapons. The measure was vetoed in Congress despite Secretary Acheson's protests that the British would soon develop the bomb anyway. Work continued on an independent British deterrent.

The Korean War

It was into this atmosphere of British frugality and of planning for Europe's defense in the more distant future that the Korean War interposed itself in June 1950. British objectives during the Korean conflict were threefold: (1) to persuade the United States to maintain adequate force levels in Europe, in case Korea proved to be only a diversionary tactic, (2) to bolster European defenses now that it was obvious no reliable assumptions could be made about the timing of the Soviet threat, and (3) to restrain the United States from precipitous use of excessive force in the Far East, especially the use of nuclear weapons or an invasion of China (or both). The first task required contributing a small British expeditionary force to the United Nations effort in Korea. More important, it required a massive increase in British defense expenditures—demanded in any case by the second objective, an enhanced European defense—in order to convince Washington that London was bearing its share of the burden. The BAOR was strengthened, and a major rearmament effort ensued.

By January 1951 Prime Minister Attlee had proposed a three-year defense allocation of £4,700 million and had increased the period of service for conscripts. These measures were clearly unpopular and were opposed by factions in Attlee's own Labour Party. Such high defense outlays were bound to undercut progress made in the economy at precisely the time some economic relief seemed to be at hand. In putting defense ahead of popularity the Labour leadership placed its electoral fortunes on the line, and Labour was narrowly defeated by the Conservatives in the general election of October 1951.

The 1952 Global Strategy Paper

The first major strategic contribution of Winston Churchill's new Conservative Government was the 1952 Global Strategy Paper. It assessed the implications of Britain's impending nuclear capability for (1) the strategic relationship with the United States, and (2) Britain's commitment to Europe. In the first context the independent British nuclear deterrent was seen as complementary to the United States Strategic Air Command (SAC), for it could be used against targets vital to British security that might not be hit in the first round of SAC strikes (the paper suggested Soviet submarine pens as an example). Thus, Whitehall did not envisage a truly independent role for the British deterrent, though it is doubtful that British planners overlooked its possible use as a finger on the United States nuclear trigger.

In the second context, Europe, the Global Strategy Paper proposed that Britain's nuclear capacity be tied in with the nation's NATO commitments. Churchill and the service chiefs had been shocked by the magnitude of the February 1952 Lisbon force goals, and had assented to them only begrudgingly. Such large conventional forces would pose a severe economic drain. Now, in the Global Strategy Paper, plans were drawn up that directly contradicted official NATO policy. Atomic weapons, it was argued, would permit the British to reduce—or at least not increase—their conventional forces in Europe, since such weapons provided a cost-effective substitute for large-scale manpower. This would be especially true after the advent of tactical nuclear weapons, whose potential usefulness had already been unveiled. Three assumptions underpinned this argument: (1) that any limited European conflict would quickly escalate into general war, (2) that Britain should therefore be interested in a posture of deterrence, not defense, and (3) that the nuclear weapons required for a deterrence posture would in the long run be less expensive than conventional forces. These assumptions guided British defense planning for some time to come.

It was not until December 1954, when NATO sanctioned planning on the basis of tactical nuclear weapons, that other Allied governments fell in line with British strategy. The Global Strategy Paper was ahead of its time; the orchestration of nuclear and conventional strategies that it proposed was unique, something neither NATO nor Washington had done until now (though NATO's conventional force plans had always presumed the ultimate presence of American nuclear air power).

On October 3, 1952 Britain detonated its first atomic bomb, a Plutonium-239 device, in Australia's remote Monte Bello Islands. Despite financial difficulties and the uncooperativeness of its major ally, Britain had become a nuclear power. In the following months the pace of British conventional rearmament slowed substantially, especially after the Korean armistice in July 1953.

British Diplomacy, 1952–56

During the halcyon years between the 1952 Monte Bello test and the Suez crisis of October–November 1956, British security interests continued to center on Europe, despite overseas "policing" efforts in Malaya (1948–57), Kenya (1952–56) and Cyprus (1954–59). After the failure of the French National Assembly to ratify the European Defense Community treaty in August 1954, British diplomacy played a crucial role in pulling together an acceptable scheme for West German participation in NATO. Whitehall feared that without such a scheme Washington—whose patience had been tried by the entire EDC episode—would contemplate reducing its commitment to Europe. At a nine-power conference in London, which began in September 1954, the Churchill government proposed reviving the old Brussels Treaty, linking it with NATO, and expanding it to include West Germany and Italy. The new grouping, to be called the Western European Union (WEU), would be empowered to fix maximum force levels for its members (in cooperation with NATO), and so would restrain Bonn from making independent use of its armed forces. The West German army would not, however, be submerged in a multinational command structure. The British hoped this arrangement would mollify French fears of German resurgence.

At a meeting in Paris in October 1954, the WEU proposal was incorporated in a series of agreements that also provided for West Germany's entry into NATO. In December the Paris Agreements narrowly gained approval in the French Assembly. What had promised to be a severe intra-Alliance crisis was avoided. West Germany joined NATO on May 5, 1955, thanks in no small degree to British efforts.

Britain also at this time played a major role in East-West diplomacy. The death of Stalin in March 1953 raised the possibility that relations with Moscow might be improved to the point of substantially reducing tensions in Europe, thus permitting London to concentrate its efforts and resources elsewhere (there was in any case a general reduction of British troop commitments to NATO between 1954 and 1957). In May 1953, Churchill repealed his 1946 Fulton speech and called for an end to the Cold War based on a guarantee of Russia's security interests in Eastern Europe. Whatever effects this might have had were quickly cancelled by Soviet suppression of the East Berlin uprising a month later, by the failure of the 1954 Berlin Four Power Conference to reach agreement on Germany's future, and by West Germany's subsequent accession to NATO. Still, a spirit of greater cooperativeness pervaded East-West relations in 1955 as the Soviet government, undergoing a sustained succession crisis, tried to encourage "moderate" sentiment in the West. The Austrian State Treaty of May 15, 1955 was followed by the Geneva Summit Conference of July 18–22 in which British Prime Minister Anthony Eden (who had succeeded Churchill as Conservative Party leader) proposed military disengagement in Central Europe based on a zone of arms limitations and on-site inspection. Eden's plan was an interesting precursor of much later proposals for mutual force reductions in Europe. In the end, however, the Geneva Conference produced no tangible progress. By early 1956 East-West relations were returning to their former tenseness.

We should note at this juncture a problem taken up more fully in chapter 10: if British diplomacy was reasonably successful in the early fifties in resolving intra-alliance problems and contributing to East-West rapprochement, it was singularly myopic in the area of Britain's political and economic relationship with the European integration movement. Although London was cognizant of its security interests in Europe, the British nonetheless balked at any suggestion of an organic political or economic linkage with the Continent. In June 1955 the Conservative government refused to participate seriously in the Messina Conference on creation of a European Economic Community. The failure to participate in Messina constituted, in the opinion of some observers, one of the two or three biggest blunders of postwar British foreign policy. As a consequence of this coolness toward European integration, London's diplomatic positions in Western Europe and the United States—which were mutually reinforcing—inexorably deteriorated after 1955.

The Suez Crisis

Perhaps no event undermined Britain's international position, or challenged assumptions about British purposes in world affairs, more than the Suez crisis of October–November 1956. The crisis began as a joint Anglo-French expedition to reassert international control of the Suez Canal, which Egypt's President Gamal Abdel Nasser had nationalized, and ended in a political disaster from which Britain never completely recovered. The ingredients of the crisis were provided by Nasser's rise to power in February 1954 at the head of a military coup, by London's agreement to a phased withdrawal of British troops from Egypt between October 1954 and July 1956, and by the United States' decision—partly in response to an arms deal between Nasser and communist Czechoslovakia—to withdraw funds from development of the Aswan High Dam on the Nile River.

The Suez Canal, a vital sea link between Europe and Asia, had been the concession of a private French concern in which the British government held a controlling interest; the Canal Zone was under joint Anglo-French administration. Nasser nationalized the canal on July 26, 1956, exactly a week after Washington's notice that Aswan funding would be canceled (and two weeks after the last British soldier had left Egypt). Revenues from the canal, announced Nasser, would compensate for American abandonment of Aswan.

The reaction not only of the Eden government in London, but also of the entire British nation, was quick. Recalls Richard Neustadt,

The British were seized by a spasm of anger, none more than the Prime Minister. For them, as for all Western Europe, the Canal was an essential artery of trade. Among other things, a great part of their oil imports came through it. To many sober citizens . . . "Egyptian" spelled "incompetent": ships would run aground, the banks would cave, the bottom would silt up. For Englishmen, moreover, and especially for Tories, the Canal had connotations apart from commerce. It was vividly symbolic: Empire, Victoria, Disraeli. Nasser, furthermore, was violating treaties in the manner of the dictators of twenty years before.*

The consensus of Eden's cabinet was that Western control of the canal had to be restored; moreover, Nasser had to be punished and, if possible, removed from power. France—cocontroller of the Canal, and rankled by Nasser's support of Algerian rebels—could be persuaded to participate in any military action.

Across the Atlantic the Eisenhower administration—with much lower stakes in Suez and the 1956 presidential election fast approaching—tried throughout August, September, and October to defuse the situation, dispatching Secretary of State John Foster Dulles to London several times, proposing peaceful solutions to the problem, and warning Britain (sometimes too cryptically) not to resort to force. These efforts were in vain. Anglo-American communication broke down as Eden concealed his real intentions from Washington, which itself vacillated in its approach to Suez. The Eden government believed, in the words of Chancellor of the Exchequer Harold Macmillan, that Eisenhower would "lie doggo" until after the presidential election. Britain and France would have a free hand.

On October 3 Eden gained approval from his cabinet for a "peacekeeping" operation in Egypt. A diplomatic cover story was devised: Israel would attack Egypt in the Sinai Peninsula; Britain and France would intervene to protect the Suez Canal from both combatants, occupying the area in the interests of world commerce. Nasser's regime was so flimsy (it was assumed) that military defeat would topple him from power. On October 16 British and French ministers met in Paris to plan the intervention. Secret coordination with Israel (whose cooperation was obviously necessary) was left to the French, who by now had transferred a substantial number of *Mystere* fighter-bombers to the Israeli Air Force.

Washington, of course, was informed of none of this activity. While the Eisenhower administration was deeply concerned about what was happening in the Middle East, its attention was now riveted elsewhere. The election campaign was drawing to a close, and Eisenhower hoped to emerge with a clear Republican majority in Congress. More important, on October 24 a popular uprising in communist Hungary turned violent. People were being killed in the streets of Budapest by the Soviet army, and East-West relations

---

*Richard E. Neustadt, *Alliance Politics* (New York: Columbia University Press, 1970), p. 12.

—the entire European security environment—became potentially very unstable.

On October 29—the same day the Soviet army temporarily withdrew from Hungary, and with the American election just eight days away—Israel marched, and the Suez operation, code-named Musketeer, was on. On October 30 Britain and France issued to Egypt and Israel an ultimatum demanding that within twelve hours both combatants withdraw ten miles from the Suez Canal and allow Anglo-French forces to occupy key points along it (the ultimatum to Israel was, of course, a charade).

Musketeer embodied a logistical nightmare from the beginning. In order to maintain the cover story and keep Washington in the dark there could be no advance accumulation of British and French forces close to Egypt. Neither Britain nor France possessed a major airlift capacity, so warships loaded with troops had to sail from Malta and even Southampton—which meant they could not reach Suez for six days. Moreover, the warships were unable to leave port until October 31, the day the Anglo-French ultimatum expired. Yet air strikes against the Egyptian air force had to be launched immediately for the protection of Israeli columns racing across Sinai, which meant that London and Paris had to drop the subterfuge of "neutrality" days before the arrival of their "peacekeeping" forces. When British aircraft joined in the bombing of Egypt on October 31, the day the ultimatum expired, London's collusion with Israel became obvious.

Prime Minister Eden quickly found himself in a politically difficult position both at home and abroad. The Labour opposition in Parliament called for a vote of censure on November 1, which failed by only a small margin. On November 2, with Israel now in control of most of Sinai and Anglo-French forces still sailing toward Egypt, the United Nations General Assembly voted a ceasefire resolution. Eden rejected the resolution the following day, though by now the fighting between Egypt and Israel had subsided anyway. On November 4 the Soviet army moved back into Budapest to crush the Hungarian revolution. On November 5 British and French paratroops finally landed around Port Said at the northern end of the Suez Canal, and the following day heavy assault forces moved ashore from the Anglo-French flotilla and began pushing south from the Mediterranean coast. The Soviet government at this point threatened to rain rockets on London and Paris, and in Washington the Pentagon—fearful of Soviet overreaction at a time of instability generated by the Hungarian crisis—cautiously moved toward an alert status.

President Eisenhower's anger on learning of British air strikes and subsequent Egyptian blockage of the Suez Canal on October 31 was profound. Why had his allies disturbed the international scene and placed him in an awkward position on the eve of the American election, especially in view of the unfolding Hungarian events? Why had they broken faith and deliberately concealed their plans from him? As it became obvious that London and Paris had adopted a plan that was militarily clumsy and politically incompetent, a plan that risked war with the Soviet Union over secondary interests, Eisenhower's anger increased. He decided to force an end to the fighting, to punish London and Paris and put them in their place. The method he chose demonstrated the wide range of coercive instruments available to superpowers in an age of increasing economic and political interdependence.

Early on Election Day, November 6, Eisenhower's secretary of the treasury, George Humphrey, gave the British Treasury an ultimatum:

As Londoners recall it, he posed the simple choice of an immediate cease-fire or war on the pound, with not a dollar to be had for oil supplies [the flow of oil had been interrupted by the Middle East conflict]. Unless they heeded the U.N., he would block their path to dollars from the International Monetary Fund, put off their hopes of credit from our [the United States] Export-Import Bank, and make no effort to align our central bankers behind sterling. If they persisted, they would face a forced devaluation, followed by petrol rationing.*

The Humphrey ultimatum was set to expire midnight, Greenwich time. There had already been a run on the pound, and the drain on British gold and dollar reserves in November alone would amount to $279 million. In a turbulent cabinet meeting that day the Eden government—confronted with an uproar in Parliament, further Soviet antipathy, and now ruin for the pound—decided to do what it was told. Whitehall ordered a ceasefire. Paris, horrified at British fickleness but unwilling to proceed alone, had no choice but to go along. At 2 A.M. Cairo time on November 7, fighting came to an end in the Middle East. British, French, and Israeli forces, which had achieved control of one-third the length of the Suez Canal, withdrew by the end of December, making way for a United Nations peacekeeping operation. Anthony Eden, ill and exhausted, resigned as prime minister in January 1957, to be replaced by Harold Macmillan.

The blow to British prestige was immense. Indeed, the failure at Suez was perhaps the biggest national setback in modern British history. London's inability to defy Washington, and its obvious difficulty in mounting a quick military operation against a nation of Egypt's modest power, indicated that Britain could no longer be counted among the premier nations of the world.

The bitterest lesson of Suez involved the United States. Since World War II both Englishmen and Americans had assumed the existence of a special relationship between their two countries. Now this seemed threatened. The failure of the Anglo-American alliance at the height of the Suez crisis— amounting, in fact, to Washington's deliberate scuttling of the British venture —pointed to the unreliability of United States pledges of military and political support and undermined the credibility of the American nuclear guaran-

*Ibid., p. 26.

tee. Further, Washington's behavior regarding Suez, if considered in train with its inaction over Moscow's brutal suppression of the Hungarian revolt, testified to a commonality of United States–Soviet interests that worked to the disadvantage of the European dependents of both superpowers.

BRITAIN AND THE ATLANTIC ALLIANCE: PHASE THREE, 1956–67

The most important British response to the Suez debacle was the White Paper presented by Minister of Defence Duncan Sandys in 1957. Motivated also by the sad state of the British economy and the need to reduce defense spending, the White Paper provided for the continued development of the independent nuclear deterrent and a reduction in conventional forces, combined with an early abolition of conscription. Large conventional forces were seen as an expensive luxury, essentially superfluous within the context of Britain's strategic position in the late fifties (London had in any case just been burned by their use). British forces in Germany were to be cut back, while Commonwealth commitments were to be met by small, highly mobile units that could be airlifted from Europe to the site of a brushfire war.

The advantages attending a continued emphasis on nuclear weapons were numerous. Nuclear weapons were still seen as more economical than conventional forces (the expensive revolution in delivery system technology had not yet occurred). In the aftermath of Suez they were deemed to have the double advantage of providing insurance against the possible unreliability of American commitments, while simultaneously helping to reestablish British prestige. In addition, some policy planners thought that the independent deterrent would be an important factor in rebuilding British morale at home, which had been badly shaken by the Suez episode.

Finally, the Sandys Paper—looking back at the Soviet threat of rocket attacks on London and Paris—admitted that there were "at present no means of providing adequate protection for the people of this country against the consequences of an attack with nuclear weapons" and stressed the shift from a defensive posture to one based on deterrence. The brunt of Britain's deterrence capability would be provided by the Vulcan, Victor, and Valiant long-range bombers ("V-bombers"), which were only now entering service in numbers and would be effective into the late sixties. Deterrence would later be provided by the Blue Streak missile, which would be fired from underground emplacements. Underscoring this aspect of defense policy, Britain's first hydrogen bomb was tested in May 1957.

The biggest problem with the Sandys Paper was that, while it provided for some drastic force reductions (including cutting the army's manpower to 165,000), it did not reduce commitments accordingly. Over the long term its effect would be to spread British forces more thinly in areas where they were already inadequate for the tasks assigned them. Thus in 1957–58 British forces remained in Germany, Cyprus, the Persian Gulf, Aden, Kenya, Singapore, Malaya, and Hong Kong.

The most important international event of 1957, one which seemed to underscore the appropriateness of the Sandys Paper's nuclear emphasis, was Soviet launching of the Sputnik satellite on October 4. It now became clear that the Soviets possessed an intercontinental ballistic missile capability and that it would not be long before cities in the United States became vulnerable to nuclear attack. Whitehall was more convinced than ever of the value of its independent deterrent; it was far from certain that the Americans would launch a strategic nuclear strike in response to a Russian assault across the Elbe, and the British deterrent provided a kind of insurance policy. Britain had to possess the ultimate means of its own defense, especially in view of American treachery during Suez.

Still, the new prime minister, Harold Macmillan, made it his first priority on taking office to repair relations with Washington. Eisenhower's anger had been largely assuaged by Britain's withdrawal from Suez and Eden's subsequent resignation; there was now a desire on that side of the Atlantic, too, to mend the damage. When Macmillan visited Washington in October 1957 Eisenhower informed him that, in response to the post-Sputnik need to pool Western "brainpower," he would ask Congress for an amendment to the Atomic Energy Act that would permit nuclear sharing between the United States and Britain. The subsequent beginning of nuclear sharing in 1958 ended a twelve-year period in which successive British governments had deeply resented Washington's violation of President Roosevelt's wartime pledges of nuclear cooperation. No doubt Eisenhower's decision in part reflected a desire to strengthen the British deterrent in view of the strategic implications of Sputnik. The British nuclear force was at this time an important supplement to American nuclear striking power.

Although 1958 and 1959 were turbulent years in terms of heightened Cold War tensions and the political crisis in neighboring France, they were relatively peaceful for Britain. True, fighting on Cyprus intensified, and there was a fresh Middle East crisis in 1958 resulting in American and British intervention in Lebanon and Jordan. But in terms of Britain's central security interests, deployment of the independent deterrent continued, and NATO units in Europe began acquiring tactical nuclear weapons. Sixty Thor intermediate-range missiles were installed in Britain during 1958, under joint Anglo-American command, but they were vulnerable to preemptive attack and were withdrawn five years later.

The fundamental assumptions and orientation of British foreign policy were at this time quietly changing. Although one major consequence of Suez, the schism within NATO, seemed to vanish in the face of sharpened Soviet belligerence, another consequence, the retrenchment of British power and interests and London's slow turn away from global responsibilities, continued to have momentum. A number of factors pointed to British retrenchment: (1) the continued emphasis on nuclear deterrence, which could be relevant only in the European context; (2) restitution of the Anglo-American special relationship, whose principal focus continued to be the security of Europe and the British Isles; (3) the determined shedding of colonial responsibilities in Africa, highlighted by Macmillan's "winds of change" speech in February 1960, which promised rapid decolonization; and (4) the Macmillan government's decision in the fall of 1960 to take Britain into the EEC, formally announced on July 31, 1961.

The Skybolt Crisis and the Nassau Agreement

The increasingly decisive impact of limited resources on British security policy became evident in late 1959 when the Macmillan government decided, mainly for financial reasons, to cancel the Blue Streak missile, which had been intended to succeed the V-bombers as the mainstay of the independent deterrent. In lieu of Blue Streak, Macmillan arranged with Eisenhower in March 1960 the purchase of a nuclear delivery system, the Skybolt air-launched missile, from the United States. Skybolt would be launched from the V-bombers and could begin equipping Britain's Bomber Command in 1965. For the first time in its history Britain was now prepared to rely on another nation for the technological means of its defense.

But the Skybolt deal did not go smoothly. When the Kennedy administration moved into the White House in 1961, the new American secretary of defense, Robert McNamara, was skeptical of Skybolt's cost-effectiveness (the missile would have only a defense-suppression role for the United States Air Force). In early November 1962, after a year of careful study, McNamara decided to scrap the project. He called in the British ambassador to tell him that Skybolt would not be available after all.

A crisis loomed. London had trusted its major ally to provide the central instrument of Britain's defense, and now that ally had reneged. Moreover, in expectation of Skybolt, Whitehall had for two years substantially slowed independent British development of nuclear delivery systems. Recent events seemed to emphasize the importance of Britain's independent deterrent. In September and October 1962 a border war between India and China raised the possibility of a British nuclear guarantee to India. Later in October the Cuban missile crisis, in which the United States consulted Britain in only the most limited way, underscored the separate strategic positions of the two countries. Macmillan decided to settle the Skybolt issue at a previously scheduled meeting with President Kennedy on December 19, 1962, at Nassau in the Bahamas. Washington had placed Britain in an untenable position, not to mention embarrassing the Conservative government in Parliament. If Skybolt would not be forthcoming, some other strategic system, perhaps the Polaris submarine-launched missile (the most advanced weapon in the United States arsenal), would have to be substituted.

London had already mentioned the possibility of Polaris to the Americans, and at Nassau, Kennedy finally offered the British, over the vigorous opposition of the State Department, a Polaris force tied to NATO Command. The United States would supply Britain Polaris missiles, while the British—with some technical assistance—would build the needed submarines and provide their own nuclear warheads. The force would be pledged to NATO from the outset, but at times of supreme national emergency it could be withdrawn temporarily from NATO for independent use by London.

There was some difference between British and American perceptions of the Nassau Agreement. The Kennedy administration, embroiled in a nuclear sharing controversy with all its NATO allies, visualized the British Polaris as ultimately part of a *multilateral* NATO nuclear force embodying a jointly financed, mixed nationality, thoroughly integrated fleet (though Washington led the British to think this was a distant aspiration). The British, on the other hand, saw their Polaris missiles as a contribution to a *multinational* nuclear force made up of national contingents controlled by their respective governments. London regarded Washington's proposal for a multilateral force (MLF) as unworkable (because it was too complicated) and dangerous (because it contemplated a West German finger on the nuclear trigger). In the end the British view of Nassau prevailed, institutionalized by the "independent use" clause, and Kennedy is said to have become unhappy with the agreement a short time after his meeting with Macmillan.

Although it is tempting to attribute French President de Gaulle's January 1963 veto of British entry into the EEC to his pique at the exclusiveness of the Nassau Agreement, this is not entirely accurate. True, London and Washington had been insensitive to the NATO alliance as a whole—and to French feelings in particular—in once again indulging in their special relationship without consulting other governments. "The French," one observer has noted, "were later to make much of the fact that Britain negotiated for sixteen months with the Common Market, but reached a major defense agreement with the United States in forty-eight hours."* But Macmillan had come away from a meeting with de Gaulle at Rambouillet on December 15—four days before Nassau—convinced that France would bar British entry to the EEC anyway. And after Nassau the Kennedy administration had made an almost identical nuclear offer to Paris, perhaps involving even broader technical assistance within a NATO Command arrangement (since the French nuclear force was not as far advanced as the British); de Gaulle, after some thought, decided to reject the offer on the same day he announced the EEC veto. Thus, while Nassau was more than just a convenient excuse, de Gaulle's actions were ultimately rooted in an enduring conception of France's political role and in a long-standing distrust of "les Anglo-Saxons." Britain's "European" credentials were more broadly questioned.

*Andrew J. Pierre, *Nuclear Politics: The British Experience with an Independent Strategic Force, 1939–1970* (London: Oxford University Press, 1972), p. 237.

Stung by de Gaulle, but reassured by the deepened strategic relationship with the United States, the Macmillan government tried to pull back to a more traditional external role in 1963–64. The attempt could not be entirely successful. As Europe's Inner Six pushed ahead with the EEC, as the military-strategic gap between Britain and the superpowers widened, and as Commonwealth support for Britain diminished, London became increasingly isolated. British policy remained effective in some areas: Macmillan successfully (and for the last time) played "middleman" during the 1963 Partial Test Ban Treaty negotiations, and London held steadfastly to a role east of Suez, intervening to suppress East African mutinies in 1964 and slowly building a military presence in Malaysia to counter Indonesian provocations there. But none of this could reverse the steady downward drift of Britain's significance in world affairs.

The First Wilson Government

The primary foreign policy issue in the October 1964 general election, which returned the Labour Party to power for the first time in thirteen years, was the future of the independent deterrent. Advocates of unilateral renunciation of nuclear weapons had badly divided the Labour Party in 1961, and from 1962 through most of 1964 the Labour leadership was carefully ambiguous about the deterrent—critical of the financial wastefulness of Conservative nuclear policies, but without promising to scrap nuclear weapons once Labour achieved power. Harold Wilson, the party leader, spoke about "renegotiating" Nassau, but the precise meaning of this was left unclear. In a trip to Washington in February 1964 Wilson talked about dovetailing Labour defense policy with what the Pentagon wanted: spending more to beef up the BAOR and less on the deterrent, and establishing centralized control of NATO nuclear weapons. The public impression at this time was that Labour would give up the Polaris and make far-reaching changes in Britain's military commitments.

Such was not the case. Wilson sought mainly to retain his freedom of action on the nuclear issue, and by the fall of 1964, as power seemed within Labour's grasp, he had second thoughts about giving up the deterrent. Construction of British Polaris submarines was now well under way, with the first submarine scheduled to enter active service in 1968. On becoming prime minister, Wilson reduced the size of the British Polaris force from five to four submarines and cancelled the TSR-2 low-level strategic strike aircraft, but he retained the deterrent under substantially the same rules that had guided its use before. This naturally displeased pro-disarmament left-wing members of the Labour Party, and the Labour government—with a narrow four-seat majority in Parliament—walked a tightrope in the ensuing months.

The Wilson government was determined at first to carry on Britain's global role; in his Guildhall speech in November 1964 Wilson proclaimed that

Britain remained a world influence and a world power. By the start of 1965 Britain had assembled in Malaysia its largest extra-European military force since the Korean War, and other global commitments were retained unaltered. But the press of limited resources on commitments continued to be a problem. By 1966 (as we shall see in chapter 10), pressure on the pound sterling and on Britain's trade position was reaching crisis proportions; a reduction of defense spending was inevitable. The February 1966 *Defence Review* argued that "Britain should continue to maintain a military presence" in the Far East and Southern Asia but announced that henceforth "major operations of war" would not be undertaken "except in co-operation with allies." A withdrawal of forces from Aden and reduction of those in Singapore and Malaysia was projected, and the British aircraft carrier program —crucial to a global disposition—was to be phased out. London was ready to recognize the de facto priorities of the past two decades by reducing Britain's global role, concentrating instead on commitments to NATO and the nation's strategic relationship with the United States. Thus in a sense Labour Defence Minister Dennis Healey carried the 1957 Sandys White Paper to its logical conclusion by carrying out a reduction in commitments commensurate with the reduction of forces.

As Britain's economic crisis deepened in 1967, the Wilson government considered further amending defense commitments, despite American pressure to retain them. In June the Arab-Israeli Six-Day War began in the Middle East, further exacerbating Britain's economic problems by closing the Suez Canal and threatening British oil supplies. Whereas in previous decades a more powerful Britain would have intervened to protect Middle East interests, now the government—mindful of British military limitations and the political repercussions of the 1956 Suez crisis—settled into hapless immobility and simply looked on. On July 18, 1967, Whitehall issued a supplementary White Paper on Defence that called for a complete withdrawal of British forces from east of Suez—Malaysia, Singapore, and the Persian Gulf—by the mid-seventies. Four months later, on November 18, Wilson finally devalued the pound, and shortly thereafter further defense reductions were announced. Withdrawal from east of Suez was now slated for 1971. Retrenchment was in hand.

By now Britain had also suffered a tremendous loss of diplomatic prestige. Wilson's refusal to intervene in force against the renegade white settler regime in Rhodesia in 1965 badly hurt London's image in the Third World, especially in the nonwhite Commonwealth (see chapter 11). In early 1967 Wilson fumbled an attempt to bring Washington and Moscow together on the Vietnam issue, with the result that London lost standing in both Soviet and American eyes. Later in the year British withdrawals from Malaysia were interpreted by President Lyndon Johnson and Secretary of State Dean Rusk as leaving the American position in Vietnam exposed, and relations between London and Washington became difficult. Meanwhile, Wilson's halfhearted support of—or at least acquiescence in—the Johnson administration's Indo-china policy earned him contempt in both diplomatic circles and among segments of the British public. By the end of 1967 Britain's fortunes seemed to be at their nadir.

BRITAIN AND THE ATLANTIC ALLIANCE: PHASE FOUR, 1967–80

In the late sixties and early seventies Britain began to move decisively toward a close relationship with Western Europe, and membership in the Common Market was gained in January 1973. At the same time relations with the United States became less intimate, so that by December 1971 Prime Minister Edward Heath had declared the effective end of the Anglo-American special relationship. At home, economic conditions did not become more permissive —in fact they were at times more restrictive than ever—and a feeling of gloom settled over British politics and the economy by the mid-seventies.

London's security policy in the period 1967–80 was dominated by four concerns: (1) deployment and modernization of the British nuclear deterrent; (2) planning for Western Europe's defense, which required maintaining an American military presence on the Continent; (3) East-West detente, includ-ing an effort to influence some aspects of the Soviet-American strategic rap-prochement; and (4) orderly reduction of British military commitments outside Europe. Since these four major strands of security policy mingled and overlapped in at times confusing ways, it might be best here to consider each strand in turn; we shall deal with areas of overlap wherever they are impor-tant.

The Nuclear Deterrent

The first British Polaris submarine began operational patrols in June 1968, just five and a half years after the Nassau Agreement. Two more Polaris subma-rines became operational in 1969, and a fourth in 1970. Each submarine, containing sixteen missiles, carried an explosive power roughly equal to all the bombs detonated during World War II and could pose a devastating threat to Soviet cities. Because of the refit time required by nuclear-powered subma-rines, normally only two vessels—but sometimes only one—could be on station at a given time. Still, the Polaris force was formidable, and by 1969 had supplanted Bomber Command as the mainstay of the British deterrent. The cost of Polaris was remarkably modest, since much of the research and development work had been done in the United States. Final costs—£162 million for the submarines, £53 million for the missiles, and annual operating expenses of £30–40 million—were slightly lower than anticipated. Of course, there was a price to be paid for such economies: Britain was now dependent upon another power, the United States, for the ultimate technological means of the nation's defense.

Although the Polaris force promised to provide a credible deterrent for some time to come, by the early seventies it seemed possible that a force of such limited size might eventually be neutralized by Soviet antiballistic missiles (ABMs). The SALT I agreement of May 1972, which limited ABM deployment by the two superpowers, effectively extended the useful life of the British deterrent. From 1973 on, however, there was growing concern about upgrading Britain's missile force, perhaps by equipping it with multiple, independently targeted warheads (MIRVs). In 1973 the House of Commons Expenditure Committee rejected British purchase of the more advanced Poseidon submarine-launched missile from the United States; Poseidon, the committee argued, was just too expensive. In that same year the Polaris Improvement Program was launched, and by 1977 a new warhead with improved capability for penetrating Soviet defenses was being fitted to British Polaris missiles.

But this was only a temporary palliative. Some means had to be found of keeping the British deterrent alive past the late eighties. One method, the purchase of more advanced strategic systems from the United States, was not necessarily available. Washington was increasingly sensitive to the possibility that nuclear assistance to its allies might disrupt Soviet-American strategic rapprochement and set a bad example in terms of limiting nuclear proliferation. Another method, the pooling of British and French nuclear resources, raised seemingly insuperable political and legal difficulties—nationalism in both countries, and legal prohibitions against passing along to France the results of Anglo-American nuclear cooperation. One thing was certain: nuclear delivery systems were now so expensive, and London—dependent on the United States—had not maintained a full range of strategic weapons research for so long, that it was extremely doubtful Britain could rejuvenate its deterrent alone. Some outside help, American or other, would be necessary (if only financial help). In the absence of such aid British policymakers would have to consider getting out of the strategic deterrent business altogether, a course of action that held out the likelihood of a further substantial loss of British prestige.

In the late seventies British leaders weighed these issues and attempted to postpone a concrete decision. They considered the relative virtues of submarine-launched missiles like Polaris and the new cruise missiles (subsonic nuclear-tipped drones that could be launched from aircraft or submarine torpedo tubes and fly close to the ground to evade enemy defenses). They also discussed amending British strategic doctrine, which in nuclear terms had inflexibly aimed at the destruction of Soviet population centers, but which in the future might incorporate more limited kinds of retaliation against military targets. Whatever options were finally selected, the choice was likely to influence relationships with Britain's American and European allies.*

West European Defense

In early 1968 the Wilson government announced an unequivocal shift to a Europeanist defense orientation. The *1968 Statement on Defence* reasoned that "the foundation of Britain's security now as always lies in the maintenance of peace in Europe. Our first priority therefore must still be to give the fullest possible support to NATO. Our contribution will be formidable . . . and will increase as British forces are brought back from S.E. Asia and the Middle East and are assigned to NATO command in Europe and the Mediterranean." The statement recognized long-standing British priorities and anticipated the benefits of a near-complete withdrawal from east of Suez. Defense efforts would be concentrated in Europe and the North Atlantic, and British military power outside Europe would come, if at all, from a vague "general capability" derived from forces maintained for European purposes.

Paradoxically, the Wilson government's decision to concentrate British forces in Europe coincided with what is generally considered the low point of NATO's history. By late 1967 the alliance teetered near dissolution. France had withdrawn from the military structure of NATO, reducing drastically the depth of alliance defenses and interfering profoundly with lines of supply and communication. The United States was preoccupied with Vietnam, and seemed to accord much lower priority to the needs and opinions of European governments, which—faced with the prospect of abandonment by Washington—felt impelled to secure their own "understandings" with Moscow. Most important, there was a general perception in Europe that the Soviet threat had diminished, that the detente policies of West European nations and liberalization in Eastern Europe might bring about a permanent thaw in East-West relations, and that NATO had therefore outlived its usefulness. Britain was as guilty of contributing to NATO's lassitude as the others. Despite Whitehall's military contraction to Europe and despite the promises embodied in the February 1968 defense statement, a full brigade was withdrawn from the British Army of the Rhine (BAOR) during 1968. It was not sent back to Germany until 1970. The British withdrawal to Europe in 1967–68 was ill-timed in another sense, too: it coincided with French rejection of Britain's second attempt to join the EEC (more on this in chapter 10).

The Soviet invasion of Czechoslovakia on the night of August 20–21, 1968, abruptly changed the perspectives of most NATO governments and

---

*For a discussion of factors influencing the viability of the British and French nuclear deterrents, see Graeme P. Auton, "Nuclear Deterrence and the Medium Power: A Proposal for Doctrinal Change in the British and French Cases," *Orbis*, 20, no. 2 (Summer 1976), 367–99.

rekindled their interest in a militarily viable Western alliance. The invasion, undertaken to end months of increasing political liberalism in Czechoslovakia, served to remind Westerners of Moscow's determination to maintain a friendly pro-Soviet "buffer zone" in Eastern and Central Europe. In early September 1968 the NATO Defense Planning Committee announced a halt to further reduction of Western forces. In November the NATO ministerial meeting agreed that the continued existence of the alliance was more than ever necessary and that NATO forces, especially conventional forces, should be improved.

London was as anxious as other governments to revitalize Western Europe's increasingly moribund defense structure, particularly in view of the introduction of twenty Warsaw Pact divisions into Czechoslovakia close to the NATO front line. In Britain's case, however, the renewed commitment to the alliance was mainly verbal; British forces in Germany were not increased. Partly this was because, while the Czechoslovak invasion had disabused all Western governments of notions about the civility of Soviet power, the Soviet action was nonetheless seen in London as preserving a stable European status quo (there were obvious differences with Gaullist French perceptions here). The Wilson government attached great importance to improving relations with Moscow, so much so that just five days after the invasion Wilson declared that "whatever the tragic disappointments of the last few days . . . we all know that the only future for the world rests upon continuing to work for detente between East and West." This sentiment was echoed in December by the NATO Ministerial Council, which argued that the alliance should still "work to promote a policy of detente."

During 1969, the first year of the Nixon administration, Washington remained preoccupied in Vietnam, and Congressional pressure for reduction of United States forces in Europe continued, despite President Nixon's pledge to resume a more active American role on the Continent. At the same time Warsaw Pact forces remained at an inordinately high level in Central Europe. This double-edged threat—American apathy and a Warsaw Pact buildup—encouraged West Europeans to develop common positions in the military field (and subsequently in detente) so that they could speak with a unified voice to the United States. The result was the establishment in 1969 of an informal group of European defense ministers within NATO known as the Eurogroup. London played a key role in its creation, indicating some ambivalence about the future of the Anglo-American special relationship.

By 1970 British foreign policy had two main objectives, which were not always compatible: (1) to strengthen the cohesion of NATO, and (2) to keep a foot in the door of the European Community. In pursuing these goals London attempted to allay the security anxieties of West Germany, reduce Anglo-French tensions and disagreements, and consolidate Europe's defense by ensuring a permanent American military presence on the NATO Central Front and in the Mediterranean. This required, among other things, adjudicating alliance disputes over burden-sharing and Bonn's *Ostpolitik* (with which the Wilson government was guardedly sympathetic), maintaining the BAOR, and adopting a patient "wait-and-see" attitude toward post–de Gaulle France.

Increasingly, however, London's special link with Washington could not be used to meet basic foreign policy goals. Transatlantic tensions were mounting: American neglect of Europe in the Johnson years was being replaced under Nixon by conflict with West Europeans not only over defense (burden-sharing, Soviet-American strategic detente, and so on), but also, and perhaps more importantly, over monetary and trade questions. Britain's turn toward Europe coincided with a decoupling of West European and American strategic and economic interests. While seeking mightily to retain Washington's military commitment to Europe, Britain also had to decide what to do if the worst should come and American forces were withdrawn. A cohesive Western Europe with Britain as a member was the best hedge against this possibility; the "two pillars" formula that was so clearly rejected in the late forties might be institutionalized after all.

The logic of Britain's foreign policy reorientation was carried to its necessary conclusion after the Conservative Party's return to power in the June 1970 general election. Prime Minister Edward Heath decisively took Britain into Europe and announced the end of the Anglo-American special relationship. The symbolic end of that relationship came in December 1971, after Heath had successfully negotiated British entry into the European Community, and after a series of shocks and surprises in American foreign policy— notably the abrupt change in Washington's China policy (about which London was not notified in advance), Nixon's August 1971 unilateral termination of the Bretton Woods monetary system, and American support of Pakistan in the December 1971 Indo-Pakistani War. Meeting in Bermuda with President Nixon, Heath let it be known that the term "special relationship" had been relegated to history, to be replaced by what he called simply a "natural relationship." The Nixon administration wanted Britain to mediate the bitter economic and monetary dispute between the two sides of the Atlantic, but Heath would have none of this; the British prime minister was unwilling to antagonize the European Community in the delicate early stages of Britain's EC membership. Nixon, Heath argued, would have to explain his own economic strong-arm tactics. The Conservative government thus made a clear choice: at a time of diminishing British power and increasing unpredictability in American policy, London had to assume as its overriding foreign policy objective an active role for Britain within Europe. This was conceived, sometimes not very easily, as supplementing Britain's commitment to NATO consolidation.

The incompatibilities between American and European (hence also British) foreign policy perspectives were catalyzed by the events of 1972–73. In May 1972 Nixon and Soviet First Secretary Leonid Brezhnev signed the SALT

I agreement curbing anti-ballistic missile deployments and setting a limit to Soviet and American offensive strategic weapon levels. This agreement, in European and British eyes, raised the disturbing specter of Soviet-American condominium. Future bilateral strategic arms negotiations might take up United States and Soviet nuclear-capable forward-based systems in Europe, raising the possibility that Western Europe's security could be jeopardized in a negotiation in which no West European government was represented. Washington's promise to consult with Europeans before reaching a final agreement with Moscow on strategic matters did not really allay these fears. Tensions within NATO increased.

On January 1, 1973, Britain formally entered the European Community. Later that month preparatory talks for the Mutual and Balanced Force Reduction (MBFR) negotiations began in Vienna, at which the prime incentive of the British (as of other West Europeans) was to forestall the withdrawal of American troops from the European Continent. On April 23, 1973, United States Secretary of State Henry Kissinger, disturbed by what he perceived as European uncooperativeness in monetary and trade matters at a time of continuing military demands on the United States, proposed a "New Atlantic Charter" that would embody European economic concessions in exchange for American military concessions. Kissinger proclaimed that 1973 would be the "Year of Europe," meaning the year in which Washington—after its long obsession with Vietnam—would once more come to terms with its European allies. But Kissinger's proposal for a New Atlantic Charter was rebuffed by the foreign ministers of the European Community who, meeting in Copenhagen, drafted a common "declaration on European identity," which was ill-received in Washington. Again, transatlantic tensions—exacerbated by continuing disagreement over international monetary arrangements—mounted.

The final straw came with the onset of a new Arab-Israeli War in early October 1973. Most West European governments—their economies heavily dependent upon Arab oil—refused to support Washington's pro-Israeli stance, imposed an arms embargo on Israel, and even denied overflight and landing rights to American aircraft carrying supplies to the Middle East. London was one of these governments. On the weekend of October 13–14 the British government refused an American request to sponsor a simple Middle East cease-fire resolution in the United Nations Security Council, and a few days later London rejected an American plan to "ostracize" through trade measures those East European governments that had facilitated the Soviet airlift of material to Egypt and Syria. On October 23, as tensions increased in the Middle East and arms poured into both sides, Washington declared a worldwide alert of American military forces. Neither London nor the Nixon administration's other NATO allies were consulted in advance, even though the alert brought the United States and the Soviet Union closer to a direct confrontation than any event since the 1962 Cuban missile crisis.

Washington's failure to consult was interpreted in Britain as symptomatic of broader difficulties. "The Middle East war," opined the London *Financial Times* on October 29, "has demonstrated conclusively, if proof were needed, that Europe's peace-time interests are not coterminous with those of the U.S."

Transatlantic relations improved in the late seventies as the oil crisis abated, and as Washington continued to participate in the European Security Conference and the MBFR talks. United States troops remained in Europe, and domestic American agitation for their withdrawal diminished in the face of a massive buildup of Warsaw Pact forces. In the economic realm, pressure to put together a replacement for the defunct Bretton Woods monetary system declined, and over time the dollar stabilized internationally. Relations between the United States and Western Europe reached a certain equilibrium as both sides openly recognized the incompatible aspects of their strategic interests and even accepted these differences as unresolvable. The dogma of Atlanticism passed into oblivion.

All of this meant that the standard postwar British formula for European security—a heavy reliance on a dominant United States—might not work beyond the immediate future. This lesson was understood quite early by France but impressed itself on Britain only in the seventies. Some alternative had to be found, and it seemed certain that this alternative would not take the form of detente with the Soviet Union. Britain and the West Europeans, while attempting to maintain American military commitments, looked to a variety of strictly European institutional frameworks for organizing defense: the old Western European Union, the Eurogroup within NATO, and the enlarged European Community. A strong indigenous European defense structure might be better able to coordinate the activities of its members and deal with the United States in such questions as modernizing the British and French deterrents, undertaking economically feasible joint weapons projects, and determining the future disposition of such new weapons as the "neutron bomb." It remained to be seen, of course, whether London and its allies possessed the political will to create such a structure.

East-West Detente

In the sixties and seventies there were two kinds of detente working simultaneously, though sometimes at cross-purposes: (1) an *immobiliste* strategic detente that attempted to stabilize the East-West division and thereby make it "safe," and (2) a revisionist political and economic detente, usually intra-European, that sought to overcome the East-West division altogether. West Germany, as the major revisionist state in postwar Europe, pursued the latter from the late sixties on. Britain, with initially conservative interests in Europe, supported the former and was much less enterprising than some of its Continental partners in its relationships with the East. By the mid-seventies

London sought to balance the danger of superpower condominium implicit in the first detente against the danger of West European fragmentation, Soviet dominance, and "Finlandization" implicit in the second. The former was still more tractable and less frightening from London's perspective.

MBFR It is not surprising, then, that from the moment the NATO Council called for Mutual and Balanced Force Reductions (MBFR) in June 1968, London was more supportive of the force reduction idea than of the less tangible and potentially more disturbing cultural and political issues bound up in the European Security Conference. MBFR, which aimed at a reduction of opposing NATO and Warsaw Pact forces on the European Central Front, (1) brought Washington safely into the center of East-West negotiations, (2) channeled detente diplomacy through existing alliance structures, thus allowing the pace of detente to be more easily controlled, and (3) provided a major incentive for Washington to avoid unilateral withdrawal of American forces. London was less interested in the goal of MBFR, the reduction of military forces, than in the *process* of the negotiations and the benefits this process could yield. After the MBFR talks began in early 1973 Britain made no major effort to break through the fundamental incompatibility between Washington's preference for "creating a balance" (that is, larger Warsaw Pact reductions since Warsaw Pact forces were larger to begin with) and Moscow's preference for "equal reductions" (maintaining Warsaw Pact preponderance on the Central Front). London was, however, anxious to keep the negotiations going. If MBFR was slow to produce basic agreement, this was undoubtedly to the liking of some Whitehall decision makers.

SALT As we have already noted, London was less enamored of the other detente negotiations. SALT, though it extended the useful life of the British deterrent, nonetheless aroused London's suspicions. Increasingly Britons wondered about the implications of strategic arms limitation agreements in view of the so-called Nixon Doctrine that predicated American support on allied "self-help"—that is, SALT's implications in terms of (1) prospective United States military withdrawals from Europe, including the possible withdrawal of nuclear-capable forward-based systems (FBS), (2) possible cancellation of American nuclear assistance to Britain, or at least the refusal of assistance beyond the strict limits of the Nassau Agreement, and (3) least important from the British perspective, a possible Soviet-American attempt to "freeze" the European status quo in defiance of revisionist European efforts to build a more organic relationship between East and West. SALT stood as a constant reminder that the United States was a global power with global interests, in the name of which European concerns could be sacrificed, while Britain was now a European power with a much more limited purview. London knew that Washington and Moscow also understood this. The SALT process had not, so far, taken in the British and French nuclear deterrents (except implicitly) because of the danger that multilateralizing the negotiations would simply stall them forever.

CSCE The Heath government at first also adopted a skeptical approach to the Conference on Security and Cooperation in Europe (CSCE, or more simply, the European Security Conference). This conference, which began in 1973, involved some of the more difficult political, economic, and cultural aspects of detente—multilateral recognition of Europe's territorial status quo, "confidence-building measures," free flow of people and ideas, and expansion of East-West trade. In London it was feared (1) that the conference would break down into empty rhetoric because of the number of governments participating (eventually thirty-five), (2) that the *appearance* of East-West normalization at CSCE would generate a sense of exaggerated security and lassitude in Western Europe, perhaps ultimately leading to Soviet hegemony on the Continent, (3) that the conference would encourage Bonn to attach even higher priority to its diplomatic outreach toward the East, with unsettling results for NATO and European Community cohesion, and (4) that an overly aggressive position at CSCE on the part of East European governments would cause Moscow to once again react to keep its satellites in line, with disturbing consequences for the East-West military balance. Britain made limited contributions to CSCE, attaching particular importance to a provision for advance notification of military maneuvers and, subsequently, to the issue of freer flow of people and ideas. In the end, British fears of CSCE's consequences were not justified. CSCE Heads of State signed a "Final Act" in August 1975, not a binding treaty, and the West did not let its guard down —largely because the entire concept of detente came under attack after 1973 in response to the Middle East crisis, the collapse of South Vietnam, Soviet meddling in Africa, the continuing Soviet strategic arms buildup, and the plight of Soviet political dissidents.

British Commitments outside Europe

The Wilson government's withdrawal from east of Suez between 1966 and 1970 was ill-planned and wasteful because the scope of the withdrawal was hastily redefined on three successive occasions (February 1966, July 1967, and November 1967). For example, forces withdrawn from Aden in accordance with the 1966 *Defence Review* were moved to the Persian Gulf; they then had to be moved from the gulf back to Europe in accordance with the July and November 1967 defense statements. Similar confusion surrounded the disposition of British forces in the Far East. The additional costs involved in all this moving were substantial. Moreover, many Britons came to see the precipitous rate of withdrawal envisioned in the November 1967 statement as unnecessary and potentially damaging to British interests, especially in Singapore and the Persian Gulf. It was no surprise, then, that the Conservative Party was particularly critical of the Labour government's east-of-Suez policies and promised in the months preceding the 1970 general election to reevaluate British military withdrawals.

After coming to power in 1970 the Conservative Heath government reversed many of its predecessor's decisions. The October 1970 *Supplementary Statement on Defence Policy* reasoned that "Britain has long-standing associations with the Commonwealth countries of South-East Asia and she shares their interest in the stability of the area." It therefore proposed to maintain a British military presence in Malaysia and Singapore and to "continue discussions with leaders in the [Persian] Gulf . . . on how Britain can best contribute to the maintenance of peace and stability in the area." By early 1971 the Heath government had decided to retain bases in Singapore and the Indian Ocean area, to renew the agreement with South Africa for the Simonstown naval base, and to deploy token forces in Hong Kong, Singapore, and the Persian Gulf. The bases on Malta and Cyprus in the Mediterranean would also be maintained, since they filled an important need on NATO's southern flank. Heath's message was clear: Britain was not completely out of the international policing business because British interests were still global in scope, though overseas commitments would take second priority behind NATO responsibilities. In Washington the Nixon administration, still bogged down in Vietnam, was pleased by these decisions—especially the decision to retain a British presence in Southeast Asia.

But there was some self-delusion in all of this, since Heath's partial reversal of Wilson's policy failed to take account of increasingly limited British resources. The November 1967 devaluation of sterling came years too late, and in the months following devaluation the domestic economy slipped into the worst extended crisis yet. The drain of resources was exacerbated by two problems: (1) the Heath government's bitter dispute with the trade unions over wage-and-price policies, which degenerated into confrontation politics in 1971–72 and brought the nation close to a general work stoppage during the 1973 coal miners' strike, and (2) the sectarian violence in Northern Ireland, which became steadily more intense after it began in 1969. The Irish problem not only drained economic resources, but also placed a direct demand on military manpower; by the middle of 1972 there were 17,000 British troops in Northern Ireland. In view of these domestic crises, the need for Britain to finance any kind of global military role was highly questionable. By 1973 even Conservatives recognized that a substantial overseas military presence would be too expensive, and a less-than-substantial presence would subject London to all kinds of liabilities without yielding many political advantages.

Britain's effective withdrawal from east of Suez occurred after the Labour Party's return to power in February 1974. Prime Minister Wilson, though mindful of British interests in the Middle East, Indian Ocean, and South Atlantic, was anxious to reduce British responsibilities as quickly as possible because the country was still embroiled in a major economic crisis. In March 1975 the Labour government announced major cuts in defense spending and overseas deployments. Nearly all forces would be withdrawn from Singapore and Malta, forces on Cyprus and in Hong Kong would be reduced, some forces would be withdrawn from the Indian Ocean, the Simonstown agreement with South Africa would be terminated (in part for political reasons), and several new defense programs would be cancelled. Roy Mason, the Labour government's defence minister, stressed that NATO remained the "linchpin" of British security and that there would be no reduction of the 55,000-man BAOR in Germany. It had to be faced, Mason argued, that the nation's global policing days were over and that Britain was now principally a European and Atlantic power.*

In sum, the evolution of British security policy involved, more than anything else, a struggle to bring commitments in line with available resources. This task was frustrated by the difficulty of predicting, from one year to the next, the exact shortfall of resources and the precise cost of new weapons projects or of continuing overseas commitments. It was also frustrated by the psychological unwillingness of Englishmen to abandon a global role that for so long had been a source of pride and prestige. We shall see in the next chapter that Britain's attempt to maintain a global security posture might have been made considerably easier if London had not insisted on two other kinds of international commitments: the commitment to a fixed-value pound sterling with international reserve and exchange functions, and the commitment to economic autonomy vis-à-vis the continent of Europe.

---

*In the general election of May 1979 a Conservative government was returned to power under the leadership of Britain's first woman prime minister, Margaret Thatcher. The Conservatives, drawing 43.9 percent of the popular vote, achieved a forty-three-seat majority in Parliament. No major shifts in British foreign policy were anticipated (the country would continue to have a Europeanist orientation), and the only immediate foreign policy problems faced by the Thatcher government were the Rhodesian question (discussed in chapter 11) and coordination with other industrialized states in fashioning a response to the growing energy crisis.

10

Political
and Economic
Reconstruction

The linkage between foreign policy and British economic recovery in the postwar era is often characterized somewhat negatively as three sets of failures: (1) the failure of the British economy to maintain a rate of growth sufficient to support the full range of the government's external commitments and defense needs, (2) the reciprocal failure of foreign policy decision makers to curtail Britain's global military commitments earlier, once the problem of a slow growth rate and low domestic investments had become obvious, and (3) the failure of British policymakers and politicians to push Britain into leadership of the European integration movement in the fifties, given the tremendous economic benefits such leadership would have yielded.

The first failure is most often attributed to a long process of British industrial decline going back to the late nineteenth century. This was a process in which the British economy suffered from an outdated industrial plant, outmoded patterns of labor relations, an anti-entrepreneurial bias among political elites, mounting competition from other industrial powers, and—with the advent of World War II—a critical loss of foreign investments. The argument based on these structural-historical deficiencies is often coupled with moral reprobation of the phlegmatic, lazy, self-satisfied British character—which is seen as the root cause of Britain's economic woes.*

The second and third failures are usually attributed to the "cognitive lag" problem discussed in chapter 9: the unwillingness of British leaders to adjust

---

*"According to the stereotype, the American businessman is gung-ho; the German, ever-efficient; the Japanese, fanatical; the Frenchman, devious; and finally, the Brit—either as manager or worker—admired for his manners, but not his drive." See Robert Samuelson, "The Lion in Winter," *The New Republic* (January 1 and 8, 1977), p. 17.

policies to the nation's reduced international role, and to accept Britain's downward slide from imperial status to being just an island off the coast of Europe. In this view, the maintenance of overseas military commitments and the refusal to join Europe were policies that exacted high opportunity costs and in the long run perpetuated the sad state of the domestic economy.

It will be argued here that all of these characterizations are at best too simplistic and at worst highly misleading. A series of contrary propositions will be advanced. First, British foreign policy was the cause—rather than the victim—of Britain's poor postwar economic performance, but this had little to do with defense expenditures (which had a major economic impact only between 1951 and 1954) or with the early refusal to join the European Economic Community (EEC). It had to do, rather, with the dogged insistence of successive British governments on retaining the pound sterling's international transaction and reserve functions at a fixed exchange rate through most of the postwar era, down to the Wilson government's reluctant devaluation of the pound in 1967. As we shall see, there were a number of powerful incentives for government intransigence over sterling, and many of these incentives were political as well as economic.

Second, Britain's refusal to join the EEC in 1957, though mistaken in hindsight, may have been throughly reasonable at the time, given the country's economic and political role in the world. Membership in the EEC was not a panacea for solving all of Britain's economic problems (government intransigence in other areas of economic policy guaranteed that), and Britain's final accession to the European Community in 1973 was on first evidence a mixed blessing—neither as damaging to British interests as critics of the Common Market contended, nor as beneficial as its more ardent supporters earlier claimed.

Third, while the "structural" argument pertaining to Britain's long-term industrial decline and the backwardness of key sectors of the domestic economy contains large elements of truth, this thesis has been frequently overstated and comes dangerously close to a kind of historical determinism that neglects the more hopeful aspects of Britain's economic picture. There is no intrinsic reason why Britain cannot have a vibrant and healthy economy.

BRITAIN'S POSTWAR ECONOMIC DECLINE

Sympathetic observers often point out that in *absolute* terms Britain's postwar economic performance was not that bad. The economy sustained a growth rate of 2.6 percent per year between 1951 and 1973, unemployment was usually held at around 2 percent until the mid-seventies, and the real buying power of the average Briton at times increased substantially. Despite occasional forebodings in the press of spiritual and economic collapse, and bouts of national self-criticism among the intellectuals, the quality of British life visibly improved. Through it all Britain gracefully withdrew from empire and maintained major defense expenditures, with defense budgets averaging 8 to 9 percent of the Gross National Product (GNP) in the fifties and 5 to 6 percent in the sixties. Added to all of this was the development of a major superstructure of public services, including health care and more education, the benefits of which were felt by all Britons. In short, the visible evidence did not support a picture of economic disaster.

Although all of this is true, it is not a convincing rationalization of Britain's postwar economic performance. Appearances can be deceiving. The fact is that it was impossible to maintain rising living standards, welfare programs, and a stable balance of payments with an annual growth rate of only 2.6 percent. Moreover, British economic performance cannot only be measured against itself, in "absolute" terms, for the simple reason that throughout the period under discussion Britain's economy was highly dependent on international systems, and its survival contingent upon its international competitiveness. Small in area, with limited resources and a dense population accustomed to a relatively high standard of living, Britain had to import half of its food and over 25 percent of its total consumption of goods. To pay for these imports the British economy had to export heavily. In postwar years imports usually amounted to between 16 and 20 percent of the GNP and exports to between 13 and 15 percent. The difference between imports and exports was made up by "invisibles" (services—mainly banking and insurance—and earnings on overseas investments), which until 1973 usually turned the trade deficit into a payments surplus. Given the British economy's tremendous reliance on the international economic system (a reliance matched by some other European states, notably West Germany and the Benelux countries), it makes more sense to look at Britain's postwar economic performance in *relative* terms—that is, to compare British performance with that of other countries at similar levels of development with comparable resources—rather than to measure it against itself over time.

Relative to the performance of its neighbors, Britain did not do well between 1945 and the late seventies. The British GNP was surpassed by West Germany in 1961 and by France in 1965, and in subsequent years this gap between Britain and its two competitors widened dramatically. By 1977 West Germany, with a population and resources comparable with Britain's, had double the GNP. In 1969 Britain's per capita GNP dropped to thirteenth among all the countries of noncommunist Europe; it retained this ranking through the late seventies, with only Italy, Ireland, Spain, and Portugal—for the most part poor Southern European countries—registering worse performances. By 1977 the per capita GNP of West Germany, Sweden, and Switzerland was approximately twice that of Britain. Even more astounding, Britain's growth rate—in terms of both GNP and GNP per capita—consistently ranked *lowest* among *all* European countries outside the Soviet bloc, including poorer Mediterranean countries. Similarly, the rate of average annual increase in output per man-hour was lower in Britain than in all its industrial competitors except the United States. Put bluntly, Britain's economic atrophy justified very pessimistic conclusions.

A partial explanation for the shortfall in British economic performance is sometimes found in the nation's military expenditures. Throughout the Cold War Britain consistently spent a larger proportion of its GNP on defense than did France or West Germany (indeed, the latter was freed from defense burdens altogether for the first postwar decade). Large-scale defense outlays began during Korean War rearmament (1951–54). As late as 1957 Britain was still spending 8.5 percent of its GNP on defense against West Germany's 4.5 percent, while allotting only 15 percent of its GNP to capital investment against West Germany's 22 percent. When the Wilson government came to power in the mid-sixties it decided to lower defense expenditures to a fixed sum of £2 billion in 1964 value, which meant that as the GNP slowly grew the percentage of it spent on defense declined—but this was still 4.9 percent in 1970 against West Germany's 3.3 percent, and in 1976, under new guidelines, it was back up to 5.1 percent against Bonn's 3.6 percent. It is argued that this channeling of more funds into defense, often in response to American pressure, reduced domestic and foreign investments and cost British export industries a larger share of world trade at critical junctures in the fifties and sixties.

But this argument can be taken too far. It is likely that defense outlays had a serious disruptive impact on Britain's investments and trade position only during the first two or three—admittedly critical—years of Korean War rearmament, 1951–54. After this the responsibility of defense expenditures for Britain's economic difficulties was probably negligible. Moreover, it must be remembered that after 1965 the national products of both West Germany and France were larger than Britain's and continued to grow at a faster rate, so that Bonn and Paris could have higher defense budgets than London and still register a lower percentage of GNP devoted to military expenditures. West Germany consistently spent more on defense than Britain after 1971, and France spent substantially more after 1974. After 1972 both West Germany and France spent more per capita on defense than Britain—a not entirely irrelevant measure of relative defense burden. In short, the extent of defense effort cannot simply be equated with the percentage of GNP devoted to military expenditure, and the decisiveness of the impact of defense costs on other sectors of the economy cannot be measured solely in this way either. It is true that for extended periods British leaders attempted to squeeze every reasonable increment of defense capability out of the economy, but Britain's defense burden—which was never so extraordinary in the sixties and seventies—could never explain the full magnitude of the economy's poor performance. As we shall see, this performance had a lot to do with the priority given by British leaders to political over economic concerns, but this only secondarily involved the defense effort.

THE POLITICS OF STERLING

One of the main causes of Britain's postwar economic difficulties was the dogmatic and at times emotional insistence of British leaders on maintaining the pound sterling's international transaction and reserve functions at a fixed exchange rate. Before examining the consequences of this intransigent monetary policy, we should understand the three major reasons it was pursued:

1 British political leaders and the Treasury were inclined to see sterling's international role as an imperial legacy, as embodying solemn responsibilities to Commonwealth governments that held sterling as a reserve asset, and as one more measure of Britain's continued great-power status. Under Harold Wilson in the late sixties sterling became a symbol of Britain's international virility and prestige, much like the independent nuclear deterrent.

2 The United States placed substantial pressure on Britain to support the Bretton Woods system, an international monetary system of fixed exchange rates and free convertibility of currencies in which the dollar and sterling served as key transaction vehicles and primary reserve assets. Bretton Woods benefited the United States immensely, and the system's continued viability depended significantly upon British cooperation in maintaining a strong sterling. Washington therefore pressed heavily during the fifties and sixties to prevent the devaluation of sterling, and to keep it at its assigned par value of £1 to $2.80 (the value of the dollar was in turn fixed at $35 to one ounce of gold).

3 Successive British governments defended a fixed, overvalued pound sterling because they feared that any devaluation (at least after 1960–61) would set off a chain of competitive devaluations as Britain's trade rivals attempted to maintain competitive export prices. Such an event might shake the international monetary system to its roots. British leaders also feared that devaluation would irremediably undermine sterling's role as an international reserve currency, a role that for political and economic reasons—prestige and an ability to run up long-term payments deficits —they wanted to preserve.

In sum, the incentives for defending a fixed international sterling were strong and were tied up in the web of international political commitments and circumstances that confronted Britain throughout the postwar era. Some of these commitments and circumstances derived from World War II itself. In economic terms, the war brought with it (1) the incursion of massive foreign debts and the large-scale loss of overseas assets by Britain, (2) a strengthening of the sterling area within the Commonwealth, with Britain at its center performing an international banker role, and (3) the conversion of British industry to wartime production, accompanied by disinvestment in the domestic economy. American Lend-Lease aid and the temporary pooling of Commonwealth monetary reserves partially substituted for Britain's foreign exchange earnings during the war, but Lend-Lease was abruptly cut off in August 1945 and the Attlee government quickly faced external payments difficulties. By this time the British external liability—largely the result of war-related spending—amounted to £3.4 billion, of which £2.7 billion was held in sterling area countries. The most obvious way to rectify this payments problem was to drastically increase British exports while holding imports to a lower level. This would uphold the external value of, and external confidence in, sterling—important, since the Treasury wanted Commonwealth governments to retain sterling as a reserve asset (Commonwealth sterling holdings eased short-term payments pressures on London).

But there were complications and competing demands. Exports could not exceed imports by such a large margin in the anomalous circumstances of the immediate postwar period, not if the Attlee government was to honor its commitment to continued domestic growth and the inauguration of expensive social welfare programs. Severe government manipulation of the relationship between productivity, exports, and domestic consumption would work a hardship on the British people, and would be politically unpopular (though some rationing of goods continued). One possible course of action was devaluation; the pound was pegged at $4.03 immediately after the war and was increasingly seen as overvalued. Devaluation would reduce the price of British exports abroad and increase the domestic price of imports, thus improving the balance of payments situation. In addition, devaluation would reduce the dollar value of Britain's external debts. But devaluation conflicted with the British Treasury's desire to maintain confidence in sterling, a desire motivated in part by the solemn commitment to Commonwealth sterling holders. In its early stages, devaluation might also disrupt the Attlee government's domestic programs.

Sterling was finally devalued in 1949, from £1:$4.03 to £1:$2.80. The devaluation came largely in response to a serious dollar shortage within the sterling area. Further measures of this kind were resisted, however, and between 1949 and 1967 successive British governments fought bitterly to prevent a further devaluation. A pattern of relationships between sterling and Britain's domestic economy was established by the early fifties that would persist well into the seventies: domestic economic growth, leading to a rise in domestic demand for imports, would repeatedly threaten the balance of payments and the international position of fixed-value sterling; the government would then repeatedly intervene to protect sterling by deflating the domestic economy and drying up the domestic money supply, in the process drying up investments and profits. These deflationary campaigns, launched ultimately for political reasons, eventually brought the British economy to the edge of disaster.

But we are getting ahead of ourselves. Well before the 1949 devaluation, Britain's desperate payments position was eased by a more direct instrument: money borrowed from the United States. Most infamous was the loan of 1946, amounting to $3.7 billion plus $672 million to cover some outstanding liabilities. The loan was to be payed back with interest over fifty years, beginning in 1951. In return for the loan, London ratified the American-supported Bretton Woods monetary arrangements—which would fix sterling exchange rates—and promised Washington that sterling would be made freely convertible into other currencies as quickly as possible. This combination of fixed exchange rates, free convertibility, and sterling's role as a transaction and reserve currency would in the long run spell deep trouble for the British economy. Two critical questions remain to this day unanswered: (1) whether London would have assented to the Bretton Woods arrangements, unaltered, if it had not needed the 1946 American loan, and (2) whether succeeding British governments would have been so unbending about maintaining sterling's fixed value and international role without the added pressure to maintain them embodied in Bretton Woods and American desires. As the Cold War intensified, the United States Congress in April 1948 approved the European Recovery Program—the so-called Marshall Plan—and loans extended to Britain under this program only further increased the country's indebtedness, political as well as financial, to the United States.

Despite these exigencies, the British economy performed creditably in the first postwar years. During the late forties visible exports increased by 75 percent over prewar levels, and Britain's trade gap (the excess of imports over exports) fell to below 10 percent, in contrast to a 40 to 45 percent gap between 1930 and 1939. Overseas investments were slowly restored, and earnings from these were supplemented by American Marshall aid. Moreover, the 1949 devaluation of the pound improved Britain's dollar position. While the country's trade performance improved dramatically, industrial production increased 30 to 40 percent in the five years 1945–50. It proved feasible to finance both postwar reconversion of the economy and the Labour government's new social welfare programs, and there was no obvious conflict at first between national growth and Labour's commitment to redistributive policies.

Unfortunately, conditions changed. By the early fifties the more efficient economies of West Germany and Japan, now fully resurgent, were gaining a steadily larger percentage of world trade while Britain's share was shrinking. From this time on Britain faced an increasing number of trade rivals. Moreover, in the three years 1951–54 Whitehall diverted substantial resources to a major rearmament effort, with inevitable opportunity costs. Another problem arose in 1958 when the pound finally became fully convertible, and therefore more vulnerable to pressure from outside the sterling area. Throughout, London continued its effort to maintain great-power status. Just as the British became overextended militarily, they likewise became overextended financially under a monetary arrangement that not only partially absolved them of international payments discipline, but also encouraged policymakers to place external financial claims ahead of domestic economic development.

British leaders regarded the sterling system—resting on fixed exchange rates, London's role as banker, and the nation's pivotal position in the Commonwealth—as a key underpinning of Britain's position as a major power; it would be possible (optimists in London contended) not only to improve living standards at home and consolidate the welfare state, but also to re-create a liberal world economic order with sterling, along with the dollar, at its center. The weight of tradition in the Treasury and among British financiers strengthened this view in the face of contrary evidence. As Stephen Blank has argued, this brought about a curious kind of political determinism in which the Treasury itself gave primacy to political over economic considerations:

Britain's international role and its international commitments were all symbolized in the pound sterling and the sterling system. The domestic economy was viewed largely in response to international developments, particularly international confidence in the pound. What this seems to indicate is an extraordinary primacy of political over economic considerations within the Treasury itself. Treasury thought was dominated by a variety of "political myths" about Britain's role in the world, sterling, and so on, which, in fact, operated against Britain's economic interests. The Treasury's approach, far from being ruled by narrow economic considerations, too often evaded such economic realities as Britain's capacity to pay the costs of its international role.*

The Treasury's highest priority, in the defense of which domestic economic growth would be allowed to suffer, was the protection of sterling's international position.

Crises were inevitable. Imports always exceeded exports in Britain, and when the domestic money supply increased and the economy showed a propensity for more-than-marginal growth, the demand for imports would rise at a faster pace than the increase in domestic productivity and exports. This would usually endanger Britain's balance-of-payments position, raise the threat of domestic inflation, and place downward pressure on the value of the pound. Hypothetically, in a system of purely free-floating exchange rates Britain's payments position would be self-equilibrating: the pound would depreciate, imports would become more expensive and British exports less expensive (therefore more competitive), and any rise in standard of living would be roughly commensurate with increases in productivity and Britain's

*Stephen Blank, "Britain: The Politics of Foreign Economic Policy, The Domestic Economy, and the Problem of Pluralistic Stagnation," *International Organization,* 31, no. 4 (Autumn 1977), 688.

external earning power.* But a floating exchange system (or even a quasi-free "dirty float" system manipulated by governments) did not exist in the fifties and sixties. The external value of the pound was fixed, confidence in it had to be maintained, and devaluation of it was unthinkable, despite its increasingly overvalued parity. This overvalued parity was especially damaging because the British economy depended so heavily on imports and exports, and overvalued sterling increased the price of British exports while making imports more competitive at home.

Deflationary Campaigns

If British governments refused to permit external devaluation of the pound (and if trade protectionism would invite retaliatory action by others), there was only one other thing they could do: suppress domestic pressure on the pound and the balance of payments by restricting the domestic economy's buying power. This is precisely what successive governments did, with ultimately disastrous consequences. From 1955 on—as the international position of sterling weakened and domestic pressure on it became more sustained, touching off frequent balance-of-payments crises—London tried to correct external payments problems through major domestic deflationary campaigns that at times required brutal internal adjustments. Each crisis would begin with external speculation against the pound and short-term monetary movements. The British government's response would be predictable: the domestic economy would be cooled down (though it was rarely actually "overheated") and spending restricted through increased taxes, a squeeze on consumer credit, and controls on installment purchases. Domestic investment would be constrained by a combination of direct investment controls, high interest rates, credit restrictions, and cuts in investment allowances for tax purposes. London launched major deflationary campaigns of this nature in 1957, 1961, and 1966. The domestic economy was simply not allowed to grow; instead, it stumbled along in a series of "stop-go" fluctuations. After 1965 the economy was in almost continuous retrenchment, and most of the incentive for economic growth was drained out of the country.

It seems phenomenal in retrospect that the stubbornness and traditionalism of British politicians and the Treasury with respect to sterling could have

---

*It should be stressed, however, that "the possibility of gain from devaluation lies chiefly in the effects of . . . relative price changes. Lower export prices will lead to increased sales; higher import prices should reduce the volume of imports. However, improvement in the balance of payments will only occur if the changes are of the right order of magnitude— that is, if the net effect of the increased export volume and decreased import volume is sufficient to offset the lower unit price of exports and the higher unit price of imports." That is, elasticity of demand is not always commensurate with fluctuations in price. See Peter Donaldson, *Guide to the British Economy* (Baltimore, Md.: Penguin, 1965), pp. 68–69.

gone so far. Through the sixties Treasury officials believed that economic growth depended principally upon strong sterling, domestic price stability, and expanded production. They were inclined to blame "stop-go" fluctuations on domestic inadequacies, especially the higher rate of wage increases compared to increases in productivity, and they in any case attached lower priority to growth than to sterling's solvency. It did not occur to them that a deflationary policy that specifically restricted investments and profits would at the same time hopelessly encumber overall economic growth. Hence, the costly adherence to a fixed international pound sterling continued.

THE 1967 DEVALUATION CRISIS

The crisis that finally brought about devaluation and began the move toward a floating pound came quickly, almost without warning, in November 1967. By this time some 20 percent of all international transactions were still conducted in sterling, and external claims on the pound amounted to £3.9 billion (not including £1.4 billion held in the International Monetary Fund). Both domestic and foreign pressure on sterling had been mounting for some time, and Harold Wilson's Labour government had only narrowly averted devaluation in July 1966. The immediate causes of the November 1967 crisis were (1) the Six-Day War in the Middle East the previous summer, which had closed the Suez Canal and forced Britain to depend for a time on more expensive Western sources of oil; (2) crippling dock strikes in London and Liverpool, which seriously disrupted exports in October and November; and (3) financial maneuvering on the European continent, especially the activities of money speculators, official nervousness about the future of the pound, and French pressure for sterling devaluation. These factors upset Britain's balance of payments, and in early November precipitated a new run on the pound in world money markets.

In previous months Wilson had doggedly insisted that he would never devalue and had even forbidden his advisers to discuss the possibility. Now he buckled under the weight of three considerations: (1) firm resistance within the Labour Party against further domestic deflation, (2) a warning from Pierre-Paul Schweitzer, Secretary-General of the International Monetary Fund, that a requested $3 billion IMF loan would have to be accompanied by extensive international monitoring and control of the British economy (a condition unacceptable to Wilson), and (3) the prospect of continuing runs on the pound sterling if measures were not taken to correct Britain's fundamental balance-of-payments disequilibrium.

On November 18, 1967—after agonizing discussions within Wilson's cabinet, with the United States Treasury, and with the international banking community—the pound was devalued from $2.80 to a lower fixed parity of $2.40 (Wilson later said that he would have preferred to float the pound, but he was apparently dissuaded from such a move). Over the objection of elements of the Labour Party (who were nonetheless mollified by the devaluation), these measures were accompanied by a new domestic deflationary campaign that indicated the government's approach to balance-of-payments problems really had not changed much.

A concerted effort was made, especially by the United States, to contain the international repercussions of the devaluation. A number of governments had assured London and Washington that there would be no competitive devaluations, but American officials were still fearful of the implications for the dollar's long-run stability (indeed, Washington had unsuccessfully pressured Wilson not to devalue). A large international credit of $2 billion was raised under American leadership to help Britain defend sterling's new parity against attack during an initial period in which the British balance of payments would be especially vulnerable. During 1968 an attempt was made, again with American backing, to prop up the reserve role of the pound in the eyes of nervous Commonwealth sterling holders through the Basle Agreement. Under this agreement, members of the sterling area "were persuaded to stay put [not sell their sterling] by a guarantee of the future value of the currency reserves which they held in sterling in London, calculated in U.S. dollars"; that is, "the Bank of England was committed to make good any further falls in the dollar value of these holdings."* The Basle Agreement served to petrify sterling deposits and prolong the increasingly moribund reserve role of sterling for only another three years, after which the weakness of the dollar itself eliminated its value as a "guarantee" currency supporting the pound.

The 1967 devaluation did not really solve any of Britain's economic problems because it was too little and too late. A larger cut than the 14.3 percent reduction to $2.40 had been advocated by some, but this was resisted by both Wilson and the Americans, with the result that drastic domestic deflationary measures had to be continued. Moreover, as Wilfrid Beckerman, one of Wilson's economic advisors, subsequently observed, "Failure to devalue earlier meant that both the deficit that had to be eliminated and the surplus that had to be aimed at in order to pay off accumulated debt were much greater than would otherwise have been the case."† The limited magnitude of the devaluation and the subsequent guarantee of the new exchange rate through the Basle Agreement meant that attention had to be focused more rigidly than ever on external confidence in sterling. Thus the domestic

---

*Andrew Shonfield, "International Economic Relations of the Western World: An Overall View," *International Economic Relations of the Western World, 1959–1971: Volume I, Politics and Trade,* ed. Andrew Shonfield (London: Oxford University Press, 1976), p. 53

†Wilfrid Beckerman, "Objectives and Performance, an Overall View," *The Labour Government's Economic Record, 1964–1970,* ed. Wilfrid Beckerman (London: Duckworth, 1972), p. 63.

economy, rather than being freed from external constraints, had to be contained and—on occasion—deflated just as much as before. But there were forces in the domestic British economy that rendered a continuation of such policies suicidal; these forces were less tolerant of the government's economic policies than they had been earlier.

THE DOMESTIC ECONOMIC CRISIS, 1968–74

Despite their tarnished reputation, British trade unions up until 1968 did not have a bad strike record. Between 1955 and 1964 Britain lost an annual average of 294 days per 1,000 workers to strikes, against 336 for France, 703 for West Germany, and 1,044 for the United States. Britain's relatively good record could in part be attributed to a broad tripartite consensus between unions, business, and the government as to the rules governing labor relations. But this consensus began to break down after 1968, when the Wilson government—frustrated over the failure of devaluation to solve fundamental economic problems, and convinced that the source of difficulty still lay in the uncooperativeness of producer groups in the domestic economy—defied tradition and directly confronted the unions by threatening to impose legal restraints on their activities. By this time the unions were more restive in any case, and most British workers were becoming impatient with the government's prices-and-incomes policies. The result of this confrontation was that between 1968 and 1974 relations between the unions and both Labour and Conservative governments were much worse than ever before in the postwar era. Strikes increased in number and severity, national union leaders lost what little control of their locals they previously had, and the breakdown of a basic agreement about the "rules of the game" in British politics brought the country to the edge of violence. Productivity inevitably suffered, and interruption of exports (damaging to the balance of trade) increased.

Union-government conflict intensified when the Conservatives returned to power in 1970 with the promise of reviving British capitalism. The Heath government introduced a new industrial relations act and pressured employers to resist wage increases. Despite these measures, runaway inflation gripped the economy and some workers suffered a reduction in real earning power. Strikes were rampant, and in 1972—with the Conservatives still in power—Britain lost more workdays to strikes than in any year since the 1926 General Strike. In late 1973 a bitter coal miners' strike forced the country to cut back production to a three-day work week; this, in combination with huge oil price increases following the 1973 Middle East War, very nearly ruined the British economy.

As a result, the Conservative government came tumbling down in the February 1974 election. Labour won a thin plurality of seats in Parliament (301 out of 635) and formed the first minority government in postwar Britain, an indication of the general malaise in British politics. Heath's economic controls were dismantled, and the new Labour government called for a "social contract" of voluntary wage constraints. This policy met with only limited success at first as trade unions, mindful of Labour's tenuous claim to power, went on a wage binge. Wage increases often averaged 30 percent, which invariably fed inflation. Still, as union demands were met the 14.8 million working days lost to strikes in 1974 dropped to 6 million in 1975 and less than 3 million in 1976. The "social contract" gradually took hold as workers themselves came to recognize the futility of inflationary wage increases. By the end of the seventies major changes were afoot.

DOLLAR DEVALUATION
AND THE END OF BRETTON WOODS

Just as earlier sterling policy had set the stage for all of this disruption in the domestic economy, the fluctuating international status of sterling between 1968 and the late seventies continued to affect Britain's overall economic fortunes. Between the Basle Agreement of 1968 and the summer of 1971 the pound fared reasonably well; overseas sterling balances grew once more, and by 1970 the currency was able to withstand a wave of bad domestic economic news. Though the new rate of $2.40 necessitated continued domestic deflation, at the international level the pound held its own.

But trouble was on the horizon. By 1969 the United States dollar came under serious pressure. The United States had abused the dollar's reserve role in the Bretton Woods monetary system for years, and the country now faced serious short-term payments difficulties (in part because of the Vietnam War). The view became widespread in international money markets that the dollar was overvalued, and speculation against it increased. Persistent dollar crises between 1969 and the summer of 1971 involved massive movements of capital and sustained runs on American reserve assets, mainly gold. Foreign central banks bought large quantities of dollars in an effort to maintain the dollar's par value (on May 5, 1971, the West German Bundesbank took in $1 billion in the first 40 minutes of trading!), but in the end the dollar faced the same fate as sterling. The pressure for devaluation was irresistible.

On August 15, 1971, President Nixon unilaterally suspended the dollar's convertibility into gold, devalued it by 10 percent, and imposed a 10 percent surcharge on certain imports. A further 10 percent devaluation of the dollar soon followed. These actions, which effectively ended the key features of the Bretton Woods arrangement, shook the international financial community to its roots.

In response, the British Treasury at first allowed the pound to float, and other West European governments also either floated or revalued their currencies. In December 1971 the Smithsonian Agreement tried to restore monetary stability by providing wider bands of exchange flexibility than the old fixed-parity system, and as part of a general realignment of currencies sterling was revalued up to $2.60. But the following summer, in June 1972, rumors of a British dock strike set off a fresh run on sterling in international money markets. The London foreign exchange market was closed for a time; when it reopened, the pound was once again allowed to float. This time the float was not temporary, and during the next five years sterling sank to steadily lower par values.

London's increased willingness to allow the pound to float in defiance of sterling's reserve role (in defiance, that is, of Britain's solemn commitment to overseas holders of sterling) was more than a result of Washington's 1971 devaluation and the weaker position of the dollar. By mid-1972 Britain had largely negotiated its way into the EEC, and one of the conditions of Common Market membership was a diminished reserve role for sterling. This condition of membership stemmed from the French argument that (1) the pound's status as a reserve currency might help Britain to escape balance-of-payments discipline and (2) the burdens of this lack of discipline—including future runs on the pound—would have to be borne by all EEC members once Britain joined the Community. Nothing was likely to diminish sterling's reserve role as effectively as an extended downward float, which would also—of course —help stabilize Britain's balance of payments.

Downward pressure on the pound was exacerbated in 1974–75 by Britain's massive external oil debt (oil costs amounted to 20 percent of the country's imports in 1974), by a decline in domestic productivity due to the coal strike, and by runaway domestic inflation (almost 30 percent in mid-1975). In March 1976 the pound dropped below the psychologically important $2.00 level, and continued its downward skid until it hit rock bottom on October 28, 1976: a par value of $1.55½. From this point on—with the benefit of a large IMF loan in December 1976—the pound began a long climb back. Efforts to maintain sterling's international value were not likely, however, to affect domestic British economic growth to the extent they had in the past.

In retrospect the ultimate costs associated with rigid sterling policies and the long allegiance to a fixed and overvalued international pound may never be known. In 1971 *The Economist* assessed these costs somewhat bluntly: "No country has sacrificed more to the great delusion of the old monetary order than Britain. In order to keep sterling standing in the front firing line of fixed exchange rates, for far longer than the Americans have now bothered to keep the dollar there, the average British family must have lost thousands of today's pounds in thwarted income over the whole decade 1957–67."* The government's monetary policies down to 1967 cannot be explained in any other terms but dogmatic traditionalism, a misdirected sense of responsibility

---

* *The Economist,* December 18, 1971, p. 13.

(mainly to Commonwealth countries), and a lingering belief in Britain's role as a great power. These same factors, as we shall now see, explain much about Britain's inability to approach the entire question of European integration in a constructive way.

THE POLITICS
OF EUROPEAN INTEGRATION

It is customary (and not altogether unjustifiable) to point to Britain's failure to take European integration seriously as a major (if not *the* major) miscalculation of postwar British foreign policy. We have argued that this view is exaggerated, that there were other—perhaps even more critical—miscalculations, and that membership in the EEC could never be a panacea for all of Britain's economic ills. Nonetheless, we must recognize the vicissitudes of Britain's economic and political relationship with the EEC as one of the dominant themes running through postwar British foreign policy. As with sterling, the British government in its approach to the EEC made decisions that had major *economic* repercussions on the basis of fundamentally *political* considerations. And as with sterling the flaws in earlier policy were not actually dealt with until the late sixties.

The reasons for British coolness toward European integration in the late forties and fifties are understandable enough, and it is unfair—with the benefit of more than two decades' comfortable hindsight—to completely fault London's thinking at the time. The principal reasons for British opposition to participation in an integrated Europe are worth recounting because most of these considerations lingered on—some in mutated form, to be sure —through the late seventies, as the debate on the wisdom of British entry into the European Community continued. There were seven major reasons for British reluctance to join an integrated Europe.

First, the concept of European unity always worried London because such unity might be arrayed *against* Britain and because it would almost certainly disrupt the Continental balance of power. Moreover, a united Europe would confront London with an unenviable choice between (1) becoming a part of "Europe" and thereby risking Britain's position as a world power and (2) staying out, with the risk of losing influence in European affairs. British interests seemed better served by the maintenance of a "traditional" Europe divided along national lines, which would pose less of an intrinsic threat to the status quo.

Second, Britain became quickly aware in the late forties that the main center of decision in world politics had shifted away from Europe to the United States and the Soviet Union. A Britain immersed in a united Europe might not be able to influence these extra-European forces. This concern was crystallized in London's preference, discussed in chapter 9, for an "Atlantic" solution to European security (involving United States domination of individual West European states) as opposed to a "two pillars" solution (involving a united Europe as a coequal partner of Washington). Taken too far, British participation in European integration might conflict with the effort to retain a permanent American military presence on the Continent.

Third, London felt it necessary—both for practical and sentimental reasons—to maintain the sympathy and cooperation of the independent Dominions (Canada, Australia, New Zealand, and to begin with, South Africa). The assistance provided by these countries was critical during World War II, and after the war British trade was heavily directed toward them. They constituted, in any case, the core of the Commonwealth idea. But these countries were also isolationist so far as Europe was concerned, and London realized that they would likely see British participation in a united Europe as inimical to their own interests. Therefore, as long as London considered Commonwealth ties centrally important, it was reluctant to move decisively toward Europe.

Fourth, Britain's recent experience stood apart from the experience of continental Europe. Britain was a victor in World War II, had stood alone against Hitler, and had derived tremendous national self-confidence from the war. At the end of the war the viability of British political and economic institutions stood in marked contrast to the bankruptcy of European political institutions and the shattered state of European economies. In the forties and fifties London remained a world power. There was no obvious reason why, even in the fifties, Britain should tie its fortunes or surrender its sovereignty to a united continental Europe. As F. S. Northedge has noted:

It was hard to believe that Britain's situation was so desperate that it was best for her to commit suicide in order to be born again into a European federation. It was almost as hard to believe that the Europeans, after all their talk and paper constitutions, really had the political ability to make a fundamentally constructive advance. It was considered that Europe, after all, owed its survival to British insularity.*

Historical experience did not support the idea of Britain as a component of an integrated Europe.

Fifth, there was the deep-seated emotional detachment of Britons from mainland Europe. The British public had an insular mentality: it saw Europe as either a place to holiday and not entirely to be taken seriously, or as a source of unpleasant military conflicts that occasionally cost Britain dearly. The detachment was cultural and historical, not simply geographic. As a consequence, neither Labour nor the Conservatives stood to gain domestic political advantage by pursuing a British role in European integration; indeed,

---

*F. S. Northedge, *British Foreign Policy: The Process of Readjustment 1945–1961* (New York: Praeger, 1962), p. 135.

the concept incurred a good many domestic political liabilities. Moreover, public biases were reinforced by elite opinion. To quote Northedge again:

From the European scene British politicians have been apt to turn with relief to their fortunate island just outside the rim of chaos, have often been deeply ignorant of European affairs and have been able to speak to British audiences as though knowledge of Europe was not an essential part of political *savoir-faire.* *

The parochialism of British attitudes toward Europe inevitably found its expression in foreign policy and was a major obstacle to a rational approach to European integration.

Sixth, the Labour government that came to power in 1945 had plans to control and reorganize the domestic economy and institute new social welfare programs. It was not about to throw away its control of the state machinery by immersing Britain in a federal Europe. In ensuing years the desire of governments—Labour and Conservative—to manage the national economy would, rightly or wrongly, constitute a major obstacle to all-out British participation in European integration. It was believed, very simply, that the British economy was idiosyncratic and that it would fair better under the close but sympathetic stewardship of the British government than under the diffuse but less benevolent influence of European integrative institutions.

Seventh, and finally, there was no persuasive reason throughout the forties and fifties for believing that European integration would be an unqualified economic success. Until 1961 Britain still had the most productive economy in Western Europe, with impressive technological capabilities, extensive Commonwealth connections, and an international reserve and transactions currency. We have seen that some of these British assets were ephemeral and overvalued, but this was not to be known at the time, and British politicians were probably not unjustified in taking a detached and even skeptical view of the EEC in the late fifties. It was only during the sixties that the consequences of much higher growth rates in Germany, France, and other European countries became obvious. Even then, it was not clear to what extent the EEC itself—as opposed to other elements of the West European economy—was the cause of rapid growth.

EARLY EFFORTS AT EUROPEAN INTEGRATION AND COOPERATION

In contrast to rejection of the idea of European *integration,* Britons were not opposed to the concept of European *cooperation.* Cooperation for limited, functionally specific purposes was considered legitimate and desirable in the immediate postwar era. At times London backed closer coordination of econ-

*Ibid., p. 134.

omies and policies through some kind of European confederation as a necessary course for Continental powers, though not for Britain. In September 1946, for example, Winston Churchill—then Opposition leader—proposed in Zurich the creation of a Council of Europe as a first step toward a "United States of Europe" (which, naturally, would exclude Britain). The following January Churchill launched the Movement of European Unity in London. This movement would stress the benefits to be gained by burying old European national antagonisms and by confronting the Soviet Union with a solid political and economic entity encompassing the western half of the Continent. Churchill's scheme was mainly visionary, of course, and it is a fair bet that he was motivated primarily by a desire to lift West European spirits in the confused months immediately following the war (it was not yet certain what form, if any, a permanent American commitment to European security would take).

The United States demonstrated its interest in European recovery in June 1947 when the Marshall Plan was announced. Ten months later Congress approved Marshall aid, and in April 1948 the Organization for European Economic Cooperation (OEEC) was created under joint Anglo-French sponsorship to distribute the funds appropriated by Congress and to administer a four-year recovery program.* London found OEEC attractive because it constituted one more instrument for tying the United States to Europe without embodying any supranational overtones.

The Attlee government was less positive about the Council of Europe proposed by France in May 1948. The Council would deal with practical problems of recovery faced by West European governments, and in the initial French scheme would have a supranational structure. To London, this idea was objectionable because it appeared to be a first move toward a "two pillars" approach to Europe's future (that is—as outlined in chapter 9—an approach that excluded the active formal participation of the United States). By the time the Statute of the Council of Europe was signed in May 1949 the British had managed to water it down to being simply an intergovernmental conference, with the principle of unanimous approval preserved for all important questions.

From this point forward Whitehall took an obstructionist position on the question of European integration and refused to countenance surrendering even part of British sovereignty to a supranational European organization. In November 1950, several months after the Schuman Plan calling for a European Coal and Steel Community (ECSC) was launched, Under-Secretary of State for Foreign Affairs Ernest Davies told the House of Commons that "there cannot be any delegation of general powers to an outside body, to an

---

*OEEC member countries were Britain, France, Austria, Belgium, Denmark, Greece, Iceland, Ireland, Italy, Luxembourg, the Netherlands, Norway, Portugal, Sweden, Switzerland, and Turkey. Britain and France assumed responsibility for West Germany within OEEC.

outside authority which might not necessarily share the view of HM Government or with which compromise was impossible, and which might even deprive HM Government of powers without which they could not carry out the wishes of the electorate." Centuries of sovereignty and tradition could not be thrown away, the British felt, under circumstances that did not seem to warrant such a move.

In April 1951 the European Coal and Steel Community (ECSC) treaty was signed in Paris, and in July 1952 its provisions went into effect. The ECSC created a common market for coal, iron, and steel among its six members (France, West Germany, Italy, Belgium, the Netherlands, and Luxembourg); its initial objective was to provide all West Europeans with a measure of control over West German industrial resurgence (see chapter 2). Britain was invited to join ECSC, but refused. Prime Minister Attlee told the House of Commons, "We on this side are not prepared to accept the principle that the most vital economic forces of this country should be handed over to an authority that is utterly undemocratic and is responsible to nobody." The Labour government insisted on maintaining firm control of the domestic British economy.

London was also cool toward the European Defense Community (EDC) proposal (which failed to pass the French Assembly in any case) and maintained a safe distance from the 1953 proposals for a European Political Community that would encompass, to begin with, ECSC and EDC. Britain was, however, instrumental in bringing about West German rearmament after the failure of EDC. This was achieved through the creation in 1954 of a Western European Union (WEU), made up of Britain, France, Benelux, West Germany, and Italy. WEU was not, of course, a supranational body. Indeed it was functionally quite specific: the channeling of West German military forces into the NATO alliance.

ESTABLISHMENT
OF THE EUROPEAN ECONOMIC COMMUNITY

The year 1955 proved to be a watershed in Britain's relationship with Europe. In June, under the prodding of the three Benelux governments, the six ECSC foreign ministers met at Messina to consider the possibility of broader intra-European cooperation. They soon announced their intention to form a European Economic Community, a customs union that would erect a common external tariff and eliminate trade barriers between member countries. The ultimate objective, decades away, was economic and then political union. A committee was appointed, presided over by Paul-Henri Spaak, to study the problems associated with broader European economic integration and to draft the text of a treaty. This committee (the "Spaak committee") met at Brussels between July 1955 and April 1956.

Britain was invited to take part in all phases of the negotiations, but London's response was ineffectual: an "observer" from the Board of Trade was dispatched to Messina but contributed little, and the British representative subsequently sent to the Spaak committee sessions was withdrawn at the end of 1955. London's position throughout the negotiations was clear: Britain would not participate in a European customs union because the common external tariff would interfere with preferential Commonwealth trade arrangements. The EEC might also, Britain feared, alienate the United States, since a customs union threatened to violate the spirit, if not the letter, of the General Agreement on Tariffs and Trade (GATT), which since 1947 had aimed at liberalization of global trade. Moreover, London would not countenance being a part of an eventual European political union. In the course of the Spaak committee's deliberations in the fall of 1955, the British representative proposed the creation of a simple free trade area—with no common external tariff—to encompass all the OEEC countries. This would obviously thwart the long-term objectives of the Spaak committee governments, however, and the British proposal was rejected (whereupon the British representative left for home).

In April 1956 the Spaak committee reported its recommendation of a customs union to the foreign ministers of the Six (France, West Germany, Italy, and Benelux). Intergovernmental negotiations began in May 1956, and on March 25, 1957, the Treaty of Rome establishing a European Economic Community was signed. The EEC began operation, without Britain, in January 1958.

While all of this was going on, London continued to pursue its free trade area proposal. Under British stimulus, the OEEC in July 1956 undertook a study of the proposal that OEEC states form an industrial free trade area supplementing the customs union of the Six. A technical report confirming the feasibility of such a scheme was issued in February 1957. Detailed negotiations on the terms of a European Industrial Free Trade Area treaty got underway in March 1957 and continued until they finally broke down at the end of 1958.

British incentives for support of a free trade area were all too obvious. London objected to the supranational overtones of the EEC, but at the same time wanted to benefit from any liberalization of industrial trade. British industry, like industry in other European countries, was feeling the pinch of insufficient economies of scale. A free trade area arrangement would force the economic policies of the Six into the wider but less demanding mold of the OEEC, in the process—perhaps—wrecking the EEC. At the same time, since the European Industrial Free Trade Area would concentrate on industrial goods and not have a common external tariff against the rest of the world, British industry could export to a wider European market while Britain continued with Commonwealth trade preferences, which provided a cheap source of food and raw materials. Thus Britain could have the best of both worlds. The governments of the Six recognized all of this and, under French leadership, finally rejected the free trade area proposal in December 1958 (just months after General de Gaulle's return to power). Anglo-French relations eroded into bitterness and recrimination.

Undaunted, the British government met in 1959 with officials of Austria, Denmark, Norway, Portugal, Sweden, and Switzerland and pulled together a plan for a European Free Trade Association (essentially made up of West European OEEC states outside the EEC). The Stockholm convention creating EFTA was signed in January 1960 and went into effect the following May. EFTA turned out to be remarkably successful in expanding trade between its members. But although it was important in its own right, its chief aim was to keep its seven members united in negotiations with the EEC. That is, EFTA was primarily an institutionalized means of maintaining pressure on the EEC to expand at terms that would be acceptable to Britain and other Association members.

THE FIRST BRITISH APPLICATION
FOR EEC MEMBERSHIP

By the end of 1960 it had become clear that the EEC was a major success. Internal trade among the Six rose more than 30 percent during 1960 alone (compared with a 16 percent rise among EFTA members), more American capital was being attracted to Continental Europe than ever before, and it proved possible to speed up the schedule of internal tariff cuts by a year.

In Britain the Macmillan government went through an agonizing reappraisal. Perhaps it would be possible for London to obstruct the supranational drift of the EEC from *within* the organization? Something had to be done. The Common Market, a growing giant of 170 million people, threatened to bypass Britain and relegate London to insignificance. In January 1961 Macmillan saw French President de Gaulle at Rambouillet to discuss Britain's association with the EEC. In June de Gaulle declared that France would welcome British membership in the EEC but that London should pose no prior conditions for entry. On July 31, 1961, Macmillan's Conservative government announced its decision to apply for British membership.

The EEC negotiations on British entry, which began in Brussels in November 1961, did not go smoothly. Britain, as de Gaulle had suspected, wanted the benefits of membership without the initial costs and attached certain conditions to its application. First, London wanted to protect Commonwealth interests and its own right to import foodstuffs cheaply from abroad. Second, it wanted to protect British agriculture and to continue the practice of direct deficiency payments to British farmers, which would keep food prices much lower than the French practice of agricultural price supports at the market level. Third, the British insisted on a suitable provision for other

EFTA countries, to which London still had a formal commitment. Fourth, there was an obvious background concern in London with maintaining the international transaction and reserve roles of sterling, a likely future bone of contention.

It proved very difficult to resolve all these issues, and just two weeks after negotiations began de Gaulle warned that although Britain was welcome to join the EEC, a choice had to be made between the Commonwealth and Europe—a choice Macmillan did not want to make. The problems of Commonwealth trade preferences and British agriculture were exacerbated in January 1962 when EEC members reached agreement on a Common Agricultural Policy (CAP), which incorporated the French preference for price supports.

In March 1962 France was relieved of a major foreign policy burden when peace was achieved in Algeria. De Gaulle was now free to launch a more vigorous diplomatic offensive in his assertion of French *grandeur,* and throughout 1962 he challenged American leadership of the NATO alliance. Britain sided with the United States against France on almost all alliance questions, and this did not help Britain's case in the ongoing EEC negotiations. De Gaulle distrusted the "Anglo-Saxons," as he referred to Washington and London, and saw Britain's role in Europe as that of an American Trojan horse. French leadership of an integrated Europe, perhaps centering on a Paris-Bonn axis, was crucial to de Gaulle's vision of France's new international role, and Britain—with special interests and close ties to Washington —did not fit into this grand design. The negotiations on British EEC membership were difficult enough; when Franco-American dissension and Gaullist nationalism were added to the equation, the prospects of success became more and more dim.

In mid-December 1962 de Gaulle met with Macmillan once more at Rambouillet and expressed grave doubts about Britain's ability to adjust to the terms of EEC membership. Macmillan left sensing trouble. A few days later de Gaulle was given the pretext for obstruction of British entry he had been looking for: the Nassau Agreement between the United States and Britain, which provided the British with American Polaris missiles (see chapter 9). Nassau confirmed de Gaulle's doubts about Britain's "European" credentials; the British were still more interested, he argued, in pursuing strategic condominium with Washington than in becoming an integral part of Europe. To a large extent, of course, de Gaulle was right. London still attached more importance to its strategic relationship with the United States than to its economic relationship with France or Germany.

On January 14, 1963, de Gaulle vetoed British membership in the EEC, shocking London. Last-ditch British negotiations with the Common Market continued for two weeks, then broke off. In subsequent months, to add insult to injury, de Gaulle rejected a West German proposal for regular consultations in Brussels between Britain and the Six. The "friendly Five," as London came to call members of the EEC other than France, kept up their support of British entry. The French continued to be obstreperous, not only over British membership but also over a variety of other EEC issues. These included agricultural policy, a proposed move (opposed by Paris) toward majority voting in the EEC Council, and the nature of supranational political consultations. Indeed, political relations within the EEC became so strained that between July 1965 and February 1966 France boycotted the Community's meetings.

The British took due note of increasing dissatisfaction with Paris among the "friendly Five," but Harold Wilson's new Labour government was less certain of the virtues of Common Market membership than Macmillan had been, and pressure for British entry temporarily abated. Wilson was doctrinally committed, as most Labourites were, to national control of the economy; supranationalism à la EEC would raise difficult problems for any coherent national development strategy.

THE SECOND BRITISH APPLICATION
FOR EEC MEMBERSHIP

The British general elections of March 1966 gave the Labour Party a Parliamentary majority of ninety-seven seats—much more comfortable than the four-seat majority in 1964—and in the following months Wilson, now much more secure in taking risky initiatives, became more positive about British membership in the EEC. It was a question of entering on the right terms. For one thing, conditions now looked more favorable to London because the Common Market had fewer supranational overtones in the aftermath of its struggle to survive de Gaulle's onslaughts. On May 11, 1967, the Wilson government submitted a new application for EEC membership. Denmark and Ireland submitted their applications to Brussels on the same day.

Whereas the Macmillan government had tried to enter the EEC quietly, almost through the back door and without making the Common Market a domestic political issue, the Wilson government's approach was very different. Throughout the summer of 1967 Wilson and high-ranking cabinet members literally barnstormed the EEC capitals to gain support for British entry. But nothing had changed since 1963: the "friendly Five" still supported British EEC membership, while France vehemently opposed it. De Gaulle reiterated his old arguments about Britain not being truly European. Enlarging the Community, argued the French president, would profoundly and irrevocably alter its fundamental nature.

On November 27, 1967—just nine days after London's devaluation of the pound, which in part was precipitated by French pressure—Paris for the second time vetoed British membership in the EEC. The reaction of other EEC governments, particularly the Dutch, was strong. Throughout 1968, while they thwarted French designs in other areas of Community policy, the Five persistently raised the issue of British membership. It was apparent to all Europeans, however, that there could be no real progress on the British entry question so long as de Gaulle remained in power in Paris.

De Gaulle's political position was badly weakened in 1968 as a result of the May Revolution (which challenged his domestic authority and badly disrupted the French economy) and the Soviet invasion of Czechoslovakia (which discredited his new entente with Moscow). Demanding a broad national mandate, de Gaulle in April 1969 staked his presidency on a national referendum (on the downgrading of the Senate and the reform of local government), which he lost. He promptly retired to Colombey-les-Deux-Eglises, and was succeeded in June by Georges Pompidou, a loyal Gaullist.

Pompidou did not have his predecessor's strong will, and de Gaulle's retirement therefore set the stage for a fresh British bid for Common Market membership. Sensitive to changed circumstances, the British Labour government in October reshuffled the cabinet to include a minister responsible for negotiating the country's entry into the EEC. London now recognized that accession to the EEC made compelling economic sense. Between 1958 and 1970 the share of British exports going to the Six rose from 14 percent to 21.8 percent, while the share going to the Commonwealth declined from 37.3 percent to 21 percent. These trends continued.

BRITAIN ENTERS THE EUROPEAN COMMUNITY

The opening shot in the campaign that finally achieved British membership in the European Community was fired by West German Chancellor Willy Brandt at the EEC's Hague summit on December 1, 1969. Brandt was adamant: "The German parliament and the German public expect me not to return from this conference without concrete arrangements on the Community's enlargement. By virtue of the [Rome] Treaty it is one of the cardinal questions of our Community, and we must not put this matter off any longer."* Pompidou's response the next day was mealy-mouthed. He suggested that the Six develop a unanimous negotiating position before dealing with Britain (a near impossibility) and hinted that these preparations could be completed by the following June.

In early 1970 French and German leaders visited London to discuss the British entry question. The French dragged their heels, but the balance of power within the Community was now shifting away from Paris, and the prospect for a successful British application seemed brighter. The Common Agricultural Policy (CAP) had been suspended within the EEC the previous

---

*Quoted in Ian Davidson, *Britain and the Making of Europe* (New York: St. Martin's Press, 1971), p. 118.

August, and in April 1970 the "friendly Five" agreed to reinstate the CAP in exchange for French agreement to reconsider the British application. Mindful of France's now weaker bargaining position and the increasing power of West Germany—which British membership of the EEC might counterbalance—Paris complied. In June 1970 Britain received from Brussels an invitation to resume negotiations; later that month, a Conservative government was returned to power in London.

At times in the following months it seemed the Conservatives were determined to get Britain into the EEC at any cost, and their chief Common Market negotiator, Geoffrey Ripon, probably made concessions on some questions that a Labour government would not have made. These concessions centered around four main issues that had to be resolved before British entry could be effected: (1) agricultural policy, including farm supports and food prices; (2) the future of Commonwealth preferences, particularly for New Zealand dairy products and Caribbean sugar exports; (3) the British contribution to the Community budget, and (4) the future reserve role of the pound sterling.

Agricultural Policy

The British public had always been guaranteed low food prices by a combination of (1) cheap Commonwealth imports and (2) a system of deficiency payments for domestic agriculture, financed by taxation. In contrast, the EEC's Common Agricultural Policy provided for (1) high tariffs on agricultural imports, which raised the price of imported food substantially, and (2) price supports for domestic agricultural products, which raised the price of food to the point where it would support relatively inefficient small farmers, most of them in France. The difference between these two approaches was basic. The British approach—financing domestic agriculture through taxation —was redistributive, since higher income individuals bore a higher tax burden while average food consumption was fairly inelastic. The EEC approach was in some ways regressive, since higher food prices—the result of price supports—were borne about equally by all food consumers, regardless of their income. It was forecast in 1970 that Britain's full adoption of EEC policies would raise the nation's food prices by between 18 and 26 percent. Such price increases would force wages up in an already inflated economy, and as food prices likewise inflated the British public would experience a cut in real income (at the additional cost, most likely, of intensified labor unrest). In order to facilitate British entry into the Common Market, EEC negotiators agreed that although London would have to accept higher food prices, the rate and magnitude of the increase would be kept down by raising external food tariffs slowly over a five-year transition period and by continuing the domestic deficiency payments to British farmers. Fuller harmonization of agricultural policies would come later.

Commonwealth Preferences

Britain felt a special responsibility to New Zealand and the less-developed Commonwealth countries of the Caribbean. By the late sixties 90 percent of New Zealand's butter exports, 78 percent of its cheese, and 88 percent of its lamb were going to the British market; these comprised a quarter of its export earnings. The high EEC tariffs on foodstuffs (as high as 45 percent) would be disastrous for New Zealand after British entry. The British government therefore felt a moral obligation to negotiate a special status for New Zealand exports to the EEC. Similarly, sugar exports to Britain by poor Caribbean Commonwealth countries provided their principal means of support; a high tariff against their sugar would spell economic disaster for them. Both of these problems were at least temporarily resolved in the Common Market negotiations. New Zealand was guaranteed a market for at least 71 percent of its butter and cheese exports until 1978, when further arrangements would be negotiated. And Britain was allowed to fulfill its sugar import obligations to the Commonwealth until the end of 1974, after which the entire question of Commonwealth quotas would be reviewed.

The EEC Budget

Given the full application of EEC rules, Britain was projected to become the single biggest contributor to the EEC budget. London would have to hand over to the Community all import levies on food, all import duties on industrial goods, and turnover tax of up to 1 percent. The Heath government was determined to make the transition to these payments as slow as possible, with very low British contributions in the early years of the five-year transitional period. But Heath's negotiators did not really meet their responsibilities here: it was absurd that Britain, with only the third largest GNP in the Community, should eventually be obligated to make the largest payments—especially since 85 percent of the Community budget was spent on CAP, which principally benefited French farmers. It was left to the subsequent Labour government to correct these inequities.

Sterling Policy

The French government, in particular, did not want the EEC to be responsible for Britain's future sterling liabilities, and Paris therefore pressed for an end to the reserve role for sterling. As we noted earlier, sterling's reserve role was reduced after June 1972 by allowing the pound to float. This role was not completely eliminated, however, and London could not force sterling holders out of the currency without compensating them with nonsterling assets, of which Britain did not have enough. A massive loan might have been raised by the EEC to reduce sterling liabilities more quickly, but the French view prevailed—that solution of the sterling problem was primarily a British rather than a Community responsibility. In the end the sterling issue did not turn out to be a major obstacle in the negotiations; the pound was, after all, floating, and it was assumed that London would eventually resolve the question through its own devices.

The accession negotiations to bring about British membership in the EEC were successfully concluded in June 1971 in Luxembourg. The accession agreement then had to be ratified by the British Parliament. In October 1971 the Conservative government's motion asking the House of Commons to approve in principle Britain's entry into the Community carried by 356 votes to 244. A year later, on October 18, 1972—after extensive and at times bitter debate, and in the middle of a national economic crisis—Commons passed the EEC bill by a much narrower margin of 267 votes to 239, the rest abstaining.

Britain finally became a member of the European Economic Community in January 1973. Denmark and Ireland joined the Community at the same time, expanding the organization from six to nine members.

THE RENEGOTIATION QUESTION

Not all Britons were happy with EEC membership. The trade unions wondered what membership would mean for them, and many businessmen thought that European competition could as easily ruin as revitalize British industry. The Labour Party leadership thought the terms of entry were too harsh. They pointed to the projected rise in food prices, to the enormously inequitable pattern of EEC budget contributions, to the ease with which the Heath government had turned its back on Commonwealth Third World obligations, and to disagreement with the European Community over such questions as redeveloping depressed areas.

During 1973 the Labour Party, which had opposed membership of the EEC in 1972, promised the British public that if returned to power it would "renegotiate" the terms of Britain's entry or, failing this, pull Britain out of the Community altogether. Labour also subsequently promised a popular referendum on membership, scheduled for June 1975. The Labour Party was returned to power in the February 1974 election, and on June 6 Foreign Secretary James Callaghan was dispatched to Luxembourg to begin the renegotiation process.

Renegotiation in 1974 and early 1975 produced some tangible benefits for Britain: the Community agreed to a complex system of adjustments that allowed London to reclaim budgetary contributions out of proportion with its share of the Community's GNP, a favorable commitment to New Zealand dairy products was obtained for the period after 1978, and progress was made on the problem of regional development strategies. The urgency was taken out of the CAP–food price issue by a general rise in world prices that reduced the gap between EEC food and food imported from outside the Community.

In March 1975 Prime Minister Wilson told Parliament that he considered the renegotiation a success and that, although problems remained, his government wanted to keep Britain in the European Community (the Labour cabinet had approved staying in by a vote of 16 to 7, one vote better than expected by pro-marketeers). Finally, in June 1975 the popular referendum was held. It turned out to be something of an anticlimax: British voters, no doubt responding to what was now bipartisan support for the EEC, elected to stay in by a decisive 2 to 1 margin.

ASSESSING BRITISH MEMBERSHIP

In subsequent years Britain's accession to the European Community appeared to be a mixed blessing. Membership did not spur the British economy to new heights of achievement or contribute appreciably to the solution of such problems as high inflation and unemployment. The British economy seemed to stabilize, but this was attributable as much to other factors—the abandonment of fixed, international sterling for one—as to participation in the Community. There was no evidence of any truly decisive improvement in the country's economic performance.

On the other hand, EEC membership was not harmful, either. The Common Agricultural Policy's effect on British food prices turned out to be trivial because (1) average world food prices increased substantially, (2) deficiency payments to British farmers still kept domestic British food prices below Continental levels, and (3) from 1974 to 1977 the level of annual CAP price fixing did not keep pace with general inflation. As a result, reported *The Economist* in June 1977, buying at world food prices instead of CAP prices would have cut the British food bill by only 2.7 percent in 1976 and 2.1 percent in 1977.* This was a far cry from the 18 to 26 percent difference predicted by anti-marketeers in 1970.

In addition, Britain's contributions to the EEC budget turned out to be far smaller than anticipated. In 1971 it had been predicted that in 1975 Britain would pay a net of £140 million to the EEC; in fact, during 1975 Britain made a profit of £54 million from the EEC, much of it in aid for depressed regions such as Scotland and Northern Ireland. Indeed, total British payments between 1975 and 1977 were two-thirds below estimates made in 1971. Payments increased sharply in 1978, the first year following the transitional period, but the corrective mechanism devised during the renegotiation was expected to keep British contributions within manageable limits after 1979.

In at least one respect EEC membership turned out to be clearly advanta-

---

*The Economist, June 11, 1977, p. 62.

geous to Britain: the nation's increasing trade deficit with the Community was reversed. Britain's deficit with the Community rose to over $7 billion in 1975 and became a cause of mounting concern in London. The deficit was reduced substantially in the two years 1975–77, however, and by 1978 Britain seemed to be back on the track to trade equilibrium with its European partners. Between 1972 and the first quarter of 1977 the value of British exports to the EEC rose by 87 percent, after adjusting for inflation; exports to the rest of the world rose by only 49 percent. "If British exports to the EEC had grown at the same rate as to the rest of the world," argued *The Economist* in 1977, "[the] total export figure would be £2.2 billion lower than it is now, at a cost of perhaps 450,000 jobs."[*] British companies exporting high technology registered especially large increases in sales to the Common Market. One company producing electronic components pushed up its EEC sales by 350 percent between 1973 and 1977, and the giant ICI conglomerate reported that 30 percent of its exports from Britain in 1977 went to the Community, as opposed to only 13 percent in 1966. It seemed likely by 1979 that membership in the Community had created more trade between Britain and the EEC than Britain had lost with other countries by joining.

This beneficial effect of the Common Market added to two other bright spots on Britain's economic horizon in the late seventies. First, it could be argued that between 1967 and 1977 the British economy had undergone the precipitous readjustment that British leaders had so stubbornly avoided in the fifties and early sixties. The experience of a ten-year "seige economy" had forced a realistic perception of economic priorities and Britain's global economic role upon governing elites; it had also, by 1976, imposed an appreciation of the dangers of low productivity and runaway inflation upon trade union leaders (though perhaps not upon the rank and file). Second, there was the discovery of North Sea oil. In 1976 North Sea oil provided 15 to 20 percent of Britain's domestic oil requirements; by 1980–81 it would cover all of Britain's needs and eliminate one major source of balance-of-payments disequilibrium. It was even possible that Britain could turn into a net energy exporter, with the EEC its principal customer.

These observations must be tempered, of course. Reform and modernization of the relationships between producer groups in the British economy, and of managerial and marketing techniques, had a long way to go. North Sea oil provided breathing space but not a panacea. And the gap between British economic performance and that of the United States, Germany, and Japan was so huge by 1979 that it was questionable whether this could ever be closed without a willingness of stronger industrial nations to reflate their economies—which was very unlikely. The costs of Britain's decades of economic self-delusion, mostly politically motivated, would not be easily made up.

[*]Ibid., p. 65.

11

Decolonization and the Third World

The process of decolonization within the British Empire began quite early, before World War I, and responded to four fundamentally important factors: (1) the relative decline of British power vis-à-vis the other major powers in the international system, (2) pressure for independence on the part of the white Dominions (Canada, Australia, and New Zealand), which gave impetus to the drive for independence among the nonwhite "dependent" colonies, (3) the inexorable rise of nationalism within colonial societies, spurred on by the experience of the two world wars, and (4) the fact that Britain remained, throughout the twentieth century, a liberal power with increasingly liberal and social welfare-oriented political priorities. The first and last of these factors played a major part in fostering British anti-imperial thought in the aftermath of the Boer War in South Africa (1899–1902). The military frustrations and enormous cost of the South African war demystified the notion of empire—that is, broke down the jingoism of an imperial ideology—in the eyes of the British public and forced a recognition of the limits of British capabilities.

DISSOLUTION OF EMPIRE
AND CREATION OF THE COMMONWEALTH

World War I also brought profound changes. In achieving victory over Germany, the British government depended heavily upon the cooperation of the Dominions, the United States, and the British working class. These three forces significantly affected British imperial policy in several ways.

1 The Dominions, along with India, had to be promised greater independence after the war in return for their wartime assistance to the mother country. In fact, the Dominions and India signed the Versailles peace treaty individually in 1919 and subsequently became separate members of the League of Nations (although London maintained control over much of their foreign policy and defense—especially in India, which was by no means fully independent).

2 The United States emerged from World War I as a major power with a fundamentally anticolonial ideology. President Woodrow Wilson's Fourteen Points centered around the principle of national self-determination of all peoples, which was inimical to the maintenance of European overseas empires. From this point forward the United States became a major source of pressure urging Britain to abandon the trappings of empire.

3 David Lloyd George, the British prime minister during World War I, had been forced to promise the British working class major social reforms in exchange for their terrible sacrifices. The war had been fought for basically elite interests with the blood and livelihood of ordinary working-class people. In its aftermath most Western societies experienced social disturbances as the public, seeing old regimes as largely discredited, clamored for domestic political and social change. Part of this change in Britain, symbolized by the rise of the Labour Party, meant attaching lower priority to imperial aggrandizement and higher priority to domestic needs and democratic principles.

The interwar period (1919–39) saw the grant of independence to the Dominions, the creation of the British Commonwealth, and the beginning of the dissolution of the British Empire as a unit of international law. Relations between the mother country and the Dominions of Canada, Australia, New Zealand, and South Africa were revised so that these states, while becoming independent, remained associated with Britain in a Commonwealth of Nations with London at the center. The Dominions were given the right to exercise most of the prerogatives of independent states, while continuing to provide allegiance and support to the British Crown. This compromise was believed to point the way to a unique federation of culturally distinct societies, which nonetheless forswore traditional notions of "nation" and "state." In 1931 the Statute of Westminister removed the last vestiges of domination by the mother country. The white Dominions became fully independent units under international law (though they continued, of course, to be active members of the Commonwealth). By the early thirties the British government, aware of the nation's declining power, saw its close association with the Dominions as the only viable alternative to a permanent alliance with one of the other major powers (the United States, the Soviet Union, or Japan). The relationship with the Dominions became, therefore, a major source of Britain's claim to great-power status.

The fate of the dependent colonies in Asia and Africa was somewhat different during the interwar period. Domestic political changes in Britain and the rise of Third World nationalism and a new international morality caused London to justify increasingly its colonial rule in terms of liberty and social reform. The purposes of colonialism came to be seen as (1) reducing the suffering of "backward" peoples, (2) preserving peace, law, and good government, and (3) preparing the colonial peoples for self-rule. Some Britons saw the grant of independence to Empire and Commonwealth countries as a "procession," with the Dominions leading the way and the colonial territories following behind several decades later. Others argued that "self-government" for the colonies meant simply domestic self-rule, with Britain continuing to be responsible for their foreign affairs and defense. As time passed it became increasingly clear that this last formula was untenable; Asian and African nationalists aimed not at a watered-down dominion status, but at complete independence.

The special status accorded India at Versailles and in the League of Nations portended a hastening of the colonies' evolution toward independence, despite some British expectations that the process might last a century. In 1929, with a Labour government in power, London declared that the natural objective of India's constitutional progress was Dominion status. The Congress Party in India responded with a demand for total independence, and in 1930–31 Mohandas Gandhi launched a civil disobedience campaign to protest British rule. Throughout the thirties India moved toward internal self-government, while the nationalist movement—spearheaded by the Congress Party—became more radical. In 1939 London reiterated the long-term goal of Dominion status for India, but the onset of World War II, in which India aided the British effort substantially, quickly changed British expectations about the timetable for Indian independence, and the process of Indian emancipation—indeed of emancipation for all the colonies—was radically contracted.

Although the Commonwealth "closed ranks" during World War II, the war nonetheless gave impetus to the decolonization process for four important reasons:

1 The loss of Singapore to the Japanese in 1942 and the collapse of Britain's position in the Far East shook London's assumptions about its influence and role in the world and demonstrated to colonial people that British power could be overwhelmed by a non-European force.

2 The Japanese occupation of Malaya and Burma aroused national awareness in those territories (as it did in French Indochina), making their postwar independence a necessity.

3 Colonial aid to the British war effort—especially the substantial use of Indian and West African military forces—came at the price of an implied promise of independence and spread nationalistic sentiments to wider segments of colonial societies.

4 American pressure for the emancipation of colonial peoples on the basis of national self-determination, a principle embodied in the new Atlantic Charter, was more successful than before since Britain depended critically upon United States aid both during the war and in the postwar reconstruction period.

The most important transformation of the forties took place, as expected, in South Asia—in India, Burma, and Ceylon. Early in 1942, shortly after the fall of Singapore, the British government called for the orderly transfer of power to an independent India once the war was over and recognized the right of free India to leave the Commonwealth. Progress toward Indian independence was complicated, however, by conflict between the Hindu majority and the Muslim minority, symbolized in the predominantly Hindu Congress Party's demand for a united India and the Muslim League's demand for minority self-government. Frustrated at the Muslim-Hindu deadlock and the general deterioration of the Indian situation immediately after World War II, Prime Minister Attlee in February 1947 announced that a definite deadline for British withdrawal from India would be June 1948 "at the latest" (in fact, British withdrawal turned out to be a good deal more rapid than this). Attlee's decision was condemned by Conservatives, who charged the Labour government with abdicating responsibility for maintaining peace and national unity in India. The Conservative opposition was also despondent over the decision's implications for the dissolution of the British Empire.

Shortly after Attlee's declaration the government managed to defeat a no-confidence motion in Parliament, and the process of granting independence to India was quickly accelerated. Desiring above all else to avoid communal civil war in India, London—over the stiff resistance of the Congress Party—finally adopted a partition solution: a separate constitution would be granted to a Muslim state of Pakistan at the same time India achieved self-government. The Independence Bill was debated and gained approval in the British Parliament in July 1947, and on August 15, 1947, India and Pakistan became independent states. The grant of independence was seen in London not as symbolizing the collapse of British power, but as the fulfillment of a democratic ideal in the creation of a multicultural Commonwealth. It was also seen as a trouble-saving expedient in view of the mounting concentration of British resources on domestic economic and social welfare programs.

Just as World War II hastened Indian self-government, the war also heightened nationalistic sentiment in Burma and Ceylon. Burma was granted independence on January 4, 1948; Ceylon became independent exactly one month later, on February 4. In both cases London realized that it could not maintain control without an unpopular and costly resort to force that would push nationalists into the hands of the communists. It was better to grant independence earlier than expected on terms that were reasonably favorable to British interests, London felt, thereby allowing the continuation of some British influence.

By early 1948 the only major remaining British possessions in South Asia were Malaya and Singapore. There could be no doubt that these territories would also ultimately have to be granted self-government, especially in view of the resurgence of nationalism following the Japanese occupation. But independence was obstructed for nine years by a communist-led insurgency on the Malay Peninsula, which broke out in June 1948 and eventually required a considerable commitment of British resources. The Malayan "emergency" passed through three phases. The first, from 1948 to 1952, saw the expansion of communist insurgent forces from 5,000 to about 10,000 in strength, and—on the other side—the consolidation of support for the British counterinsurgency effort and for the moderate nationalist movement. The second phase, from 1952 to 1954, saw government forces taking advantage of Malaya's relative insularity to isolate and then break the communists' organizational and military strength. During this period the Malayan army, under London's command, was built to around 30,000 regulars supplemented by 30,000 reservists; it benefited from extensive British air and naval support. The third phase, between 1954 and 1960, involved a mopping-up operation in which the few remaining insurgents were driven back to the desolate mountains and jungles along the Thai frontier. By 1955 the situation had stabilized sufficiently for London to permit internal self-government in Malaya. In 1957 independence was granted to the Malayan Federation under the leadership of Tunku Abdul Rahman, and in August 1958 a self-governing State of Singapore came into being (Malayans had resisted union with Singapore because the majority of Singapore's population was Chinese). The process of British decolonization in South Asia was now complete, only thirteen years after World War II.

It seems clear in retrospect that the evolution of the British Empire into a Commonwealth of Nations was complete by the late forties. This evolution had at least three distinct facets. First, independence was granted to the white dominions in the twenties and thirties, and in subsequent years they became a prime source of support for Britain's continued global role (and also, therefore, a prime cause of self-delusion on the part of British foreign policymakers). Second, India, Pakistan, Burma, and Ceylon gained independence by 1948, and a similar course for Malaya was seen as inevitable. India's decision to stay within the British Commonwealth—and London's willingness to accept India's membership as a republic—legitimized the concept of a multiracial, multicultural association of states spanning Asia and the West (the importance of the multiracial aspect of the Commonwealth was subsequently seen in South Africa's forced retirement from the "club"). Third, in the late forties London had accepted the inevitability of some form of self-government for the dependent colonies in Africa. There remained two problems: that of deciding what form self-government in these territories should take, and that of safeguarding the future of white minorities in Rhodesia and East Africa while adhering to democratic principles.

In dismantling its empire, the British government demonstrated in the first half-decade following World War II a remarkable flexibility—a flexibility reflected in the total lack of any "master plan" for decolonization. This flexibility meant that London gave in to demands and made concessions when necessary to prevent violence and shore up the power of moderate nationalists. Often the grant of independence came earlier than expected because to wait longer would only play into the hands of radical movements and enhance the likelihood of violent confrontation. There can be no doubt either that Britain's flexibility derived in part from the nation's altered position in the global balance of power. The emergence of two dominant superpowers (both of them opposed to European colonialism), the preeminence of intra-European security concerns, and the imposition of the logic of Cold War bipolarity upon Third World regions all meant—when combined with a tidal wave of Third World nationalism—that the future role of Britain as a colonial overseer, like that of its European partners, was severely circumscribed. All of these factors must have been recognized in the British Foreign Office, though their impact was lessened by a pervasive sense of colonial responsibility and a misperception of the pace at which change would likely occur.

THE MIDDLE EAST

No account of British policy in the Third World can be complete without some mention of British activity in the Middle East during the period 1945–58. It is appropriate that we take up this matter now, before proceeding to African decolonization and Britain's peacekeeping role in the sixties.

The strategic significance of the Middle East as the geographic crossroads between Europe, Asia, and Africa was enhanced by the Suez Canal (which was a major communications and trade lifeline) and the discovery of oil in the Persian Gulf area. British objectives in the region were threefold: (1) to keep open the communications and trade link with the Empire, (2) to protect British access to Middle East oil, and (3) to contain the intrusion of Russian power and influence. These interests persisted throughout the Cold War era.

After World War I Britain assumed control of Palestine, Jordan, Iraq, and the southern shoreline of the Persian Gulf. In addition, though granting self-government to Egypt in 1922, London maintained military forces in the Suez Canal Zone. But the British position in the region was quickly complicated by the question of the future of Palestine. In assuming the League of Nations mandate in November 1917 the British government had pledged to support on certain conditions the creation of a home for the Jews in Palestine. British acceptance of this goal was motivated by ulterior considerations (especially opinion in America and Bolshevik Russia, and the need to establish a British naval base in the Eastern Mediterranean). Controlled emigration of Jews to Palestine took place after World War I, and by the early thirties it was obvious that the Jews were not content to remain a minority there. At the same time the Arabs refused to let them become more than a minority. The objectives of the two groups—Jews and Arabs—became more and more incompatible, and as a result British governance of Palestine became increasingly difficult. A revolt by Palestinian Arabs in 1936 resulted in a British proposal for partition of the mandate, but this proposal was rejected by Arabs and Jews alike. At the outbreak of World War II the issue was left unresolved; Jewish emigration to the Middle East slowed to a trickle.

During World War II, Zionist organizations continued their pressure on London to permit a majority Jewish settlement in Palestine. By the end of the war their arguments were bolstered by the appalling spectacle of the Nazi extermination campaign, which underlined the moral requirement for a safe Jewish homeland outside Europe. When the Attlee government came to power in 1945 it faced an immediate demand by Jewish organizations and the United States government for the relocation of 100,000 Jewish refugees to Palestine. But Attlee and Foreign Minister Bevin at first resisted such a move, and proposed a smaller and slower Jewish emigration. Accession to the Jewish and American demand—which would undoubtedly be followed by further demands—would almost certainly ruin Anglo-Arab relations. Rejection, on the other hand, would also exact a price, as London quickly learned from the increasing scale of Jewish violence in Palestine during 1946. There seemed to be no easy way out, no middle course between satisfying Washington and protecting British interests vis-à-vis the Arabs. A joint Anglo-American inquiry begun in 1945 did not point to any realistic way to overcome the impasse. President Truman rejected London's 1946 "provincial autonomy" plan for Palestine that would have given in to the demand for settlement of 100,000 Jews but would have restricted further immigration.

By late 1946 London's attitude had toughened. The minimum Jewish demand was now for Jewish sovereignty in a sizable area of Palestine, which conflicted with the minimum Arab demand for an independent Palestine with a permanent Arab majority. London was convinced that a solution could only be worked out over a considerable period of time. Washington, however, which had persistently meddled in British policy in the Eastern Mediterranean, was not willing to allow London the luxury of an extended period of accommodation and peacemaking.

The situation in Palestine grew steadily worse, with violence mounting daily. In April 1947 London was forced to call a special session of the United

Nations General Assembly. The British made it clear that they would not impose by force of arms a solution in Palestine that was not acceptable to both Arabs and Jews. In November 1947 the General Assembly, under American and Soviet prodding, voted for a partition plan—the creation of a Jewish state and an Arab state. London promptly announced that it would not implement the scheme (which was not acceptable to either faction in Palestine) and would instead withdraw all British forces from the mandate by August 1948.

The British withdrawal from Palestine has subsequently been seen as playing into the hands of the Arabs, since London made no attempt to provide lasting security for the Jewish settlements. Yet it is undeniable that the Jews were no less anxious than the Arabs to see the British go and that Jewish terrorist groups such as the Stern Gang and the Irgun Svai Leumi were directed against British rule as much as against Arab Palestinians.

On its part, London was eager to wash its hands of an impossible situation that had been made even more difficult by American interference. At the end of 1947 there were 80,000 British troops in Palestine. The cost of maintaining British forces there between 1945 and 1948 was £100 million, and 338 British subjects were eventually killed. The mood in London was one of cutting losses as quickly as possible. It is probably also true that the British assumed the Arab invasion of Palestine following the British evacuation would drastically reduce the area allotted to the Jews in the United Nations plan and that a good Anglo-Arab relationship would thereafter be preserved. Thus the final success of the Jews in the February–April 1949 armistice, which resulted in a viable Israeli state larger than that envisaged by the United Nations, was something of an embarrassment to London. Tensions between Britain and the Arab states increased as Arabs—like their Jewish opponents—blamed Britain for the evolution of events in Palestine.

In the years between the Palestinian crisis and the 1956 Suez debacle London attempted to maintain a close relationship with Arab states and to support some Arab governments militarily. This policy encountered a number of obstacles, however. Middle East leaders quickly suspected what was true enough: London's support stemmed partly from a desire to contain the consequences of Arab nationalism and partly from an attempt to align Arab nations behind the effort to limit Soviet influence. At the same time London's limited supply of arms to Egypt, Iraq, and Jordan was viewed negatively in Israel and with some degree of suspicion in Washington. In May 1950 the United States, France, and—with some cajoling—Britain signed the Tripartite Declaration, which decried the arms race between Israel and the Arabs and limited arms transfers in the Middle East to defensive weapons. This was immediately interpreted by Arab governments as an attempt to cement the status quo and protect Israel, which in turn reinforced Arab reluctance to join the West in an anti-Soviet defense pact.

In February 1955 the Baghdad Pact was formed by Britain, Iran, Iraq, Pakistan, and Turkey. Its intent was to provide a *cordon sanitaire* keeping

Soviet influence out of the Middle East. In July 1958, however, a coup in Iraq was followed just two days later by Anglo-American intervention in Jordan and Lebanon, where civil war threatened. Iraq's sympathy with the West declined, and in 1959 Iraq withdrew from the Baghdad Pact. The pact thus lost its only Arab member, and the alliance subsequently became—with the addition of the United States as a new member—the largely ineffectual Central Treaty Organization (CENTO). Meanwhile, the 1956 Suez crisis (discussed in detail in chapter 9) succeeded in alienating even moderate Arab governments from Britain and France for a time and bolstered the Soviet Union's political influence throughout the Middle East.

At the same time, British control of the Mediterranean island of Cyprus was becoming increasingly precarious. Virtual civil war broke out in May 1955, with Greek Cypriots—four-fifths of the island's population—demanding union with Greece, and Turkish Cypriots—the other fifth—demanding either partition of the island and their union with Turkey or continued British rule. A state of emergency was declared in November 1955 as violence became more intense and British authorities were forced to be more repressive; in March 1956 the Greek-Cypriot leader, Archbishop Makarios, was deported to the Seychelles. Conditions became worse in 1956, just as the British and French were using the island to support the Suez invasion, and throughout 1957 the trouble continued. Finally, in February 1959 an agreement was reached establishing Cyprus as an independent republic, with Britain retaining two sovereign military base areas. Independence came in August 1960, and Archbishop Makarios became president. It was not long, only until 1963, before factional violence flared anew on the island and the British bases took on the role of safe havens for refugees.

DECOLONIZATION IN AFRICA

As in Asia and the Middle East, the rapid changes that brought independence to Britain's African colonies had their roots in World War II. Political awareness and national consciousness grew as African soldiers were recruited by the British to fight in North and East Africa and in Burma. West Africa was used as a major supply route between the Allies and the Middle East and South Asia, and African labor was employed to build airports and expand port facilities. National consciousness spread. At the end of the war a new kind of African political leader appeared, represented by Kwame Nkrumah in the Gold Coast and Nnamdi Azikiwe in Nigeria. Trained in England or America, such leaders fostered the sympathy of the African masses and made radical demands for political reforms and ultimately independence. London at first thought that this new nationalism could be mollified by partial concessions, but this proved not to be the case. Full independence was the demand, and Britain's necessary response.

The transformation was especially swift in the Gold Coast and Nigeria, British colonies in West Africa. The area had been less thoroughly colonized by the Europeans, but experienced major changes during World War II.

In 1948 riots erupted in the Gold Coast, led by war veterans protesting poor economic conditions. Shocked by the disturbances, the Attlee Labour government in 1949 began the colony's transition to responsible self-government. In 1956, after some delay occasioned by conflict between the two major Gold Coast political factions, a newly elected national legislature passed a motion asking for independence. Under its new name of Ghana, the colony became an independent state within the British Commonwealth on March 6, 1957. Unfortunately, the Westminster model of competitive parliamentary democracy did not last long in Ghana. By 1959 Ghanaian politics degenerated into a cult of personality centering on the ruthless President Nkrumah and a single-party mass mobilization campaign. Ghana's economy suffered from mismanagement, and in February 1966 Nkrumah was overthrown by a military coup d'etat. This pattern would unfortunately become a familiar one in African politics.

Decolonization also proceeded fairly quickly in Nigeria, though here independence was delayed by factional and regional conflicts that subsequently brought disaster to the country and posed a major problem for British foreign policy between 1967 and 1970. Nigeria's problems originated in the way the colony was founded. In the nineteenth century the European colonizers in Africa usually marked out for themselves territorial claims that bore no relation to the historically significant boundaries between indigenous societies and ethnic groups. Those African states that gained independence in the sixties were therefore defined, territorially and ethnically, by the pattern of earlier European penetration on the continent. Artificial creations, these states faced almost insuperable problems of national identity and national cohesion. Nigeria was one such artificial state. It encompassed three distinct ethnic groups that historically had clashed with each other: the Hausa-Fulani in the north (who were Muslims), the Yoruba in the southwest, and the Ibo in the southeast (who were predominantly Christians).

Prior to Nigerian independence the most significant conflict was north-south, between the Muslim Hausa-Fulani and the other two groups. Although the north was larger than the other two regions in both population and area, and controlled a majority of the Nigerian legislature, it nonetheless feared domination by the non-Muslim south, and in the fifties resisted a quick transition to independence. Hopeful that Nigeria's national cohesion could be maintained, London opted for a federal constitution under which each region would have its own prime minister and potential full autonomy. On this basis the eastern and western regions (in the south) were granted internal self-government in 1957, and the northern region in 1960. Nigeria thereby gained its independence and with a population of 32 million became the fourth largest state in the British Commonwealth.

But Nigeria's problems were just beginning. The bonds that held the federation together were tenuous—they were vulnerable to perceptions of discrimination against one region or another by the federal administration, and weakened still further by corruption and nepotism in the central government. In particular the Ibo southeastern region—which contained many of Nigeria's economic resources, including oil—became disaffected by 1965, fearful that a crude alliance between the north and the southwest might be operating to its political and economic disadvantage. In mid-January 1966 Ibo officers of the Nigerian army staged an unsuccessful coup; from this point on compromise became very difficult. Ibo claims amounted to a demand for outright secession in late 1966 and early 1967, and in July 1967 civil war broke out, with the Ibos under the leadership of the charismatic Colonel Odumegwu Ojukwu. After an initial period in which Ojukwu's forces came very close to Lagos, the Nigerian capital, they were thrown back into their own eastern region where they steadily lost ground.

The civil war in Nigeria presented awkward problems for British foreign policy. British interests there—especially oil interests—were substantial, and London endorsed Nigerian national unity in principle as the only viable alternative to a breakdown into tribalism. But Ojukwu was supported by powerful European money interests and by the French government, and throughout the period 1967–70 he was able to launch a major propaganda campaign in Europe and America that supported the breakaway Ibo state of Biafra and denounced British and federal Nigerian "atrocities." Despite Biafra's increasing isolation as federal forces gained ground, Ojukwu refused to negotiate or to be resupplied by road; he would only allow relief aircraft to land at night—since this provided cover for aircraft flying in French arms—and the result was mounting shortages leading to widespread starvation among the Ibo.

The British government suffered a bad image through the whole affair, since it continued to supply Nigerian federal forces with certain types of arms. Yet London was in fact being blamed for Ojukwu's own stubbornness. Prime Minister Wilson, who faced mounting criticism over Biafra from within the Labour Party, tried repeatedly to arrange an organized settlement —always to no avail. He faced a difficult dilemma: if he abandoned the central Nigerian government, the latter would simply receive increased support from Moscow (which was also supplying arms), and there would be no guarantee of a British voice in negotiating a just postwar settlement. Wilson stuck by his guns, and when the secessionist Biafran forces were finally overrun in January 1970 he was able to preserve a major British role in the postwar relief effort. The Nigerian experience underscored two important lessons: first, that London had to be prepared for the skillful and at times highly misleading use of world media by its opponents (Biafra had been supported by public relations experts in Geneva); second, that London could retain residual responsibilities in former colonies long after their independence.

East Africa

The British experience in East Africa was different from the experience in West Africa in important respects. Whereas the tropical climate of West Africa made Nigeria and the Gold Coast inhospitable for European settlers, the moderate temperatures, ample water, and sparse population of the high plateau country of Kenya and Uganda seemed to make these territories ideal for permanent white settlement. (Tanganyika, which Britain acquired as a League of Nations mandate after World War I, was less desirable.) As late as 1923 Kenya was thought of as potentially a white colony, and long after this (until 1960) white settlers retained special landholding rights in the Kenya highlands, though the vast majority of the population was—of course—black African. In Kenya's case (though much less so in Uganda and Tanganyika) the special interests of an entrenched white minority had to be considered before independence could be granted; in the Gold Coast and Nigeria this kind of impediment did not exist. Moreover, in both Kenya and Uganda the process of decolonization was further complicated by the existence of a large Asian minority.

During World War II the campaign against the Italians in Ethiopia was mounted from Kenya, and for a period the fighting was carried to Kenya itself. As in the Gold Coast and Nigeria, the experience of the war had the effect of reinforcing nationalist tendencies in all four British East African colonies (Kenya, Uganda, Tanganyika, and Zanzibar). At the end of the war London faced a dilemma in Kenya. In Britain's eyes, the question became very simply whether 50,000 whites should continue to rule over 5 million Africans, and—if not—what kinds of safeguards ought to be built up over a long period of time to protect the Europeans. But black Kenyans, like black Africans elsewhere, were not willing to wait a long period of time. The Kikuyu tribe, which was more advanced than other East African tribes, assimilated Western nationalism fairly quickly, and under the leadership of Jomo Kenyatta this nationalism developed into the Mau Mau movement of fanatical resistance to British rule. The Mau Maus began to resort to open violence in 1952, and in the three years 1952–55, 7,800 members of the Mau Mau, 510 members of the security forces, and 1,365 civilians (most of them Africans) were killed. Kenyatta was jailed, and thousands of Kikuyu tribesmen were placed in government prison camps. As could be expected, a substantial investment of British police power was required to quell the rebellion.

The Mau Mau uprising had long-term political effects. In 1954 a new constitution was introduced providing for participation by all ethnic groups (Africans, Europeans, and Asians) in Kenyan politics, though not at first on a proportional basis. Further reforms followed. The logic of political reform in Kenya involved a basic compromise: as it bacame evident that majority black rule was inevitable, the European population had to "bargain the best deal" in order to protect its interests after independence. The primary incentive for reform came, of course, not from Kenya, but from the outside world —specifically from London.

What happened in Kenya in the late fifties and early sixties reflected, in microcosm, the full range of Britain's colonial policies in Africa. In early 1960 the Conservative Macmillan government announced a general acceleration of African decolonization. Speaking in Ghana, Macmillan talked about a "wind of change blowing through Africa" and affirmed the mother country's willingness to encourage the movement toward independence. London recognized the principles at stake in the African striving for self-government; more important, it recognized the constraints imposed on British colonial policy by the desire to maintain a constructive posture in other parts of the world. There were considerations of British self-interest. Macmillan realized that he would have to take the initiative in Africa and dissociate his government from white settler regimes and racist South Africa in order to retain the support of the Commonwealth and avoid chaos in the remaining colonies. The longer he delayed, the stronger the radical elements in African nationalist movements would become. London could either defend the prerogatives of white settlers in East and Central Africa, and thereby endanger the Commonwealth, or obey political necessity and sacrifice the white minorities. Macmillan's decision in the turbulent world of the early sixties was a foregone conclusion: the white minorities would have to be sacrificed.

Consequently J. N. Macleod, Macmillan's new colonial minister, ordered preparations for land reform in Kenya, granted amnesty to suspected Mau Maus, and ended the seven-year state of emergency in the colony. In February 1961 there were elections in which Jomo Kenyatta's Kenya African National Union (KANU) won. Kenyatta was released from detention and led the country peacefully to independence on December 12, 1963.

Tanganyika, meanwhile, had gained independence in December 1961 under the leadership of Julius Nyerere, an outspoken critic of the "multiracial" concept of constitutional advance advocated by the British before 1960. The following year, in 1962, Uganda gained self-government under the leadership of Milton Obote. (Ten years later, following a coup that brought Idi Amin to power, Uganda proved to be a source of embarrassment for Britain when persecution of Uganda's Asian minority there resulted in their claim of British citizenship and the emigration of 20,000 Asians to Britain. This aroused racist sentiments in British domestic politics, leading to discriminatory—and morally embarrassing—immigration restrictions.)

Britain maintained an active role in East Africa for some time after the colonies achieved independence. When elements of the Tanganyikan, Kenyan, and Ugandan armed forces staged mutinies in January 1964, all three governments requested British troops to restore order. London subsequently negotiated the continuation of British base rights in Kenya and provided training for East African military personnel. East African bases took on added importance after, first, stepped-up Soviet naval penetration of the Indian Ocean and, second, the 1967 closure of the Suez Canal, which forced shipment of Middle East oil around the Cape of Good Hope.

Central Africa

By "Central Africa" we mean, of course, the former British colonies of Southern Rhodesia, Northern Rhodesia, and Nyasaland (now Zimbabwe, Zambia, and Malawi respectively).

After World War II, the white settlers in the two Rhodesias and Nyasaland pushed for a federation of the three territories, which—they argued—would create an economically stronger and administratively more efficient Central African dominion under white leadership. Africans in the three colonies vehemently opposed such a federation: they argued that Southern Rhodesia would dominate it and that the federation government would deprive black inhabitants of all three territories of the direct protection of the British Colonial Office. In London, the Attlee Labour government thus refused a quick adoption of the federation plan, though it agreed to study the proposal.

In 1953, with a Conservative government led by the old colonialist Winston Churchill in office, London finally granted the white settlers' wish, and the Federation of Rhodesia and Nyasaland (or Central African Federation) was created. The federation was created, however, on the condition that dominion status (i.e., independence) could not be granted unless the "inhabitants of the Territories so desired," a provision that ostensibly protected black African interests. The British Labour Party opposed the federation in Parliament but could not muster sufficient votes to defeat it; meanwhile some Conservative MPs, aping their white brethren in Rhodesia, argued that "African opinion does not exist" and (more moderately) that a "dual policy" preserving two racial communities could succeed. The Central African Federation's legislature itself embodied, as African spokesmen had predicted, white domination, and extended white supremacy to Northern Rhodesia and Nyasaland. White Rhodesians defended this arrangement by invoking the racist slogan of "equal rights for all civilized men" (again, they were echoed by some Conservatives in the British Parliament) and by arguing that Africans might assume a larger policymaking role in the distant future (how "distant" was never specified). Black opposition to the federation culminated in violent resistance between 1958 and 1960. The resistance was at first strongest in Nyasaland, where Doctor H. K. Banda inspired the Nyasaland National Congress to outbreaks of violence in 1959, which in turn led to white political repression and Banda's arrest. There was also organized resistance in Northern Rhodesia, where the United National Independence Party was established in 1960 under the leadership of Kenneth Kaunda.

In response to this rising dissidence, the Macmillan government dispatched a commission of experts to Nyasaland in 1959. The commission produced a report that described Nyasaland as a "police state," argued that Banda's National Congress had popular backing, and criticized white Rhodesian misrepresentation of the facts of the situation. The report seemed to turn Macmillan against the white settlers and their leader, Sir Roy Welensky; it certainly reinforced those considerations that led to the prime minister's "wind of change" speech in early 1960. It was in any case unthinkable by now —as we noted earlier—that Britain could repress black African nationalism and flout world opinion; the structure of British interests would not allow it. In late 1960 the Monckton Commission reported again that the Central African Federation was strongly opposed by black Africans; it argued that the eventual breakup of the federation was made inevitable by white supremacy in Southern Rhodesia and that Nyasaland and Northern Rhodesia should be allowed to secede. By 1962 London came to accept this view, and during 1963 the federation—which had served, paradoxically enough, as a catalyst of African nationalism—was allowed to dissolve. Nyasaland became independent under the new name of Malawi on July 6, 1964, and on October 24 Northern Rhodesia achieved self-government as Zambia. The independence of these two territories now focused attention on Southern Rhodesia, the last remaining British dependency.

The Rhodesian Problem

The white Rhodesian backlash against the unsettling events since 1959, and against London's evident decision to support black nationalism, took the form of repression and extremism. As control over events in the federation slipped between the fingers of white Rhodesians, and as black nationalism reared its head in Southern Rhodesia after 1958, the white settlers came to see any concession to the Africans as dangerous. There was increasing sympathy for abridging the civil rights not only of blacks but also of liberal white settlers. In the Southern Rhodesia election of 1962 the white electorate voted into power the right-wing Rhodesian Front, headed by Ian Smith. Smith advocated outright white supremacy, maintained if necessary by force of arms.

The Smith regime promptly set about pressing Britain to grant independence to Rhodesia. The government argued that London had broken faith with the white settlers and that the future of the territory had to be determined in Salisbury, not London. In fact, of course, the Smith government feared that if independence were not quickly granted, Britain would make constitutional arrangements with Rhodesia's black majority that would undercut the dominant position of the whites. These fears grew worse after the return of a British Labour government to power in 1964; it was likely that white Rhodesians would receive even less sympathy from Harold Wilson than they had received from Macmillan. In October 1964 a "referendum" of Rhodesian voters (90,000 whites and 13,000 Africans, of whom 61 percent voted) resulted in a 90 percent vote for independence from Britain. Most enfranchised Africans, a tiny minority of the total African population, abstained.

London's response to Smith's challenge was predictable: there could be no grant of independence unless there was ample evidence of genuine African support for it, and there had to be a guarantee of reasonable progress toward black majority rule. Democratic suffrage meant "one man, one vote," and London insisted that this principle be embodied in the Rhodesian constitution. Tensions between Salisbury and the British Labour government steadily increased through early 1965. In October 1965 Smith met with Wilson in London, and it quickly became clear that there could be no easy way around the impasse; the British and white Rhodesian positions were mutually incompatible. Smith feared for the very existence of the white Rhodesian community. In his view, it was a zero-sum situation in which any major concession to black Rhodesians was bound to damage white settler interests. On October 11, after three days of talks between the two leaders, Smith returned to Salisbury with nothing accomplished.

Ominous signs emanated from Salisbury: the Rhodesian government, exercising its police power, was making arbitrary arrests and curtailing freedom of the press. At the same time there was clear evidence that Ian Smith was prepared to declare unilaterally Rhodesia's independence, even though such a move would be illegal and would risk British armed intervention. In a final effort to avert drastic action by the Smith regime, Prime Minister Wilson flew to Rhodesia in late October. Further negotiations with the white Rhodesian leader proved fruitless, and Wilson returned home in a pessimistic mood.

On November 11, 1965—less than two weeks after Wilson's return to London—the Rhodesian government announced its Unilateral Declaration of Independence (UDI). Smith declared a state of emergency throughout Rhodesia, and government officials were vested with wide powers of arrest, search, interrogation, censorship, and detention without trial. In the years to follow this "state of emergency" was extended again and again.

In London the Wilson government faced a difficult decision. Britain declared the UDI illegal and refused to recognize Rhodesia as a sovereign state, but this was not enough. There had to be sanctions to force Smith back into the fold. Black Commonwealth states and several Labour Left MPs demanded that London intervene militarily to put down the rebellion, but this would have been an unpopular move in Britain as well as a tactically difficult operation. London's eventual refusal to take military action angered Africans, who recalled those instances in which British military power had been promptly used to suppress black uprisings. Nine African states—including Ghana and Tanzania (formerly Tanganyika)—broke off diplomatic relations with Britain.

Instead of using military force, the Wilson government decided in 1966 to apply economic sanctions through the United Nations. These sanctions were broadened in 1970 to include suspension of all "diplomatic, consular, trade, military and other relations" with Salisbury. Such measures had only a limited impact, however: between 1968 and 1974 Rhodesian per capita income grew by 5 percent each year, and consumer goods remained plentiful as traders used their ingenuity to circumvent the United Nations embargo. In the end it was the mounting military costs associated with the Salisbury government's counterinsurgency effort—estimated at $700,000 to $1 million a day in 1977—that, in combination with a global economic slump, put a real dent in Rhodesian growth.

Truly effective opposition to the Smith regime had to come from within Rhodesia or from the surrounding African states. By 1962 there were two major black nationalist movements in Rhodesia, led by Joshua Nkomo and Reverend Ndabaningi Sithole. But these two groups dissipated much of their energy in conflict with each other, principally over the question of whether to sit down and negotiate with the Smith regime or undertake massive guerrilla warfare against the entire white society of Rhodesia.

Beginning in 1968 the Rhodesian government encountered increasing acts of violence at the hands of guerrilla bands, many of them based in Zambia and Mozambique. Guerrilla incursions increased in frequency and scale through the seventies, and by 1978 guerrilla activity was reaching the outskirts of Salisbury. Although Rhodesian military and police forces were well equipped, the country was surrounded by hostile regimes in Angola, Zambia, and Mozambique, and it became clear—even to Ian Smith—that concessions would have to be made to moderate black leaders if the growth of violence and political radicalism was to be reversed.

Britain continued to feel some responsibility for the constitutional evolution of Rhodesia, and most governments continued to see Britain as technically having sovereignty over the territory. In 1971 Ted Heath's Conservative government reopened negotiations with Salisbury, but ultimately to no avail. Other attempts at reconciliation followed. In 1977 the British presented an Anglo-American plan for transition to majority rule, which would include a United Nations peacekeeping force, but this proposal produced no agreement.

Perhaps the best hope for change at this point lay within the Rhodesian regime. In 1976 Smith declared that in principle he agreed with the goal of "one man, one vote" and could envisage a Rhodesian political system based on universal suffrage. In November 1977, after rejecting the Anglo-American initiative, Smith began negotiations of his own with moderate black nationalists—Reverend Sithole and Bishop Abel Muzorewa—aimed at a fair political arrangement between the country's 260,000 whites and 6.3 million blacks. Of course, Smith still had to contend with the more radical guerrilla leaders— Joshua Nkomo and Robert Mugabe—who vowed to reject any settlement produced by black moderates and who wished to continue fighting even if it meant black civil war. Smith's visit to the United States in 1978—intended to drum up American support for a "moderate" settlement—did not alter these basic conditions, and Rhodesian security forces continued to battle domestic sabotage and terrorism as well as guerrilla military strikes mounted from neighboring Mozambique. In April 1979, as part of Smith's "internal solution," black Rhodesians voted Muzorewa's United African National Council into power. Whites retained inordinate control over the government, however, and the election was rejected by guerrilla leaders and most foreign governments.

PEACEKEEPING EAST OF SUEZ

In chapter 9 we noted that Britain sought throughout the postwar era to maintain a military presence in the Third World that was not solely connected to former colonial responsibilities. Until the late sixties London saw itself as a global power with an obligation to assist its major ally, the United States, in maintaining the stability of the international system (though it was in the Third World that British and American interests frequently clashed). This global peacekeeping role derived from Britain's great-power legacy more than from its colonial legacy.

Thus, Britain became involved in two kinds of military operations in the Third World: those that were incidental to decolonization, as in Palestine, Cyprus, and Kenya, and those that involved an effort to maintain the stability of the postcolonial world, as in the Sino-Indian conflict of 1962 and the Malaysian-Indonesian confrontation of 1963–66. Of course, there was some overlap here: violent confrontation during decolonization sometimes resulted from London's desire to remain in a territory for the sake of broader, non-colonial strategic objectives (Cyprus and Palestine are examples), and post-colonial applications of British power tended to center on those former colonial areas that had traditionally been considered within Britain's ambit (India, Malaysia, and Nigeria are cases in point).

Perhaps the most well-known British peacekeeping operation east of Suez was the support given to the former colony of Malaysia during the Indonesian confrontation. In September 1963 the Federation of Malaysia—merging Malaya, Singapore, and the North Borneo territories of Sarawak and Sabah—was proclaimed. Indonesia, which claimed the North Borneo territories for itself and was ideologically opposed to Malaysia, quickly broke off diplomatic relations with the new federation. In subsequent months President Sukarno of Indonesia adopted a militant posture and announced his intention to "crush" Malaysia with the help of arms supplied by the Soviet Union and China. All through 1964 Indonesian guerrilla activities intensified, especially in North Borneo, and in August and September 1964 a small group of regular Indonesian forces—including paratroops—was landed in the Malayan province of Johore.

It now became obvious that Indonesia posed a real threat to the future of Malaysia, and Britain decided to beef up its military commitment to the federation. The tactic adopted by London was to avoid actual military conflict with Indonesia for as long as possible but to confront Sukarno with a show of force sufficient to deter him from invading Malaysia. By early 1965 Britain had deployed six infantry battalions to North Borneo and dispatched eighty naval vessels (including aircraft carriers) and a force of V-bombers to Singapore. A successful counterinsurgency effort was mounted along the thousand-mile jungle frontier separating the Malaysian and Indonesian parts of Borneo. By midyear Indonesia's worsening economic condition, combined with a shortage of spare parts for Soviet- and American-supplied aircraft and naval vessels, caused hostilities to subside. In October 1965 a successful antigovernment coup in Djakarta unseated Sukarno, and on August 11, 1966, the new Indonesian government officially announced the end of the confrontation. Meanwhile, in August 1965, Singapore dropped out of Malaysia, though the rest of the federation remained intact.

There were other British peacekeeping ventures east of Suez. Britain intervened to support Kuwait in its confrontation with Iraq in 1961, provided extensive military support to India during the 1962 Sino-Indian war, and tried to mediate the Indo-Pakistani conflict of 1971. In none of these instances could British behavior be related solely to former colonial responsibilities; London attempted, quite simply, to maintain the capabilities of a global power.

But fulfilling a global role meant (as we noted in chapter 9) that British military commitments became the object of a vexing allocative dilemma. Commitments in the Third World clearly had lower priority than Britain's contribution to West European security, but despite shrinking resources, it was not until the 1967 sterling crisis that Whitehall committed itself to withdrawing from Malaysia, Singapore, and the Persian Gulf. And even then the Heath government temporized, suspending the withdrawals between 1970 and 1974. By this time most of Britain's former colonies had achieved independence, and only fragments of empire—Hong Kong, Belize, the Falkland Islands, and so on—remained. Moreover, the British navy, now much smaller, had lost much of its overseas capability. British power in the Third World rested increasingly upon London's diplomatic and moral influence— ambivalent at best—among the former colonies.

CONCLUSION

There will always be a heated debate over why Englishmen clung to the illusion of global power for as long as they did—why, that is, there was such an obvious "cognitive lag" between British perceptions of London's international role and the limitations of the role itself. Part of the reason can be found in the relatively smooth dissolution of the British Empire. Britain gave up its overseas possessions without any major crises—such as those of the French in Indochina and Algeria—and without any large-scale domestic political repercussions. Without any cathartic "shocks," Englishmen could for the first two decades of the postwar era nurture a feeling of continuity.

Yet, historically, the British Empire was always destined for early independence because a nation of Britain's small size and meager resources could not retain control of such far-flung and populous possessions for a longer period. Thus Britain was never completely secure in its imperial role. As rival great powers emerged—some of them much better endowed—London had to ultimately follow the path of least resistance and harmonize its policies with pressure in the colonial areas for national identity and independence. In the end this meant not only granting independence to overseas colonies but also —in the late twentieth century—turning a back on white settler societies predicated on racial supremacy doctrines. London accommodated itself to the global tidal wave of nationalism. This, ultimately, was the logic of British decolonization and of Britain's political relationship with the Third World.

12

Foreign Policy and Domestic Politics

Foreign policy inevitably has a major impact on domestic politics in advanced industrial states; in turn, domestic attitudes and conditions invariably influence foreign policy. Foreign policy issues had a deep effect on West German domestic political cleavages throughout the postwar era, and French domestic politics suffered a series of jolts caused by such foreign policy predicaments as the wars in Indochina and Algeria. Moreover, all three of the countries we have studied in this book underwent crises of national self-definition that were complicated by the inertia and traditionalism of domestic public opinion.

In Britain's case the linkage between domestic politics and the external environment, while profound, was less obviously problematic than in the West German and French cases. We have already noted a variety of instances in which this linkage played a major role for Britain:

1 The British public's expectation after World War II that the nation would continue to have major global responsibilities and play a great-power role undoubtedly slowed the country's external adjustment to its new, more subordinate international position. Political elites—especially the leadership of the political parties—wanted to avoid contending with the domestic repercussions of a more rapid wind-down of Britain's global responsibilities. The result was a foreign policy that overextended British resources and that ignored important opportunities for the fulfillment of tangible British interests.

2 Conversely, the British public's postwar demand for more extensive social welfare programs—which coincided with a general reorientation of domestic political values—limited the resources available for defense and foreign policy purposes and dictated a further retraction of British power. This was especially true during the years of the Attlee government, 1945–51.

3 One of the most crucial internal-external linkages stemmed from sterling policy. The commitment of several British governments, both Conservative and Labour, to maintaining a fixed-value pound sterling with key international transaction and reserve functions generated successive deflationary campaigns at home, and ultimately brought the domestic economy close to disaster for the sake of an external commitment involving international prestige. This was made even more important by the general concentration on economic issues of British domestic politics throughout the postwar era.

4 The issue of British membership in the Common Market focused direct attention on the overlap between domestic and foreign policy; it also gave rise to reservations and anxieties on the part of special interests in the domestic economy and forced these interests to reconcile themselves more fully to Britain's changing international role. In the end the Common Market became a major domestic political issue, one that not only divided the two major political parties but also generated unprecedented tensions within each party.

In most of these instances the impact of foreign policy upon domestic politics was not as well articulated and direct as it was at times in West Germany and France, but this impact was nonetheless very great. When domestic and foreign policy objectives clashed, as in these cases, one could not predict with certainty which would prevail. Domestic objectives centered around political expedience and economic priorities; international objectives centered around strategic needs, national prestige, and the very survival of the nation-state. Most postwar British governments spent more time and energy on foreign policy issues than on domestic affairs. Among postwar prime ministers only Attlee devoted the bulk of his personal time to domestic needs, delegating the conduct of foreign policy to Foreign Secretary Ernest Bevin. All of the others (possibly excepting James Callaghan) concentrated almost excessively on foreign affairs, often ignoring—as in the case of sterling policy—the domestic repercussions of specific foreign policy decisions.

Yet the priority attached to foreign policy was necessarily implicit. The growing democratization of British society led to increasing electoral constraints on governmental expenditures for defense and imperial responsibilities, since domestic political priorities focused on social security and higher standards of living. As Joseph Frankel has noted, in electoral terms domestic demands were "hard" whereas defense requirements were "soft"; governments often had to devote resources to the former at the expense of the latter, for they would pay dearly politically if they did the reverse.* Consequently, the changing character of British society—its shift toward mass culture, mass consumption, and the democratization of access to social goods—had an inevitable impact on the British government's position and power in the international system.

POLITICAL DOCTRINE AND FOREIGN POLICY

In France and West Germany there were large doctrinal differences between political parties, which translated into polarized foreign policy positions (especially during the early years of the Cold War). In Britain, however, few such differences existed, and where they did exist they did not run along classic party lines. There was a broad foreign policy consensus between Conservative and Labour leaders, and in most elections there was no substantial divergence between Conservative and Labour foreign policy positions— only differences in emphasis and timing. This consensus paralleled, in some respects, the consensus over domestic issues. Hence continuity rather than discontinuity generally marked the changeover from Conservative to Labour governments, and vice versa. Just as the Conservatives did not dismantle the welfare state or reverse the Attlee government's commitment to decolonization (indeed, Macmillan hastened the independence of Britain's African colonies), neither did Labour governments challenge the basic capitalist structure of the British economy or abolish so doctrinally anathema an instrument of foreign policy as the independent nuclear deterrent. Both parties nurtured the "special relationship" with the United States, maintained British forces on the European continent, adhered to a fixed international sterling until 1967, adopted a cautious view of the Soviet Union, and pursued smooth but rapid decolonization. The Suez crisis of 1956 and Labour's insistence in the early seventies on renegotiating the terms of British Common Market membership stand out as the two major instances in which the foreign policy consensus failed.

The reasons for this consensus—an agreement about foreign policy goals that prevailed throughout the postwar era—are not hard to fathom:

1 Leaders of both major parties found "doctrine" per se anathema, preferring a pragmatic and incremental approach to foreign policymaking. A great deal has been said (much of it exaggerated, to be sure) about the "pragmatic" style of British politics. This pragmatism—which, as we noted in chapter 9, made long-term planning and the imposition of an overarching rationale on foreign policy impossible—eliminated most

---

*See Joseph Frankel, *British Foreign Policy, 1945–1973* (London: Oxford University Press, 1975), p. 18.

doctrinal haggling and restricted partisan disagreement about foreign policy to questions of tactics rather than goals.

2 Policy in both parties reflected a broad foreign affairs consensus on the part of the British public and a desire by both Conservative and Labour leaders to cushion public opinion against too precipitous a recognition of Britain's international decline. This meant that the consensus was at times poorly informed and rested in part on an acceptance of common myths about Britain's role in the world. These common myths were the closest most Englishmen came to some sort of foreign affairs "doctrine."

3 Foreign policy implementation was largely in the hands of a professional bureaucracy that was homogenous in terms of its training and cultural perspective and that could operate with impressive singleness of purpose. According to Joseph Frankel, American models of "bureaucratic politics . . . generally do not apply to British politics. Here co-ordination, although rather informal, is the pattern, and major policy issues are much less frequently affected by a tug-of-war between competing institutions, as in the United States."* The pattern of bureaucratic decision making had its source in, and in turn supported, a broad consensus about political "rules of the game" and the structure of British national interests.

4 British foreign policy was severely constrained by external conditions over which London exercised little or no control, and these constraints rendered moot many of the conceivable doctrinal differences over foreign policy orientations. Both major parties recognized, for example, the limits placed on policy options by Soviet military superiority in Europe and the consequent reliance of Britain on the United States for ultimate military security.

Serious foreign policy dissent in postwar Britain came mainly from the left wing of the Labour Party. While the Conservative Party was socially cohesive and disdained abstract doctrine, the Labour Party was socially heterogenous and contained some small but vociferous ideology-oriented elements. One could distinguish within the Labour Party a working-class group that was closely connected to the Trades Union Congress (TUC), a middle-class group that had moved from blue-collar into nonmanual jobs, and an intellectual group composed of professionals. It was the professional intellectual wing—under the leadership of men like Aneurin Bevan, Richard Crossman, and Michael Foot—that formed the dissenting Labour Left and that was most likely to break with the Labour leadership during important votes in the House of Commons. Under the Attlee government the Labour Left exhibited its displeasure in Parliament by either willfully abstaining (an act of defiance in Parliamentary tradition) or casting negative votes on a number of critical foreign policy issues: the American loan and the Bretton Woods monetary

*Ibid., p. 28

agreement (1945–1946), peacetime conscription (1946–48), the administration of Germany (1947), Palestine (1947–48), and the NATO pact (1949). Labour governments in the sixties and seventies experienced similar dissent within the Labour Party over the nuclear deterrent, Rhodesia, Common Market membership, and a number of other issues.

In most cases, Labour Left Members of Parliament justified their dissent by referring to so-called "socialist" principles of foreign policy—internationalism (the attempt to transcend national sovereignty), international working-class solidarity, anticapitalism, and antimilitarism. Such principles, grounded in traditional (and, after World War II, outmoded) conceptions of international socialism, were intended to further the interests of world peace and economic justice. In practice these principles were unworkable, and the Labour leadership—which frequently paid lip service to them while it was out of office—abandoned them as empty doctrine whenever it held power.*

All Labour leaders faced a difficult balancing act. They had to reconcile the more conservative proclivities of most Labour voters, especially rank-and-file trade union members, with the at times radical demands of the doctrinaire left wing of the party. Harold Wilson and James Callaghan were effective leaders because they could perform this balancing act relatively well; other Labour leaders, like Hugh Gaitskell, were less successful.

There were also, of course, doctrinaire groups on the political right—groups that were nationalistic, militaristic, neo-imperialist, or (as in Enoch Powell's campaign against colored immigration from South Asia and the West Indies) based on populist racism. These factions seemed to draw support from the steadily worsening state of the British economy in the late sixties and early seventies. They never, however, achieved any significant size, and their impact on British politics and foreign policy was minimal. Extremist conservatism had to be distinguished, of course, from resurgent British "Gaullism," which in a much more moderate way simply institutionalized a sometimes justifiable distrust of the United States and of Britain's West European partners.

ELECTORAL POLITICS

Foreign policy issues played a minor role in British electoral politics throughout the postwar era; they simply were not judged to be critically important by the voters. The decisive defeat of Churchill and the Conservatives in 1945 was as much as anything a vote against the candidate who, of necessity, had placed foreign policy above domestic needs since 1940. The Labour victory

---

*For a fuller treatment of socialist principles of foreign policy, see Michael R. Gordon, *Conflict and Consensus in Labour's Foreign Policy, 1914–1965* (Stanford, Calif.: Stanford University Press, 1969), pp. 13–43.

reflected a strong popular desire to return to normality, to undertake the construction of the welfare state, and to raise the domestic standard of living. Even in the second postwar election—in 1950, well after the beginning of the Cold War—the major issues remained domestic economic development and the welfare state. The Labour Party, which had begun instituting far-reaching social welfare reforms (with the help of American Marshall Plan aid), won a clear Parliamentary majority. The public's desire to stress domestic needs over foreign policy was sustained also in the 1951 election, in which the Attlee government lost a close race and was voted out of power in the aftermath of its massive—and unpopular—increase in defense spending.

Popular noninvolvement in foreign policy had other causes, of course. British political elites typically rejected the notion of a "democratic foreign policy," and kept very much in mind de Tocqueville's famous dictum:

Foreign politics demand scarcely any of those qualities which are peculiar to a democracy; they require, on the contrary, the perfect use of almost all those in which it is deficient. . . . a democracy can only with great difficulty regulate the details of an important undertaking, persevere in a fixed design, and work out its execution in spite of serious obstacles. It cannot combine its measures with secrecy or await their consequences with patience.*

Many foreign policy issues were simply too complicated and sensitive to be subjected to the ebb and flow of electoral opinion. A successful foreign policy had to be conducted discreetly and patiently, and that usually meant divorcing it from domestic party politics. This was obviously a more enduring concern, by the way, than the more short-term one of softening the impact on postwar public opinion of Britain's declined international stature.

Perhaps the clearest example of the limited domestic impact of foreign policy was the popular reaction to the 1956 Suez crisis, one of the few postwar foreign policy issues that did arouse public passions. Polls taken by the British Institute of Public Opinion before and after the crisis indicated that 70 percent of all Labour voters disapproved of the military action, while a consistent 20 percent of Conservatives also disapproved. Yet the electoral impact of the crisis was negligible. The Conservatives, who were responsible for the Suez affair, suffered only minor setbacks in the fourteen by-elections between November 1956 and November 1958, and in the 1959 general election they picked up twenty new Parliamentary seats. As before, the electorate was principally concerned about domestic matters, especially the state of the economy (in a sense Macmillan was rewarded in 1959 for a period of moderate economic growth). The passions aroused by the Suez adventure quickly subsided.

A similar pattern emerged in the general election of 1964. Two foreign

*Alexis de Tocqueville, *Democracy in America, Vol. 1* (New York: Knopf, 1945), pp. 234–35.

policy matters seemed to dominate the campaign in the months preceding the election: the future of the independent nuclear deterrent, and the prospect of British membership in the EEC. The Labour Party had been deeply divided over the independent deterrent during 1960–61, and in October 1960 the party's annual conference passed two resolutions calling for unilateral renunciation of nuclear weapons. Hugh Gaitskell, leader of the Labour Party, managed after intensive lobbying to reverse this position. On the eve of the 1964 election, however, the nuclear issue was still very much alive. Alec Douglas-Hume, the Conservative leader, launched a campaign to "save" the deterrent, and concern for it dominated his speeches in the weeks leading up to the election. Noted one of his colleagues, "Every P.M. has one issue he cares about more than anything else. Alec's is the bomb. He'd even be prepared to lose an election on it."* Yet a National Opinion Poll taken in the last week of the election campaign showed that only 13 percent of the voters thought the nuclear deterrent was an important issue, despite Douglas-Hume's intense interest in it and the earlier divisiveness in the Labour Party. In contrast, 72 percent of the voters thought the cost of living was a major issue, and 29 percent thought education should be a focus of attention. More general defense and foreign affairs questions ranked even lower in the public mind than the specific question of the deterrent. A similar lack of public interest was evinced with respect to Common Market membership, even though Labour and the Conservatives had been depply divided over the issue in Parliament in 1961–62, and despite the fact that the Conservative Macmillan government had suffered a humiliating setback at the time of de Gaulle's veto of British entry in January 1963. The issues that carried the Labour Party into power in 1964 revolved more than anything else around the domestic economy and, secondarily, the balance of payments. It should be remembered, of course, that there was a substantial divergence between elite and mass perceptions of what issues were important, a divergence in part explained by the conscious effort of British political elites to shield the public from the more pessimistic ramifications of Britain's declining international power position.

The 1966 general election, which resulted in a major victory for Labour, was not tangibly different from the elections that preceded it. Despite the Rhodesian crisis, Vietnam, and the mounting debate over commitments east of Suez, the overriding public concerns were again domestic. The only foreign-related issue that served as a major irritant during the election campaign was colored immigration. By the mid-sixties there were 800,000 West Indians, Pakistanis, and Indians in Britain—concentrated in a few urban areas—and their numbers were increasing. The Labour Party's opposition to statutory limitation of this inflow generated some white backlash votes for the

---

*Quoted in Anthony King, "Great Britain: The Search for Leadership," *European Politics I: The Restless Search,* ed. William G. Andrews (New York: Van Nostrand, 1966), p. 64.

Conservatives, but even this had a negligible electoral impact. Labour won 47.9 percent of the popular vote against the Conservatives' 41.9 percent, and 57.6 percent of the seats in Parliament against the Conservatives' 40.2 percent.

Similar observations can be made about the 1970 election and the two anomalous elections of 1974. Although it is tempting to attribute the Conservative victory in 1970 to the Labour government's abandonment of Britain's world role (devaluation in 1967 and the planned military withdrawal from east of Suez), it would be highly inaccurate to argue along such lines. By the late sixties (as pointed out in chapter 10) the British economy was in chaos and the fundamental consensus between labor, management,and government about the "rules of the game" seemed to be breaking down. This, far more than Britain's increasingly subordinate international position, was the focus of public attention. It was the focus of attention again in 1974, when the trade unions and the Heath government were approaching open war with each other. Disgusted by the inability of either major party to put the domestic economy in order, a large proportion of the electorate—25 percent in both February and October—voted for third parties. Labour was forced to put together a minority government. The chief public concerns were inflation, employment, housing, and social welfare programs—the same issues that dominated all postwar British politics. Even Labour's criticism of the terms of Britain's 1973 entry into the EEC cannot be said to have been preeminent in either of the 1974 elections.

Why did foreign affairs play only a very limited role in British electoral politics throughout the postwar era? We should note first of all that it may be misleading to pose the question in this way. To compare—as this book attempts to do—Britain with West Germany and France may give the impression that the limited impact of the external environment on British electoral politics was the exception, and the more direct impact of international affairs on West German and French domestic politics was the rule. But it is more likely that the British experience was the norm. West Germany underwent the unique experiences of national dismemberment, occupation, and—as the Cold War unfolded—a truly critical security dilemma. West German sovereignty was spawned by Western security needs, and the problem of national reunification—while in one sense a domestic issue—had far-reaching international ramifications. France also experienced defeat and occupation, and after World War II the French people went through an acute national crisis of confidence. It was in the midst of this crisis of confidence that the Indochina and Algerian wars took place, and as a result these conflicts had major domestic psychological and political repercussions. Britain underwent nothing like either the West German or the French experience. Instead the British passed through a sort of slow-motion crisis, which while gentler in its immediate effects, was in other respects more debilitating. There was no cathartic questioning of Britain's international role or of its national identity, and foreign policy issues correspondingly played a limited role in domestic politics. It was to be expected that domestic concerns would predominate at election time; there was no reason why they should not, especially in view of the increasing democratization of British political life.

If the limited impact of foreign policy on British domestic politics was "normal," it was normal precisely because of those factors we have already discussed: (1) the complex and convoluted nature of foreign policy problems, a complexity that necessarily yielded to over-simplistic notions when subjected to the domestic political arena, (2) the desire of political elites to decouple external affairs from domestic political campaigns, (3) the fact that the broad goals of foreign policy were often not clearly articulated (even for the foreign policy elite itself), and so did not lend themselves to intelligent domestic debate, (4) the secrecy with which much of foreign policy was necessarily conducted, and (5) the ascendance of social welfare-oriented priorities in domestic politics. Added to all of these factors was the negligible *immediate* domestic relevance of most British foreign policy decisions, in contrast to the quite tangible domestic relevance—for extended periods—of external policy in West Germany and France.

THE FOREIGN POLICY ELITE

In earlier chapters we discussed at length the crucial role of the British foreign policy elite, not only in formulating policy but also in shaping to a significant extent public perceptions of Britain's international position. If in Britain's case the first major characteristic of the relationship between the external and internal environments is the limited impact of foreign affairs on domestic politics, the second major characteristic is the fundamentally elitist nature of foreign policymaking. In this, of course, Britain is not unique: all governments that hope to operate effectively in a Hobbesian international system must centralize, rationalize, and coordinate their foreign policy processes. This centralization requires a hierarchical decision-making structure that can, barring bureaucratic dissonance, generate and implement a set of national priorities. Yet just as hierarchy and centralization yield important benefits, they also constitute a source of vulnerability, since the misperceptions of a small number of decision makers may result in a hopelessly misdirected foreign policy. It becomes important, therefore, to understand the precise capabilities and characteristics of the foreign policy elite

Under British law the conduct of foreign policy is the peculiar concern and responsibility of the executive—that is, the cabinet and the professional bureaucracy that the cabinet directs. Not only is there no pretension to a democratic foreign policy (a concept invoked in Britain during the thirties, and still sometimes invoked in the United States), but there is also no requirement for the executive to seek the legislature's advice and consent in foreign policy matters. Parliament's *direct* control of the foreign policy apparatus is limited to approval or disapproval of the basic financial arrangements, and even here the potential for control is intermittent at best.

David Vital has summarized the constitutional positions of the British executive and Parliament in foreign policymaking:

In fact, although Parliament exercises some influence on the making of foreign policy this influence is very slight. Above all, Parliament is in no sense a regular participant in the process, either by right or by custom.

Even those matters which are most crucial and which, at first sight, seem the most appropriate subjects for legislative checks on the Executive—the making of war and peace and the making or ratification of treaties—are, in British constitutional law, termed Acts of State and are undoubted and exclusive prerogatives of the Crown. Certainly no modern government will refrain from bringing its intention to make war before Parliament and, latterly, the practice of laying the texts of treaties and other major international documents on the table of the House of Commons has become somewhat more frequent. Nevertheless, since, in the strict sense, neither the making of war nor the making of treaties require legislation, or even Parliament's approval, and there is therefore no equivalent to the "committee stage" in which Parliament subjects Bills to detailed scrutiny clause by clause, the legislature once again has only the revolutionary alternative of rejecting government policy *in toto.* In short, the monopoly which is accorded the Executive in the sphere of foreign affairs *de jure* is consistent to a remarkable degree with the general supremacy of the contemporary Executive over Parliament *de facto.*

The making of foreign policy, then, is the business of the Executive and for almost all practical purposes the Executive is unfettered in its exercise of this function.*

That this kind of executive domination stands in marked contrast to the democratic principles underpinning the British Constitution is testament to the traditional separation of foreign and domestic affairs. Of course, as Vital notes, the preeminent constitutional position of the executive in foreign policymaking parallels the de facto trend toward cabinet and even prime ministerial government in postwar Britain.

The control of foreign policy, then, tends to be in the hands of a group of powerful men who occupy key positions in the professional foreign affairs bureaucracy and in various cabinet committees. This group—usually trained at elite private schools and at the universities of Oxford and Cambridge—shares common assumptions to the point of not needing to articulate them and wields sufficient ad hoc influence (quite outside constitutional structures) to block unacceptable policies and preserve the status quo. It is a self-selecting, self-perpetuating elite, peculiarly cohesive and—when it chooses—remarkably impervious to external pressure.

The style of leadership yielded by the training of a relatively closed and

*David Vital, *The Making of British Foreign Policy* (New York: Praeger, 1968), pp. 48–49. Reprinted by permission of George Allen & Unwin Ltd.

homogenous elite results in the implicit (though not programmatic) continuity of foreign policy. Ideally the committee system of foreign policymaking incorporated in cabinet government recognizes public needs and national priorities, and also guards against the excesses that might result from one-man formulation of foreign policy. But there are costs as well as benefits. The steadily increasing concentration of power in cabinet committees in recent decades, combined with the homogeneity of an elite foreign policy bureaucracy, has caused indecisiveness and a serious lack of innovative thinking. Moreover, British leaders have erected cultural and emotional blinders that have interfered with or warped the flow of information to and from the outside world. Solution of these problems is difficult so long as control of British foreign policy remains predominantly in the hands of the same self-selected elite. Unfortunately, as Vital has pointed out, the constitutional setting of foreign policymaking renders any sustained challenge to that elite unlikely.

The Cabinet

No real understanding of the domestic setting of British foreign policy decision making can be achieved without an appreciation of the changed role of the cabinet. "Cabinet government" became the norm in the past few decades as new national programs increased the amount of Parliament's time devoted to government (as opposed to private) measures. The cabinet, sponsoring government bills, not only takes up most of Parliament's time but also decisively influences Parliamentary (and therefore national) priorities. The members of the British cabinet—the prime minister and his chief ministers—are simultaneously the symbolic heads of government, leaders of their party in Parliament, managers of the business of Parliament, and chiefs of the major administrative departments. It is from these multiple roles that the cabinet derives its collective responsibility and power; the cabinet is, in all important respects, the executive.

In the past the cabinet could delegate authority for the conduct of foreign policy to a minister with special expertise in the area, who could then pursue a policy bearing his personal imprint and exercise considerable freedom of maneuver. Palmerston, among other nineteenth century foreign ministers, exemplified this tradition. Today, however, such personalized diplomacy is no longer possible. We have seen in the preceding chapters that British foreign policy decisions in the postwar world frequently involved far more than the formal apparatus of the Foreign Office. Foreign policy was effectively influenced and even "made" by a variety of government departments, including—most notably—the Treasury and the Ministry of Defence.

This broadening of responsibility for foreign policy formulation did three things: (1) it deprived the Foreign Office of the monopoly over external policymaking that it had previously enjoyed, (2) it required coordination of the activities of the separate agencies and departments involved in external affairs, and (3) it required increasing coordination of domestic and foreign policy, especially in the economic sphere. The cabinet thus took on a dual role so far as foreign policy was concerned: to coordinate the external activities of the various agencies of the British government, and to reconcile domestic policy and needs with external policy and requirements. Some writers have argued that the cabinet system made possible the increasing subordination of foreign to domestic affairs. We have seen, however, that this has not always been the case. The sterling policy of successive postwar governments clearly subordinated domestic needs to external commitments, and the cabinet system was an important tool in implementing such priorities.

The Prime Minister

The prime minister affects the conduct of foreign policy in three important ways. First, he is a direct participant, sometimes taking on the role of "super-foreign secretary." Macmillan, for example, personally negotiated the Nassau Agreement and assumed major responsibility for his government's application to the Common Market. Wilson traveled to Nigeria in an effort to achieve a negotiated settlement of the civil war there and to Rhodesia in a last desperate bid to head off its unilateral declaration of independence. In 1966–67 he barnstormed the capitals of Western Europe to drum up support for Britain's second Common Market application. Where a prime minister is an active participant in foreign affairs (as most prime ministers since Attlee have been), foreign policy invariably bears the imprint of his personal style and approach.

Second, the prime minister chooses his foreign secretary and determines what the role of the foreign secretary will be in his government. Prime Minister Attlee mainly concerned himself with domestic policy and allowed Ernest Bevin almost free reign as foreign secretary (though Attlee insisted on being informed). Prime Minister Eden, in contrast, was an extremely active participant in foreign policy and relegated his foreign secretary to a support role. Again, the crucial factor is as much as anything the personalities of the individuals involved.

Third, the prime minister has wide latitude in deciding how to respond to a particular foreign policy crisis or event. He may consult with his foreign secretary, with the entire cabinet, or with a cabinet committee (an "inner cabinet"). A cabinet committee, carefully selected, can on occasion be used to circumvent the full cabinet. The choice between these options will inevitably affect the content of the response to a particular problem and will be dictated by considerations of efficiency (it ordinarily requires two days' notice for the full cabinet to meet) and the prime minister's personal power and influence.

These factors give the prime minister considerable power, and the principle of the cabinet's collective responsibility also ensures the prime minister that a subordinate minister will not publicly dissent from a decision reached by the cabinet as a whole. Conversely, of course, the prime minister is himself bound by a cabinet decision even if he does not support it, but instances of cabinet "coups" are rare. Although the British prime minister is not as secure in office as an American president, and may for this reason be reluctant to pursue controversial policies, his power in the realm of foreign affairs is nonetheless considerable.

The Bureaucracy

The professional foreign policy bureaucracy in Britain is beset by the same difficulties that afflict all entrenched bureaucracies. Because of its preference for pragmatic, short-run thinking it has not been able to guarantee the formulation or implementation of a completely rational foreign policy. There is substantial overlap between the responsibilities of different ministries, and in some cases—as in the relationship between the Foreign Office and the Ministry of Defence—a serious dissonance exists between the perceptions of different agencies. The bureaucracy has also, as we saw with respect to sterling policy, been encumbered by its own doctrinal blinders.

The specific components of the general problem are familiar enough. First, a rational foreign policy requires the articulation of long-range goals, the specification of alternative means of achieving these goals, and the selection in each instance of those means best suited to the attainment of a specific goal. The British foreign policy apparatus, however, tends toward short-run thinking, a pragmatic reactive stance, and a distrust of doctrinal consistency. In some ways these tendencies are rooted in the British national character, in the tradition of "muddling through." In another sense they have been historically determined by the requirements of exercising global imperial responsibilities despite a limited domestic resource base. A pragmatic policy orientation worked well with respect to decolonization of the dependent Empire; it was an impediment, however, to the formulation of an effective security policy and a realistic policy toward the continent of Europe. Whatever its sources, the pragmatic bent in British foreign policy runs directly counter to the trend toward systems analysis, long-range planning, and the explicit consideration of future alternatives. Although it might be argued that the anarchic and unpredictable nature of the international system does not allow detailed long-range planning, this does not absolve foreign policy decision makers of their responsibilty to forge a set of long-term national priorities. Such priorities have not always been well articulated in Britain's case.

Second, a rational foreign policy requires that responsibility for the achievement of specific goals be placed squarely in the hands of identifiable and fully accountable agencies of government that can follow policies through to their conclusion. In Britain this requirement is not completely met, though the ideal of bureaucratic rationalization is closer to achievement than in the United States. One finds in the British government substantial overlap of authority and responsibility between, for example, the Foreign Office, the Treasury, the Board of Trade, and the agencies responsible for domestic economic development. Each of these departments of government is likely to look at the same problem in a slightly different way and to recommend somewhat different solutions to it, though—as noted earlier in this chapter —it is unlikely that they will indulge in the kind of "bureaucratic politics" found in the United States. Sometimes bureaucratic dissonance occurs because the rational constraints on a policy affect one department of government before they affect another. For example, the Foreign Office has been able to plan a traditional foreign policy largely unfettered and to give verbal support to traditional commitments, while the Ministry of Defence—which is called upon to support policy through the concrete commitment of men and resources—has been the first to encounter budgetary and resource limitations and the need to revise traditional outlooks. The result, inevitably, has been interdepartmental conflict stemming from the incompatibility between policy planning and implementation.

Third, a rational foreign policy must be formulated by a bureaucracy committed to a thoroughly dispassionate assessment of facts. In the postwar era the British foreign policy bureaucracy has consistently tripped over its own prejudices and emotions. The most obvious shortcoming has been the inability of responsible bureaucrats to reconcile themselves to Britain's less powerful international position, an inability that has contributed directly to such blunders as Suez and the Skybolt dilemma. As already noted, the professional bureaucracy in Britain is socially homogenous—middle or upper-middle class, with leaders drawn overwhelmingly from Oxford and Cambridge —and the result has been an amazing imperviousness to change. Pressure for reform has usually come not from within the bureaucracy, but from Parliament and the cabinet.

The problems raised by these observations are crucial. The question of who controls the civil service—that is, whether we are dealing in Britain with party government or a largely autonomous administrative government—does not have an easy or obvious answer. As Anthony Sampson has noted, when "a new party comes to power in Britain, only about a hundred politicians move into Whitehall to run the 800,000 civil servants."* The senior civil servants, endowed with a continuity in office not possessed by the politicians, wield considerable power—power sufficient to foil government policy. Shortcomings in the British foreign policy process and bureaucracy are therefore of critical importance.

*Anthony Sampson, quoted in Michael R. Gordon, "Civil Servants, Politicians, and Parties: Shortcomings in the British Policy Process," *Comparative Politics*, 4, no. 1 (October 1971), 47.

A DEMOCRATIC PROCESS?

We noted at the beginning of this chapter that domestic conditions in Britain are profoundly affected by the international environment. This is to be expected in a nation as small and densely populated as Britain, dependent for its very survival on international trade, and with a long maritime and imperial tradition. Yet we have also pointed out that the planning and execution of British foreign policy is fundamentally elitist and that foreign affairs have had only a minor impact on British electoral politics. We must ask whether there is not a contradiction between the democratic pretensions of the British constitution and the concentration in a few hands of control over an external policy that must indirectly affect millions. In an interdependent world in which domestic political and economic systems are increasingly "penetrated" by the conditions of the international environment, the question "who makes foreign policy" may have broad-ranging domestic repercussions. The allocation of political and economic goods in a society is undoubtedly influenced (and sometimes determined) by external policy decisions, despite the fact that those decisions are made by a very small number of people. In chapter 10, for example, we saw that a few politicians and Treasury officials managed for eighteen years to maintain a fixed international sterling, even though measures taken to uphold this monetary system ultimately hurt the vast majority of Britons. Democratic institutions and safeguards simply did not extend to the conduct of external monetary policy.

It can be argued, of course, that the British foreign policy elite is committed to the nation's best interests and that because of its special expertise the elite is entitled to identify those interests. It can also be argued that the broadly articulated "public will" gains expression in the attitudes of politicians and civil servants, who have a sense of *noblesse oblige*. Finally, one might contend that—given the apathy of the average British voter with respect to foreign affairs—the British public ultimately gets what it deserves, and furthermore that there is no essential barrier to a more partisan and publicly active approach to foreign policy. Indeed, the Labour Party's campaign for renegotiation of Britain's entry into the EEC and the public referendum that followed seemed to point to a new kind of popular involvement in external affairs.

All of these arguments must be looked at circumspectly, however. The fact is that control of British foreign policy is not in the hands of the public, not even indirectly. This could change, though it is not likely to. Certainly a democratic foreign policy would have no guarantee of being more successful than the present one, and might even be less so.

CONCLUSION

13

Transatlantic Relations, Economic Interdependence, and the Confluence of Domestic and Foreign Policy

In this chapter we will reflect on three themes that have run through the book, but that have not been given sustained treatment. These themes follow logically from our concerns with military security, economic development, and the relationship between foreign policy and domestic politics. They are (1) the relationship among the three secondary powers—West Germany, France, and Britain—and their superpower ally, the United States, (2) the accelerating process of economic interdependence among these three countries and throughout the industrialized world, and (3) the alignment of external and internal politics and policy processes.

SECONDARY POWERS AND SUPERPOWERS

One of the major themes of this book is the relationship between the United States and its three major European allies. Over time serious transatlantic tensions developed between Washington and Bonn, Paris, and London—with Franco-American relations beginning to deteriorate much earlier than Anglo-American or German-American relations. Given historical perspective and the changing conditions of the postwar international system, this evolution of American–West European relations was largely predictable. The growing incompatibility between American and West European interests emerged from geopolitical factors, developments in military technology, and the enormous difficulty of understanding and then somehow holding together a highly dynamic international economic system. With respect to the latter, the combination of Europe's newfound economic strength with the growing importance of economic security questions seemed to assure transatlantic divisiveness.

In the first postwar decade American and Western European interests were largely compatible. The European continent lay shattered and disillusioned, confronted at the same time with enormous Soviet military power. The requirements of reconstructing a healthy Europe and containing the Soviet Union were the same. The United States, the undisputed economic superpower and architect of a new international monetary system, provided goods and money for reconstruction and, as the largely invulnerable possessor of the only viable nuclear force, guaranteed West European military security without great immediate risk to itself. Yet, as Henry Kissinger pointed out long ago, American political, military, and economic hegemony was destined to be as short-lived as the conditions that brought it about at the end of World War II.

West Germany and the United States

In West Germany's case, America's role was critical. The United States actively supported—both politically and economically—German reindustrialization. Washington also encouraged West European integration as a means of sublimating traditional European antagonisms and fears of German revival. Finally, American pressure was instrumental in bringing about West German rearmament and with it Bonn's sovereignty, against the resistance of France and the reluctance of Britain. And while the strategic purpose of American forces in Germany was not always perceived in the same way in Washington and Bonn, both governments—responsive to a broad commonality of interests within the Atlantic alliance—wanted those forces to remain in place.

Only with respect to the reunification issue, nuclear sharing, and (later) certain aspects of Bonn's economic policy was American support more reserved. While Washington gave lip service to the ultimate goal of reunification, especially during the Adenauer years, Germany's division was at least tacitly accepted as permanent and—from the standpoint of ensuring European stability—viewed as beneficial by many American officials. One goal of the Adenauer government, to obtain a finger on a multilateral NATO nuclear trigger as a bargaining tool to hasten reunification, was not supported by Washington at all. The MLF proposal, advanced partially to mollify Bonn's alleged clamoring for a nuclear role, was ultimately dropped by the United States, and West Germany had to settle for an active role in the NATO Nuclear Planning Group. Tension between Washington and Bonn over nuclear matters continued through the late sixties, as Bonn delayed signing the nuclear nonproliferation treaty in an effort to retain yet another bargaining chip for use in its dealings with the East. American differences with Bonn over economic matters—part of broader American differences with the European Community—were tempered by the fact that between 1969 and 1971 West Germany made greater efforts than any other country to cushion the United States against constant onslaughts on the dollar. Of course, Bonn in part felt impelled to do this by the threat of United States troop withdrawals. What is surprising in retrospect is that the United States, finding the status quo in Europe quite tolerable, and West Germany, seeking to overcome the status quo to advance reunification, managed to cooperate as fully as they did throughout the postwar era. This cooperation was a testament to the ultimate concern in both governments with Western Europe's military security. It also demonstrated that West Germany saw its political and economic future so closely tied to the West that a see-saw policy between East and West became inconceivable.

France and the United States

In France's case, the roots of conflict with the United States were seen easily enough in de Gaulle's wartime relationship with Roosevelt and Churchill. In the immediate postwar period, Washington, concerned about French political stability and the size of the French Communist Party, extended economic and moral support to Paris and in 1953–54 even provided the bulk of the funding for the French Indochina War. But American officials could never view France in the same way they viewed Britain—France's wartime collapse and post-war political instability guaranteed that—and Washington's rejection of de Gaulle's September 1958 demand for equality within the Western Alliance was almost predetermined.

Franco-American conflict intensified as Paris wrestled against the idea that a global superpower balance had displaced a regional European power configuration—one no longer supported by overseas empires. In significant respects this conflict presaged a broader transatlantic dissensus, one based on fundamental incompatibilities between American and West European strategic and economic positions. Washington, concerned about maintaining its control over NATO nuclear weapons, staunchly opposed development of the *force de frappe*, which de Gaulle viewed as a primary instrument of French diplomatic independence. As the danger from the East diminished, de Gaulle felt more confident charting his own course in international politics; he pushed ahead with the *force de frappe*, launched his own brand of detente with the Soviet Union, and in 1966 pulled France out of NATO. Always, however, there was the presumption of an American military presence in Europe—a presence that, paradoxically, allowed Paris more freedom than it otherwise might have had.

Britain and the United States

Relations between Britain and the United States were close from the beginning, but the Anglo-American "special relationship" was a residual of wartime cooperation and not a permanent feature. At first British leaders fostered close ties with Washington because they perceived the United States as a necessary counterweight to Soviet power in maintaining a European balance. In addition, American aid was crucial in financing both Britain's haphazard economic recovery and new social welfare programs. Americans in turn found British diplomatic experience and contacts useful, and saw in London's far-flung commitments an asset for global peacekeeping (though American and British policies were in frequent conflict outside Europe).

To Washington's dismay, Britain stayed out of the EEC in the fifties and sixties. As the Community's burgeoning growth contrasted starkly with Britain's flagging economy, Washington developed more interest in maintaining close direct relations with the European continent; Britain's role as a spokesman for American interests in Europe, a tenuous role in the first place, vanished. Moreover, by the mid-sixties Britain's nuclear capacity was no longer an important supplement to American strategic forces, and Whitehall's abandonment of overseas responsibilities eliminated Britain's value as co-peacekeeper. Britain's entry into the European Community in the early seventies coincided with generally severe European-American tensions that reinforced the collapse of the Anglo-American special relationship, signaled by Edward Heath in December 1971. By the late seventies the only remnant of the special relationship was Anglo-American nuclear sharing, principally embodied in the provisions of the Nassau Agreement, and the future of this arrangement was uncertain.

The Breakdown of the Atlantic Consensus

None of these developments should have surprised the Germans, French, British, or Americans. There were "systemic imperatives" that virtually guaranteed some degree of transatlantic conflict; and the anomalous circumstances of the first postwar decade—which originally brought the Atlantic alliance together—could not last forever. The United States and Western Europe occupied distinct geopolitical and therefore strategic positions, and the dogma of Atlanticism (meaning, from Washington's perspective, continued United States predominance) could not paper over these differences.

If we combine the experiences of Bonn, Paris, and London, we can discern three broad developments that broke down the Atlantic consensus. First, the evident vulnerability of the United States to Soviet nuclear attack after the early sixties forced Washington to qualify the automaticity of its nuclear guarantee to Europe, impaired the credibility of that guarantee, and ultimately brought the strategically distinct positions of America and Europe into clear focus. This was the long-term effect of the American flexible response doctrine. The Pentagon—interested in establishing a firebreak between limited East bloc provocations and all-out devastation of American cities—accepted the possibility of a limited war in Europe, which from a European perspective would be total war. Deployment of tactical nuclear weapons did not really change this fact. West European governments had to take refuge in the "hostage" value of American forces on the Continent, and in the nuclear triggering potential of tactical nuclear weapons and the British and French national deterrents. Moreover, as the United States commitment became more qualified, the incentive for maintaining European nuclear forces became stronger in some circles, and this further exacerbated transatlantic tensions since Washington viewed national European deterrents as disturbing the stability of Soviet-American strategic rapprochement.

Second, the breakdown of the monetary and trade consensus in the late sixties had a devastating impact on Alliance unity. As the United States Federal Reserve resisted repatriation of overseas dollars, Europeans grew impatient of accumulating dollars and surrendering tangible assets to American interests in exchange for paper money that increasingly lacked reserve backing. More extreme European critics, such as Jacques Rueff, saw the Federal Reserve as running a "paper mill." Yet the dollar was protected against devaluation by its privileged position within the rigid Bretton Woods monetary system. Europeans could not be convinced that this privileged position absolved the United States of balance-of-payments discipline, or that the United States was acting as a global investment banker, "borrowing short and lending long." Washington, of course, also had economic complaints. The United States argued that Europeans had too conservative an attitude toward long-term credit and investment and that the allegiance to gold of European central banks smacked of economic atavism in an age of complex postindustrial economies. Washington resented, too, trade discrimination by the EEC, and in 1973 Henry Kissinger accused the Community of violating GATT and betraying the principle of Atlantic free trade. There was some degree of hypocrisy in this: the United States government, under pressure from organized labor and less competitive industry, had become increasingly protectionist. It seemed ironic in any case that Americans—now chafing under EEC discrimination—had earlier pushed so adamantly for European integration.

Confronted with trade and monetary differences with Europe, Washington tried in 1973 and 1974 to establish a link between United States military commitments on the Continent and European economic concessions. Europeans dragged their feet and finally rebuffed the idea; after all, West Germany was already making large offset payments to Washington to redress the United States balance-of-payments deficit on its military account. In some ways a linkage between economic and defense policies made sense, however: the distinction between "low politics" and "high politics" was becoming progressively blurred in Atlantic diplomacy, a fact that made the European-American relationship even more convoluted and difficult. The consummate blurring of this distinction came in 1973, when West Europeans refused to support the United States, militarily or any other way, at the time of the Arab-Israeli War and the subsequent United States global alert. Again it was a question of fundamentally different positions. The United States was not critically dependent upon Middle East oil for its economic survival; Europe was. This difference in economic circumstances dictated conflicting American and European stances across the entire spectrum of diplomatic activity.

The third force pulling the transatlantic consensus apart was the fact that the immediacy and intensity of the Soviet threat diminished in both European and American eyes after the early sixties, allowing centrifugal pressures within the Western Alliance freer rein. American planners still saw NATO's prime functions as *military* (deterrence and defense), but by the mid-sixties they no longer considered a Warsaw Pact assault on Western Europe probable, and devoted the bulk of their attention to Vietnam. In contrast, West Europeans, with a similar view of the Soviet threat, saw the prime functions of NATO as *political*—that is, ensuring a continued United States commitment to the political and economic future of Europe, and thus ultimately also guaranteeing the Continent's military security. When the intensity of American concern for Europe's military security diminished, this was interpreted in European capitals as a reduction of the level of political commitment. During the late sixties and early seventies Europeans became anxious as Washington was bogged down in Vietnam and American pressure on Europeans to build up their conventional defense seemed to be a prelude to United States military withdrawal. As a result—though also in response to a general relaxation of East-West tensions—West Europeans made their own political and economic arrangements with the East bloc. If American support was no longer reliable, then it was necessary to come to terms with the behemoth in the East. This intra-European detente and its dynamics for overcoming the East-West division sometimes conflicted with the more static strategic detente between the two superpowers, which sought only to stabilize the East-West division (that is, make the division "safe" rather than overcome it). Washington was not completely comfortable with its allies' contacts in the East, since these contacts could not be easily controlled. In turn West Europeans were mistrustful of bilateral Soviet-American rapprochement, which promised to produce agreements occasionally detrimental to the allies of both superpowers.

By the late seventies Americans and Europeans alike had come to a more mature acceptance of the basic differences in their positions and perspectives. The dogma of Atlanticism, which treated European-American conflict as illegitimate or at least abnormal, no longer held sway. Many of the economic conflicts that so bitterly divided the alliance between 1969 and 1974 abated, though tension persisted over floating exchange rates and Middle East oil policy. West European–American differences over detente were muted after 1975 by the general decline of detente itself in the face of a Soviet arms buildup and new Soviet stridency in Africa and the Middle East.

ECONOMIC INTERDEPENDENCE

Closely connected with transatlantic relations are the other two themes that have run through this book: economic interdependence and the confluence of domestic and foreign policy.

In focusing on the foreign policy goals of Germany, France, and Britain, we implicitly stressed the importance of the nation-state and its institutions. The idea of the national interest continued to be a central element in postwar international politics, and the international system remained an interstate system in many of its essential features. But at the same time equally powerful forces were at work in international politics that curtailed or in any case modified the role of the nation-state. These developments—usually summarized by the term *interdependence*—were in part the result of the changing nature of the nation-state itself and in part the result of new ways in which nation-states interacted. The three countries we have examined were strongly affected by processes of interdependence—as we have seen at many points in our previous discussion—and their foreign policies cannot be fully understood without underlining the significance of this phenomenon.*

The Prerequisites of Interdependence

Interdependence required a permissive context. It was possible only in a type of international system that allowed it. Liberalization of trade and money flows, minimal interference with transnational investment activities, absence of protectionism, and other liberal economic preferences—as well as the political purposes and ideological justifications connected with them—were prerequisites for a highly interdependent political and economic system. Although technology shrank the world, politics kept it that way. International economic systems, as much as military-strategic and political systems, reflect the influence and interests of their predominant members. The international economic and monetary arrangements of the postwar period were essentially the creation of the United States, which emerged from the war as the undisputed economic and monetary superpower. Although conceived initially as a worldwide arrangement of liberalized trade and monetary relations (a global "open door" for the United States), following the onset of the Cold War the arrangement began to revolve around trilateral relationships among the United States, Western Europe, and Japan, with the communist economic-monetary system becoming a regional subsystem. This trilateral combine was subjected to increasing stress during the sixties and underwent major changes

*For a fuller discussion, see Wolfram F. Hanrieder, "Dissolving International Politics: Reflections on the Nation-State," *American Political Science Review* (December 1978), pp. 1276-78.

in the early seventies, with the result that the United States had to share its predominant position with Western Europe and Japan. A new international monetary and trading system slowly developed, its shape still ambiguous, under the uncertain impact of the North-South conflict and of OPEC's monetary resources.

In addition to a permissive external context, interdependence required a permissive internal context. National political systems needed political, institutional, and ideological attitudes that accepted processes of interdependence. By and large this condition was met in the three countries we have examined. In the case of West Germany, the United States had enormous leverage—first as an occupation power and later as the alliance superpower—to foster attitudes and create institutions that were receptive to economic internationalism. This was in fact welcomed by Konrad Adenauer and Ludwig Erhard, and may have been a major factor in Germany's speedy economic recovery. In the case of France and Britain, American influence was more subtle but nonetheless inescapable. Both countries needed American aid; and the string attached to that aid was French and British willingness to liberalize trade and money transactions. The United States exerted its influence to create an international economic order that corresponded to American political and economic interests.

Germany, France, and Britain were not only similar with respect to their openness to international economic processes and the types of demands their citizens made on their governments, but they also had available similar means of directing, containing, expanding, or otherwise affecting domestic as well as international economic processes: trade and monetary policy, fiscal policy, income policy, wages policy, labor policy, taxation policy. Similar challenges were tackled with similar policy instruments.

But there were also significant differences. The division of labor between state and society, the mix between public, semipublic, and private structures, the relationship between interest groups and bureaucracies, the uses of taxation, sensitivity to inflation and unemployment, attitudes on economic growth, preoccupation with national security—to mention only a few examples—were significantly different in West Germany, France, and Britain. Their domestic political and economic structures, and the explicit and implicit codes that defined the appropriate role of government in the economy and society, were quite divergent. In each country there were entrenched administrative practices that were unique and resisted international coordination. While the bureaucratic instinct might be universal and timeless, it could not be stripped totally of its local historical and institutional context. All these traditions, and their structural manifestations, were different. The differences appeared in their starkest form in welfare concerns rather than in security concerns. Although governments everywhere were pressured to direct the solution of economic and social problems, their impulses and capacities to act were energized and inhibited in different ways.

Divergence and Integration

These differences made it difficult at times for Germany, France, and Britain to coordinate their foreign policies. In the context of European integration as well as in the context of the Atlantic alliance, two contradictory processes (at times of unequal intensity) were visible: a process of divergence and a process of integration. We have dealt with a number of examples of divergence as well as integration: de Gaulle's decision to remove France from the unified command structure of NATO (as well as other Gaullist foreign policy projects) is an example of policy divergence, whereas the decision to establish structures for a European Community (within which conflicting national interests would be adjusted) is an example of an integrative type of policy.

There is no question that in many important respects the political systems of West Germany, France, and Britain became more and more alike. Yet these similarities did not impel them toward greater integration, but at best toward greater coordination of national policies. This was so not only because of internal domestic obstacles to integration but also because each member of the European community—and especially the three countries we have dealt with—had a distinctly different relationship with the United States. At the same time these governments had to turn to the international arena in order to satisfy the demands pressed upon them by their electorates, demands ignored only at the risk of being removed from office. It was primarily for this reason that coordination of policies became a central issue in intra-European as well as transatlantic relationships. The similarity of domestic developments and problems required some form and measure of international cooperation, but since greater integration was unacceptable to many members of the European Community for a variety of reasons, coordination appeared to be the only alternative. Policy coordination became a substitute for integration.

Moreover, as the European Community became larger, the prospects for deeper interaction diminished (and promised to diminish further as the Community grew still larger in the future). By the late seventies there was a legitimate question as to whether there existed any compelling reasons to give Community institutions more power or whether it was sufficient to solidify and streamline these institutions. Important industrial and commercial interests in the Community appeared to be interested primarily in conserving and sustaining the present level of integration, seeing their interests adequately served by the status quo and shying away from the uncertainties and readjustments that would attend changes in the scope and intensity of supranational arrangements.

The possibility for coordination in the area of security issues was uneven and the record was mixed. The Western response to the issues presented by the European Security Conference was well coordinated, but this was so in large part because West Germany's *Ostpolitik* and the resulting treaty arrangements had already resolved issues that were of concern to the Soviet Union and Eastern Europe. Throughout the seventies a coordinated European foreign policy program was as remote as it had ever been, and it was difficult to imagine events that could push the Community in that direction, especially in a decade in which governments were less inclined to pursue grandiose schemes for global and regional power rearrangements than in the sixties.

EXTERNAL AND INTERNAL
POLITICAL ALIGNMENTS

The processes we have described reflect a dialectic of independence and interdependence. In advancing their interests, governments and subgovernmental groups—society as well as the state—brought about interdependence. Interdependence was sustained because these interests did not allow disintegration of interdependent relationships toward a more fragmented and contentious international system, though they also did not propel the system toward greater integration. Interdependence, and the coordination required for its operation, was a halfway house between disintegration and integration of political and economic processes. Interdependence was the prototypical phenomenon of an international system that derived its dynamics from the pursuit of national interests as well as other interests that were either narrower or larger than national interests.

All this made it very difficult, and perhaps meaningless, to distinguish between domestic and foreign policy. From the beginning of the postwar period, external international factors had a strong influence on the domestic political process of the three countries we have studied. This was especially visible in the case of France and Germany, but it was noticeable also in the case of Britain. In general, especially in the fifties, but extending into the sixties as well, German and French decision makers and important pressure groups saw the nature of their respective domestic societies strongly influenced by foreign policy issues and consistently evaluated foreign policy problems in terms of their impact on the domestic socioeconomic and political scene. This meant that foreign policy problems were carried over into the domestic political process, leading at times to a striking similarity between patterns of political alignment on external and internal matters. In Britain, where a broad foreign policy consensus prevailed, foreign policy elites fashioned the country's external adjustment to radically altered international conditions so that this adjustment's impact on public sentiment—on national self-confidence—would be minimal. The result was that British foreign policy evolved too slowly and in a piecemeal way.

West Germany

In the case of West Germany, in the late forties and throughout the fifties the domestic conflict over foreign policy was polarized because the apparent incompatibility on the international scene between security, rearmament, recovery, and the return of the Saar on the one hand and unification of East and West Germany on the other posed basic and painful choices of priority. The core issue in this setting was widely perceived to be rearmament versus reunification. At the same time, limited agreements and ad hoc coalitions among the major political parties and interest groups lessened and occasionally obscured this fundamental split. It was the polarization of viewpoints on how to achieve unification, combined with the overlapping patterns of preference on related subissues, that characterized domestic politics in West Germany before the mid-fifties. The polarization in the domestic contest over rearmament and reunification was essentially imposed by the polarization of the Cold War international system, even though its meaning for Germans derived from the conflicting blueprints that the contending parties advanced for the nature of German society.

Important changes in the international system took place after the mid-fifties, producing corresponding shifts and realignments in the domestic pattern of consensus or dissensus. When it became apparent that Germany's reunification could not be achieved, the major impediment to a partial consensus on foreign policy was overcome. The partial and ad hoc elements of agreement among political parties and major interest groups, which had existed all along, could now move into the foreground and coalesce into an informal and incomplete, but nonetheless significant, consensus.

In the late sixties and early seventies, the domestic political process in Germany was still very much affected by foreign policy issues, but in a fundamentally different way. Again, the international context within which Germany had to operate had an important bearing on this development. In the seventies, Cold War confrontations between the United States and the Soviet Union (and their respective alliances) abated in an era of detente, tensions lessened between the superpowers, the military threat of the Soviet Union diminished, and the status quo in Europe became acceptable to most European countries (especially with respect to territorial arrangements). As a result, economic well-being and related social issues became more predominant relative to military-security issues and large-scale political concerns. Willy Brandt's *Ostpolitik* made an essential contribution to this development, although his Eastern policy was also subject to intense scrutiny by his opposition in Bonn and raised a good deal of public debate. This highly dramatic German policy of reaching an accommodation with the East was in a sense the last remnant of the big, "classical" foreign policy issues that had preoccupied West Germany for two decades. More and more, in Germany as well as in other European countries, economic and monetary issues came to the foreground, and it became increasingly difficult to draw distinctions between foreign and domestic policies. Aside from the reasons already mentioned, this development was pushed forward by interdependence in world and regional politics and further enhanced by the processes of European economic integration. Increasingly, foreign policy and domestic economic and social issues became fused in a highly intricate way, leading to a change in the way foreign policy issues were debated and evaluated on the domestic political scene.

France

A remarkably similar process was taking shape in France. During the Fourth Republic the French political process was also strongly affected by foreign policy issues, and this held true as well during the time de Gaulle was in power in the first stage of the Fifth Republic. Even so, there were significant differences between France and Germany. In the first place, French foreign policy goals in the Fourth Republic were not as diametrically incompatible and polarized as in the German case. No clear-cut alternatives, such as rearmament or reunification, were visible in the French case. But, in contrast to Germany, the French goals of political recovery and economic recovery were largely incompatible. The quest for political and diplomatic mobility and independence, which was the distinctive element of the French goal of political recovery, conflicted sharply with the need to accommodate the United States—dictated by French dependence on American economic aid, without which the long-range goal of economic reconstruction and self-sufficiency could not be achieved. Thus, far from being complementary and reinforcing, as was the case in Germany, the political recovery and economic recovery goals of France were largely incompatible.

The contradictions in the late forties between the pursuit of French security toward Germany and security toward the Soviet Union made it difficult to pursue policies with which to implement either set of goals. Success in one set of goals was bound to be achieved at the expense of success in the other. Because the Cold War polarization between the superpowers fragmented the French goal of security by giving it an anti-Soviet as well as anti-German dimension, France was unable to play the role of independent mediator. French weakness was underlined by dependence on the United States and the alliance structures that Washington had established for the containment of communism. Thus security considerations with regard to the Soviet Union as well as Germany stood in the way of the kind of political recovery France had envisaged—becoming an independent, flexible power, involved on a global scale and prominent on the Continent. France was forced into an accommodation with Germany that was not made much more palatable by the fact that it took place within the context of integrative European structures, sponsored by the United States.

The necessities of security in the Cold War context were also incompatible with the goal of retaining the French empire. The decomposition of the empire, although irreversible in any case, forced upon France the choice of either acquiescing benevolently or fighting tenaciously. Once the latter alternative was chosen, there was a drain on French military, economic, and psychological resources to the point of collapse. These resources could have been put to more effective use in strengthening the French position relative to the superpowers and relative to Germany.

Yet the fact that central aspects of French foreign policy goals were incompatible did not mean that they could be organized and compressed into relatively clear-cut alternatives. Here the contrast with Germany during the early Adenauer years is instructive. The contest in West Germany over the core issue of security and recovery versus reunification, which characterized the foreign policy disagreements between government and opposition, was largely imposed by the international context of the Cold War. Although the alternative supported by the Social Democrats—a flexible, essentially neutral foreign policy intended to preserve and enhance the chances of reunification —may have had little chance of success, the alternatives nonetheless were relatively distinct. But it was in the nature of French foreign policy goals, especially those of security and political and economic recovery, that the international context did not impose upon them polarized alternatives— regardless of whether one or the other alternative might have had chances of success. Thus, although French goals and the context in which they were pursued were contradictory and highly intractable, they were not clearly defined as opposing choices. This also meant that no strongly complementary goals developed, as had been the case in Germany with the goals of security and recovery during the first decade of the Bonn Republic.

Of course, the fact that French foreign policy goals (and the instruments toward their realization) could not be articulated as polarized alternatives need not have been intrinsically negative. As the German case indicates, polarization into clear-cut alternatives most likely develops when foreign policy goals are strongly incompatible. Moreover, in the postwar years the French clearly preferred diplomatic flexibility and freedom of maneuver, which would automatically have been inhibited if diametrically opposed policy choices had presented themselves. The absence of polarized foreign policy alternatives meant, however, that a fragmented domestic political system met with an equally fragmented set of foreign policy preferences. Neither the external nor the internal political setting compelled or encouraged the development of an internally consistent, interlocking foreign policy program, with the result that domestic political forces could not be marshaled effectively for policy alternatives. A responsible and plausible simplification of foreign policy alternatives, which might have resulted either from the incontrovertible realities of the international context or from distinct divisions of opinion in the domestic political context, could not be constructed. During the Fourth Republic, fragmentation rather than polarization characterized the external as well as internal dimensions of French foreign policy goals.

Under de Gaulle in the Fifth Republic, foreign policy became more streamlined. De Gaulle's foreign policy program, although not devoid of certain contradictions, was nonetheless coherent and well-considered. The major problem was that this program could not be implemented. Still, domestic opposition to de Gaulle's foreign policy remained ineffectual because the forces of opposition were not effectively channeled. Foreign policy issues became, for all practical purposes, depoliticized. Under de Gaulle's successors, foreign policy issues once again became politicized. Economic interdependence meant that foreign policy issues and domestic socioeconomic issues became closely intertwined. The domestic political process was compelled to adjust to this development. Party alignments and cleavages depended on whether the issues were matters of purely domestic policy, traditional foreign policy, or mixed domestic-foreign policy. A highly complicated political pattern developed, leading to different configurations of consensus and opposition depending on what kind of foreign policy issue was at stake.

Britain

The impact of foreign policy issues on the British political process was somewhat different from the case of France and West Germany. Foreign policy had a limited *direct* influence on British electoral politics. Nonetheless, the internal and external dimensions of British politics and foreign policy overlapped significantly, especially in the economic realm. As with West Germany and France, this overlap was reciprocal: foreign policy concerns and the conditions of the external environment profoundly affected the context of domestic politics, and domestic political concerns had a great impact on the direction and tenor of foreign policy. On balance the increasingly domestic focus of party politics had a negative impact on the formulation of external policy, causing successive governments to avoid any fundamental rethinking of that policy until change was unavoidable (and, sometimes, too late).

The overlap of external and internal facets of British policy was most evident in the psychological impact of Britain's declining world role. Many of the British were reluctant to accept this decline and experienced a kind of "cognitive lag" between their own perceptions and the conditions of the real world. This cognitive lag was strongest among the mass of British voters, whose traditional view of British power was bolstered by the experience of World War II and who perceived the need for changing Britain's external orientation more slowly than foreign-policymaking elites. From 1945 until the mid-sixties successive governments avoided drastic foreign policy changes and kept the public from recognizing Britain's new circumstances. This made Britain's long-term readjustment more difficult.

In the area of defense policy, readjustment took place earliest and with the clearest perception of British capabilities. Economic policy was a different matter, though it was impossible to shield the British public from the realization that the nation lacked the resources commensurate with great-power status. External economic problems—persistent balance-of-payments difficulties and the effort to sustain sterling's value—constantly intruded into the domestic economic and political life of the country. Nonetheless, the domestic impact of external events and commitments was frequently ignored, with damaging consequences.

In many respects, British reluctance to face the realities of diminished power was symptomatic of attitudes that prevailed in all three countries. While Britain clung to traditional notions of great-power status (including military power and global diplomacy), that option was unavailable to Germany because of its defeat and discredited past. Instead the Germans turned to the compensations of economic and monetary power in the context of European and transatlantic integration. Following France's demise in World War II, at first Paris also sought to redefine the nation in traditional power terms. But the American pressure for European integration, the demoralizing experience of Indochina and Algeria, and economic necessity sensitized France to the fact that for secondary powers the meaning and applications of power had shifted to economic sources.

West Germany, France, and Britain initially pursued foreign policy goals that derived from a more traditional measure of international influence. But these notions had to be revised in the light of military-strategic and economic developments. In the context of new necessities, the opportunities and costs of being secondary powers began to emerge.

For Further Reading

WEST GERMANY

GROSSER, ALFRED, *Germany in Our Time: A Political History of the Postwar Years*. New York: Praeger Publishers, 1971.

HANRIEDER, WOLFRAM F., *The Stable Crisis: Two Decades of German Foreign Policy*. New York: Harper & Row, 1970.

HANRIEDER, WOLFRAM F., *West German Foreign Policy, 1949–1963: International Pressure and Domestic Response*. Stanford, Calif.: Stanford University Press, 1967.

HANRIEDER, WOLFRAM F., ed., *West German Foreign Policy, 1949–79*. Boulder, Colo.: Westview Press, 1979.

KAISER, KARL, *German Foreign Policy in Transition: Bonn Between East and West*. London: Oxford University Press, 1968.

KELLEHER, CATHERINE MCARDLE, *Germany and the Politics of Nuclear Weapons*. New York: Columbia University Press, 1975.

MERKL, PETER H., *German Foreign Policies West and East: On the Threshold of a New European Era*. Santa Barbara, Calif.: ABC Clio, 1974.

MORGAN, ROGER, *The United States and West Germany, 1945–1973: A Study in Alliance Politics*. London: Oxford University Press, 1974.

OSGOOD, ROBERT E., *NATO: The Entangling Alliance*. Chicago, Ill.: University of Chicago Press, 1963.

RICHARDSON, JAMES L., *Germany and the Atlantic Alliance: The Interaction of Strategy and Politics*. Cambridge, Mass.: Harvard University Press, 1966.

VALI, FERENC A., *The Quest for a United Germany*. Baltimore, Md.: The Johns Hopkins Press, 1967.

WHETTEN, LAWRENCE L., *Germany's Ostpolitik: Relations Between the Federal Republic and the Warsaw Pact Countries*. London: Oxford University Press, 1971.

FRANCE

DE CARMOY, GUY, *The Foreign Policies of France, 1944–1968*. Chicago, Ill.: The University of Chicago Press, 1970.

FREYMOND, JACQUES, *The Saar Conflict, 1945–1955*. New York: Praeger Publishers, 1960.

GROSSER, ALFRED, *French Foreign Policy Under de Gaulle*. Boston, Mass.: Little, Brown and Co., 1965.

HARTLEY, ANTHONY, *Gaullism: The Rise and Fall of a Political Movement*. New York: Outerbridge & Dienstfrey, 1971.

HOFFMANN, STANLEY, *Decline or Renewal? France Since the 1930's*. New York: Viking Press, 1974.

HORNE, ALISTAIR, *A Savage War of Peace: Algeria 1954–1963*. New York: Macmillan, 1977.

KOHL, WILFRID L., *French Nuclear Diplomacy*. Princeton, N.J.: Princeton University Press, 1971.

KOLODZIEJ, EDWARD A., *French International Policy Under de Gaulle and Pompidou*. Ithaca, N.Y.: Cornell University Press, 1974.

KULSKI, W. W., *De Gaulle and the World: The Foreign Policy of the Fifth French Republic*. Syracuse, N.Y.: Syracuse University Press, 1966.

MORSE, EDWARD L., *Foreign Policy and Interdependence in Gaullist France*. Princeton, N.J.: Princeton University Press, 1973.

VON ALBERTINI, RUDOLF, *Decolonization: The Administration and Future of the Colonies, 1919–1960*. Garden City, N.Y.: Doubleday, 1971.

WILLIS, F. ROY, *France, Germany and the New Europe, 1945–1967*. Stanford, Calif.: Stanford University Press, 1968.

BRITAIN

BEER, SAMUEL, *British Politics in the Collectivist Age*. New York: Alfred A. Knopf, Inc., 1965.

CALLEO, DAVID, *Britain's Future*. New York: Horizon Press, 1968.

DAVIDSON, IAN, *Britain and the Making of Europe*. London: Macdonald and Co., 1971.

FRANKEL, JOSEPH, *British Foreign Policy, 1945–1973*. London: Oxford University Press, 1975.

GORDON, MICHAEL, *Conflict and Consensus in Labour's Foreign Policy, 1914–1965*. Stanford, Calif.: Stanford University Press, 1969.

PIERRE, ANDREW, *Nuclear Politics: The British Experience with an Independent Strategic Force, 1939–1970*. London, New York: Oxford University Press, 1972.

ROSECRANCE, RICHARD, *Defense of the Realm: British Strategy in the Nuclear Epoch*. New York: Columbia University Press, 1968.

VITAL, DAVID, *The Making of British Foreign Policy*. New York: Praeger Publishers, 1968.

WALLACE, WILLIAM, *The Foreign Policy Process in Britain.* London: George Allen and Unwin Ltd., 1977.

CONCLUSION

BLAKE, DAVID H., AND WALTERS, ROBERT S., *The Politics of Global Economic Relations.* Englewood Cliffs, N.J.: Prentice-Hall, 1976.

BUCHAN, ALASTAR, ed., *Europe's Future: Europe's Models of Western Europe in the 1970s.* New York: Columbia University Press, 1969.

CALLEO, DAVID, ed., *Money and the Coming World Order.* New York: New York University Press, 1976.

CHACE, JAMES, AND RAVENAL, EARL, eds., *Atlantis Lost: U.S.–European Relations After the Cold War.* New York: New York University Press, 1976.

COHEN, BENJAMIN J., *Organizing the World's Money: The Political Economy of International Monetary Relations.* New York: Basic Books, 1977.

HANRIEDER, WOLFRAM F., ed., *The United States and Western Europe: Political, Economic and Strategic Perspectives.* Cambridge, Mass.: Winthrop Publishers, 1974.

HOFFMANN, STANLEY, *Gulliver's Troubles, Or the Setting of American Foreign Policy.* New York: McGraw-Hill, 1968.

SOLOMON, ROBERT, *The International Monetary System, 1945–1976.* New York: Harper & Row, 1977.

Index